IGNATIAN HUMANISM

A Dynamic Spirituality
for the 21st Century

RONALD MODRAS

JESUIT
WAY

an imprint of
LOYOLAPRESS.
CHICAGO

an imprint of
LOYOLAPRESS.

3441 N. ASHLAND AVENUE
CHICAGO, ILLINOIS 60657
(800) 621-1008
WWW.LOYOLABOOKS.ORG

Cover images: St. Ignatius—Ars Jesuitica ©2000 the Jesuits of the Missouri Province. Karl Rahner—Catholic News Service (CNS). Friedrich Spee—Stadtbibliothek Trier. Pedro Arrupe—Missouri Province Archives, St. Louis Missouri. Mateo Ricci—courtesy The Society of Jesus, Rome.

Cover and interior design by Kathy Kikkert

Library of Congress Cataloging-in-Publication Data
Modras, Ronald E.
  Ignatian humanism : a dynamic spirituality for the 21st century / Ronald Modras.
    p. cm.
  Includes bibliographical references and index.
  ISBN 0-8294-1986-1
  1. Spirituality— Catholic Church 2. Ignatius, of Loyola, Saint,
1491–1556. Exercitia spiritualia. I. Title.
BX2350.M663 2004
255'.53—dc22
                                                      2003022959

Printed in the United States of America
05 Bang 10 9 8 7 6 5 4 3 2

For my colleagues and students at Saint Louis University

I have learned much from my teachers, and from my colleagues more than from my teachers, but from my students more than from them all.

Babylonian Talmud, Tractate Ta'anith 7a

CONTENTS

INTRODUCTION

Ignatian Humanism: A Spirituality for the Twenty-first Century

Book titles commonly call for some explanation. This title all but cries out for one. Virtually every word of it raises questions.

First, *Ignatian.* Ignatius Loyola, the founder of the Jesuits, a humanist? If humanism implies anything, it implies a high regard for human freedom. Wasn't it Ignatius Loyola who wrote something to the effect that what he sees as white he will believe to be black if the Catholic Church hierarchy says so? That hardly sounds humanistic. Putting together the words *Ignatian* and *humanism* is curious, to say the least. What do I mean by humanism?

Or by spirituality, for that matter? Doesn't spirituality have to do with escaping from life's temptations and challenges by going off someplace where people pray all day? What does that have to do with life in the twenty-first century? Don't Ignatius Loyola and the Jesuits go back to the sixteenth-century Protestant Reformation, when they battled Protestants as part of the Catholic Counter-Reformation? Most Catholics and Protestants have risen above those old quarrels. What does the sixteenth century have to say to the twenty-first? Answers to some of these questions simply raise more questions.

Most of this book is devoted to five Jesuit humanists. In that case, why not just call it *Jesuit Humanism?* Or, if it's about spirituality, why not *Jesuit Spirituality?* Why Ignatian? Again, for that matter, why *Humanism?* Most of these questions will be addressed in the chapters that follow. Some will take the entire book to answer adequately. Others, like the last, can be dealt with at the outset.

A book with *Ignatian Humanism* in the title will not, I hope, mislead librarians into cataloging it next to Bertrand Russell, John Dewey, or Jean-Paul Sartre. This book assumes, on the contrary, that humanism is more encompassing than its narrower, purely secular subspecies. And it makes dual claims. One is that Ignatian spirituality is rooted not in the Catholic Counter-Reformation conflict with Protestantism but in sixteenth-century Renaissance humanism, indeed that its humanistic features are so numerous and intrinsic as to justify calling it a form of humanism. The second claim is that those humanist features make it exceptionally relevant for anyone—not just Roman Catholics and maybe not just Christians either—looking for a way to live a responsible spiritual life at the dawn of a new century, in which the only constant seems to be change.

For a clearer understanding of the two foregoing claims, the reader deserves some immediate explanation of what I mean by three words under discussion here: *spirituality, humanism,* and *Ignatian.* The first two have evolved from ideas that reach back deep into the history of Western culture. They have come to acquire disparate, sometimes competing definitions, necessitating the addition of modifying adjectives that point to their particular historical provenance. The third word is one of those adjectives.

Spirituality

Spirituality is a word moderns tend to identify with matters otherworldly and exotic. It conjures up images of hermits in deserts and gurus on mountaintops. When modified by Catholic adjectives like *Benedictine, Carmelite,* or *Trappist,* it brings to mind clicking rosary beads and silent cloisters. In the early 1960s, Protestant theologian Paul Tillich lamented that the words *spirit* and *spiritual* had lost any meaning for modern Western culture. Books surveying the religious landscape spoke of secular cities and the death of God. Spirituality was associated with matters pious and churchy. Anyone could see that the churches were in trouble and that the 1960s were anything but pious.

If he were alive today, Tillich would express pleasant surprise at the comeback spirituality has made in the last thirty years in North America—but then quickly add, he knew we couldn't do without it. Bookstore shelves are crammed with titles ranging from the classics of Western spirituality to Eastern mysticism, Blessed Mother Teresa, and New Age. Without much reflection on the difference, people—the younger generation in particular—identify themselves as being spiritual but not religious. Though church life is in decline, interest in spirituality is thriving—which is not to say that the moguls of popular culture acknowledge it as something central to the human enterprise. The mass media still tend to see spirituality as a fringe phenomenon best ignored except at Christmas and Easter or at times like the 9/11 terrorist attacks when "God bless America" came so easily to the lips.

The resurgent interest in spirituality merits reflection, if only because it tells us something important about ourselves. At the same time that science and technology are creating new forms of life and already have the basic knowledge and skills to clone human life, we are experiencing a need to talk about ourselves in terms other than DNA molecules and genes. When biologists demonstrate how little genetic difference there is between human beings and higher primates, when anthropologists discover the bones of ancestors that we share with those primates on our evolutionary family tree, we are drawn to focus on that difference. There is something at our core that resists being reduced to merely bigger brains and clever thumbs.

The word *spirit* is how we talk about that core. The English—along with the Italian and Spanish—goes back to the Latin *spiritus*, which, like its Hebrew and Greek counterparts, has to do with wind, the air we breathe, and, as a result, life. Spirit is what the prescientific ancients saw as the difference between a living person and a corpse. In German, *Geist* links spirit to the *Geisteswissenschaften,* the "sciences of the spirit" that study the full range of human endeavor and its achievements. The French *esprit* suggests that spirit has something to do with being fully alive. All these cognates give us some idea why spirit and spirituality resisted being swept into the dictionary's dustbin for obsolete words. They point to something inalienable and central to who we are. They point to that difference, that something more, that makes it possible—how did someone put it?—for the rubbing of horsehair over gut to come out as Beethoven's First Violin Sonata. They point to that which makes us unique . . . which makes us human.

It is also in that dimension we call the human spirit that we experience what we in the West, under the influence of the Judeo-Christian tradition, call the Holy Spirit. That familiar but confusing compound is translated more prosaically as holy wind or holy breath. Because the Hebrew for holy *(qadosh)* refers to that which is out of the ordinary, Holy Spirit became the way the Hebrew and Christian scriptures talk about God not far off in some seventh heaven but as a mysterious power (like the wind) that is beyond the ordinary and yet experienced as a presence (like the breath we inhale and feel deep within us).

Spirituality is about the experience at the core of our beings of something—a power, presence, drive, longing—that is beyond the ordinary. Defined in this way, spirituality is not about something at the fringes of human life. It is not a leisure-time activity or option for people with a taste for the exotic. It is about what one thoughtful author has called the "holy longing" or "dis-ease" (St. Augustine called it a "restlessness") at the heart of human life.[1] It is about the *eros,* the energy or drive within us that shapes our actions and ultimately our lives. Seeing spirituality this way makes it a "nonnegotiable," more basic than religion:

> Long before we do anything explicitly religious at all, we have to do something about the fire that burns within us. What we do with that fire, how we channel it, is our spirituality. Thus, we all have a spirituality,

whether we want one or not, whether we are religious or not. Spirituality is more about whether or not we can sleep at night than about whether or not we go to church. It is about being integrated or falling apart, about being within community or being lonely, about being in harmony with Mother Earth or being alienated from her.[2]

This view of spirituality is obviously at odds with those who see it as something only for churchgoers or devotees of the paranormal. But does that make it so broad as to become meaningless? Is it an abuse of the word to say that people who do not pray are spiritual? (Whether or not their spirituality is adequate or complete is another question.) But how else do we take people at their word when they say that they are spiritual though not religious? How else do we interpret Albert Einstein, when—though not one to frequent a synagogue—he tells us that, as a scientist, he wanted to know God's thoughts? How else do we understand Spinoza, the seventeenth-century Dutch philosopher, being regarded both as an atheist and as "God-intoxicated"? How else do we explain researchers who make their science a religion, or self-styled atheists with a totally selfless commitment to justice? For the prescientific ancients, spirit was what held a body together, keeping it from disintegrating. For us moderns, as individuals or in communities, spirituality can still be a way of talking about what holds us together, what keeps us from disintegrating.

Humanism : *humanity w/o Religious additives; @ its core.*

Humanism is another word with a complicated history. But it has an even wider range of possible meanings that, if left unmodified, make it hopelessly ambiguous, some might even say useless. To resolve the difficulty, some authors argue that its unmodified use should be restricted to the eighteenth-century Enlightenment's rejection of religion and to themselves—the modern proponents of that rejection—who would include signatories of the 1933 and 1973 Humanist Manifestos; the members of

—7 *PURELY human.*

various national humanist leagues, such as the American Humanist Association, which publishes *The Humanist*, and those who agree with the notion that <u>humanism constitutes an alternative to religion with a term less negative than atheism</u>.

Atheistic (a.k.a. secular, rational, or ethical) humanists are not the only ones to advocate limiting the word exclusively to themselves. There are conservative Christians of various churches and denominations who happily cede the word to secularists for the sake of having an unambiguous label for the enemy camp. Televangelists of this stripe, for example, blame all that is wrong in America and modern culture—from public education to the feminist movement—on humanism, regarding it with the same animosity as they do liberalism, their other (or is it the same?) bête noire.

Despite such efforts at simplification, however, humanism remains stubbornly ambiguous. *The Oxford English Dictionary* offers several different subdefinitions, which one scholar of the word's usage and history finds to be only a fraction of the various senses and contexts in which it has been applied. Its range extends, as he puts it, "from the pedantically exact to the cosmically vague." One of those vague but, I would argue, legitimate extended meanings refers to humanism as an evaluation of human achievements and cultivation of human enrichment. But in addition to that nondescript, nonthreatening definition are meanings that carry powerful positive or negative connotations, depending on one's ideological allegiance.[3]

The word, in a word, is loaded. For those who salute it, humanism stands for human freedom and dignity, synonymous with the best of modern Western culture. At the other end of the playing field, postmodern critics of the Enlightenment fault the word for masking its users' restriction of full dignity and freedom to a particular race (white), gender (male), and class (fellow aristocrats, landowners, or nationals). Like the Athenian Greeks whom they emulated, the colonial founding fathers who announced American independence with a declaration that "all men are created equal" owned slaves. In the course of Western history, full humanity at various times has been denied to women, children, those who did not speak Greek (or more recently English), and Jews. For its critics (like Theodor Adorno), the Enlightenment's rationalist, humanist enterprise came to its logical conclusion at Auschwitz. For more recent postmodern critics of the word (Michel Foucault, Jacques Derrida), the humanity to which humanism appeals and on which it is based is little more than a pretentious metaphor.

That's a lot of baggage for a word first coined to describe an academic reform. In the early nineteenth century, a group of German educators began promoting a curriculum that gave pride of place to what they regarded as the wellsprings of Western civilization and culture, the literary classics and achievements of ancient Greece and Rome. They called their program *Humanismus,* a word evocative of the Italian Renaissance *umanisti,* who advocated replacing Aristotle and scholastic theology with the study of Cicero, Virgil, and other Latin and Greek classic texts. The fifteenth- and sixteenth-century *umanisti* were speech and letter writers for the nobility and ruling magistrates of their day. But they were also the teachers of grammar, rhetoric, history, and ethics, who cultivated what they called—borrowing a phrase from Cicero—the *studia humanitatis,* or what today we call the humanities. Needless to say, the word has wandered far beyond the precincts of academe or the fifteenth-century Italian taste for literature.

Renaissance humanism will be treated at some length in chapter 2 of this book. Suffice it for now to say that virtually all the Renaissance humanists were practicing Christians. They did not renounce religion or Christian faith. But they did criticize the Latin style and pedagogy of the "scholastics," who dominated university faculties at the time. And some humanists could be quite forthright in criticizing the state of the church, clergy, and popular piety, most notable among these being the acerbic priest Erasmus and his friend Thomas More. Both, though critical Catholics, would stoutly rebuff any aspersions cast on their Catholic loyalty or humanist credentials. Other Christians with substantial humanist claims are, to name but a few, Florentine Platonist Pico della Mirandola, Luis Vives and Fray Luis de León in Spain, Jacques Lefévre d'Estaples in France, and John Milton and John Donne in England. The word can also be justifiably ascribed to more recent, though heterogeneous, Christian thinkers such as Gabriel Marcel, Thomas Merton, Paul Tillich, and (Erasmus redivivus?) Hans Kung.[4] Obviously humanism cannot be simply identified with irreligion.

But what do the ideas and writings of the above Christian humanists have to do with those heroes of secular humanism for whom Christianity and the church were not objects of loyal criticism but contempt? One thinks here of Diderot (for whom Christianity was "the Great Prejudice"), David Hume ("Christian superstition"), and Voltaire ("*écrase l'infame*"). Humanists less polemical but just as averse to all forms of religion were Karl Marx ("opium" for the oppressed masses) and Sigmund Freud ("neurosis"). Clearly we have here two very different strains of a bifurcated intellectual tradition, both laying claim to be legitimate heirs of the Renaissance humanists.

The genesis of the secular humanist tradition is to be found in the writings of the eighteenth-century British freethinkers and French *philosophes* who made up what came to be called the "Age of Reason" or "Enlightenment" (*siècle de lumières; Aufklärung*). The Renaissance *umanisti* had immersed themselves in alternative topics of interest (the humanities) from the narrower, theological discourse (divinity) of the Middle Ages. The events of the late sixteenth and early seventeenth centuries contributed to transforming that alternative taste into a distaste for religious discourse altogether.

The religious wars that followed the Reformation and the imposing achievements of scientific reason (Copernicus, Galileo, Newton) gave ample grounds for Enlightenment philosophers to forego interest in contentious religious doctrines and concentrate on matters human and empirical. (Alexander Pope summed up the attitude of the age famously: "Presume not God to scan; the proper study of Mankind is Man.") Those in England who did give thought to religion gave rise to Deism, which rejected revealed religion in the name of reason and a natural theology that was sure that God and the afterlife were quite capable of rational demonstration (John Locke, *The Reasonableness of Christianity*; John Toland,

Christianity Not Mysterious). From first polite and then undisguised indifference to religion, there followed the hostile contempt exemplified by Diderot, Hume, and Voltaire, cited above.

In Germany, Immanuel Kant put an end to natural theology with his critique of rational attempts to prove the existence of God or an afterlife. He also formulated what became the classical definition of Enlightenment as emancipation from religious authorities who would presume to shackle human reason ("the end of humankind's self-imposed infancy"). Without dwelling any further on its historical evolution, secular humanism today can be described in terms of four basic assumptions. As articulated by a leading historian and representative of secular humanism, those four assumptions are: that we humans are on our own, that this life is all there is, that we are all responsible for our own lives, and that we are responsible for the lives of our fellow human beings.[5] One will notice that these are all faith assumptions—but a faith, their author would argue with a nod to Kant, within the limits of reason alone.

The Enlightenment tradition uncoupled the concept of human dignity from its moorings in the biblical belief that human beings are created in the "image of God." It has been argued (John Pawlikowski) that this disconnect and the "death of God" in Western culture (Friedrich Nietzsche) are what made it possible for the Nazis to attempt to overthrow the Judeo-Christian values that underpinned European civilization, providing the most horrific example of what has been called the "anti-humanism" of modernity.[6] Totalitarian nation-states came to claim the allegiance once reserved for religion. But the issue need not be belabored here. This book is not a critique of the Enlightenment or secular humanism. It seeks rather to illustrate an alternative humanist tradition, one, I would argue, with equal claim to the title and the Renaissance legacy.

The ambiguity of the word *humanism*, left unmodified, should be clear enough by now. There are too many disparate kinds of humanism, which may share enough features to justify the generic noun but still differ enough to require adjectival specification. Chapter 2 will look in some detail at those common features. Several of the specifying adjectives have already been encountered. There is, of course, the original Renaissance or literary humanism, and the classical humanism of Greece and Rome that the *umanisti* emulated. There is Enlightenment or secular humanism, also referred to, according to one's preferred nuance, as scientific, rational, atheistic, agnostic, or ethical humanism.

The term *religious humanism* is no less ambiguous than the unmodified noun, since theists and nontheists alike have used it to describe themselves. Christian humanism (which secular humanists generally regard as an oxymoron) stands alongside Buddhist, Confucian, Hindu, Islamic, and Jewish humanisms. (Martin Buber, Abraham Heschel, and Emmanuel Levinas come to mind as Jewish humanists; Gandhi as a Hindu humanist.) Other kinds of humanism one finds in the literature are German romantic, liberal, existentialist, Marxist, philanthropic, and socialist. And, as if those adjectives were not enough, here I am suggesting another—Ignatian.

Ignatian

In this book I will try to make the case that the spirituality that began with Ignatius Loyola and the founding of the Society of Jesus was and remains so deeply imbued with distinctive features it absorbed from the Renaissance humanism of the day that it deserves to be called a kind of humanism. I will illustrate how this humanism has evolved over the centuries, thanks to an aptitude for accommodation prized in Renaissance education and inherent in the spirituality and ethos of the Society of Jesus (hence the "dynamic" in the book's subtitle). But if that is the case, why Ignatian humanism? Why not Jesuit? Because Ignatian spirituality is broader than the Jesuit spirituality embodied in the Society of Jesus. One does not have to be a Jesuit to embrace the principles and practices of Ignatian spirituality.

Ignatian spirituality has its origins in the *Spiritual Exercises* of Ignatius Loyola. Jesuit spirituality does too, but also in the *Constitutions of the*

Society of Jesus, which give it a decidedly distinctive coloring. The Jesuits are a religious order of men tied together by vows, including a distinctive fourth vow that gives them a special relationship to the popes. Ignatian spirituality embraces a wider spectrum of adherents—laymen and lay-women without vows, non-Jesuit diocesan priests, congregations of religious women founded by Jesuits and influenced by their spirituality, in fact anyone who has taken the time to make the Ignatian Spiritual Exercises either completely or in part. That means not only Roman Catholics but also a variety of Christians who have no ecclesial ties to the bishops of Rome—Anglicans, Episcopalians, Lutherans, Methodists, Presbyterians, members of the United Reformed Church, Mennonites, and Quakers.[7] All of these non-Jesuits constitute what I like to call, borrowing a phrase from the (1995) Thirty-fourth General Congregation of the Society of Jesus, the "extended Ignatian family."[8]

Though not a Jesuit, I consider myself a member of this family on a number of counts. I have taught at a Jesuit university for nearly a quarter of a century and try to provide my students with the vision and values of a Jesuit education. Several years ago, over the course of nine months, I made the Ignatian Spiritual Exercises in a so-called (nineteenth annotation) "retreat in daily life." It was during the course of that experience that I decided to research and write this book for anyone, like myself, drawn to or interested in Ignatian spirituality. The members of that group for whom this book is not specifically intended are the Jesuits themselves, although even those learned men may discover some forgotten nugget of wisdom among the familiar chestnuts or a new insight gleaned from a perspective more distant than theirs.

In addition to readers drawn to Ignatian spirituality, this book is also for my colleagues and students at Saint Louis University; their counterparts at other Jesuit colleges and universities; alumni, boards of trustees, and supporters of Jesuit institutions; in short, anyone involved in Jesuit education or ministry. That includes my Jewish, Muslim, Hindu, and Buddhist colleagues and students and those uncertain of any faith, who—perhaps without knowing why (though I hope this book will help give some answers)—find themselves at home in a Jesuit academic setting.

That's a good reason why Ignatian spirituality deserves to be called a kind of humanism, and why Ignatian humanism needs to be seen in the broader context of a "spiritual humanism," as I have called it elsewhere.[9] There are persons I know whose spiritual eros or energy is not nourished or directed by any church or organized religion, but whose integrity, commitment to justice, and concern for the needs of their fellow human beings all bespeak a depth appropriately described as spiritual. Ignatian humanism—I will try to show in the chapters that follow—argues for a God at work in the lives of people even when they give up on religion or the notion of God.

The organization of my argument is simple enough. The first chapter describes Ignatian spirituality in the context of its origins in the life of Ignatius Loyola. The second outlines the characteristics of Renaissance humanism and their influence on Ignatian spirituality and the founding of the Society of Jesus. Chapters 3 through 7 will illustrate how that humanism has continued to evolve, exemplified in the lives and ideas of several notable Jesuits. These are Matteo Ricci, who pioneered interreligious, intercultural dialogue in China; Friedrich Spee, a pre-Enlightenment champion of human rights; scientist and visionary Pierre Teilhard de Chardin; Karl Rahner, who plumbed the theological depths implied by Ignatian spirituality; and Superior General Pedro Arrupe, who brought the Society of Jesus into a new era by returning it to its roots. A concluding chapter will attempt to draw together the lessons of the preceding chapters, arguing that the Ignatian humanism that has evolved over the centuries has a distinctive relevance for our own times.

In virtually every sphere of cultural criticism, analysts seem agreed, we are living in a time of transition. The by-now-overused word *postmodern*—however one defines it—presupposes that an era has come to an end. Whether it happened in World War I, at Auschwitz, or Hiroshima, the rationalist dogmas that constituted the foundation of modern Western culture have come into question. We no longer take it for granted that progress is inevitable or that science and technology alone will save us. Our computers give us more information than we know how to handle. The Hubble telescope brings onto our living room coffee tables color photographs of galaxies colliding and stars being born millions of light-years away. People from continents and cultures once oceans away now move into our neighborhoods and study or work at desks across the hall.

For the closest analogue to our own day, I would suggest, one must look to the Renaissance. That too was a time of wider horizons and new knowledge overturning former certitudes. Though it looked to the past for guidance, the Renaissance became the bridge to modernity. We in the postmodern, early twenty-first century could do worse for guidance than to look to the Renaissance and its humanist values, as embodied in Ignatian spirituality. Ignatian humanism may not be the answer for everyone looking to live a responsible twenty-first century spirituality or faith-life. I don't claim it is the only way, but it is one way. Its humanism is an aspect of Ignatian spirituality that I personally find helpful and appealing, one that I trust the reader will too.

I don't claim that this book tells the whole story of Ignatian spirituality (let alone Jesuit history), or that the Jesuit humanists I treat here even begin to exhaust the possibilities. Other candidates worthy of consideration are scientists Christopher Clavius (who designed the now universally adopted Gregorian calendar), Athanasius Kircher (Egyptologist and inventor of an early film projector), and Roger Boscovich (who in the eighteenth century anticipated modern atomic theory by more than a hundred years). In the arts, poet Gerard Manley Hopkins comes to mind, as well as the lesser known Domenico Zipoli, who in 1716 gave up composing Baroque oratorios for Italians to write music for natives at Jesuit missions in what are now Paraguay and Bolivia. An entire book could be written on American Jesuit humanists like pioneers Jacques Marquette, Pierre De Smet, and Eusebio Kino. Pioneering intellectuals in such a book would include freedom of conscience champion John Courtney Murray;

ecumenist Gustave Weigel; and philosopher-theologian Bernard Loner-
gan. But arbitrariness is unavoidable in an enterprise such as this, and an
author must draw lines somewhere.

My only regret is that, in telling the story of Ignatian humanism, I find
myself writing exclusively about Jesuits and therefore celibate males.
Women were among the most formative influences on the life of Ignatius
Loyola. (It is doubtful he would have survived his reckless penitential
excesses were it not for the women of Manresa.) Women were among his
earliest supporters and among the first to "make" his Spiritual Exercises.
His letters to women fill a hefty volume.[10] But until recently, Jesuits were
almost the only interpreters and developers of Ignatian spirituality. Happily, that is changing.[11] The histories of the many religious orders of women
inspired by Ignatian spirituality have yet to be written. I would hope that
a volume like this one might encourage research in that direction, enriching the concept of Ignatian humanism with a feminist perspective.

Books this wide-ranging do not get written without help from generous colleagues. Nor in this instance, from a generous and supportive university. When I conceived the idea that eventually became the *Shared Vision*
video series on Jesuit education, it was J .J. Mueller and Thomas Rochford
who collaborated in refining and realizing the project, Saint Louis University that underwrote it, and Jesuits James Blumeyer and Lawrence
Biondi who supported it. Research on *Shared Vision* prompted me to write
a 1995 article in *America* magazine entitled "The Spiritual Humanism of
the Jesuits." Among the letters in response to that article came a suggestion to expand it into a book. The rest, as they say, is history.

I am particularly grateful to Saint Louis University for financial support in the way of research grants from its Marchetti and Mellon Funds
and for a research leave and sabbatical that allowed me to bring this book
to a timely conclusion. My sincere thanks also to the staff of the university's Pius XII library, especially archivists John Wade and Randy McGuire
and theology specialist Ronald Crown, and to my research assistants over
the last several years, Andy Matthews, Dennis Durst, Brett Huebner, and

Daniel Dunivan. I would be remiss if I did not acknowledge the inspiration afforded me by Renaissance historian John O'Malley, whose book on the first Jesuits intrigued me enough to venture a book along these lines.

Colleagues and friends who have been willing to read and offer helpful criticism of parts of this manuscript or who have made helpful suggestions include Bernhard Asen, Claudia Carlen, Paul Coutinho, Marian Cowan, Philip Fischer, David Fleming, Paul Garcia, Mary Garvin, Philip Gavitt, Dolores Greeley, John Haught, Thomas King, Vincent O'Keefe, John Padberg, Robert Phillips, Carl Starkloff, Bill Stauder, Kenneth Steinhauser, James Voiss, Xiaoxin Wu, and the members of the Seminar on Jesuit Spirituality, in particular Robert Bireley and G. Ronald Murphy. I wish to acknowledge George Lane, Jim Manney, my copy editor Rebecca Johnson, and the staff at Loyola Press for their support of this project. Special thanks too to my manuscript editor, L. B. Norton, for her sharp eye and wise counsel. Any shortcomings in these pages are, of course, my responsibility and not theirs. Finally, for the English teacher's skills she honed in a previous life and for her unflagging moral support in this one, my love and thanks to my wife, Mary Elizabeth Hogan. This book is dedicated to those colleagues and students at Saint Louis University who have enriched both our lives with their spirituality, humanism, and friendship.

ONE

~

IGNATIAN SPIRITUALITY

Up to the age of twenty-six he was a man given to the follies of the world; and what he enjoyed most was exercise with arms, having a great and foolish desire to win fame.[1]

So begins a largely unremarkable account of a most remarkable man, Iñigo López de Loyola, more commonly known as St. Ignatius Loyola. The original title of the narrative, *Acta Patris Ignatii,* has been variously translated as the testament, memoirs, or autobiography of Ignatius. He dictated its contents reluctantly, only after his Jesuit lieutenants repeatedly pressed him for it. They wanted a kind of life story that would inspire his followers with a model for them to emulate. After putting them off for months, Ignatius finally gave in to their appeals. He would pace back and forth and recall the events that shaped his life, referring to himself in the third person as "the pilgrim"—an apt metaphor for a man who preferred forging ahead to looking back.

It was Jesuit Fr. Luís Gonçalves da Câmara who for more than two years had the unenviable job of badgering Ignatius to talk about his past, while he listened, took notes, and later wrote down what he had heard—some

1

parts in Spanish, others in Italian. Da Câmara confessed that, for the sake of faithfulness to Ignatius's exact words, he sometimes had to sacrifice clarity.[2] The same could be said for literary grace. Given the haphazard method of its composition, it's no surprise that the finished product was deemed clumsy and so embarrassingly inelegant that for centuries the text lay all but ignored in the archives of Jesuit headquarters in Rome. Today it is generally recognized as a spiritual classic, not only because of its author and subject matter, but precisely because of the unvarnished honesty revealed in its clumsiness.

Ignatius Loyola is a major figure not only of Catholic but also of world history. Even in an age of Renaissance genius and monumental achievements, he stands out for the impact he made on his own and subsequent centuries. He had a vision that continues to change people and the way they see their lives. During his lifetime he aroused both suspicion and devotion, reflected in the contrasting, sometimes contradictory images historians have painted of him (which is not to say that even today his partisans or critics completely understand him).

Ignatius Loyola has never been easy to categorize.[3] The stereotype of an ex-soldier founding a military order to fight Protestantism is inaccurate and misleading. The metaphor of the Christian as a "soldier of Christ" was a commonplace in the sixteenth century, found in the works of the scholarly Erasmus as well as those of Ignatius. Indeed, the romantic novels Ignatius read as a teenager probably had a far greater influence on his ideas about doing chivalrous deeds in God's army than did his brief exploit in battle. That's why his *Spiritual Exercises*[4] and the spirituality that it fosters are more easily described than defined and why the genesis of his spirituality, not only the specific exercises but also its entire worldview, needs to be described in terms of his life experiences. Ignatian spirituality is profoundly biographical.

EARLY LIFE

Ignatius was ailing and in his last years when he began dictating his memoirs, and many of his Jesuit confreres were already regarding him as a saint, but his memories took him back to a time in his life marked by anything but sanctity. He was born in the Basque region of northern Spain almost certainly in 1491, the year before Columbus set sail for new worlds, and so at the waning of the Middle Ages.[5] His home was a fortresslike castle situated among the pine-covered foothills of the Pyrenees, about a mile from the town of Azpeitia. There he was baptized Iñigo López, a name by which he was known until he was in his late forties, when increasingly he began signing his name Ignatius.

Documents going back to 1180 describe the Loyolas as one of the ten great families of their province, declaring the family's unbroken loyalty and service to the kings of Castile and their right on certain occasions to be invited to the king's court. Iñigo's father fought with the king against the Moors at Granada. Two of his brothers fell in battles at Naples and in Mexico; a third died fighting Turks in Hungary. For the men in their class, (UPPER) a sword and dagger were an essential part of the dress code, and knowing how to use them a requisite part of every young man's education.

But the Loyolas were known for more than military prowess. Iñigo was his parents' eleventh child, and in addition he had a half-brother and a half-sister fathered out of wedlock. His mother's death, shortly after Iñigo was born, could only have intensified the masculine ethos of the household. Machismo, vendettas, and bloody family feuds were part of the Loyola heritage, amorous displays of virility no less so. As one biographer bluntly put it, fathering illegitimate children was a family pastime.[6] This included Iñigo's brother Pedro, who was a priest. In short, the Loyola pedigree was better suited to producing a swashbuckler or Don Juan than a saint. ✶

As the youngest of several brothers, Iñigo had no prospect of inheriting any part of the family estate, all of which went to the eldest living son. He would have to shift for himself, making a career in keeping with his social rank by performing aristocratic service, preferably to the Spanish crown, whether on the battlefield or at court. That he might learn the skills of a courtier, his father sent him at about age fifteen to Arévalo and the household of Juan Velázquez de Cuéllar, chief treasurer to King Ferdinand and Queen Isabella. With that the adolescent Iñigo exchanged the relative comforts of the lower nobility for the splendid opulence of the court.

Under the tutelage of Velázquez, Iñigo set about acquiring the poise and manners of a page. He learned to move with ease among Spain's highest aristocratic circles, including visiting members of the royal family. He developed a taste for music and literature, especially the romantic tales of chivalry still in vogue among Spanish nobles. He tells us in his memoirs that his head was "all full of tales like Amadís de Gaul, and such books" [17]. They told of knights setting off in search of adventures, slaying ogres, and rescuing fair ladies. Beneath the feudal trappings of these tales, however, lay an idealized notion of the relationship that joined a knight to his liege lord. Each assumed obligations to the other, the vassal-knight promising service, the lord promising friendship, and both of them under high expectations of mutual allegiance and generosity.

But as one would expect of a Loyola, Iñigo preferred living real adventures to reading about imaginary ones. He worked at developing his skills in fencing and riding. For diversion he also enjoyed gambling, including, it seems, high-risk adventures of the heart. At one point, we learn, he had to hire two bodyguards to help defend him against a rival intent on killing him for what was most likely his part in a love triangle. Juan de Polanco, Ignatius's secretary in his later years, tells us "he especially indulged in gambling, dueling, and romances with women."[7]

Young Iñigo must have cut a dashing figure. By his own later admission, he was vain about his appearance—fastidious about his nails and the look of his shoulder-length hair. Apparently women found him attractive, and he found them compliant. The records also indicate that on a visit to Loyola in 1515, when he was twenty-four, he was arrested for some mysterious affair (a prank? a brawl?) and placed for a time in confinement.

And yet, as he later related to his secretary, Polanco, he was "attached to the faith." It would seem that young Iñigo was a typical Spanish gentleman of his day—fiercely Catholic without being terribly consistent about what that might mean. At Arévalo an elderly aunt, a nun, warned him, "Iñigo, you will not learn nor become wise until someone breaks your leg."[8]

While he was in his early twenties, Iñigo's career prospects took an abrupt turn for the worse. Velazquez fell out of favor with the royal family and lost his post. With the old man's death, Iñigo was advised to offer his services to the Duke of Nájera, a distant relative who was also viceroy of Navarre. He took the advice and left for Navarre and its capital city, Pamplona, where his life would change.

The duke welcomed Iñigo into his company and set him to work honing his diplomatic skills. Despite the common misconception, Iñigo was never a professional soldier, though he would, if the need arose, take part in military expeditions. The young man proved a proficient diplomat, though in one instance at least, impulsiveness got the better of good judgment. For whatever reason, a group of ruffians insulted his honor and pushed him against a wall; Ignatius drew his sword and chased them down the street. If not restrained, he would likely have killed one of them, or they would have killed him. Ignatius was clearly not someone to trifle with. But neither could he claim to have inherited a temperament for cool-headed deliberation.

This brings us to the opening passage of Ignatius's memoirs, with the subject in his late twenties, given to worldly vanities and craving fame. Iñigo had been serving the duke for some five years when Navarre, long a battleground between France and Spain, once again came under attack by French forces. When the two armies arrived at Pamplona, the disparity between them was overwhelming—a little more than 1,000 Spanish troops to 12,000 French. The townsfolk, seeing the hopelessness of the situation and anxious to save their lives and homes, urged their defenders to surrender. As seasoned soldiers, the commandant of the Spanish troops and his officers also wanted to give up. But the fiery Iñigo had never been one to back off from a fight, no matter how desperate the odds, and his courage proved infectious. He was willing to resist to the death and filled the other defenders with the same fire.

The battle for Pamplona lasted some six hours. The fortress's defenders acquitted themselves well. French losses were considerable. But the fighting came to a quick end when Ignatius, sword in hand at the center of the fray, fell wounded. A shot from a French cannon shattered one leg and seriously injured the other. At the time Iñigo would surely have preferred death to the humiliation of being a cripple, but death at Pamplona was not his destiny.

Like the famed "shot heard round the world" at Concord, this earlier one at Pamplona reverberated down the centuries. It strains the imagination to think how history would be different if the French cannon had missed him and Iñigo had escaped the battle uninjured. He would likely have remained a cavalier, or perhaps become a conquistador in Spain's expanding colonial empire. At most he would have been a footnote in Spanish history. How would things have turned out, if he had died or escaped untouched? Or, for that matter, if he had been made of lesser stuff? He could just as well have become a bitter, self-pitying old man, weeping for what might have been. As it was, Ignatius's mettle was never more tested than after his wounding.

Despite the losses they had suffered because of him, the French forces treated Iñigo kindly. They set his legs and, once he was well enough, had him transported home to Loyola. There he came under the care of his older brother Martin, heir of the Loyola estates, and his wife, Magdalena de Araoz, who was as much a mother figure to Iñigo as a sister-in-law. Despite their best efforts, Iñigo's shattered leg was not healing. Physicians and surgeons were brought in and determined that the leg needed to be broken and reset correctly. The "butchery," as Ignatius called it in his memoirs, had to be endured without anesthesia. He gave no sign of pain other than his clenched fists [2].

It is safe to say that Iñigo earned his reputation for being a tough hombre honestly. Just how tough—and vain—is apparent by what happened next. The trauma of the second surgery was such that he almost died. The doctors advised that his condition was critical, and Iñigo was given the last rites, but he survived the operation. He was making good progress toward health when it was discovered that one leg was shorter than the other; a bone below the knee was riding on another. And, if that were not bad enough, the bone protruded.

Skintight breeches fitted into boots were the style of the day for swaggering young men like Iñigo, who liked to show off the muscles of their thighs and calves. Iñigo's deformity humiliated him. The doctors informed him that the protruding bone could be cut away, but that the ordeal would be even more excruciating than what he had already endured. The bone had healed, and cutting it would take time. Ignatius chose the surgery. Better to be "tortured" than humiliated by deformity [4]. *SHALLOW!*

The surgeons cut away the flesh and excess bone and, when these began to heal, Iñigo submitted to having his shorter leg stretched so that it would be even with the other. Despite the agonies, he continued to recover. He even felt fit, though he could not put any weight on the bad leg and had to remain in bed. Rarely has a convalescence had more consequence.

CONVERSION

It was 1521, the same year that a papal decree excommunicated a German monk named Martin Luther. Iñigo was bedridden on the upper floor of the Loyola castle for nine months. Averse to inaction by temper and training, he was compelled by his doctors to endure long days of idleness. Out of boredom he asked for some books—romances like the ones he had enjoyed reading at Arévalo. But the Loyolas were not given to building up libraries. The castle contained only two books, both brought by his brother Martin's wife, Magdalena, with her dowry.

One was a four-volume Spanish translation of a life of Christ by a medieval Carthusian monk known as Ludolph of Saxony. It retold the Gospel stories, embellished with descriptive details drawn from the author's imagination. The other was *Flos Sanctorum,* a Spanish edition of Jacopo de Voragine's *The Golden Legend,* a popular collection of lives of the saints. The prologue in that edition described the saints as *caballeros de Dios* (knights of God), a notion Iñigo would naturally find appealing.[9] Both books were devotional—not what he had asked for, but there was nothing else. The hours went by slowly, and Iñigo passed much of the time daydreaming. When that became tiresome, he read about Jesus and the saints.

Iñigo grew fond of the two books. He tells us he read them many times over, putting them aside sometimes to think about what he had read. The convalescent had plenty of time to muse and would daydream for three or four hours at a time without realizing it. He became absorbed thinking about a "certain lady," higher in station than a countess or duchess. That would make her a princess, putting her quite beyond the prospects of someone from the lower nobility like him. He would imagine "the quips—the words he would address to her; the feats of arms he would perform in her service." Iñigo has reminded more than one commentator here of Cervantes's Don Quixote, fantasizing adventures and impossible dreams. But when the reality of his situation once again dawned on him, he became depressed [6]. The word he would come to use was "desolation."

Less dispiriting were his musings about the life of Jesus and saints like Francis and Dominic. Iñigo envisioned the heroic deeds that the saints had done for God and, with his customary bravado, thought, *I can do that.* The more difficult the exploit, the surer he was that he could match it. If St. Francis had tried to convert Muslims, he could too. If saints had given up eating meat and lived on vegetables, he could too. No rigors were beyond his capacities to withstand. And when he daydreamed about doing great feats for God, he felt "consoled."

Iñigo had the time to become introspective enough to notice something about himself. When he thought about his old life at court—the banter, the feats of arms—he felt dispirited. But thoughts of doing great things for God and Jesus, as the saints had, excited him. These imaginings left him "satisfied and joyful." He reflected on this difference between what he called "spirits" stirring within him. Here at Loyola was born what

Ignatius would call the discernment (*discretio*) of spirits. He was sure that the deflating spirits came from the devil and the uplifting ones from God. Not surprisingly, Iñigo thought in the categories of a sixteenth-century Catholic, not a modern-day psychologist. He had no idea that, by cultivating the practice of reflecting on his interior experiences and consciousness, he was pioneering into a future science.

In addition to his interior experiences, Iñigo began contemplating his situation. He was thirty years old with little to show for it. He had his honor but little else, at least for someone with ambition enough to daydream about princesses. He lived at a time when heroic achievements were almost commonplace. Spanish adventurers were charting new seas and pushing deeper into new continents. Men showed what they were made of by deeds of courage and endurance in service to some prince or pursuit of some glorious cause. Iñigo was confident of his mettle and ability to endure hardship. But to what lord and cause should he devote himself? What should he do with the rest of his life?

What is usually called Ignatius's conversion was the beginning of a literal and spiritual journey. The former would take him to foreign lands, the latter to the uncharted seas of his deepest self. He had reason thirty years later to look back at his life and think of himself as a pilgrim. His nine months of convalescence were the beginning of a lifelong habit of intense introspection, punctuated by experiences so extraordinary as to deserve being called mystical.

Iñigo began thinking less about a career at court and more about imitating saints. He wanted to do penance for his past sins and was especially taken up with the idea of making a pilgrimage to Jerusalem, to see for himself the places about which he had daydreamed while reading Ludoph's life of Christ. One night these "holy desires," as he called them in his memoirs, "were confirmed by a spiritual experience" [10]. He described it in terms of a vision of Mary with the child Jesus, followed by a "very great consolation" that lasted a considerable time. The connection between desires and consolation would remain pivotal in his thinking for the rest of his life.

The experience of having his "holy desires" confirmed by consolation left Iñigo a changed man. His family noticed the difference as he began talking about God with members of the household. He continued reading from the lives of Jesus and the saints and in a copybook began writing down passages that he found especially significant, using red ink for the words of Jesus and blue for those of his mother Mary.

With his leg gradually improving, Iñigo began to move a bit around the house. He gave considerable time to prayer, gazing out a window for hours at the night sky and stars. He became restless, anxious to be off and on his way to Jerusalem. And when he thought about what he would do after that, the idea came to him of becoming a Carthusian monk like Ludolph, spending the rest of his life in a monastery doing penance. He tells us that recalling his past life filled him with loathing.

By February 1522, Iñigo was well enough and impatient to begin his pilgrimage to Jerusalem. He told his brother Martin he was going to Navarrete, where his patron, the Duke of Nájera, was staying. Iñigo had kept his pilgrimage plans to himself, but Martin suspected he had more in mind than returning to the duke's service. Martin pleaded with him not to throw his life away, but Iñigo was not to be deterred. With his sights set eastward, toward the port city of Barcelona and eventually Jerusalem, he left Loyola castle, properly armed and dressed as a gentleman, astride a mule and accompanied by two servants. He traveled to Navarrete, where he collected back pay from the duke's treasury and paid some debts. Then he sent the servants back to Loyola so they could tell his brother that he had indeed told the truth and gone to Navarrete. (He was becoming scrupulous about matters like telling the exact truth.) But first he confided in them that he was going on to the shrine of Our Lady of Montserrat, which just happened to be on the road to—and only a short distance from—Barcelona.

"He set out alone on his mule from Navarrete for Montserrat," Ignatius recalled and then went on to relate one of the most intriguing incidents in all his memoirs [15–16]. On that first leg of his journey, he found himself accompanied by a fellow traveler, also astride a mule; the man was a Moor, one of the so-called "new Christians" converted from Islam. (In 1502, Spain's Muslims suffered the same fate Jews had ten years earlier, compelled to convert to Catholicism or leave.) Iñigo and the Moor chatted amicably as they rode along together, until the conversation turned to theology. The Moor said that he believed Mary did indeed conceive Jesus virginally, without human intervention (a Muslim doctrine contained in the Qur'an), but he did not see how she could have retained her physical virginity during childbirth. Iñigo argued with the Moor and tried to convince him otherwise but without success. The discussion must have become heated because, we are told, the Moor then went ahead so quickly that Iñigo lost sight of him. The Moor was obviously no fool.

The argument had aroused such "indignation" and perplexity in Iñigo that he had to stop and ponder what he should do. He felt that the Moor had insulted the honor of the Virgin Mary and that he was duty-bound to defend it. His inclination was to catch up with the Moor and stab him for what he had said. Old habits die hard, and Iñigo was new at imitating saints. He could not make his mind up, and after a while he tired of deliberating. There was a fork up ahead, with one road going to a village, where the Moor said he was stopping, and the other a highway going on further. Iñigo decided to leave the reins slack and let the mule choose which road to take. The village road would mean searching out the Moor and stabbing him. Fortunately on many counts, the mule took the highway, saving the Moor from death and Iñigo from spending the rest of his life as a prisoner in the galleys.

Relating his memoirs, Ignatius could look back at conversations with princes and popes but said little about them. He told the story of his encounter with the Moor, he said, so that we could understand how God dealt with his soul. Despite his ecstasies and desires to serve God, he was still capable of premeditated murder. Ignatius came to see his experiences, including this one, as typical of how God works in people's lives. He was not disposed to see conversion as an instantaneous, once-and-for-all, "I'm-born-again" event that could be dated. He and any number of saints and mystics like him have persuaded Catholic tradition that conversion is

LiFE iS
a long and often uncertain process, a spiritual pilgrimage filled with initial excitement and enthusiasm but open as well to wrong turns and sidetracks. Ignatius did not hide his lapses; he wanted those making the journey after him to learn from his mistakes.

Heading south and east, Iñigo eventually viewed the splendid sawtooth mountain of Montserrat rising in the distance. He stopped in a nearby town, where he commissioned a robe made out of sackcloth and purchased a staff and gourd, the traditional emblems of a pilgrim. Climbing up the steep incline, he came to the Benedictine monastery-shrine that housed the venerated wood-carved Black Virgin, Our Lady of Montserrat. The statue had made the monastery a popular place of pilgrimage for several centuries already.

The monks received Iñigo kindly and agreed to his request to make a general devotional confession of his whole life. The monastery's late abbot, Garcia de Cisneros, required novices, before making their final vows, to spend two weeks preparing for a general confession.[10] Iñigo made a modified version in three days. To assist him he was given a copy of Cisneros's *Book of Exercises for the Spiritual Life.* The title of Cisneros's book seems to have influenced Iñigo in the choice for his own.[11]

Iñigo was well acquainted with the centuries-old custom that a new knight embark upon his chivalrous service with a vigil at arms. He decided to begin his own service by improvising on the customary protocols. He first donated his mule to the monastery and arranged for his sword and dagger to be hung as votive offerings to the Madonna. He then took off the splendid attire of a Spanish gentleman and put on the pilgrim's tunic he had purchased. He gave his fine clothes to a beggar, never to wear finery again. He spent his last night at the monastery kneeling and standing at turns before the Madonna's altar, like a knight of old, a pilgrim's staff in hand instead of a sword.

At daybreak Iñigo quietly left the monastery, taking every precaution to preserve his anonymity. So he was dismayed when, after only a short distance, he found someone hurrying to catch up with him. He was told that the authorities were holding a beggar under suspicion of stealing a gentleman's fine clothes. The beggar claimed he had been given the clothes. Was this true? Iñigo confirmed the beggar's story, we are told, with tears streaming from his eyes "in compassion" for the beggar's plight.

The remark about Iñigo's tears merits reflection. A man who only a year before had merely clenched his fists when doctors sawed into his bones, now wept for the misfortune he inadvertently caused to befall a beggar. Iñigo Loyola was becoming a far more complex person than the tough hombre who roused the Spanish troops at Pamplona.

MANRESA

The onset of Iñigo's pilgrimage coincided with the election of a new pope, Adrian VI, the former Cardinal Adrian Boeyens of Utrecht. Although Dutch, he was a Spanish subject, a former tutor of Emperor Charles V and for a time his regent.[12] The election delighted the Spanish aristocracy but left Iñigo in a quandary. Barcelona would be teeming with nobles taking ships to Rome for the papal coronation. Someone would certainly recognize him, and his pilgrim's garb was sure to cause a sensation among his old acquaintances from court. He decided to put off going directly to Barcelona and spend a few days in the vicinity of Montserrat. In any case, he wanted to make some notes in his copybook. He would set out for Barcelona later, when he wouldn't be noticed. So leaving the road that led to the sea, he traveled around to the other side of the mountains, to a town on the banks of the Cardoner River called Manresa.

Iñigo began living by the kindness of strangers. Not so much from his memoirs but from testimonies given after his death for his canonization, we learn of the "women of Manresa," especially Inéz Pascual who, with her friend Jerónima Calver, met the limping Iñigo on the road from Montserrat to Manresa. They directed him to a small hospice that Jerónima ran, where he slept and helped out occasionally for his keep. They with other women of the town provided him with food and shelter, taking him into their homes when necessary. Inéz in particular, a widow of a Barcelona merchant with houses in both Manresa and Barcelona, proved a life support to the new pilgrim. Out of her own means and with money she collected from friends, she helped to support Iñigo in his later student days in Paris.[13] Ignatius's memoirs tell us also of an elderly woman known for her holiness. Impressed by Iñigo's fervor, she said to him, "Oh! May my Lord Jesus Christ deign to appear to you someday." The remark startled Iñigo, who took the words literally as a prophecy [21].

The days and weeks at Manresa assumed a pattern. Mornings Iñigo attended Mass and evenings vespers and compline. Each Sunday he would go to confession and receive Holy Communion. Frequent communion was unusual for the sixteenth century, but Iñigo had been recently introduced to Thomas à Kempis's *Imitation of Christ,* which encouraged the practice. Most of his time Iñigo spent in a cave overlooking the river valley, where he could see Montserrat in the distance, the play of sun and clouds painting soft gray and rose hues off its craggy heights. He could look out at the splendid colors of creation or into a cave whose shadows symbolized the forces with which he was about to struggle. He tells us only about the latter, nothing of the former. The few days he intended to stay at Manresa stretched into ten months, the most important of his life.

The regimen Iñigo chose for himself consisted of seven hours of meditative prayer a day. To this he added a program of penance for his past sins calculated to ensure that no similar transgressions would occur in the future. The kind of resolve he showed against the French at Pamplona, he now turned against himself. He denied himself all but minimal food and sleep. Only on Sundays would he eat meat or drink wine. He scrutinized not only his actions but his thoughts and motivations, determined to discipline anything in himself that appeared unruly.

Iñigo set about "punishing every aspect of himself and his behavior that had once been a source of satisfaction to him," uprooting all attachments by acting exactly contrary to them.[14] Having already given away all his money and belongings, the once proud nobleman now humbled himself even more by imitating St. Francis and begging for alms so he could eat. In his days at court, the young Iñigo had been vain about his flowing hair and carefully manicured nails; now he let them grow dirty and unkempt [19]. Vanity had no place in his image of a poor and humble Christ, and he was determined to crush any appearance of it in himself.

The exterior calm and regularity of his life at Manresa belied the turbulence within him. At first Iñigo experienced what he described as an "interior state of very steady joy." But then came serious questions about the new identity and life he had chosen. Would he be able to endure such hardships and privations for the rest of his life? Iñigo had no doubt that the devil was tempting him, and he exorcised his doubts "with great vehemence," he tells us. But then came mood swings. He would suffer periods of depression, feeling out of sorts and finding no peace in saying his prayers or attending Mass. Then this "sadness and desolation" would leave him, and he would feel euphoric. Iñigo found this new emotional agitation profoundly disturbing [21].

Then came the obsessive concerns about his past sins generally known as scruples. Had he been as clear and complete as possible in confessing to the priest? Had he omitted any necessary details? Despite the care with which he had been making his confessions, Iñigo began having doubts about them. He felt compelled to repeat his former confessions, to be even more meticulous in describing his failings. But rehearsing his old transgressions brought him no relief, and his sharper focus on minutia only intensified his anxieties [22].

As a child of his time, Iñigo knew nothing about the destructive power of psychic impulses. Even so, he realized that these obsessions about sin and guilt were doing him no good. A psychoanalyst might say he was dealing with the irrational drives of an aggressive superego. Iñigo knew only that he was suffering severe emotional distress and that he was helpless to do anything about it. He began learning a difficult lesson in humility. The self-assurance of the knight and would-be saint had been faltering for some time already and now was shattered.

Despite prayers for deliverance, none came. The scruples continued unabated, becoming so relentless that he began to be gripped by thoughts of suicide. Only because of its sinfulness did he resist the idea. After

depression? Religious Schizofrenia?

several months of this kind of agony, he decided in desperation to subject himself to even more extreme penances. He began denying himself food and drink altogether, still persisting, however, in his regimen of seven hours of prayer a day, including a vigil at midnight.

After a week of these extremes, Iñigo told a priest in confession about his new penitential regimen, and the priest commanded him to break his fast immediately. Iñigo obeyed, and for a few days at least he felt relief. But then once again the obsessive memories of his sins, and the compulsion to repeat them in confession, returned. Once again he felt self-loathing and the urge to give up. This time, however, came deliverance. As he later related in his memoirs, he had an experience in which he awoke "as if from sleep." He realized that these scruples and compulsions could not possibly be from God. They were evil and had to come from some other source. Once again he examined "the diversity of spirits" at conflict within him and "decided with great lucidity not to confess anything from the past anymore." From that day on the scruples left him [22–25].

Iñigo continued his daily routine of prayers, freed now from recurrent anxieties about sin. He found himself interrupted occasionally by visitors whom he would help by conversing with them about "spiritual matters." Once again he experienced serenity in his prayers and "great spiritual consolations." But often these came to him just as he was about to go to sleep. So Ignatius did something that was becoming a habit with him. He "examined" this phenomenon. He had allotted himself little time for sleep as it was, and now he was losing sleep because of these apparent "consolations." He began to question whether these distractions from sleep were indeed from God. He decided that it would be better to ignore them and to sleep instead.

Gradually Iñigo came to what can only be considered an astonishing conviction. As he expressed it years later in his memoirs, "God treated him at this time just as a schoolmaster treats a child whom he is teaching" [27]. He could not say why he thought God was doing this. Was it his lack of education or wit? Or his strong desire to serve God? Whatever the divine reasons or design, Iñigo became convinced God was indeed instructing him in the innermost center of his being. And he was sure that he would be offending God if he were to doubt it.

Iñigo did not claim such extraordinary certainty without extraordinary experiences, the kind we associate with that select circle of people called mystics. And like other mystics who try to describe what they invariably insist is indescribable, Ignatius spoke of visions, "interior eyes," rays of light, and "great spiritual joy." He wrote of experiencing God as being like the harmony of "three musical keys." And this experience, to use his own words, "brought on so many tears and so much sobbing that he could not control himself." Another time he experienced God as creating the world. And one day at Mass he experienced as never before the presence of Christ in the Blessed Sacrament [28].

So powerful were these mystical encounters, so much did they strengthen his convictions, that Iñigo was confident that, if need be, he could lay down his life for his Christian faith. He was sure he could do so simply on the basis of what had occurred within him, even if there were no Scriptures to teach us that faith, he added without any apparent sense of audacity [29]. Along with the consolation of these extraordinary experiences came the profound satisfaction of seeing that his conversations about God were bearing spiritual fruit in people's lives. God was using him to help them. And seeing it, he gave up the extremes of his former ways and began cutting his hair and nails again. TRUE CONVERSION? copy

spir. fulf. ment.

But one experience at Manresa stood out from all the rest. Ignatius tells us in his memoirs, "even if he gathered up all the various helps he may have had from God and all the various things he has known, even adding them all together, he does not think he had got as much as at that one time." He was on his way to a chapel a short distance from Manresa. At a spot where the road goes by the Cardoner River, he "sat down for a little while with his face toward the river, which ran down below." There, without any apparent cause, "the eyes of his understanding began to be opened; not that he saw any vision, but he understood and learned many things, both spiritual matters and matters of faith and of scholarship and this with so great an enlightenment that everything seemed new to him" [30].

Ignatius's memoirs do not give us any further details about this experience at the Cardoner, except that he now had "a great clarity in his understanding." As he looked down at the rushing waters below him, things suddenly seemed to fit together. For more than a year, ever since his convalescence at Loyola, he had been wrestling with the question of what he should do with the rest of his life. Now he knew that he wanted to serve God by teaching people what God had taught him. He wanted to help them better their lives, to distinguish between good and evil spirits, to choose between God and the devil, whom he would come to describe simply as "the enemy of the human race."

The Cardoner experience was one that Ignatius described not only in his memoirs but also later in life in his conversations with others, such as his secretary, Juan de Polanco. In his own retelling of Ignatius's life, Polanco wrote of Ignatius being "illuminated by a flood of light" at the Cardoner. "Thereupon he set himself to devise a plan or method for purifying the soul from its sins . . . for meditating on the life of Christ . . . and for progressing in everything which tended to inflame the soul more and more with love of God. In this way he created a little book of very great profit for the salvation of his neighbor."[15]

Everything came together at the Cardoner. Iñigo called it an illumination, not a vision, but it gave him a vision. Manresa made him a changed man; at the Cardoner he was given a purpose.

CONVERSATIONS

His excessive fasting and sleep deprivation left their marks on Iñigo's once robust health. At one point a fever put him into a state where he thought he would die [32]. He began to suffer stomach pains that would vex him periodically the rest of his life. The winter cold brought him, in his weakened condition, an illness that caused alarm to women in the town who had come to hold him in "deep regard." They forced him to dress warmly, wear shoes, and cover his head. As he improved, he would converse with them "on spiritual matters" [34]. As soon as he sufficiently recovered, Iñigo began his newfound mission in life to talk to people about God. And the first people he found were women.

After ten months at Manresa, Iñigo became restless to resume his pilgrimage. He headed once more for Barcelona, from where he would first sail to Italy and then proceed to Rome to receive the pope's permission to make the journey. His intentions were to place his trust solely in God by making the pilgrimage without money or provisions. In Barcelona he found a ship's captain whom he convinced to give him free passage. The captain agreed only on the condition that Iñigo bring his own food. Iñigo gave in to this request and begged for his provisions in the city. But just before boarding ship, he discovered he had five or six coins left from what he had received begging from door to door. Ignatius tells us that he left the coins on a bench by the shore [36]. He made his entire pilgrimage that way, begging in imitation of St. Francis and trusting God in imitation of Jesus.

Having received the pope's blessing to make the pilgrimage, Iñigo begged his way to Venice. There he met a wealthy Spaniard who was taken with him and his plan and introduced him to no less than the city's highest magistrate, the doge of Venice. The doge in turn arranged for his passage to Cyprus. From there he boarded a pilgrim ship to Jaffa, on which, he tells us, "he brought no more for his maintenance than his hope in God, as he had done on the other" [44]. Iñigo's entire pilgrimage to Jerusalem, symbolic of the spiritual journey that was the rest of his life, was based completely on trust that God would provide his daily bread. It was a faith that was more than intellectual.

Ignatius is laconic in describing his stay in Jerusalem, saying little in his memoirs about his visit to the holy sites. He tells us instead about his intentions to remain in the Holy City and "help souls" [45]. By this he presumably meant to engage in conversation with Muslims with an eye to making them Christian converts, an activity expressly forbidden by Islamic law. Iñigo announced his first intention, to remain in Jerusalem, but not the latter, and apparently he did not need to. The resident Franciscan friars who supervised Catholic pilgrims must have seen him as something of a loose cannon. When he declared that he was going to remain in Jerusalem and no physical force could change his mind, the Franciscan leadership ordered him to return home with the other pilgrims. They had the pope's authorization to excommunicate any Catholic who disobeyed their orders, and they would use it. Did he want to see the papal documents for himself? He declined, knowing he was bested [46–47].

Iñigo was forced to conclude that remaining in Jerusalem, at least for the time being, was not God's will for him. He returned to Italy and then Barcelona, trusting in God and begging for alms, the same way he had left. He had come to realize that, if anything he said was to be taken seriously, he would need further education. So once again Iñigo did violence to what shreds were left of his old vanity. In Barcelona the former swordsman, now thirty-three, sat in a classroom and studied Latin verbs with preadolescent schoolboys. He found concentrating difficult, however, when his mind wandered to spiritual matters that moved his heart. He decided they were distractions, not inspirations, and proceeded to dismiss them. Finally, after two years, his teacher assured him that he had enough Latin to understand the lectures at the University of Alcalá. He could now study the "liberal arts," which is to say, the humanities [56].

At Alcalá he began his studies of logic and physics, depending as before on hospitality and alms. But he did not limit his activities to lectures and books. Over the year and a half he stayed there, "he was engaged in giving spiritual exercises and teaching Christian doctrine, and this bore fruits for the glory of God" [57]. Iñigo's conversations began drawing crowds, and he was joined by three companions who dressed in the same coarse garb that he wore. Word of their activities spread through the region and eventually reached the inquisitors at Toledo. Did Iñigo and his companions belong to the *alumbrados,* those heretical "enlightened" mystics who had no need of the church or church authorities because of their direct revelations from God? An examination of the four young men found no error in their teaching, but they were told to dress like the other students and stop wearing the same uniform, since they were not religious. Iñigo dutifully complied with the order.

Some months later there was another investigation, followed by Iñigo being put under arrest. Two noblewomen, a widow and her daughter, to whom he had been giving spiritual advice, were missing. They had left unaccompanied and on foot. Iñigo admitted to the authorities that he advised the women. They wanted to go about the world serving the poor in one hospital and then another; he had tried to dissuade them from that course and to convince them to serve the poor at home in Alcalá.

Iñigo was blamed for persuading them to attempt something foolish and dangerous, and was put into jail, where he eventually spent forty-two days. "He did the same things as when he was free, teaching and giving exercises," he tells us. When Iñigo was finally released, it was with the proviso that he study for four more years before speaking publicly about matters of faith [60–63].

Iñigo decided to try his luck elsewhere and to study at the University of Salamanca. There, after only a few days with his companions, the local Dominican friars invited him to Sunday dinner. After the meal one of the friars began to question him about his preaching. We don't preach, Iñigo replied, we simply talk to people about the things of God. But the friar was not about to be put off by subtle distinctions. What things of God do you speak about? About some virtue or other, praising it; or some vice or other, condemning it, Iñigo answered. At that point he realized that this was not a friendly conversation but an interrogation, and by someone more skilled in logic than he was. "'You are not learned men,' said the friar, 'and you speak about virtues and vices; but no one can speak about these except in one of two ways: either through learning or through the Holy Spirit'" [64–65].

Iñigo decided to end the exchange, but it was too late. Once again he found himself arrested and imprisoned under suspicion of being an *alumbrado*. After several days he was summoned before four judges, all of whom had already seen his book of spiritual exercises. They asked about one of the early points in the book where he distinguishes between mortal and venial sin. From where was he getting his ideas, if he had not studied? What did he know about sin or grace?

This time his imprisonment lasted twenty-two days. His judges found no error in his life or teaching but demanded that he spend four years in further studies before he tried to define the difference between mortal and venial sin. Iñigo was dismayed. The verdict meant he would have to stop giving people spiritual exercises. To that he could not agree. He resolved to find someplace new to study, outside Salamanca where the verdict had no force and where he could continue engaging in spiritual conversations.

On his release Iñigo decided to leave Spain and continue his studies at the University of Paris. It would mean coming under the authority of his former enemies, and there were still hostilities between the French and Spanish. But Iñigo felt safer dealing with French soldiers than with the Spanish Inquisition.

He arranged for his three companions to wait in Spain and see if he could find some means for all of them to study. In Paris he hoped to find a few more like-minded men willing to share his mission. He set out alone, his memoirs tell us, taking some books, among them his own early *Spiritual Exercises*.

THE SPIRITUAL EXERCISES

The Spiritual Exercises are predicated on a number of logically unverifiable assumptions, but for Iñigo they were based on experiences so real and profound they were unassailable. For one, at Manresa he became convinced that God was not only speaking to him in his heart but also teaching him like a schoolmaster. That led him to see his entire life as full of lessons. Some, like learning to discern spirits, would serve as guidelines; others— like his excessive penances and struggle with scruples—as learning from his mistakes. Another assumption is the conviction that God's will for us can be found in our deepest authentic desires. One of Iñigo's earliest desires was to make the pilgrimage to Jerusalem, later to help people find God's will for them in their own deepest desires.

Iñigo became convinced that experiencing God in a direct and immediate way was not a special favor reserved for a few select mystics. If God was willing to speak directly to a sinner like him, God would speak to anyone—anyone, at least, who was willing to take the time to be still, listen, and pray. If people were willing to spend an extended period of time in solitude and prayer, daydreaming about Jesus the way he had at Loyola and Manresa, then he, Iñigo, could help them experience God and learn God's will for them. This, he became convinced, was his mission from God: to help people experience God's presence and learn God's will by directing them in making the Spiritual Exercises.

The substance of the Spiritual Exercises existed, at least in outline, by the time Iñigo left Manresa, but he continued to gain insight from his successes and failures at directing others in prayer. His memoirs tell us that he was already giving people spiritual exercises in Alcalá, and in Salamanca his judges were already familiar with his initial manuscript. It started out simply as notes for himself, to aid him in his own efforts at helping people to pray and discern spirits. But his notes eventually evolved into a manual for people who had made the exercises under him, so they could now in turn give the exercises to others. By Alcalá he came to see the task entrusted to him as requiring more than his individual labor. His was a service to be shared.

Iñigo continued to refine his text for the next twenty years, making such revisions and additions as he saw fit based on his further theological education and reflection. Finally in 1548 he was satisfied that it could be put into print. Since that first publication, *Spiritual Exercises* has come to constitute one of the most read and utilized books ever written. It has been published some 4,500 times, an average of once a month for 400 years. The number of copies printed has been estimated at some 4.5 million—despite the fact that the book is about as dull as a teacher's manual of lesson plans. And that is exactly what *Spiritual Exercises* is—a teacher's handbook with detailed directions on how to help people look at their lives, pray, take note of what's going on in themselves and their lives, and make a decision. Amid conflicting inclinations, how can one hear the voice of a God who speaks in the stillness of the heart? Amid our many options, how can we discover our deepest, authentic desires, God's way of calling us?

Like its author, the *Spiritual Exercises* is often misunderstood. Iñigo never intended the Exercises to be given only by Jesuits to other Jesuits. He was a layman when he began directing people through the Exercises, and he gave them to anyone he thought would profit from the experience. He directed women and men, lay people and priests, students and doctors of theology in Paris, high ecclesiastics and reformed prostitutes in Rome. He gave the Exercises to anyone he thought would profit from them: people with seriously sinful pasts desirous of making a change in their lives and already-devout Christians sincerely interested in a deeper experience of God.

Anyone who picks up *Spiritual Exercises* looking for inspiration is sure to be disappointed. The text is wooden. With its examens and points, it reads like a book on counting calories to lose weight or, better yet, a handbook for personal trainers at a health club. For that's what it is—an instructor's manual—but instead of directions on the proper way to do sit-ups and leg exercises, there are directions on how to meditate, contemplate, rid yourself of "disordered affections," and listen for the voice of God.

However, *Spiritual Exercises* is not a self-improvement, do-it-yourself book. Iñigo believed that to avoid the mistakes he had made and profit from the Exercises, a retreatant needed direction from a seasoned veteran. He wrote his book for people who had already made the Exercises themselves and aspired to help others do so. Ignatius Loyola invented the so-called directed thirty-day retreat, indeed the retreat altogether, though he would never claim he was the inventor. All the credit would go to the divine "schoolmaster." What he himself had grasped only slowly and painfully, he simply passed on to others.

Some of these others, like Pierre Favre, an early companion and friend, gave the Exercises to others, and they in turn to still more. Not unlike Zen masters and their disciples, Iñigo's profitable "little book" represents a living tradition, an unbroken chain of recipients-become-directors engaged in a praxis extending back more than four and a half centuries, ultimately back to Ignatius himself.

The *Spiritual Exercises* opens with twenty so-called "annotations," introductory explanations meant to assist the retreat director with practical guidelines [1–20].[16] Several of them grew out of Iñigo's personal experiences at Loyola and Manresa and the lessons he drew from directing others. As such the annotations encapsulate a number of distinctive characteristics of Ignatian spirituality. One of the first and most typical, for example, advises the director on how to help retreatants "relish" making the Exercises so that they get more out of the experience than information. "For, what fills and satisfies the soul consists, not in knowing much, but in our understanding the realities profoundly and in savoring them interiorily" [2]. The Exercises are meant to speak to the whole person—not just the intellect but also the imagination, affections, and will—so that God's presence might be relished by all the senses. We are not angels. Ignatian spirituality is decidedly incarnational in its engagement not of disembodied spirits but flesh-and-blood human beings.

Another hallmark of Ignatian spirituality is summed up in the directive to "allow the Creator to deal immediately with the creature and the creature with its Creator and Lord" [15]. Iñigo instructs directors not to plant any ideas into the head of an exercitant.[17] They are not, for example, to try persuading retreatants into a vocational decision, like religious life. Iñigo's own personal experience became a touchstone for those who would follow in his path. So profound was Iñigo's respect for his own religious experience (such that he was sure he could die for his faith even if there were no Scriptures), that he wanted to impart a similar reverence for the religious experiences of others.

One of the most striking features of these introductory notes is Ignatius's encouragement, indeed insistence, that the Exercises be adapted to the persons making them. The Exercises are not "one size fits all." The director needs to consider the retreatant's age, education, physical health, and whether or not the exercitant is at a crossroads in life and needs to make an important decision. Iñigo divided the Exercises into four groups, which he calls weeks; he thought that for some people the first week was sufficient. Retreatants were to be given only the Exercises that would help them in their spiritual life, and no more [18].

Ignatius conceived the Exercises ideally as a thirty-day retreat, during which a person withdraws from ordinary daily life to be alone with God, living in silence except for conversations with the retreat director. But he took into account that the occupations or family responsibilities of some people don't allow them to take off for that length of time. For such people he recommended making the Exercises for an hour and a half of prayer a day, extended over a longer time span [19]. Thanks to Iñigo's insistence on flexibility, retreatants today can take a week or a weekend to make part of the Exercises, individually directed or preached to a group. They can also make all the Exercises in thirty days or extended within the context of normal daily life over the course of nine months, a so-called "nineteenth annotation retreat."

Another prefatory comment Iñigo inserts into his text is a piece of advice he calls a "presupposition." Its intent was to help improve the quality of conversation between the director and recipient, though it can prove useful for any relationship: "Be more eager to put a good interpretation on a neighbor's statement than to condemn it." One can't help but recall here Iñigo's encounters with the Spanish Inquisition, particularly his experience at Salamanca with the Dominicans, who fretted about his orthodoxy regarding mortal and venial sin. To faultfinders and heresy-hunters of any stripe, he gives the humane advice to judge people and their words in a way that presumes the best, not the worst, and gives them the benefit of any doubt. And if correction is needed, he says, do it with love [22].

With all preliminaries duly noted, Ignatius states that the purpose of the Exercises is to help retreatants bring order into their lives and overcome any obstacles to spiritual growth. This is particularly the objective of the first week, to become free of disorderly attachments so as to be able to give oneself more generously in service.[18] Although the Exercises focus extensively on sin, love is the underlying theme—learning to love in a way that is a generous self-giving, not a mask for self-interest. The opening exercise consists of reflecting and praying over what is called the "principle and foundation," at first glance simply a list of statements about God creating humankind and our purpose in life in the context of creation. The purpose of the "principle and foundation," though, is to confront retreatants with the big picture, so that they can more easily attain a "right-ordered" freedom and make a "right-ordered" decision to give their lives in self-giving love. Iñigo's early life was not consistent with his faith. He would have retreatants look at how consistent their lives are with their faith, going from the big picture to big questions.

After his experience at the Cardoner, Iñigo saw creation not as an event in the distant past but as something going on right now, like the river flowing below him. God is at work, Iñigo perceived, creating us, cherishing us, and desirous of using us as part of a "project."[19] That project holds that we and everyone and everything come from God and are meant to return to God. Ignatius asks if we are making God and God's plan for us the center of our lives or if we are putting something else there instead—health, riches, or honor. What do you love? Or, as Martin Luther put it, what do you hang your heart on?

Hanging your heart wrongly, loving unwisely is the theme that runs through the first week's meditations. One thinks here of the opening words of Iñigo's memoirs with their references to vanity, warlike sport, and the desire for fame. Against the backdrop of God's generosity in creating us, giving us all we are and have, Iñigo asks exercitants to take a long look at their lives. One author has described it as a journey through the hell of self-knowledge. We are to look at the history of sin and the ravages of evil in the world and realize how we have contributed to it. Iñigo then has retreatants imagine themselves in the situation of a knight who stands before his king and his whole court, aware he has "grievously offended him, from whom he had received numerous gifts and favors" [74]. The point is not to look at oneself and wallow in self-recrimination or shame but to look at God and realize that one is loved and graced despite all failures and offenses.

The first week culminates, if it is called for, with contrition, conversion of heart, and perhaps a general confession. One thinks here of the general confession Iñigo made at Montserrat. At the abbey Iñigo looked back at his entire life and set it in a new direction. At the end of the first week, he invites retreatants to do the same.

The metaphor of the knight and his king suggests that Jesus, though hardly mentioned in the first week's Exercises, is very much at the heart of the first week, just as Jesus is incorporated more explicitly in the rest of the Exercises.[20] Iñigo invites retreatants to reflect and ask themselves: "What have I done for Christ? What am I doing for Christ? What ought I to do for Christ" [53]? Implicit in that "what ought I to do for Christ" is the word "more," in Latin, *magis*. The word is emblematic of Ignatian spirituality, an obvious cognate of *majorem*, "greater," as in the Jesuit motto, *ad majorem Dei gloriam* ("For the greater glory of God").

These words or their equivalent appear time and again in the writings of Ignatius. Behind them lie Iñigo's education as a courtier, where the ideal was to distinguish oneself in greater service to one's lord. Iñigo was a creature of his era and upbringing, but was now serving someone greater than the Spanish king or his treasurer.

The dynamic of the second week of Exercises proceeds around two focal meditations. The first, "The Call of the King," presents Jesus as a royal crusader calling his people to join him—sharing his food, drink, and labors—and "conquer the whole land of the infidels" [93]. The second, a meditation on "The Two Standards," presents Jesus as the "supreme commander of the good people," calling them to rally around his banner on a great plain "in the region of Jerusalem." On another plain "in the region of Babylon" is Lucifer, "leader of all the enemy," calling the forces of evil to his flag, to tempt people to sin with riches, vain honor, and pride. Jesus calls those around his standard to share his life and lot, which for Iñigo, in opposition to the enemy, meant poverty instead of riches, criticism and rejection instead of honor, humility instead of pride [136–148].

Experts on Ignatius widely regard these two meditations as the heart of the *Spiritual Exercises* in its earliest form. Both have their genesis in Iñigo's conversion at Loyola, while reading Ludoph's life of Christ and Voragine's lives of the saints. The Spanish edition of the latter, which Iñigo would have read, featured on the title page a picture of Christ crucified. An introduction by the translator read, "Whoever reads this book should grasp the crucifix with his right hand and hold it aloft as a royal standard . . . as an emblem which armed the chivalrous hearts of the saints for a courageous conquest of the world, the flesh, and the devil . . . ."[21] Here too one reads about St. Augustine and his classic *City of God*, in which Augustine "treats of the two cities, Jerusalem and Babylon, and their kings, for Christ is the king of Jerusalem and the devil of Babylon."[22] Iñigo's images of Jesus obviously reflect his own late medieval times more than our own, but they are true to the Jesus of history at least insofar as they present him as someone with a mission, inviting friends to share his way of life in exchange for companionship.[23]

So they could better know what it means to share Jesus' way of life, Iñigo has retreatants do the same thing he did convalescing at Loyola. They read about events taken from the Gospel stories and daydream. He has them imagine themselves at Mary's home in Nazareth, at Jesus' birth in the stable at Bethlehem, at the shores of the Sea of Galilee when Jesus calls his first disciples. Iñigo instructs the exercitants to "see the place," to use all their senses in placing themselves into the Gospel stories. He has them enter into conversation with God, Jesus, or Mary, and even instructs them on what favors to ask for.

Not only the second week, but also the Spiritual Exercises as a whole culminate in a consideration of what it takes to make a "sound and good election," which is to say, a decision about what to do with the rest of one's life [169–89]. Everything else leads up to or away from it. For people at a crossroads, like Iñigo at Loyola, the election may entail choosing a state of life—like marrying, remaining single, or entering religious life. For those with no such decision to make, the choice entails how to become a better Christian, to bring one's life more into line with the gospel values one experiences in reflecting on the life of Jesus. Experts on Ignatian spirituality generally see the "election" or decision, in one or the other form, as the essential purpose of the Exercises.[24] It amounts to a second conversion, this time not *from* sin but *to* a more focused discipleship.

Ignatius expects retreatants to make their decision by discovering God's will for them. This they do by probing their deepest, authentic desires and discerning—which is to say distinguishing—between the spirits that move within them. In his rules for discernment of spirits, Ignatius identifies God's will with what brings "genuine happiness and spiritual joy," in contrast to "the enemy" who induces "sadness and turmoil" [329]. Whatever "weakens, disquiets, or disturbs the soul" comes from the evil spirit. Whatever brings "happiness and spiritual consolation" comes from God, particularly if it is a "consolation without previous cause." The ambiguity of the latter phrase has been a cause célèbre for Ignatian interpreters but seems to suggest that making the Exercises entails not only one's conscious imagination, intellect, and will, but unconscious dynamics as well.[25]

DECISION

In the view of many Ignatian experts, the third and fourth weeks are meant to serve as a confirmation of one's decision. Exercitants in the third week contemplate the last days of Jesus so that they might intensify their identification with him. To remedy what could be an overly romantic vision of discipleship, Ignatius gives them a healthy dose of realism. They are to imagine how Jesus felt entering Jerusalem for what he knew would be his last supper, the agony in the garden, the minute details of Jesus' passion and death. Retreatants are asked to foster an attitude of heartbreak, banishing any joyful thoughts even if they are good and holy [206]. Affectivity here is the key to strengthening resolve and identifying oneself with the trusting surrender of the rejected and crucified Christ.[26]

Just as identifying with Christ's suffering is the focal point of the third week, identifying with his Easter joy is the focus of the fourth. Iñigo has retreatants reflect on the various resurrection stories in the Gospels and instructs them to ask for a share in the gladness of Jesus' exaltation to glory. He tells them to recall and reflect on "things which bring pleasure, happiness, and spiritual joy." He suggests they go outdoors and seek pleasant experiences in nature according to the seasons, enjoying "refreshing coolness in summer or the sun or heat in winter" [229]. The advice serves as an apt segue to the contemplation on love that follows, with its celebrated Ignatian principle of "finding God in all things."[27]

Serving as the climax and conclusion of the four weeks, the "contemplation to attain love" aims at helping retreatants learn to love the way God does. It mirrors in many ways the "principle and foundation" with which Ignatius began the first week's Exercises, by placing the retreatant before all creation. But now everything is seen as grace, as the gift of a gracious God.

The contemplation opens with the oft-quoted Ignatian dictum, "Love ought to manifest itself more by deeds than by words." Ignatius, as noted above, had nothing against feelings, but he was more interested in cultivating a love that serves and gives, even when we don't much feel like it. He saw this kind of love as rising out of gratitude. He has the retreatants reflect on all that they have received, not only all that they are and have but, indeed, God's very Self. And in gratitude for God's self-gift, Iñigo has us respond in kind with our own self-gift, expressed in his oft-quoted prayer, known by its first word in Latin, *Suscipe:* "Take, Lord, and receive all my liberty, my memory, my understanding, and all my will—all that I have and possess. You, Lord, have given all that to me. I now give it back to you, O Lord. All of it is yours. Dispose of it according to your will. Give me your love and your grace, for that is enough for me" [234].

The prayer is almost a summary of Ignatian spirituality. Unusual for his times, the first thing Ignatius has us offer, before any of our intellectual faculties, is our liberty, viewed by many modern thinkers as that which is most basic to us as human beings.[28]

The contemplation has us look at the world through the eyes of the protagonist in George Bernanos's *Diary of a Country Priest* who whispers as he dies, *Tout est grace* ("Everything is grace"). Everything is "from above"—each day of life, each person in our lives, each kind word, smile, flower, tree—all of it is gift. Like a composer-conductor reaching the coda of a symphony, Ignatius brings all the instruments into a final three-note crescendo [235–237]. First realize that all creation—everything we are and have and see—is given as token of God's self-gift. Second, realize that God is present in all creation—dwelling in the elements, plants, animals, and us. Finally, realize that God is not only present but "laboring" in all that exists—creating, conserving, concurring.

In each of the concluding three points of the contemplation, Ignatius writes, "I will reflect on myself." God is present in us, working in us, self-giving in us. The Exercises end, and we return to our routines filled with a sense of divine immanence—in the world, in our lives, and in our labors, no matter how busy or mundane. The Ignatian ideal is that now we can recall and relive an experience of "union and familiarity" with God that uplifts and sustains us no matter the distractions of our work or banality of our lives.[29]

Here is the basis for finding God not only in all things but also in the flurry of everyday life. Nothing human is merely human. No common labor is merely common. Classrooms, hospitals, and artists' studios are sacred spaces. No secular pursuit of science is merely secular. The hand of the creator can be detected by looking at galaxies through telescopes or examining cellular life in laboratories. Retreatants return to their supposedly dull, humdrum lives with a new vision and appreciation of God's operative presence. Like Ignatius after his experience at the Cardoner River, we see things differently. We get a new sense of what Jesuit poet Gerard Manley Hopkins meant when he wrote, "The world is charged with the grandeur of God."[30]

TRANSLATING THE SPIRITUAL EXERCISES

Even from this brief description, it is evident that the *Spiritual Exercises* shows its age, or, more precisely, the age in which it originated. As mentioned already, Iñigo de Loyola has reminded more than one commentator of Cervantes's Don Quixote. Born in the last days of chivalry, Ignatius conceived of himself and the retreatants he directed as knights-errant, serving in the ranks of a crusader Christ. In an age of conquistadors, he pledges his fealty to a Jesus he perceives as "supreme commander" and king of

Jerusalem, making claims not to mere continents but all humankind. Opposed to this enterprise is Lucifer, "seated on a throne of fire and smoke" situated on "the great plain of Babylon." With both combatants rallying their forces around their raised standards, Iñigo invites all who will give him the time to reflect and choose the banner under which they will stand.

There are images and categories in the *Spiritual Exercises* that, from a twenty-first-century perspective, are foreign and problematic. The "land of the infidels" that Iñigo wanted to conquer in the name of Jesus belonged to God-fearing Muslims, who, more often than not, behaved much more decently to the peoples they conquered than did cross-bearing Christians. The crusader metaphor poses difficulties in our pluralistic global culture, even if spiritualized and mounted against the forces of evil. The cosmic dualism that pits Jesus against the devil has a more prominent place in Iñigo's worldview than it has in the Gospels' or our own. And when Iñigo has us imagine the Triune God gazing down at a world overrun with sinners, the heavens as he saw them hung much closer to earth than do our own.

The bridges over the Cardoner River have seen a lot of water flow under them in the last 450 years. Our universe is vastly larger. Evolution is part of our scientific and cultural worldview. Evil is still mysterious but less likely to be projected outside ourselves onto a fallen angel. Catholic church leaders today speak of Jews and Muslims not as infidels but as children of Abraham related to Christians by a "spiritual bond." We read the Bible, including the Gospel stories, with greater awareness of what is history and what is not, appreciating better than Iñigo or our forebears could the role that symbols and symbolic stories play in expressing faith.

All of which is to say that we need to read the *Spiritual Exercises* against the backdrop of its origins. Such a reading requires that we first situate it within its own historical context and then translate its meaning for our own time and culture. As noted above, Ignatius gathered companions around himself so they could help him help others make spiritual exercises. When he wrote the *Spiritual Exercises* to help them in that task, he counseled them to accommodate themselves to circumstances. Early on

Jesuits took Ignatius at his word.[31] They accommodated the Exercises not only to the situation of individual retreatants but also to particular cultures. Taking a cue from the tradition, female Ignatian experts have begun adapting the Exercises by accommodating them to the contours of feminine spirituality and culture.[32]

Jesuits have translated and adapted the *Spiritual Exercises* to the disparate cultures of Latin America, Asia, and Africa, as well as postmodern Western Europe and North America. Some attempts in this direction entail simply a more modern reading of the text.[33] Others essay a complete paraphrase, replacing the images of Ignatius's late medieval and Renaissance worldview with those more accessible to our own. To illustrate this latter form of adaptation, one could hardly do better than to look at the overhaul that has been given to "the examen," the daily examination of conscience. The practice is an ancient one, predating Christianity, but it has been reconditioned into what has been called "the most postmodern prayer."[34]

Of all the various spiritual exercises, Ignatius was particularly keen on the examen. He practiced it regularly himself and wrote into the constitutions, which directs the lives and practices of the Society of Jesus, that Jesuits are to do it twice a day. Though he dispensed sick Jesuits from other exercises like meditation, he hardly ever dispensed anyone from the examination of conscience. Of any practice in the *Spiritual Exercises,* only the examen received this kind of approval rating. Ignatius obviously agreed with Socrates that the unexamined life is not worth living.

And yet not only for Jesuits but also for most people attracted to Ignatian spirituality, the examen became a sterile routine. Of all the spiritual exercises, it was the most easily relinquished. Blame it on Freud and fear of neurotic guilt or simply greater sophistication about the inner workings of the subconscious. Nitpicking one's memory for moral failings appeared spiritually unproductive and psychologically unhealthy . . . until at least one Jesuit spiritual director remembered that in Spanish, and so for Ignatius, *consciencia* meant not only "conscience" but also "consciousness."[35] Whereas examining one's "conscience" has narrow, moralistic overtones related to what we have or have not done, examining "consciousness" entails looking at what is being done to us: how we are being affected and moved (often quite spontaneously) deep in our affective consciousness. We look back at what is going on in our lives and pay notice not so much to faults as to feelings.

One avid supporter of examining one's consciousness has described the exercise as "praying backward through your day" and offered the following five steps as a way of doing it.[36] Each step is a prayer.

1. One begins with a prayer for light, perhaps to the Holy Spirit. The examen is not merely about remembering, it's about insight into the mystery that we are even to ourselves. The purpose of the exercise is a graced understanding of when and where and how the Spirit of God has been leading us. It makes sense to ask God for help to see ourselves, not so much as others see us but as Christ does, who sees into the deep recesses of the heart.

2. Next comes a review of the day with, as one Jesuit slogan puts it, an "attitude of gratitude." Rooted in the contemplation on love that concludes the *Spiritual Exercises,* gratefulness is a prominent feature of Ignatian spirituality. The examen provides an opportunity to count the gifts of the last twenty-four hours—everything from a morning cup of coffee to a chance meeting with an old acquaintance. All is gift and calls for thanks.

3. As we walk through the day, though, beside the gifts we note the gaffs. Small pleasures bring to mind sore spots; pleasant surprises conjoin with annoying frustrations. These too call for prayer. Feelings, whether positive or negative, are an index to what is going on in our lives and force us to look not so much at our actions or failures as the motives and reasons behind them.

4. This kind of review of the day may conjure up a welter of feelings, or maybe only one. Even if several come to mind, one usually stands out, calling for particular attention and focused prayer. Envying someone may call for praying for that person.

Shame at one's insensitivity calls for sorrow. Anger, defensiveness, and self-righteousness . . . the examen calls for a self-critical assessment of one's spontaneous feelings, which tell us who we are and perhaps what we need to do. Feelings may be spontaneous, but that does not mean they are beyond control.

5. The examen closes with a look to the future, sometimes evoking a sense of determination and a resolve to try again. But other feelings could rise up just as well, and these too can be turned into prayer, for whatever comes most readily. Spontaneous sentiments are usually the deepest, where, St. Paul says, we find the Spirit of God praying within us (Rom 8:26–27).

The examen ends, as do most exercises, with the Lord's Prayer, expressing trust and asking for forgiveness and deliverance. Whichever sentiment speaks best to the heart at the time depends on what transpired in the previous quarter-hour. Gratitude for gifts may have held center stage, or a worrisome feeling, or concern for the future. Whatever the focus, Ignatian spirituality encourages that we adapt our prayer to our particular circumstances at the time, allowing a free interplay of our most personal experience, reflection, and action.

As one can see from the foregoing, there is considerable difference between conscience and consciousness. Jesuit translators have transposed a moralistic search for sins into a prayerful review of God working in one's life. But in doing so, have they taken too many liberties? Whatever one's view of the matter, there is no doubt that they have interpreted the mind of Ignatius. They had no choice. Cultures and their languages change. Every day new words are born, some old ones die, and still others acquire new and different meanings. To refuse to translate an ancient or classic text is to risk misunderstanding it. And understanding it requires putting it into its historical context. Words like *persons* (with respect to the Christian understanding of God), *jihad,* and *crusade* are problematic for us today because we do not think like fourth-century Greeks, seventh-century

Muslims, or twelfth-century Roman Catholics. Neither do we think like sixteenth-century Spaniards.

Translating, as all who have tried their hands at it know, requires making choices. Once you understand a word or text within its historical context, how do you express it in today's quite different situation? Biblical scholars know the dilemma. How do you translate the Hebrew *Yahweh Sabaoth* of Isaiah's vision of God (Is 6:3), cited verbatim in the Sanctus of the Latin Mass? Literally as "Lord of the armies," or figuratively as "Lord of power and might"? How do you translate the Greek addresses of Paul's epistles? Literally as "brothers," or inclusively as "brothers and sisters"? The challenge faced by translators and interpreters is fidelity to the spirit and mind of the text and its author, distinguishing between negotiable forms and nonnegotiable substance, between what is at the heart of the matter and what is a matter of mere cultural expression. That said, what stands behind the image of a crusader Christ? What are the nonnegotiables of Ignatian spirituality? What are the characteristics that define it?

The foregoing consideration of Ignatius's life and the origins of the *Spiritual Exercises* have already given us a few clues.[37]

SOME DISTINCTIVE FEATURES OF IGNATIAN SPIRITUALITY

For being quite a slender volume, the *Spiritual Exercises* has generated whole shelves of commentary. There are books that probe each idea, parsing virtually every word and relating them to Ignatius's other writings like the *Constitutions of the Society of Jesus* and his thousands of letters. Because Ignatian spirituality arose out of a life experience, some of the most valuable analysis explores the historical origins of its various characteristics. One such distinctive feature, for example, is generosity, as articulated in the recurrent theme of doing "more" (*magis*) for the "greater" glory of God (*ad majorem Dei gloriam*). We can see from Iñigo's memoirs how this arose from the idealized notions of knighthood he imbibed reading romances at the court of Juan Velázquez de Cuéllar. Generous service was expected of a vassal-knight in response to the generous patronage and friendship of his temporal liege-lord. How much more for the friendship of the eternal "universal Lord"?

Given the massive literature on the subject, it would be unrealistic to attempt an extensive analysis of Ignatian spirituality here. But a summary outline of its more salient features may be helpful. The crux of this study is to examine the influence of Renaissance humanism on Ignatian spirituality. But, at the risk of some repetition, what can be distilled from the considerations made thus far? Obviously there is much about Ignatian spirituality that is generic. Rooted in a 1500-year-old Catholic tradition, it has features in common with other, earlier forms of Christian spirituality. But even those common features have a slant to them that, taken together, make them distinctively Ignatian.

1. Centeredness on a Christ with a Mission

Clearly there is nothing exceptional about a Christian spirituality being Christ-centered. But there is a wide variety of aspects of Jesus' person and life described in the Gospel stories—his forty days in the wilderness, his teaching and healing, his poverty and passion. These have all led to various schools or kinds of spirituality. Despite all they have in common, there are distinctive features to the spiritualities associated with St. Benedict, St. Francis of Assisi, and St. Dominic. The same can be said of Ignatian spirituality. Its Christ is not the one whose time apart in a wilderness inspired early Christian hermits or gave rise to cloisters; the Ignatian Christ is a man on the move.

It is worth noting how relatively few of the Gospel stories assigned for prayerful reading in the *Spiritual Exercises* have to do with miracles compared with those that have to do with Jesus teaching people and engaging them in conversation. Ludolph's life of Christ that Iñigo read while convalescing at Loyola presents a Jesus who reveals and mediates God to a fallen humanity. Ludolph invited his readers first to seek forgiveness and renewal of spirit in Christ and then to read and reflect on the events of his life in such a way as to experience and imitate him. Taking Ludolph at his word, Ignatius did just that, and in the *Spiritual Exercises* he invites retreatants to do the same.

Behind the medieval metaphors of competing armies and a crusading king lies the idea of a divine project or master plan, expressive of what St. Paul's epistles describe as a divine "mystery."[38] This mystery is that Christ's mission is to unite all things in himself and thereby to God (1 Thes 5:9; Col 2:2; Eph 1:9–10). In Christ the world is reconciled to God (2 Cor 5:19). Paul's vision is panoramic. "All [things] are yours. And you are Christ's, and Christ is God's" (1 Cor 3:22–23). According to the project, as both Paul and Ignatius understood it, the church continues the reconciling work of Jesus. It exists to carry on his mission and thereby do him service. Every Christian is called to some particular aspect of that service, to do his or her part in the divine project.

The first week of the Spiritual Exercises opens with fundamental questions of existence: Why does anything exist? What is my purpose? How do I fit in? In the "principle and foundation" of the *Exercises,* Ignatius responds to those questions with answers as basic as the first pages of a catechism or Sunday school reader: we were created to "praise, reverence, and serve God our Lord"; all creation exists to help us attain that end. Ignatius connects St. Paul's cosmic vision with the quite individualized invitation of Jesus to "come, . . . follow me" (Mk 10:21). What exactly following Jesus means varies from one person to another. Ignatius gradually grew sure that God did not intend a monastic existence for him. He gleaned this as he looked back at the unfolding course of his life history and listened to what for him was God speaking in the deepest desires of his heart. In the *Spiritual Exercises* he invites retreatants to do the same.

2. Trinitarian Sweep

There is a Trinitarian sweep to Ignatian spirituality. No distant watch-maker/architect or self-absorbed thinker, God in the *Spiritual Exercises* is "one who is laboring," [236] not only creating the universe but also rec-onciling it in and through Christ. As for the early Christians, so for Ignatius too, reflection on Christ had Trinitarian implications. Who is Jesus? How does he relate to the God he called Father? Who or what is the Holy Spirit? Not that Iñigo explicitly thought out these questions. For him the Triune God of Catholic tradition was more a reality of experience than a question for pondering. He tells us in his memoirs [28] that he had "great devotion" to the Most Holy Trinity and that one day he experienced God as three keys on a musical instrument making one harmonious chord. The experience moved him to tears, something that occurred often in his later life, particularly if he happened to see three instances of anything.

There is nothing original about the Trinitarian imagery of the *Spiritual Exercises*. In some ways it is naïve in its portrayal of the Triune God "seated, so to speak, on the royal throne of their divine majesty" [106]. God is "the Father," seated "above." Jesus, who is both above and below, is the "eter-nal King" who mediates for us with the Father, revealing and accom-plishing God's master plan. Both, together with the Holy Spirit, are "God our Lord" or the "Divine Majesty." What is striking about the *Spiritual Exercises* is Iñigo's panoramic view of salvation history, in which the entire universe is viewed as proceeding from God and returning to God, link-ing the ongoing creation to its consummation. There is a Trinitarian cir-cularity to Ignatian spirituality. The end of the *Spiritual Exercises* corresponds to the beginning. The creating God of the opening "principle and foundation" is the "same Lord" who, in the "contemplation to attain love" concluding the *Exercises,* "desires to give me even his very self, in accordance with his divine design" [234].

It is often noted that there is little mention of the Holy Spirit in the *Spiritual Exercises*. In fact, there is only one explicit reference, in which

Ignatius describes the Holy Spirit as one who governs and guides the church [365]. This makes the Spirit latent but not absent. Taking as an example the just-cited reference to God desiring to give "even his very self," one can argue that allusions to the Holy Spirit abound throughout the text, and not only at their climax in the "contemplation to attain love." The discernment of spirits looks not only to the inner motions or dynamics within our psyches but also to their causes. Consolation, which is central to the Exercises and at the heart of the discernment of spirits, is regarded by Christian tradition as the work of the Holy Spirit. So too is the indwelling of God's presence in ourselves and all things, which is a hallmark of Ignatian spirituality.

The image of God as Father or Creator points to God as transcendent, beyond creation and "above." The image of God as spirit—meaning both "breath" and "wind"—points to the immanent God whose power, like wind, is beyond telling and whose presence, like one's breath, is experienced "within." Ignatius was not careful in making Trinitarian distinctions. More than once in the *Exercises* he describes Jesus as "Creator and Lord," and attributes to him the Spirit's traditional "office of consoler" [224]. We can excuse Iñigo's lack of linguistic precision here. In Christ the meaning of creation and the purpose of consolation flow together like the waters of a river, revealing the One God who is at once Creator and Consoler, Giver and Gift.

3. Liberality of Grace

Grace is one of the most distinctive and pivotal concepts of Christian theology and spirituality. Recurring time and again in the epistles of St. Paul, there can be no self-reflective Christian spirituality without it. Yet, in the so-called "rules for thinking with the church" of the *Spiritual Exercises,* Ignatius warns directors against speaking "so lengthily and emphatically about grace that we generate a poison harmful to freedom of the will"

[369]. He explains the caution in terms of the controversies besetting the church at the time with regard to human responsibility and predestination.

The sixteenth-century debates over grace arose out of the theology of St. Augustine, named by subsequent centuries the Doctor of Grace. God's grace for him was primarily an unmerited supernatural help to convert from sin or resist temptation. Augustine knew the weakness of his own human nature and his own need for God's help; he interpreted that help as grace. With all due respect to the Doctor of Grace, that notion of grace, while correct as it stands, is much too narrow. The biblical understanding of grace is far richer and more wide-ranging, as St. Thomas Aquinas later noted and as the several cognates of the word suggest.

The Greek word for grace, *charis,* lies at the heart of both *charisma* and *Eucharist.* The Latin *gratia,* the root of the Spanish *gracias* and Italian *grazie,* is also at the heart of English words like *gracious, graceful, gratitude,* and the concept of a grace before meals. The word has three interrelated levels of meaning. Its primary reference is to the "graciousness" or generosity of one who gives and, in the case of debts or wrongdoing, forgives. Its secondary reference is to the "gift" that is given. With respect to gifts from a gracious God, the word may point to the natural talent of a gifted musician, the gracefulness of a dancer, or the charisma of a speaker. In the case of debts or wrongdoing, the gift is that of mercy and forgiveness, the meaning favored by Martin Luther. In the case of those unable to resist temptation or do the right thing on their own, the gift is God's supernatural help, the meaning St. Augustine preferred. The Catholic Middle Ages focused on the gift of God's love, viewed as something poured into our hearts. More recently, thanks greatly to Karl Rahner, Catholic theology gives more attention to the Self-Gift that is God's indwelling Spirit. As a response to all these gifts and the graciousness from which they flow derives the third basic meaning of *grace,* "gratitude," the expression of thankfulness to God that is the focus of a grace before a meal or the canonical eucharistic prayer of the Mass.

Ignatius may have been wary of dwelling at any great length on the subject of grace, lest he raise a red flag for inquisitors suspicious of his orthodoxy. But allusions to all three levels of meaning behind the word abound in the *Spiritual Exercises*—God's graciousness and gifts, and our duty to respond with gratitude. But here too there is a distinctive Ignatian slant. St. Augustine was impressed by the amount of sin in the world; humanity for him was a *massa damnata*. That seems to imply that grace is not only unearned but bestowed sparingly. Ignatius, on the other hand, was impressed by the fact that God spoke to him despite his sinfulness. That implied a liberality to God's giving and forgiving. If God would speak to him, he would speak to anyone. And from a conviction of abundant grace springs what has been called Ignatian optimism. The "contemplation to attain love" is a veritable hymn to grace, aimed at stirring the soul to "profound gratitude" by reflecting on God's generosity as Giver and Gift [233]. If Ignatian spirituality seeks and finds "God in all things," it is because everything is grace.

4. Faith as Trust

Faith is as central to Christian life and spirituality as grace is. Jesus in the Gospels makes it requisite for entry into God's reign. There can be neither discipleship nor healing without it. For St. Paul, Christians can be identified simply as "believers" or "the faithful." And yet, like grace, the word *faith* became a red flag for Catholics in Ignatius's day, after Luther seemed to disparage love and good works by making grace and faith alone the essence of the gospel. So again, in the "rules for thinking with the church" of the *Spiritual Exercises,* Ignatius warns against speaking too much or too emphatically about faith, without any further distinction or explanation [368].

Ignatius was giving sound advice there. Faith requires explanation, because the word is ambiguous. It is one thing to have faith or believe *that* a statement is true or *that* someone is telling the truth. It is something else altogether—involving the whole person and not just one's intellect—to have faith *in* someone or to believe *in* something, in other words, to trust.

Faith in the Hebrew Bible (*amoona,* a cognate of *amen*) means being able to lean on someone or something that is trustworthy, like a rock. Trust in himself and his message is what Jesus claimed could move mountains (Mk 11:23). Their trust in their moms and dads is the reason Jesus tells his disciples to become like little children (Mk 10:15). For the Hebrew Bible and the Jewish Jesus, trust is the primary and basic meaning of faith.

But the disciples' trust in Jesus, especially after Easter, required explanation and argument. Faith *in* him led to expressions of faith *that*—that he is the Risen Christ, Lord, Son of God. Verbalizing one's trust and the reasons for it invariably leads to the secondary meaning of faith as intellectual acceptance and avowal of a statement as true. As the Jewish-Christian church entered into the cerebral world of Greek culture and became more gentile, it was this intellectual understanding of faith that became dominant. "The faith" became identified with dogmatic formulas and creeds, and the virtue of faith was defined as accepting them as revealed and true. Trust—in God, in Jesus, in God's providence and promises—became more identified with the virtue of hope. The ambiguity of the word was at the heart of much of the debates about faith in the Reformation era, and Ignatius found it wise not to become embroiled in these debates. But trust is very much a central feature of Ignatian spirituality, just as it was for Luther.

Trust became a focal point for Luther out of his reading of St. Paul. It became a focus for Ignatius out of his reading of Gospel stories, for there he encountered a Jesus who had nowhere to lay his head. Jesus' poverty is central for Ignatius's Christology; it is at the heart of his being "Eternal King" and "Lord of all the world." In the meditation on the "two Standards," riches are the allurement of "the enemy." One stands with Jesus by one's willingness to share his poverty. Recall here from his memoirs how determined Iñigo was to live by begging while on his pilgrimage to Jerusalem, going so far as to leave behind his few remaining coins before boarding ship. On a later leg of his journey as well, he trusted God would provide and "brought no more for his maintenance than his hope in God" [44]. He might have said *faith,* but because the word in Catholic tradition had become so intellectualized, he said *hope.* But whether articulated as faith or hope, he was talking about trust, which was indispensable both for the literal kind of pilgrimage he made to Jerusalem and the spiritual one he invited people to make in the *Spiritual Exercises*. Call it faith or hope, it took trust to risk either pilgrimage, just as it takes trust to say the suscipe and really mean it.

5. Service in the World

If the suscipe sums up Ignatian spirituality, it disproves any allegation that the Spiritual Exercises are an attempt at self-salvation. Ignatius's prayer is a quintessential expression of a faith that acknowledges the priority of grace: all that I have and possess, you, Lord, have given to me. But then the prayer entrusts everything back to God: all of it is yours, dispose of it according to your will [234]. In the meditation on the kingdom, Ignatius has retreatants, like vassal-knights, consider how they "ought to respond to a king so generous and kind" [94]. He invites them to respond with generous desires and generous service.

Service is at the core of Ignatian spirituality, encapsulated in a phrase that Ignatius used more than any other in his writings: "helping souls." The phrase appears in the first paragraphs of the *Constitutions of the Society of Jesus* as its purpose for existence. But Iñigo gave spiritual exercises to lay people long before there was a Society of Jesus; as early as his stay in Alcalá, the widow and her daughter he directed were moved by the exercises to a desire to serve poor people in hospitals. Service appears at the culmination of the *Spiritual Exercises* in the "contemplation to attain love," where it is described as the love that manifests itself "more by deeds than by words" [230]. The Christ of the "Meditation on Two Standards" sends his servants and friends out "to aid all persons" [146]. The "election" of the second week—to which everything prior leads and from which everything after proceeds—is a decision about what form one's service will take, discerning God's will in one's deepest desires.

For that decision to be truly authentic, Ignatius put a premium on freedom. To discern those deepest desires amid the pull and tug of competing interests and attractions, he counseled retreatants to cultivate a quiet equilibrium (a state he termed "indifference"). He also insisted that directors allow God "to deal immediately" with retreatants without interference [15]. They were not to persuade exercitants toward one form of service or vocation over another, not even to the religious life or priesthood. This would eventually lead to criticism of the *Spiritual Exercises* for not favoring religious vows over married life. But Ignatian spirituality implicitly recognizes the validity and value of all vocations and all forms of service. Jesuits were accused of borrowing from Protestants by describing their various forms of service as ministries.[39] But the biblical term, thanks to the Second Vatican Council, is now an integral part of Catholic theology and spirituality, linking the episcopal and presbyterial ministries of bishops and priests to those of the laity, whose service is no less vital or necessary to the church for being called lay.

Helping souls as a characteristic of Ignatian spirituality does not (and never did) mean ignoring people's bodies. And the reader will note the modesty implied in the word "helping" rather than "saving" souls. But it is the openness of the *Spiritual Exercises* to people both inside and outside religious life that makes Ignatian spirituality particularly apt for a twenty-first century marked by increasing lay involvement and leadership in the Catholic church. If, as Ignatius put it in the Jesuit constitutions, we can and ought to "seek God our Lord in all things," then there is no aspect of life or human endeavor that is outside of grace or inappropriate for Christian service.

Seeking and finding God in all things, Iñigo and his Jesuit companions went where they saw needs. They would ask the pope to send them where he saw the greatest needs. And they would elicit the assistance of laymen and laywomen to help them in their response to those needs. "The world is our home," said Jerónimo Nadal, Iñigo's close associate and someone he credited with truly understanding what the *Spiritual Exercises* is all about. With the world as their home, Jesuits and those who shared their spirituality (the "extended Ignatian family") more often than not found themselves where the people and their needs were most numerous—in city centers. Serving people anywhere in the world and finding God there, Ignatius—again to cite Nadal—became a "contemplative in action." The phrase has become a classic expression of the Ignatian spiritual ideal.

6. Praying with Discernment

Is there anything distinctive about prayer in the Ignatian tradition? "Contemplative in action" has become a slogan in Ignatian circles. Is Ignatian prayer peculiarly contemplative? Not if one understands the word, as most people do, as prayer that is free-flowing and without images. Ignatian prayer is highly structured and teems with images. In the second week of the Spiritual Exercises, Ignatius asks retreatants to contemplate ("look at") the birth of Christ, using all their senses. One is to imagine the road, feel the wind, listen in on the conversation between Mary and Joseph, gaze at the newborn infant—all activities intended to arouse the affections. An exercise with a very different aim is the meditation on hell, which asks retreatants not only to imagine the pain but see the fires, hear the wailing blasphemies, and smell the sulphurous smoke and rot.

Given such appeal to all the senses, one might say that prayer in the Ignatian tradition is peculiarly holistic. Contemplations employ the imagination so as to speak to the heart. In meditations one thinks discursively by reasoning, reflecting, and reckoning so as to bring about a firm decision by the will. The examination of consciousness and "contemplation to attain love" both rely on memory to stir up a sense of gratitude. Ignatius has retreatants pray for sorrow, tears, shame, serenity, consolation, knowledge of God's will in one's deepest desires, and the affections necessary to pursue those desires.

This broad appeal to the spiritual faculties does not imply that Ignatius forgot the body. He gives advice about eating, sleeping, and what time of day or night certain exercises are to be made. He makes recommendations on one's posture while praying (standing, sitting, kneeling, walking about, lying face up or prostrate on the floor), when to close the shades to keep out the sunlight or go outside to feel its warmth. There is even an exercise that calls for taking a breath between each word of the Our Father. Focusing on breathing while praying is something we ordinarily associate with yoga.

None of these methods or recommendations for prayer is original with Ignatius or peculiar to Ignatian spirituality. They are found in earlier schools of Christian and non-Christian spirituality. If anything is peculiar about the Ignatian slant on them, it is the freedom with which they may be used or ignored. No directive is sacrosanct, unless it is that of "whatever helps." Ignatius's approach to prayer is pragmatic. (Spiritual exercises on humility prove more beneficial to aristocrats and ambitious clerics than self-deprecating commoners.) Whatever works to bring a retreatant to conversion, consolation, and deeper love of God and neighbor, that is the kind of prayer to be recommended—at the director's discretion.

Discretion is another way to translate that most idiosyncratic of Ignatian terms generally rendered as *discernment*. Both words come from the Latin verb *discerno,* meaning "to sever or separate." It subsequently came to mean "to distinguish, discriminate, comprehend, and judge." Ignatius used the substantive form of the verb to mean not only discernment and discretion, but also insight. Keenness of insight and skill in discriminating are accurate representations of what Ignatius meant by the word.[40]

Praying in the Ignatian tradition pays attention and discriminates. The director pays attention and discerns what is going on within the retreatant, so as to be able to counsel which exercises to recommend and which not. Retreatants pay attention and discern what is going on within themselves, discriminating between what causes true inner peace and what causes distress. Discernment is the key to moral conversion, for only from self-knowledge can there come self-discipline. Discernment is also the key to discovering what kind of service one is being called to offer. Service in the world, as pointed out above, is characteristic of Ignatian spirituality. But what kind of service? The answer is discovered by discerning what constitutes the "greater" glory of God.

Coupled with the word *discernment* is that other peculiarly Ignatian word, *magis*. Translated as "more," the word has been mistaken to mean that Ignatian spirituality calls for constantly giving more and more of oneself in a kind of messianic enthusiasm that can lead to burnout. Nothing could be further from Ignatius's mind. Seeking the *magis* in Ignatian spirituality means paying attention to means and ends and discerning what is "more conducive" to achieving the end results desired. It's a matter of discriminating between options and choosing the better of the two. (Burnout is not a reasonable option.) Thus one prays over one's choices, looks at one's gifts, considers the needs, and then decides where can one do the greater good.

These six are only some of the traits usually described in commentaries as distinctively Ignatian. More could be said about respect for freedom or the emphasis on God's mercy in the sacrament of penance. Some elements of Ignatian spirituality (like the *examen* or the focus on poverty) were borrowed from earlier sources. And others, if distinctive at one time, are no longer so (like frequent Holy Communion). But, to return to the thesis of this book, it was more than Iñigo's life experiences that gave shape to the *Spiritual Exercises* and the spirituality arising from it.

His memoirs tell us what Iñigo remembered, not what he took as much for granted as the air he breathed. That air included the assumptions and attitudes embedded in the culture of his day. It included the education he and his companions received as university students at Alcalá and Paris. The spirituality codified in the *Spiritual Exercises* is a product both of Ignatius's experiences and Renaissance humanist culture. It is that influence that warrants calling it Ignatian humanism.

TWO

～

THE RENAISSANCE
ORIGINS OF IGNATIAN
HUMANISM

Already by this time they had all determined what they would do, go to Venice and to Jerusalem and spend their lives for the good of souls; and if they were not given permission to remain in Jerusalem, then return to Rome and present themselves to the Vicar of Christ, so that he could make use of them wherever he thought it would be more for the glory of God and the good of souls. They also planned to wait a year in Venice for passage; but if there was no passage for the East that year, they would be free of their vow about Jerusalem.[85][1]

Except for the word *vow*, one would hardly think from this passage in Ignatius's memoirs that anything exceptional had occurred on that August 15, 1534. He mentions the occasion almost as an afterthought, inserting it into his narrative after forgetting to include it earlier. Only benefit of hindsight allows us to view the day as one that changed history.[2]

Ignatius and his six companions were all at or near the end of their studies at the University of Paris. A kind of informal fraternity of seven, they called themselves *amigos en el Señor*, "friends in the Lord." Like most students at graduation, they were at a crossroads. What would they do with the rest of their lives? They might simply have said their good-byes and gone their separate ways, but Ignatius had already directed five of the others in making the Spiritual Exercises and planned to do the same for the sixth. They decided to remain together, live poorly, and serve God by doing good. With the enthusiasm of youth, they set their sights on Jerusalem, the holy city that they, like most Europeans, still regarded as the center of the world.

Ignatius had taken to escaping the raucous, narrow lanes of the Latin Quarter, where most university students made their home, by climbing up the Montmartre, just north of the city, for some quiet prayer. Halfway up the rustic slope he discovered the small, cryptlike chapel of Notre Dame, so different from its imposing Gothic namesake at the center of the city. It was perfect for their purposes. On August 15, the feast of Mary's Assumption, the seven *amigos en el Señor* climbed up to the small chapel, where they vowed to spend their lives together for the "glory of God" and the "good of souls"—two phrases that would recur time and again in Ignatius's writings. One of their number, Pierre Favre, ordained a priest just a month earlier, said Mass. After some time in prayer, they found a spot near a brook and celebrated the holiday with a picnic.

Their ages ranged from nineteen to forty-three, and their social backgrounds, personalities, and temperaments differed just as widely. Pierre Favre had been a shepherd boy in Savoy, in the southeast of France; a friendly scholar, recognizing his intellectual abilities, tutored him in the Greek and Latin classics.[3] At nineteen Favre came to the University of Paris, where at the Collège Sainte-Barbe his roommate was Francis Xavier, a student cut from a different cloth altogether. A Basque nobleman from Navarre and already a cleric, Xavier was intelligent, athletic, and dashing, and his success in a cushy ecclesiastical or academic career seemed all but assured. But then another Basque student came into his life. Xavier and Favre acquired a new roommate, a member of the lower nobility who dressed like anything but and harbored no doubt that God had given him a mission.

Favre, who wanted to become a priest, had suffered for some time from severe scruples. Under Ignatius's guidance, Favre made the Spiritual Exercises and learned how to cope with his religious anxieties. The worldly and ambitious Xavier was (as Ignatius put it later) a harder nut to crack. He stubbornly resisted Ignatius's goading to examine his life and motivations: What do you want to do with the years you have left? How do you measure success? Ignatius prodded Xavier to be more consistent and to discern the spirits in his heart. At the time of their vows at Montmartre, Xavier was the only one not to have made Ignatius's Spiritual Exercises, postponing the retreat until he completed the lectures he was giving to support himself.

Ignatius met Diego Laínez and Alfonso Salmerón in a chance encounter on the streets of Paris. Newly arrived from Spain, each had spent five years at the University of Alcalá just after Ignatius had left. Laínez, who had heard of Ignatius and wanted to meet him, came from a wealthy family in Castile, his great-grandfather a convert from Judaism. Salmerón's origins were humbler; his parents were village people from the environs of Toledo. Neither knew much French, and both were happy to join Ignatius's small circle of friends. In the winter of 1534, under Ignatius's direction, they also made the Spiritual Exercises.

Rounding out the group of *amigos* were Simón Rodrigues and Nicholás Alonso. Rodrigues was Portuguese, one of fifty young noblemen to receive scholarships from Portugal's King John III to study at Sainte-Barbe. He would later become Ignatius's biographer. Alonso, known as Bobadilla after his native village in Northern Spain, came from an extremely poor family, but he completed a degree at Alcalá. After teaching philosophy for a time, he came to Paris to complete his studies. The irascible and outspoken Bobadilla would become the *enfant terrible* of the nascent Society of Jesus.

But all that lay in the future for the unsuspecting *amigos* that August afternoon. On that day they were simply seven university students about to graduate who had resolved to keep up their companionship and do something with their lives by serving God and helping people. After finishing their studies and taking care of whatever personal business they had, they decided to gather in Venice and set sail for Jerusalem.

The first people they planned to help were Muslims in the Holy Land, intending to convince them of the error of their ways. The project, if pursued, would have cost them their lives. Islamic law allowed Christians to live in Muslim lands but did not permit proselytizing. Apparently the *amigos* did not pay much attention to that detail. Or at least not as much as they did to the practical question of what to do if no ships were sailing to the Holy Land. Strained relations between Venice and the Turkish Empire often delayed sailings indefinitely. How long would they wait? The seven *amigos* accommodated their vow to the circumstances. If after a year they could not find passage to the Holy Land, they would go to the pope for instructions as to where they could best be of service to God and help souls.

As remarkable as their vow was in its own right, its conditional clauses make it more so. Considered from our perspective of more than 450 years later, those clauses appear quite peculiar, but it's unlikely the *amigos* gave them a second thought. The fact of the matter is that Ignatius and his companions did not think like us. Steeped in the culture of their times, they had studied and cultivated the skills of rhetoric, the ancient art of writing and speaking persuasively. Despite Plato's scorching criticism of its Sophist ancestors, rhetoric was a central discipline in Roman education and no less valued in Renaissance Europe. Ignatius and his companions had learned the rhetorical necessity of accommodating their words to their audience, and their actions to their circumstances. For these university graduates in sixteenth-century Paris, readiness to accommodate to changing circumstances was something they took for granted, even when making a vow.

RENAISSANCE HUMANISM

Ignatius and his companions lived during some of the most turbulent and pivotal decades in the history of the West. Navigators were circling the globe for the first time in human record and discovering that it was larger than anyone had imagined. In art and letters it was an age of genius with the likes of da Vinci, Michelangelo, and Erasmus. Inaugurating a century of religious upheaval and wars, Martin Luther, John Calvin, and Henry VIII each put his personal stamp on the dissolution of medieval Christendom. And to the East, Polish astronomer and mathematician Nicholas Copernicus began the overthrow of a naïve faith and worldview that put the earth and humankind at the center of the universe.

Though they would later become identified with the Catholic response to the Reformation, Ignatius and his friends did not occupy themselves with either the events in Germany or King Henry VIII's divorce of England from Rome. The year, 1534, was not yet in the era of the "Counter-Reformation," and the *amigos* were headed for Jerusalem, not Wittenberg or London.

From the perspective of some centuries later, the Renaissance appears as a bridge from the Middle Ages to modernity. But those who were building the bridge looked back. They viewed their age primarily as a revival of the past, a rebirth of arts and letters modeled after the glories of Greece and Rome. And though the Renaissance is now thought of in terms of its achievements in art and architecture, it started off as a literary movement, a revival of appreciation for the classics first of ancient Rome and then of Greece. It began, as one pundit put it, when the fourteenth-century Italian poet Petrarch put down his Latin translation of Aristotle and picked up a book of Cicero.

The Italian academics who coined the word *Rinascimento,* or "Renaissance," had little regard for those centuries they labeled the Middle Ages, a period that Petrarch himself called "dark ages." Both terms betray the bias of fifteenth-century Italians who wanted to distinguish their own more creative times from the centuries after the fall of Rome, during which Italy, compared to northern Europe, had been a cultural backwater. These scholarly Italians were not philosophers or theologians. Their interests were pre-Christian Latin literature, the city of Rome, and the ideal of republican virtue.[4] Borrowing a phrase from Cicero, the professors and students of these subjects called their discipline the *studia humanitatis*—what today we call the humanities—in contradistinction to theology, the study of divinity. Just as their colleagues in canon law or the arts were called *canonisti* or *artisti,* the student slang of Italy's universities dubbed the practitioners of the humanities *umanisti*. From these humanists came the later concept of humanism.[5]

Renaissance humanism was not a school or system of philosophy. It was rather a cultural and educational program whose focus of interest can be roughly described as literature—the Latin and Greek classics. This was not exactly an unprecedented innovation. The medieval grammarians had cultivated Latin authors, and the scholastics at the universities had been reading Aristotle in Latin translation since the thirteenth century. But the Renaissance *umanisti* had a far more comprehensive and intense interest in ancient literature than any of their medieval forbears or, for that matter, most academics today.

Most *umanisti* were active either as teachers of the humanities or as secretaries to princes or city authorities. For these latter writers of speeches and letters, pursuit of the classics was not just a matter of taste but of practical and professional self-interest. Learning to speak and write well, they believed, required studying and imitating the ancient authors, above all Cicero. Cicero's writing on rhetoric provided the theory for attaining literary elegance, and his orations provided the models. Soon enough, though, high regard for the literary form of the Latin classics extended to their contents as well. Humanists began to turn to and quote classical authors for the insight and value of their ideas. Their writings became the gold standard for any aspiring orator or writer, viewed as embodying the ideal marriage of eloquence and wisdom.

The humanist movement gradually developed from a cultivated appreciation for good Latin into a veritable educational revolt.[6] Because they embodied the highest level of human achievement and contributed so much to human understanding, the classics, from the humanist point of view, deserved center stage in any program of education. No one could claim to be a serious scholar without being steeped in them. But, university politics and personalities being then what they are now, not all academics were of the same mind—particularly those still wedded to the more traditional methods of pedagogy and curricula.

Enamored with the elegance of Cicero, humanists disdained what they regarded as the medieval authors' debased Latin.[7] But where Italian humanists were content simply to ignore medieval letters and learning, humanists in northern Europe were decidedly explicit in their scorn. Most notable is Erasmus of Rotterdam (1469–1536), who was scathing in his assaults on the practitioners of Scholasticism, the so-called *via antiqua* or "old way" of doing things. To his mind the medieval system of education was largely responsible for all that was wrong in the church and in society. Ever since the last days of the classical authors and church fathers, religion and learning, he believed, had been in decline. Only a return to the original sources—Scripture and the tradition of the church fathers—could produce the reform that was generally recognized as imperative for the times. But the foremost impediment to that reform, as Erasmus saw it, was Scholasticism.[8]

The humanists' contempt for Scholasticism is the main reason that later generations have misunderstood what they were about. Humanism was not a new philosophy; even less was it an attack against Christianity or religion. The anti-Scholasticism of the humanists was the attempt by practitioners of one discipline to overcome the intellectual domination of another. Their efforts in this vein did not make them either crypto-atheists or pagans, although that is a frequent misreading of their enterprise. Though "humanism" in the last century has come to be identified with atheism and irreligion, its original meaning was quite different.

Recent scholarship finds that practically all the Renaissance humanists were genuinely Christian. Charges of "paganism" or "atheism" hardly make sense in the context of a pervasively Christian culture such as that of Renaissance Europe.[9]

Still, in comparison to the narrower, explicitly religious discourse of the Middle Ages, a return to the pagan classics did provide humanists with alternative and competing topics of interest and consideration. At its core, the humanist movement was neither religious nor irreligious but simply literary. Some humanists chose not to engage themselves with religious issues; others had a genuine concern for religion and the church and brought their humanist training to bear on theology. And when these theologically engaged humanists—most notably Erasmus—called for a return to the classics, they included in their appeal the Christian classics, both the Bible and the writings of the church fathers.

SOME DEFINING CHARACTERISTICS OF RENAISSANCE HUMANISM

When Ignatius Loyola and the other six *amigos en el Señor* made their informal private vows on Montmartre, they were in the process of completing their university studies at a major battlefield in the Scholastic-humanist wars. Ignatius spent altogether more than seven years being imbued with Paris's Renaissance culture and with it the humanist ideas and values that constituted its most pervasive component. The *amigos* did not need to be conscious of the impact humanism had made on them to become conduits of the humanist ethos. But it is helpful for us to recognize how the characteristics of that ethos affected not only Ignatius and his companions but also Ignatian spirituality and what would become the Jesuit philosophy of education. Without any claim to be exhaustive, the following are some of humanism's more salient features.

1. Classicism

Humanism was the dominant constituent of Renaissance culture and the foremost characteristic of the humanist movement was a cultivation of the Greek and Latin classics.[10] With classicism came the Renaissance taste for literary elegance, neatness, and clarity of form.

The humanist movement generated a veritable passion for finding and collecting ancient Greek and Latin books and manuscripts. Both before, but particularly after, the fall of Constantinople (1453), Byzantine scholars migrated to the West, bringing their books. Italian humanists also traveled to the East to collect Greek manuscripts for themselves and their patrons—such as Cosimo de' Medici and Tommaso Parentucelli, the future pope Nicholas V, whose own collection became the basis for the Vatican library. The literary monuments of Greek antiquity were viewed as the wellsprings of knowledge, and the humanists set about making Latin translations of the Greek classics, since Latin was the common language of any educated European at the time. The humanists then went on to study and translate Hebrew and Arabic classics as well.[11]

2. Educating the Whole Person

From classicism followed other humanist characteristics such as the ideal of becoming a well-rounded or whole person. The very name for their discipline, *studia humanitatis,* implied a claim that an education in classical literature served to cultivate a certain desirable kind of human being, a person developed as far as possible in all forms of virtue. Petrarch criticized any education that was merely cerebral. He faulted Aristotle's ethics for informing the mind without setting the heart on fire, for not inspiring the reader to love virtue and hate vice. "What is the use of knowing what virtue is if it is not loved when known?" The true moral philosophers are those who sow in their readers' and hearers' hearts love of the best and hatred of the worst.[12] That good literature produced good persons was a central tenet of the humanist credo.

The ideal of being a whole person gave rise in turn to the humanist ideal of striving for excellence in a variety of pursuits, becoming a *uomo universale,* or so-called "Renaissance man," many sided and passionately devoted to developing all aspects of the human personality. It was an age of merchant-statesmen, artist-inventors, and poet-scholars. The *uomo universale* was someone who attempted to master as much of the learning and skills as the culture had to offer. The ideal also sought to conjoin theory to practice and private to civic virtue.

3. An Active Life of Civic Virtue

Studying such classical authors as Cicero and Seneca, who were orators and statesmen, led naturally to the humanist ideal of cultivating a life characterized by civic virtue. To achieve a full measure of *humanitas* required one to develop practical as well as cognitive skills, and no skills were prized more than those associated with good oratory—memory, eloquence, the ability to persuade, and the ability to accommodate one's message to one's audience. The ideal product of a humanist education was someone accomplished in these rhetorical skills, someone whose oratory was admired not only for its aesthetic qualities but also for its ability to shape public opinion and thereby fulfill the civic duties of a statesman. From the perspective of medieval intellectuals who appealed to the Gospel story, Mary chose the better part over Martha; monastic contemplation and insight were superior to a secular life of action. From the humanist perspective, the two were complementary: insight without action was sterile, and action without insight was primitive. Contemplation and the monastic life were not the only or best way to live one's life and secure one's salvation. An active life of civic virtue could also stake a valid claim.

Contrary to the popular stereotype, the Renaissance was not "godless" or "pagan" or any more immoral than any other age. And Renaissance humanists were not agnostics or secularists doubtful of an afterlife. Many of them devoted considerable time speculating on the immortality of the soul,[13] but they did not flee the world or reject responsibility for the here and now. Renaissance culture was predominantly the product of urban centers, created by city-dwelling laity and the churchmen recruited from their ranks. These Renaissance urbanites were quite sure that happiness in the hereafter did not preclude what Cicero called the "art of living happily and well" in the here and now. The Ciceronian ideal did not mean living comfortably so much as virtuously, both as a public and private person, as a member of society and as an individual.

4. Individualism within Community

The very idea of being a private person has long been associated with the Renaissance. Scholars in the nineteenth century wrote of the period as giving rise first to individualism and later to our more modern ideas of individual rights. They argued for sharp contrasts between the Renaissance value of the individual and the more corporate culture of the Middle Ages, when people drew their identity primarily from a group—a family, a guild, or a social class.[14] More recent scholarship has shaded these sharp dichotomies by recognizing a continuity between the two periods. There was more individualism in the Middle Ages than was formerly acknowledged, and more corporate thinking in the Renaissance, which was as much the "waning of the Middle Ages" as the dawning of modernity.[15] The Renaissance was a time of transition. As such it embodied traits of both medieval and modern culture, making it an amalgam of competing values in polar tension. One of those polarities was that between individualism and a sense of communal identity and responsibility.

People living in a Renaissance urban culture continued to nourish a strong sense of membership in a community; one's identity and responsibilities were still determined by corporate ties to family and class. But there was also a new sense of being an individual, a *uomo singulare*, with feelings and opinions worthy of expression. The newly invented sonnet form of poetry encouraged the expression of inward personal experience. Biography and portrait painting, though neither was a new genre, thrived as never before. As voyagers and geographers explored and described newly discovered peculiarities about the outside world, humanist authors explored and described the peculiarities of the human condition.

5. Human Dignity and Freedom

Class differences in fifteenth-century Italy, though undoubtedly real, were not as sharp as those elsewhere in Europe, which may explain why the Italian Renaissance gave birth to a heightened sense of human dignity. The Middle Ages had a fundamentally negative view of human nature. Under the influence of St. Augustine, medieval culture regarded humankind as a *massa damnata* (fallen race), exiled from paradise because of its sinfulness. Humanists had no illusions about the human capacity for vice. One need only read Machiavelli or study the faces in Michelangelo's *Last Judgment* to appreciate that the Renaissance artists could be just as pessimistic about human nature as St. Augustine. But despite widespread immorality, the humanists were dogged in their conviction of the exalted place human beings hold in the universe. Medieval scholastics accepted Plato's and Aristotle's thinking about humankind standing midway between the realms of matter and spirit, but the Renaissance development of the idea was more sustained and systematic than anything that had come before.

For humanist Pico della Mirandola, the central place humans hold in the "universal chain of Being" makes our situation at once exalted and precarious.[16] In what became a highly regarded oration on human dignity, Pico singled out human freedom as making us the envy of angels and brutes alike. We are the only creatures fundamentally unfettered by nature, that is, endowed with the privilege and the responsibility of shaping our destinies. To be a human being is to face a moral choice: to lead a life of virtue or depravity. With our God-given freedom of choice we can fashion ourselves either to become more like God or more like the beasts we are meant to govern.

6. The Unity and Universality of Truth

Pico's oration on human dignity made allusions to the Bible but also to Plato, Horace, and even Muhammad. The humanists cited truth wherever they found it. With a newfound appreciation for classic authors, they found themselves confronted by the same problem that the church fathers (and St. Thomas Aquinas) had faced earlier—that of reconciling faith with pre-Christian ideas. In translating and reviving Plato and other philosophers and thinkers, the humanists put an end to the monopoly Aristotle had held over intellectual life since the thirteenth century. They followed the example of Cicero, himself an eclectic.

Amid this philosophic ferment and welter of opinions, the humanists drew on the medieval confidence in a harmony of faith and reason, philosophy and theology. Thomas Aquinas provided useful guidelines: God, who is the author of all truth, ensures a unity of truth.[17] This Scholastic principle gave rise to the Renaissance idea that truth is where you find it. And because of the universality of truth, there is a wisdom that pervades the entire history of human thought. Along with the Bible and Christian tradition, pre-Christian and non-Christian thinkers and traditions can also articulate this "perennial philosophy," which exists beyond any particular doctrine or philosophical school. Humanists granted that false ideas can obscure the truth, but the mere possibility of human error does not contradict its existence. On the contrary, the coexistence of human wisdom and error requires us to recognize and integrate every element of truth we find, wherever we come across it.

The seeds of humanism, composed of ideas and attitudes like these, germinated in Italy and by the mid-fifteenth century had spread into virtually every area of European culture. But not all humanist ideas received the same welcome. The Lutheran and Calvinist insistence on human depravity, for example, may represent in part a reaction to the humanists' allegedly exaggerated ideas of human dignity and freedom. But humanist classicism cut across religious and national divides, setting standards of excellence for students at Protestant Oxford and Catholic Salamanca.

If humanism was the most pervasive component of Renaissance culture, it was not only because of the prestige enjoyed by the classics, but also because most scholars received a humanistic education in secondary school before beginning professional training at a university. This certainly was the case for Ignatius Loyola and his companions. Whatever the differences in class and national origin, the *amigos en el Señor* were all educated by humanists. The influence of their instructors and the humanist culture they assimilated at Alcalá and Paris remained with them as individuals and as a community, entering into the very fiber of the Jesuit ethos.

The Humanism of the Early Jesuits

People are not generally prone to think of Ignatius Loyola as a humanist. He obviously doesn't fit the secularist mold or the stereotype of a Renaissance neo-pagan. But if one thinks of humanism as an orientation in education and culture, with all the characteristics enumerated above, then Ignatius and his companions can be described as first the products and then purveyors of humanistic education and culture.

Ignatius, Laínez, Salmarón, and Bobadilla were all exposed to the humanist movement at the University of Alcalá, renowned at the time and under the sway of the writings of Erasmus.[18] Apparently without anyone to direct his studies, Ignatius tried to take in too many subjects at one time and found himself assimilating little of what he studied. Encounters with the Spanish Inquisition, a brief sojourn at the University of Salamanca, and an order not to talk about such matters as mortal and venial sin until he had completed his education convinced him to go to Paris to what was still the most prestigious university in Europe. In the spring of 1528, at the age of thirty-seven, he began his university studies all over again.

More so than Alcalá or any city in Spain, Paris was a crossroads. With a centuries-old reputation for excellence and comprising more than fifty "colleges" (partly autonomous residences), the University of Paris drew students from all over Europe. Some students pursued advanced professional studies in the so-called "higher faculties" of theology, law, and medicine, but most enrolled in the "lower," preliminary faculty of arts, where they studied grammar, rhetoric, and philosophy. Ignatius recommenced his study of Latin grammar at the austere College of Montaigu, where both Erasmus and the young John Calvin had preceded him.

Montaigu had flirted with Renaissance humanism earlier in the century, but by the time Ignatius arrived it had become a bastion of Scholastic intransigence. The "master of the house," Noël Beda, chafed at Erasmus's criticism of medieval education and would have no truck with humanists, whom he regarded as little more than crypto-Lutherans. At Montaigu Ignatius studied Latin grammar according to Scholastic, not humanist, methods. The slenderness of the record prevents us from knowing for sure where his sympathies lay, but they don't seem to have been on the side of Master Beda. After only a year and a half, Ignatius left Montaigu and entered the rival college of Sainte-Barbe.

The humanism that Beda found deplorable pervaded Sainte-Barbe; its master, André de Gouvea, championed humanist ideas and principles. Instructors adopted the latest methods imported from Italy to teach languages as well as other subjects. Students studied whole works, not mere compilations of quotations, and primary texts written by church fathers, not just scholastic commentaries. For three and a half years Ignatius studied philosophy at Sainte-Barbe, where he encountered the *modus Parisiensis* or "Parisian style" of pedagogy—a succession of graded stages that would eventually become a model for Jesuit education.

After completing his oral examinations in philosophy, Ignatius earned his Licentiate in Arts in 1533 and the next year the more honorific degree of Master of Arts. By that time he had already begun his study of theology with the Dominicans on the Rue Saint-Jacques. The Dominican house, long renowned for scholarship, had replaced the standard medieval textbook in theology, the *Sentences* of Peter Lombard, with the *Summa Theologiae* of St. Thomas Aquinas. Ignatius studied the *Summa* for eighteen months and found the opinions and outlook in it congenial to his own. He would later demonstrate his admiration in the *Constitutions of the Society of Jesus* by endorsing the study of Aquinas by Jesuit students.

Ignatius's choice of Aquinas as the principal theological authority for Jesuits might seem, on the surface, to undermine the claim that Renaissance ideas and values pervade the Jesuit ethos. Who, after all, better personifies medieval Scholasticism? But Renaissance Italians, especially in Rome, had long held Aquinas in high esteem. They admired him for such classical virtues as simplicity of expression, clarity, and order. They valued Thomas's insistence that there is no capriciousness in God's governance of the universe. The fact that for Thomas "the world was nothing if not ordered" was congenial to humanists, for whom the mark of wisdom, human and divine, was the ability to produce order.[19]

Ignatius found Thomas's well-tempered universe appealing, especially his theology of grace. Grace does not contradict or oppose nature, according to Thomas, but builds on it. This view of compatibility between the two coincided with Ignatius's own experience and convictions. When he came to write the constitutions, Ignatius prescribed that, when ministering to others, Jesuits should not presume to rely only on God's grace but make use of all possible natural human means as well.[20]

The principle that grace builds on nature lies at the heart of Ignatian humanism. Without that principle—or something akin to it—there can be no spiritual or religious humanism, Christian or otherwise. Believing in the affinity between creation and grace explains why the church fathers could borrow freely from the categories and insights of pagan Greek and Roman authors. It explains why Dante could revere Virgil and why Petrarch wished he could count Cicero a Christian. Individuals first have to affirm the possibility of truth outside their own community before they can look and learn outside of it. On the basis of that Thomistic principle, Jesuits would insist on teaching "pagan" classics and resist all efforts to oppose it.

The subsequent evolution of Ignatian spiritual humanism is unintelligible unless one assumes an affinity between nature and grace, science and religion. Faith does not require fear of scientific inquiry or building barriers to how far one can question authority or explore the universe. For Renaissance humanists like the early Jesuits, God is the author both of nature and grace, faith and reason. One need not give up one for the sake of the other.

HUMANISM IN THE *SPIRITUAL EXERCISES*

Conviction about the compatibility of nature and grace, the influence of Renaissance culture, and a humanist training are all apparent in the subsequent lives and careers of the early Jesuits. The same can be said of the *Spiritual Exercises,* which Ignatius began at Manresa but continued to work on after completing his education in Paris. Even the book's title suggests the Thomistic affinity of nature and grace. The person making the Spiritual Exercises—waiting, asking for grace—does not do so idly. Distractions must be set aside, unruly desires overcome. Spirits, no less than bodies, require the time and effort of disciplined exercise.

Accommodation—promoted by humanist instructors as a basic principle of good rhetoric—is plain not only in the vow that Ignatius and his companions made on Montmartre but also throughout the *Spiritual Exercises.* Time and again, as pointed out in chapter 1, the director is advised to adapt the Exercises to the circumstances and spiritual condition—as well as age, education, and ability—of the person making them [18]. In an explanatory note introducing the Exercises (the nineteenth annotation), Ignatius explicitly allows for people unable to take thirty days away from their responsibilities to make the Exercises over an extended period of time, an hour and a half a day [19].

This constant adaptation of the Exercises to the situation of retreatants reveals an individualistic bent to Ignatian spirituality. The exercitant draws away from family and friends to face God alone, if only for a while—not to escape society, but to know one's place and calling in it; not to run away from life, but to discover what one most deeply desires out of it. Humanist awareness of the individual coheres with the profound respect for the retreatant that the Exercises require on the part of the director. The director does not intrude but allows God to work and speak within the soul of the retreatant [15].

Consciousness of human dignity requires a director to respect a retreatant's experience, opinions, and freedom and to interpret these in the most favorable light [22]. Though we can't be certain why Ignatius required this respect, his unhappy experiences with the Inquisition, including the Dominicans at Salamanca, seem to have contributed.[21] Whatever the reason, the "presupposition" calls for what psychologists today call "active listening," which makes the relationship between the director and the retreatant not hierarchic so much as dialogic.

Spiritual Exercises fosters such humanist values as respect for individual experience, freedom, and human dignity. The "presupposition" tacitly assumes the Renaissance conviction that the one truth can find expression in many voices. Equally clear is the humanist concern for the whole person; the Exercises address more than the intellect, for "it is not knowing much, but realizing and relishing things interiorly, that contents and satisfies the soul" [2]. Exercitants are to use all their faculties and senses not only to think but also to imagine, see, hear, smell, taste, and feel. The Exercises engage the whole person in his or her spiritual encounter.

Classicism, very much at the heart of the humanist enterprise, entailed a return not only to the classics of Greece and Rome but also to the foundational texts of Christianity—sacred Scripture and the church fathers. In the same vein, the *Spiritual Exercises* gives central focus to a devout reading of Gospel texts on the life of Christ. But Ignatius's humanist education surfaces as well in the so-called "rules for thinking with the Church," a kind of appendix to the *Spiritual Exercises* most probably composed toward the end of Ignatius's years in Paris.[22] There, in the eleventh rule [363], Ignatius commends both "positive and scholastic learning," both the church fathers (Jerome, Augustine, Gregory) and the medieval Schoolmen

(Thomas Aquinas, Bonaventure, Peter Lombard). He refuses to take sides between the humanists and their Scholastic adversaries, preferring instead to see their two kinds of theology as complementing one another. Taking his own advice, he puts the best interpretation on both, approving the medieval scholastics for their clarity and precision and the church fathers for their ability "to stir up our affections toward loving and serving God our Lord in all things."

Despite this attempt to be evenhanded, Ignatius and his companions differed from the Scholastics, including Thomas Aquinas, on one crucial issue. Theology, as Aquinas described it in the *Summa* and as the scholastics practiced it, was a "contemplative" or academic discipline, highly intellectualized and speculative. Such speculation, as the humanists regularly pointed out, was addressed to the head, not the heart. No less than their humanist contemporaries, the early Jesuits were critical of reducing theology to speculation alone. Theology for Ignatius was not a theoretical discipline but a way of bringing people into relation with God. Renaissance historian John O'Malley put it this way:

A strong case can be mounted for the opinion that the most pervasive aim of Ignatius's life after his conversion was his desire to move others "to love and serve God our Lord in all things," which is precisely how he described patristic theology and which could equally be applied to the theological reform advocated by Erasmus and others. It was also the most fundamental aim of the *Spiritual Exercises,* and it was an aim directed at the affections, at the human heart. It was the aim of his ministry.[23]

But if the eleventh rule for thinking with the Church supports the humanist reform, the thirteenth appears to raise the most serious challenge to any claim that Ignatian spirituality is humanistic. Here, in the last pages of the *Spiritual Exercises,* we read: "What I see as white, I will believe to be black if the hierarchical Church thus determines it [365]."

Outside their context, these words seem to require a blind obedience to church authority, patently at odds with human dignity and the right of an individual to express conscientious dissent. But Ignatius did not express these sentiments in a historical vacuum, nor is his choice of words—"What I see as white, I will believe to be black"—merely unfortunate and easily misunderstood. Written during his years in Paris (1528–34), they are a pointed reference to a passage by Erasmus, around whom a storm of controversy raged throughout the years of Ignatius's study.

Our understanding of Ignatius's attitude toward Erasmus—and by extension toward humanism—has labored under the legend that he was "chilled" by reading the Dutch humanist's *Enchiridion*, cast the book aside, and forbade anyone in the Society of Jesus to read anything by Erasmus. Modern scholarship has dispelled that story as a myth.[24] There is no denying that the kind of biting satire one finds in Erasmus's *Praise of Folly*—skewering high churchmen and lowly monks alike—was foreign, not to say offensive, to Ignatius's temperament. But one cannot deny that there is much that Ignatius and Erasmus had in common as church reformers, not the least being their thinking on the discernment of spirits.

Erasmus raised the issue in his heated exchange with Luther, converting it from the question of good and evil to that of truth and error. How did Luther know his interpretation of Scripture was the correct one? How was truth to be decided? On the basis of one's experience? On the strength of one's conviction? The question was not new, nor was the language in which it was phrased. Skeptics argued with Stoics about the issue in the first century B.C., and Cicero phrased it like this: "How can it be said distinctly that anything is white, when it may happen that what is black appears white." Erasmus, commenting on the limits of papal authority, used the same language when he noted wryly that "black would not be white if the Roman Pontiff were to say so, which I know he will never do." Ignatius's thirteenth rule was a direct response to Erasmus's jibe, without in fact contradicting it. The issue was a matter of discerning truth, not fabricating it.

Although the wording is problematic for our times, the idea of believing something contrary to appearances was not at all controversial in the sixteenth century. Against all empirical evidence, Luther and Ignatius alike believed Christ to be truly present in the Lord's Supper. Protestants and Catholics alike believed the revelation of God could be perceived in a crucified Jesus of Nazareth. For all its potential for misunderstanding from our perspective, the thirteenth rule for thinking with the church is basically a rephrasing of the first rule, which serves as the principle underlying all the rest. "With all judgment of our own put aside, we ought to keep our minds disposed and ready to be obedient in everything to the true Spouse of Christ our Lord, which is our Holy Mother the hierarchical Church" [353].

Here Ignatius certainly parts company with Luther and, with respect to his sarcasm, with Erasmus. Ignatius had no illusions about the need of the Roman Catholic Church for reform, but it was the moral reform of its members—including those in the highest places—that he made paramount. He had no patience for Luther's contempt or Erasmus's ridicule of ecclesial authorities, even though he had personally suffered more at the hands of churchmen than either of them. He was the object of no fewer than eight legal investigations by church authorities, several of them entailing arrest and imprisonment, one lasting for twenty-two days.[25] Still, Ignatius had a love and reverence for the institutional Catholic church, warts and all. As retreatants came to the end of their Spiritual Exercises, Ignatius wanted them to acquire the same kind of disposition, if their directors deemed there was need of it. The Latin and Spanish original referred not to "thinking" in the sense of a purely rational act but to a "genuine attitude" (*sentido verdadero*) that is affective as well as intellectual, a "knowing with the heart," a thinking with the church that is also a feeling for the church.[26]

There is a decidedly ecclesial aspect to Ignatian spirituality. Not only the Jesuit constitutions (with their fourth vow of obedience to the pope) but also the *Spiritual Exercises* call for caring about the church. Neither for Ignatius nor those Jesuits who came after him did this ever mean standing by in acquiescence to the status quo. Obedience meant respectful listening and sometimes suspension of one's judgment, but never did it mean going contrary to one's conscience. Never did it mean not trying to reform what needed to be reformed, whether that meant improving church practices (preaching, religious instruction, frequent Holy Communion) or changing the way priests ministered to the faithful (showing kindness rather than severity in the confessional, accepting alms but taking no payment for services).

An affective, thoughtful caring about the church today requires a different articulation from the guidelines Ignatius set down in the rules.[27] As the following chapters will show, what those rules meant to the Ignatian humanists treated here was anything but servile conformity to regulations. (A wisecrack from yesteryear has it that one of the things even God does not know is what Jesuits mean by obedience.) The fact of the matter is, that for all their reverence for the hierarchical church, Ignatius and those who joined him intended to reform it (in some ways not unlike Luther, but without using the word). Reform was what the Renaissance humanists were about—especially Erasmus, who, for all his sarcasm, developed a humanistic spirituality not totally unlike that of Ignatius.

For a last word on the matter, here is how Renaissance historian John O'Malley puts it:

> From the very beginning and at the core of the humanist movement was spiritual and moral reform, even though these features might at times have become obscured. The movement eventually developed a rather coherent spirituality that achieved its apex in the writings of Erasmus. For centuries that aspect of Erasmus was scorned rather than studied, and only in the past two decades have we begun to discover the depths of his spirituality—and, I might add, its many similarities with the spirituality of the first Jesuits, unaware though most Jesuits seem to have been of these similarities.[28]

As the foregoing arguments suggest, the *Spiritual Exercises* and the spirituality it engenders actually appropriated the defining traits of Renaissance humanism. Giving the Spiritual Exercises was the early Jesuits' proto-ministry and became the paradigm for all their other work. And because this entailed engaging retreatants as whole persons, humanism influenced the rest of their lives as much as it did their vow on Montmartre.

MINISTERING TO THE WHOLE PERSON

Their vow called for the *amigos* to meet in Venice and embark from there on a ship that would take them to Jerusalem. Again—as in the case of the cannonball that shattered Ignatius's leg—one can only wonder how differently history might have turned out had there been a ship that year to transport them to their original destination. As it happened, they did not all arrive in Venice until midwinter, when no ships sailed. Ignatius had set out for Spain in the spring of 1535 to make what would be his last visit home; the other six companions remained behind in Paris until all had completed their studies. Under the direction of Pierre Favre, three other university students made the Spiritual Exercises—Claude Jay, Paschase Broët, and Jan Codure. The new recruits joined the *amigos* in their resolve to give their lives to the service of God by helping souls.

That phrase—"helping souls"—sounds quaint to our ears, like an echo from a bygone era. It rings of the Neoplatonic philosophy that dominated Christian spirituality and thinking for centuries, the view that a human being is essentially a spirit encased in a body, as in a cage or tomb. We've grown out of that kind of dualism and its implied disregard for the body. But what exactly did "helping souls" mean for Ignatius and his first companions? The phrase appears in so many words on virtually every page of the early Jesuit record.

Synecdoche is a figure of speech in which a part becomes a metaphor for a whole ("lend me your ears," "all hands on deck"). This is the explanation for what Ignatius and the early Jesuits meant by "helping souls," as they demonstrated during the time they spent in Venice. Their labors there were clearly not for the benefit of disembodied spirits. And their collective experience there lives on, arguably second only to Ignatius's experience at Manresa in its impact on subsequent Jesuit history.

Ignatius had been in Venice studying theology privately for little more than a year when the nine companions joined him in January 1537. They had made the journey across France and over the snowy passes of the Alps on foot. Together once more, they waited for fairer weather and a ship that would take them east. They divided themselves into two groups of five, with one group working at Sts. John and Paul hospital, the other at the hospital for incurables, where most of the patients suffered from syphilis.

One should not confuse our contemporary idea of a hospital—all antisepsis and clean sheets—with hospitals in the sixteenth century, bereft of either anesthesia or indoor plumbing. The groaning, screams, and smells can only be imagined. Receiving no payment save their room and board, Ignatius and his companions scrubbed floors and emptied slop buckets, dug graves and prepared corpses for burial. One of their number, Simón Rodrigues, later described the experience as one of hunger and exhaustion, revulsion at their surroundings, and fear of contagion.[29] If there is a popular image of Jesuits today, it's that of the priest-professor, an intellectual with chalk on his hands but clean fingernails. Outsiders unfamiliar with their history do not ordinarily think of Jesuits nursing victims of sexually transmitted disease. But long before taking charge of classrooms, they were involved in any number of such tasks guaranteed to get their hands dirty.

Making a pilgrimage to the Holy Land required the pope's blessing. For reasons of diplomacy, Ignatius stayed behind in Venice but sent the others to Rome, where they made a favorable impression. Pope Paul III blessed their journey and even provided them with some unsolicited funds. More important, however, he gave his permission for them to be ordained. They returned to Venice, and on June 24, 1537, six of them, including Ignatius, were ordained priests. Then, after forty days spent in seclusion and prayer, and taking their cue from the New Testament stories of the apostles, they separated into groups of two or three and traveled to the towns near Venice, where they preached in the streets.

Political tensions between Venice and Turkey prevented any pilgrimage ships sailing to the Holy Land that year. The *amigos* continued to wait and to preach in the open air. They needed an answer to the question that people were putting to them with more and more frequency: Who were these priests who scrubbed floors, dug graves, and preached on street corners? They gave serious thought to the question. They were not monks or friars, who spent a good part of their day praying in common. The people called them *preti reformati,* reformed priests. Their own view of who they were was rather more like comrades.

To describe themselves they chose the Spanish word for companions, *compañeros,* bound together into a company, a *compagnia.* And because they had no exemplar other than the Jesus of the Gospels, who in the course of the Spiritual Exercises called them to share his mission and lot, they chose the name *Compagnia di Gesù.* The Spanish translated into Latin as *Societas Jesu,* in English the Society of Jesus. *Compagnia* later received a military connotation, though there is no reason to believe that was the original intention behind the choice.[30] And some critics deemed it presumptuous for them to name themselves after Jesus, when other groups were named after mere saints. As is often the case in such matters, it was their critics who first called the *compañeros* Jesuits. (Similarly, it was their students in the United States who first called them Jebs, and those in Britain who nicknamed them Jays.)

By November 1537, with winter approaching, it was clear there would be no ship sailing to the Holy Land within the year they had stipulated in their vow. With the other companions scattered around in various cities of Italy, Ignatius, Favre, and Laínez headed down to Rome. In accord with the proviso of their vow, they were determined to go wherever the pope sent them. He would know best where they could do the most good. On the outskirts of the city, the trio stopped at a wayside shrine in the hamlet of La Storta. At this shrine, Ignatius had a religious experience that was to have a profound impact on his sense of mission. As the story has come down to us, he had a vision of Jesus carrying a cross and saying, "I wish you to serve us." The voice of God then said, "I will be propitious to you in Rome." Ignatius took it as divine confirmation of the name the company had chosen for themselves and the direction they were taking.

Ignatius was heartened by their reception in Rome, especially by Pope Paul III. The pope assured them that more than enough work waited for them in Italy. Two years later, when the idea of going to Jerusalem came up again, he reproached them for holding on to their old ambition. Rome could be their Jerusalem, he told them. Certainly there was more than enough work for them to do there. Ignatius had seen himself and his companions as pilgrims on the move, ready to go wherever they were needed, but others of the company would have to fill that description. Ignatius would spend the rest of his life in Rome, the headquarters from which the other pilgrims were sent.

In Rome, the first Jesuits settled into a city that had been a center of Renaissance humanism for well over a century. Humanists from Florence and elsewhere in Tuscany were drawn to Rome first for its classical associations and ruins and then by the patronage of the papal court, the Roman curia with its various branches. Latin was the language of all curial business. Humanists could find themselves positions composing not only letters and official documents but also histories, orations, and poetry. At least two fifteenth-century popes (Nicholas V and Pius II) were themselves humanists, and others saw patronizing the humanist enterprise as a means of building up personal prestige and the papal office. The first Jesuits had entered a city already forever altered by the architecture of Bramante, the paintings of Raphael, and the sculpture of Michelangelo.[31]

As in Venice and its environs, so now in Rome and throughout Italy, the *compañeros* engaged in a variety of ministries. The pope assigned Laínez and Favre to lecture in theology at the University of Rome. Ignatius gave the Spiritual Exercises to members of the papal court. The companions taught catechism to the young and unlettered, heard confessions, and preached as they imagined Jesus and the apostles did—in public squares, marketplaces, hospitals, prisons, wherever people gathered. At a time when preachers made every effort to alarm sinners with dire warnings about hell-fire and damnation, and sensitive consciences suffered from scruples and heightened religious anxiety, the companions strove to comfort their hearers. The *Spiritual Exercises,* with its heavy accent on God's grace, became the prototype for their other dealings with people. And, following the humanist ideal, they spoke not just to the head but also to the heart.

The *Spiritual Exercises* speak of showing one's love for God "more in deeds than in words." Nursing the sick and dying was only the beginning of that kind of Jesuit ministry. The first Jesuits also tried to influence the rest of the staff to treat patients in a manner that was more helpful and humane.[32] Working as prison chaplains, they comforted the poor who were imprisoned simply because of debt and consoled prisoners awaiting sentencing and execution. Jesuits working in remote villages found fierce blood feuds that had raged for years; making peace among warring parties became a special concern for the early Society of Jesus, later formulated in their constitutions as "reconciling the estranged."

Ignatius and his companions had been in Rome for only a year when the city was struck by an unusually severe winter. Famine drove hundreds of people from the countryside into the city. People lay in the streets half-frozen and exhausted from hunger. Ignatius and the other Jesuits responded to the crisis with more than prayers. Accustomed to begging for their own bread, they now begged for the homeless. They moved as many as they could into their own quarters as well as into other shelter and did what they could to feed them. Several of the companions had been members of the lower nobility, and they knew how to deal with people of means. With their connections and access to the powerful, they were able to bring relief to people with none. Their response to that winter of 1539 would become an archetype for their future activities and a component of Jesuit self-identity.

The question of that identity grew more pressing. Who were these priests who called themselves "companions of Jesus"? A new religious order? If so, they needed official Vatican approval. And for some centuries already church authorities were reluctant to allow any new orders. More-over, members of religious orders were required to spend hours each day chanting the psalms of the divine office. Such a practice would obviously interfere with helping souls in the manner the early Jesuits saw as their "way of proceeding."

A series of deliberations in 1539 resulted in documents that would become the *Constitutions of the Society of Jesus*. Despite the hesitations of some Vatican officials, and despite the novelty of omitting choral chant of the divine office, on September 27, 1540, Pope Paul III gave the Society of Jesus formal approval. With it emerged a new concept of religious life, more activist and worldly than any thus far conceived.

That year Pierre Favre was assigned to a mission in Germany, and Francis Xavier left first for Portugal and then for the Orient. The companions of Jesus branched out and multiplied, doing whatever was needed to help souls. One of the lesser known of those early Jesuit ministries began in 1543 in Rome with the opening of Casa Santa Marta, a kind of halfway house for women driven by circumstances into prostitution. Did Ignatius feel a special responsibility to women in that oldest of professions because of his own personal failings before his conversion? Whatever the motivation behind it, at least in the clergy-ridden city of Rome, the effort was aimed at church as well as social reform. Jesuits elsewhere followed suit and organized efforts to help the former prostitutes find housing, work, and even husbands. Casa Santa Marta and the similar projects it inspired enlisted the support and assistance of non-Jesuits, especially of laywomen. Organized into confraternities, they eventually took the work over altogether. This too became a pattern for the Jesuit way of doing things—beginning a ministry and then turning it over to lay supporters.[33]

SCHOOLS THAT MAKE A DIFFERENCE

Pilgrimage was Ignatius's preferred metaphor for explaining what he and his companions were about. He wrote in the Jesuit constitutions [304] that their vocation was "to travel through the world and live in any part of it whatsoever," wherever there was an opportunity to give greater service to God and help souls. But the image of itinerants, ready at any moment to pull up stakes and break camp, ran into conflict with a different reality when Jesuits became sedentary schoolteachers. Taking charge of classrooms was not exactly what Ignatius had in mind when he first conceived of his companions of Jesus, but it fit in with his hopes. What better way of making a difference for God?

Jesuits had been involved in any number of ministries when the city fathers at Messina, Sicily, asked Ignatius to send them some teachers to open a *collegio,* or secondary school, for their sons. The Jesuits had already been educating their own recruits and lecturing on a temporary basis in other institutions. The idea of founding their own school to form young men who would have an impact on the church and secular society was appealing. Because of their Renaissance upbringing, the early Jesuits believed in the power of education or "good letters," as they put it. Studying the pre-Christian classics, such as Cicero, provided a model not only for eloquence but also for moral inspiration. Ever since Petrarch, it had been a humanist commonplace that good literature produces good persons. And no institution was more characteristic of the humanist enterprise than the school.

In 1548, fourteen years after the vow on Montmartre, Jesuits opened their first college. They didn't anticipate that they would quickly become identified with their schools; educating youth was just one more way to help souls. But Ignatius had the foresight to send some of the Society's best men to staff the school at Messina, and the venture proved to be an immediate and resounding success. Invitations to found schools began to pour in from other cities in Italy and then from abroad. Before long, education became the dominant activity of the fledgling society. Within twenty-five years after their approval as an order, Jesuits were staffing schools from Portugal to Poland. Sharing success stories and learning from one another's mistakes, Jesuit teachers eventually put together a detailed course of studies that would be codified in an official *Ratio Studiorum.*

Every alumnus of a Jesuit school was compelled, as a rite of passage, to wrestle with Cicero, Horace, Virgil, and Ovid (without the racy parts).

Their schools provided Jesuits with useful centers for their other activities. The schools also gave them entrée into the civic life of communities that they would never have had otherwise. Educating young men was an ideal way of influencing the next generation of leaders, as well as their families. True to their own humanist training, the early Jesuits were critical of instruction that was purely speculative or abstract. Education, like other Jesuit ministries, was to address the whole person—character and morals, not just cognitive faculties. Ignatius wrote into the constitutions that Jesuit teachers were to show *cura personalis* (personal concern) for their students, getting to know them as individuals and being concerned about their total development as human beings.[34]

In 1551 Ignatius founded the Collegio Romano. A sign on the door read simply: "A school of grammar, humanities, and Christian doctrine. Gratis." The humanities are still at the core of Jesuit education, so the fact that they were there from its inception comes as no surprise. But given the cost of Jesuit education today, the word *gratis* certainly does. That Jesuit education was originally free of charge clearly explains at least some of their schools' early popularity. The Jesuits accepted only room and board for themselves and enough of a stipend to allow them to educate their new recruits. If wealthy individuals or a city government wanted the Jesuits to open a school in their locale, they first had to provide an endowment to allow the Jesuits to teach without requiring tuition.

The early Jesuits were not bent on fomenting social revolution, but they were conscious of being reformers. They saw education as a means of producing good leaders and citizens for society and good priests for the church. Because Ignatius insisted that all Jesuit ministries should be offered without charge, Jesuit education was the first systematic, widespread effort to provide large numbers of people with free schooling.[35] Though the Jesuits had no intentions of breaking down traditional roles or class structures, by opening their schools to all who were qualified they had a transformative impact on society. Especially in the beginning, their schools brought together a mix of social classes, the sons of merchants and cobblers with the sons of aristocrats.

Though some became universities, most Jesuit colleges remained secondary schools, the equivalent of the French *Lycée* or German *Gymnasium*, a program encompassing the United States' equivalent of high school and junior college. But even at these levels, Jesuits were engaged in secular disciplines—the humanities (grammar, rhetoric, the Greek and Latin classics) and, under the rubric of "natural philosophy," the natural sciences (mathematics, astronomy, and physics). Jesuits began not only teaching science but also writing scientific books, going on to establish observatories and laboratories.

In good humanist tradition, Jesuit schools put a premium on teaching the art of public speaking, which led them to introduce drama into their curriculum. Jesuits began writing and directing plays aimed at honing the students' rhetorical skills and leaving actors and audience alike better instructed on the rewards for virtue and the wages of sin. Thus was born one of the more lasting, if dubious, Jesuit contributions to modern civilization—the school pageant (an achievement all the more remarkable when one considers that the original productions were completely in Latin). As a diversion for those parents and relatives in the audience without an ear for classical Latin, the Jesuits began inserting musical interludes between acts. With time and increasingly larger audiences, performances evolved into spectacular productions that incorporated music, dance, and even opera, as Jesuits began seeing their spiritual mission as having a cultural component.

ENGAGEMENT WITH CULTURE

The original companions could hardly have foreseen the impact their schools would have on their company's ethos. Even though engagement with culture was not a goal of the Society at its inception, it has become a Jesuit hallmark, integral to the Society's self-definition. An evolution in that direction was not a fluke, however. Cultural engagement was a natural and logical outgrowth of their humanistic values. A willingness to accommodate to circumstances carries its own dynamic, amenable to further evolution. A God at work in all things can be found on a stage as well as in a sanctuary. Neither random nor incidental, the Jesuits' cultural engagement germinated systemically from the humanist seeds at the heart of their Ignatian spirituality and an evolving understanding of ministry in an Ignatian context.[36]

The Jesuits' schools and their sense of cultural mission would eventually bear consequences beyond the confines of Europe and the Renaissance. For example, when Pope Gregory XIII needed advice on how to revise the Julian calendar in 1582, he turned to a Jesuit mathematician at the Roman College, Christopher Clavius (from the German Klau). Clavius's solution required suppressing ten days in the Julian calendar and every four-hundred years omitting the extra day of what otherwise would be a leap year. English Protestants declared the whole idea a "Jesuit plot," but the formula worked, and virtually all nations around the globe have adopted the Gregorian calendar as their secular system for reckoning dates. Clavius enjoys little celebrity today, except for a crater named after him on the moon (a distinction he shares with some thirty other Jesuit scientists and mathematicians).

Along with their schoolteacher colleagues in Europe, Jesuit missionaries also saw themselves as having a cultural calling. Georg Kamel, a Moravian Jesuit, worked as a missionary-pharmacist in the Philippines. He would send plant specimens peculiar to the Orient back to Europe so they could be studied and compared. How many moderns know that Carl Linnaeus, in recognition of Kamel's contributions to botany, named a species of the tea family after him—the camellia? Or that quinine—taken from the cinchona tree that missionaries in the tropics sent back to Europe for its remarkable ability to bring down fever—was once called "Jesuit bark"?

Jesuits were the first explorers with higher education, and the first Europeans altogether to venture into the interiors of Mexico, Mongolia, and the Amazon. It is fair to say that, were it not for the research and writings of early Jesuit missionaries, geography and ethnography would not have become serious branches of study as early as they did. As the next chapter will point out, Jesuits were the first Europeans to study Sanskrit in India and to write grammars in Chinese. They did the same with the native languages of Brazil. In fact, Jesuits have been credited with doing the foundational work for the grammars and dictionaries of ninety-five languages.

True to their origins, the Jesuits focused on spirituality—helping people find a deeper relationship with God. But faith in a God whose grace builds on nature entails openness to self-expression in art. In Italy "Jesuit architecture" was an early name for the Baroque style that helped to define an entire era. And while their Italian counterparts were building Baroque churches, French Jesuits were teaching ballet at their school in Paris. The first serious treatise on ballet was written by a Jesuit, Claude François Menestrier. It was said of French theater at the time of Louis XIV that "there is no one like the Jesuits for doing pirouettes."[37] At the same time, in the interior regions of Paraguay, Jesuit missionaries taught the Guarani natives the musical skills to perform operas.

What was literally true for Jesuit missionaries became figuratively true for its scholars. In the words of Ignatius's lieutenant, Jerónimo Nadal, "the whole world is our home." Ignatian spirituality—seeing God as deeply immersed in all creation and all human endeavor—became increasingly worldly and humanistic. Ignatian spirituality has the capacity to embrace the celebrated humanist dictum first penned by the Roman, pre-Christian playwright Terence, *humani nil a me alienum puto* ("I consider nothing human foreign to me"). For Ignatian spirituality, nothing human is merely human. And no enterprise, now matter how secular, is merely secular. We live in a universe of grace. From that Ignatian perspective, it follows that holiness and humanism require each other.

Because of their humanistic spirituality, Jesuits, from their inception, have been at the intersection of science and religion, secular culture and faith. That put them at a boundary that enabled them to speak in a worldly way about piety—and piously about the world. They could not and did not always live up to the ideals of their origins, but they did it often enough to find themselves in the middle of any number of cross fires.

Jesuit treatises on meditation enjoyed widespread popularity in Elizabethan England, as they did on the continent, but in England the treatises had to be anonymous or falsely attributed. The Jesuits were outlawed and forced to work underground. Given those undercover operations, it is perhaps not surprising that the *Oxford English Dictionary* gives as a secondary meaning to the word *Jesuit,* a "dissembling person." To be "Jesuitical" was to be deceitful. For anticlerical humanists like Diderot and Voltaire, the Jesuits were too spiritual. Because of their humanist optimism about grace, Blaise Pascal and the Jansenists found them too lax. But the Jesuits have a knack of outliving their enemies, and *Jesuitical* as a pejorative term has virtually died out of the English language.

Ignatian spirituality is not the same as it was when Ignatius first published the *Spiritual Exercises.* Its openness to accommodation gives it a dynamism that allowed it to evolve, as encounters with new cultures and scientific discoveries broadened the horizons of the Jesuits who gave the Exercises and wrote theological reflections on them. And, despite efforts to the contrary, Jesuit schools persisted in teaching pre-Christian classics. It became almost a motto of Jesuit education, made sacrosanct by being attributed to its origins—better to teach first-rate pagan than second-rate Christian authors.

Its humanist origins informed the Jesuit ethos, even if Jesuits did not always realize it. Ignatian spirituality and the Jesuit "way of proceeding" were rooted in the Renaissance. For centuries thereafter and to this day, that has made a difference.

The Jesuit mission, when encountering a non-Xtian is to make them more Buddhist or more Hindu etc...

THREE

~ "The traveler":

MATTEO RICCI

1. Realization of existing values of which acc. to him he was going to convert or "bring"
2. Realization of human common spiritual values.
3.

The science of ethics with them is a series of confused maxims and deductions at which they have arrived under the guidance of the light of reason. The most renowned of all Chinese philosophers was named Confucius. This great and learned man was born 551 years before the beginning of the Christian era, lived more than 70 years, and spurred on his people to the pursuit of virtue not less by his own example than by his writings and conferences. His self-mastery and abstemious ways of life have led his countrymen to assert that he surpassed in holiness all those who in times past, in the various parts of the world, were considered to have excelled in virtue. Indeed, if we critically examine his actions and sayings as they are recorded in history, we shall be forced to admit that he was the equal of the pagan philosophers and superior to most of them.[1]

This is how Matteo Ricci, the man who coined the name Confucius as a translation of K'ung Fu-tzu ("Master Kung"), introduced China's greatest sage to the Western world. Ricci (1552–1610), an Italian Jesuit, studied the classical literature of China much as he had studied Cicero and Horace as a schoolboy. He mastered the language enough to have some of his own writings eventually included in a canon of Chinese classics.

More than an author, Ricci was a pioneer. He won entrée into cities and circles where few outsiders had been welcomed before. He brought Western mathematics and science to China and wrote the first detailed descriptions of Chinese life and culture for the West. Along with titles like Renaissance man and humanist, he can lay claim to being the father of sinology. But because he was also and foremost a missionary, his contribution to secular culture has often gone unnoticed.

Ricci had high regard for Confucius, waxing eloquent with words like *virtue, self-mastery,* and even *holiness* to describe him. More to the point here, he classified Confucius as a philosopher, "the equal" of the pre-Christian philosophers of Greece and Rome and "superior to most of them." Ricci's journals reveal a similar admiration and respect for the Chinese and their culture altogether, though he could be critical of what he saw as their peculiar character flaws and failings. Theirs was a civilization that predated Christianity by centuries. And, if their ethics consisted of confused maxims, it was nonetheless an ethics derived "under the guidance of the light of reason."

While this reference to the light of reason may not seem particularly important at first reading, its significance becomes apparent later in his journals, where Ricci describes the ancient Chinese as worshiping one Supreme Being and teaching that every human action should hearken to the dictates of reason.

One can confidently hope that in the mercy of God, many of the ancient Chinese found salvation in the natural law, assisted as they must have been by that special help which, as the theologians teach, is denied to no one who does what he can toward salvation, according to the light of his conscience. That they endeavored to do this is readily determined from their history of more than 4000 years, which really is a record of good deeds done on behalf of their country and for the common good.[2]

Ricci faced the same culture shock that other sixteenth-century explorers and missionaries did on discovering lands and peoples previously unknown to Europeans. But unlike most of the earlier missionaries to follow Spanish and Portuguese explorers, Ricci had the advantages of a classical humanist education. He encountered in China not a culture of hunters and gatherers but a civilization largely dominated by Confucian scholars, a class of humanists like himself, given to reading classic texts. The Chinese, he learned, had been printing and devouring books for four hundred years before Johannes Gutenberg gained celebrity for introducing movable type in the West.

It had been the long-held Christian conviction that there was no salvation outside the Christian church.[3] Medieval Europeans were quite sure that the gospel had already been preached to the ends of the earth. Theologians in the Middle Ages speculated about the unlikely scenario of a solitary child surviving in a wilderness without hearing about Jesus Christ—how could such a person be saved? According to the medieval mind, Jews and Muslims who refused to accept Christianity did so by their own choice and through their own fault. But this was palpably not the case with the Chinese. Ricci was confronted with the reality of millions of people who for thousands of years had lived and died without ever having had the chance to hear of Christianity or Jesus Christ. Were they all doomed? How could millions of people be faulted, let alone damned, for lacking faith in a Savior they had never heard of?

Catholic theologians had already begun adjusting their theories to new realities, and Ricci could appeal to their teachings about natural law and conscience to buttress his confident hope in the mercy of God. The new thinking was of more than just theoretical interest for him. In his mission deep in the interior of China, Ricci found flesh-and-blood people for whose sake he had left family, friends, and native land. His journals reveal that he had come to regard any number of them as friends.

As a missionary to the East, Ricci took the same difficult sea journey that Francis Xavier, the Jesuits' protomissionary, did. But in more ways than one, Ricci went beyond Xavier, taking up where the latter left off.

Xavier died on a deserted island just off the coast of China, waiting for a ship to take him to the mainland. That was in 1552, the same year Matteo Ricci was born.

In the Footsteps of Francis Xavier

When King John of Portugal heard about Ignatius and his companions, he wrote to the pope and asked him to send some Jesuit priests to his Portuguese colonies in the Indies. The companions had vowed to go wherever the pope sent them, and Ignatius decided on Simón Rodrigues and Nicolas Bobadilla for the task. But then Bobadilla fell ill, and everyone else in the fledgling society was either sick or away on papal service. A disconcerted Ignatius found that he had no one left to send but his secretary and close friend, Francis Xavier. The two longtime comrades parted, knowing that they would never see each other again this side of the grave. Their only means of communication would be letters.[4]

Xavier left Rome for Lisbon in March 1540, and the following year set sail for the Portuguese colony of Goa on the western coast of India. The journey lasted thirteen months, six of them spent on the island of Mozambique waiting for the right winds. In May 1542, Xavier arrived in India and found in Goa what he described as "a completely Christian city, something to behold."[5] In the hands of the Portuguese since 1510, the city already boasted a monastery of Franciscan friars and several churches, including an "ornate cathedral." Xavier began his missionary enterprise by walking through the streets ringing a bell and drawing the curious, mostly children, into a church. There he would teach them lessons and prayers using rhymed verses and popular tunes—a teaching method he would use, with modifications, wherever he went for the rest of his missionary career. But Goa was a Portuguese city, and Xavier taught his lessons in Portuguese. It was a European enclave with a European culture, and the natives who became Christian were expected to adopt a European culture as well.

After five months in Goa, the governor asked Xavier to work among the Parava villages on the opposite coast of India, across from Sri Lanka. The higher castes of Hindus looked down upon the Paravas, who scraped together a meager living from fishing. They had become Christian several years earlier but knew next to nothing about their new faith. No Portuguese lived in the area, because of its poverty, and the natives spoke only Tamil, the principal language of south India.

Xavier was accompanied by three young men preparing for the priesthood, native Tamil-speakers who had come to Goa as boys and learned Portuguese. With their help Xavier prepared a Tamil version of the Ten Commandments and the Apostles Creed, with a brief commentary on each point. Neither Xavier nor his young helpers had sufficient command of the language, and their translations proved to be poor,[6] but that inadequacy does not take away from the significance of the deed. Even if one gives some credence to stories shrouded in legend, for the first time in a thousand years, Christianity was being translated into the language of a non-Western culture. Though Xavier seems to have been unaware of it, he was crossing a cultural frontier.

Even before he died, Xavier's missionary successes had become the stuff of legend. Hagiographers inflated the number of his conversions into the tens of thousands. Despite those later exaggerations, however, there is no disputing his ability to attract people to himself and to the Christian faith—first in India, then Malaysia, Indonesia, and finally Japan. By all accounts, he had a personality that people found charming, even when they could not fully understand him. Later tales to the contrary, Xavier was not a linguist, and he rarely preached without an interpreter. His deficiencies in language were compensated by his charisma and the urgency with which he preached. Xavier was still locked into a medieval paradigm of faith. Unless these natives accepted Christian faith and baptism, they would be damned. For Xavier "the prayers of pagans are displeasing to God, all the gods of the gentiles being demons." Salvation was to be found in an explicit faith in Christ alone.[7]

Xavier wrote in his letters how his voice would go hoarse from preaching, his arms sore from baptizing. Still how many were the souls perishing for lack of Christian missionaries to save them from hell. He complained about the students at the University of Paris, more concerned about their academic careers than with the fate of these idol-worshiping pagans.[8] Even more did he complain about the greed of the Portuguese colonists and their exploitation of the Christian converts.[9] Like missionaries after him, he learned that efforts to convert pagans could be seriously impeded by the immorality of Christians.

Xavier's first seven years in the Orient were spent in Portuguese colonies, first in India, then Indonesia. His letters from these colonies express both aversion and disdain for the religious practices of the local peoples, for Hinduism, Islam, and the native religion of the Indonesian tribal peoples. And though he expressed fondness for his converts and tried to protect them from exploitation by the colonists, he had little regard for their culture. He describes these indigenous peoples, at least those whom he had encountered thus far, as ignorant and barbarous. Writing Ignatius to send more Jesuit recruits, Xavier asked only for young men of good health and solid virtue; to be a missionary in this part of the Indies, no great learning was needed. He wrote Ignatius of his eagerness to sail to Japan, where there was a "race that is most inquisitive and eager to know what is new, both with respect to God and to other, natural things."[10] But converting the Japanese required more than virtue and health.

In Japan, Xavier faced the challenge for the first time of presenting Christian faith to people without the political backing of Europe's colonial powers. Here too he first encountered a high culture strikingly dissimilar to his own. In good humanist fashion, he accommodated and began making deliberate, conscious changes in his missionary methods. From the onset of his stay in Japan, Xavier set his sights on Kyoto, where he intended to meet and convert the emperor, sure that all Japan would then follow suit. After only a year in Japan, he and a companion, a Japanese convert, set out on foot for the imperial palace. In simple pilgrim dress, they endured the hardships of winter, often sleeping in wet clothes, sometimes scorned or even stoned when seeking hospitality on the way. In Kyoto he learned the painful truth that the emperor had no real power and very little wealth. Central authority in Japan had broken down, and the various provinces were ruled by great lords or barons, called daimyo, each ruling autonomously with an army of samurai knights.

Xavier realized that, to convert the Japanese, Christians would need the sympathy and support of the daimyo. On his futile journey to Kyoto, he was received kindly by one such lord, Yoshitaka, the daimyo of Yamaguchi. Xavier requested a second audience. This time he appeared before Yoshitaka dressed not in his shabby Jesuit habit, but in silk, and he presented the daimyo with letters of recommendation, impressively written on illuminated parchment and introducing him as the ambassador of the Portuguese governor in India. Xavier also presented the daimyo with a variety of gifts, some of them never before seen in Yamaguchi—a clock, a telescope, a three-barrelled musket, a pair of spectacles, pictures, books, and cut glass. Yoshitaka was impressed and offered gifts in return, but Xavier refused, asking only for the daimyo's permission to preach about the Christian God in his dominions. The daimyo granted the request and gave Xavier and his companions an empty Buddhist temple for their headquarters.[11]

With two Jesuit brothers, Japanese converts, Xavier spent the next six months in Yamaguchi, entering into conversations and debate with bonzes, the Buddhist monks of the city. Only a few bonzes became Christian, but one at least proved to be quite important to the mission because of his ability to teach Xavier and the others about Buddhism. Xavier's Japanese companions up to this time had not been educated at any depth in Buddhist theology or philosophy—and translating the Christian message into Japanese proved just as challenging a task as it was in Tamil. To give just one example, how should one translate the credal statement that Jesus sits at the right hand of the Father, when in Japanese culture the place of honor is at the left?

Even more troublesome was finding the proper word for God. Xavier had depended on one of the Japanese converts, a former samurai, to find the appropriate Japanese words to translate his message. From his background in the Shingon sect of Buddhism, the former samurai chose to translate the word "God" as *Dainichi.* The Shingon bonzes were pleased at the choice and invited Xavier to their monastery, where they received him with honor. Xavier became suspicious and then quite upset when better educated converts informed him that the *Dainichi* worshiped by the Shingon sect was not at all a personal God, but the impersonal matter beneath things. To make matters worse, the word also connoted the male sex organ.

Determined to avoid any similar embarrassment in the future, Xavier chose simply to modify *Deus,* the Latin word for God, into Japanese. The God of the Christians became *Deusu,* as if it were a proper name. The bonzes, no longer sympathetic to Xavier, struck back at their new competition. You could tell Deusu was a fraud by his very name, they taunted, since it sounded almost exactly like *daiuso,* which means "great lie."[12] Clearly, translating Christian vocabulary into another culture could be a discouraging as well as daunting task.

Xavier found much in Buddhism to remind him of Catholic Christianity—vestments, incense, rosaries, prayers in choir. And the Japanese found something in Xavier's preaching that reminded them of Buddhism—a belief in hell. But those in the Buddhist hell could be released by the bonzes' prayers; one needed only to give the bonzes alms to have them pray for deceased loved ones. Jesuit controversies with the bonzes centered on the nature of hell and the bonzes' claims. The Japanese converts were impressed by Xavier's teaching that hell was eternal, and by the fact that he had come from so great a distance to save them from it. They grieved, however, for their deceased parents, relatives, and friends who, according to Xavier's teaching, could not be freed from hell by anyone's prayers.[13] Xavier seems not to have noticed the similarities between the Buddhist hell and Catholic purgatory.

Xavier observed how, when hard pressed in an argument, time and again his Japanese conversation partners would appeal to the authority of the Chinese. To the Japanese mind, "if the Christian religion was really the one true religion, it surely would have been known to the intelligent Chinese and also accepted by them."[14] Xavier became convinced that if

China became Christian, Japan would follow. And to convert China, all he would have to do was convert the emperor of China. With God's grace all things are possible. As soon as he was sure that his small but growing community of Japanese Christians was safe, he took the opportunity to leave them and return to Goa.

After a short stay, during which he saw to the affairs of the province, Xavier set sail for China. In late August 1552, he arrived on the island of Sancian at the mouth of the Pearl River, not far from Canton. There he waited patiently for permission to enter the mainland. China was closed to foreigners, and illegal entry was punished with prison. He waited for three months, but permission never came, and the Portuguese merchants would not risk landing him illegally. In mid-November he wrote a friend that, God willing, he soon would be found in Beijing, at the court of the "king of China." Either there or imprisoned in Canton.[15]

Toward the end of the month, Xavier fell seriously ill. Less than two weeks later, on December 5, 1552, he died, hoping almost to the end to get an audience with the emperor. He had no idea of the distance to Beijing, nor of the audacity of his project. The Great Wall of China was as much a symbol as a defense: China was a closed society. Virtually no one saw the emperor, not even the Chinese. There were reasons why the imperial palace was named the Forbidden City.

That within one lifetime after Xavier, a Jesuit would be entering those hallowed precincts, speaks volumes to the genius of Matteo Ricci. But it speaks as well to the vision of Alessandro Valignano. He recognized in Ricci the qualities necessary for the journey to Beijing and had the astuteness to perceive how Ricci was to get there.

THE VISION OF ALESSANDRO VALIGNANO

Everard Mercurian, a Belgian, had been elected general of the Jesuits only a few months when he appointed Alessandro Valignano visitor to the Jesuit missions in the East. The choice occasioned surprise and no little grumbling. Valignano, with little administrative experience, was only thirty-four years old, and this was one of the most important positions in the entire Society. The murmurs came from those who expected a Portuguese, not an Italian, to fill the post, because the Jesuit missions in the East were either part of Portugal's colonial empire or within its sphere of influence. The visitor was expected to work with the royal and ecclesiastical authorities in Lisbon. The general clearly wanted to forge a new mission policy in the East—but in appointing Alessandro Valignano, he got more than he bargained for.

Valignano (1539–1606) came from a distinguished family with good connections.[16] After studying law in Padua, he went to Rome to pursue a comfortable career at the papal court. His plans dramatically changed, however, with the death of his would-be patron, Pope Paul IV, followed by a brush with the law in Venice. Valignano protested his innocence, but the judges could not come to a decision one way or the other. The young aristocrat was compelled to sit in prison for sixteen months awaiting judgment. How much that experience affected his life is hard to tell, but in 1566, two years after his release, he was back in Rome and petitioning the Society of Jesus for admission.

Valignano spent the next six years in Rome, first as a Jesuit novice and then as a student. His superiors must have perceived his leadership qualities, since shortly after his ordination as a priest, and even before he had completed his studies, he was made master of novices. He held the position only briefly, but was there in August 1571 when the nineteen-year-old Matteo Ricci entered the Jesuit novitiate. The following year Valignano was appointed rector of the college in Macerata, Ricci's hometown. The correspondence indicates that at this time Valignano asked to be sent to work in the missions in India.[17] He could hardly have anticipated that the general would put him in charge.

Even before setting sail for India, Valignano had to confront challenges to his new authority. The Portuguese Jesuits in Lisbon worked closely with the royal court and were staunch supporters of Portugal's national interests. They were concerned about the unprecedented number of new Jesuits

Valignano was taking with him to the colonies, most of them Spanish. Valignano insisted on training the recruits himself without Portuguese interference. He insisted too that henceforth all correspondence from the missions would go directly to the Jesuit procurator, an Italian, not to the Portuguese provincial. Valignano and Mercurian were clearly intent on breaking the stranglehold that the Portuguese colonial system had on the Jesuit missions in the East.[18]

In March 1573, Valignano sailed from Lisbon with forty-one Jesuits destined for various missions in India and the Far East. Like Xavier before him, he first stayed in Goa, the capital of the Portuguese East Indies. Portugal had succeeded in creating a home away from home for its conquistadors and for the colonists who followed in their wake. The missions were simply another part of Portugal's colonial enterprise, an extension of its European culture on Indian soil. Converts were expected to assume both a new faith and its European trappings, in effect cutting themselves off from their native culture and heritage. Such was the case not only in the Portuguese East Indies but also in the Spanish colonies in the Philippines and in the New World as well.

When converts were poor and illiterate, scantily clothed or polygamous, weaning them from their native cultures was seen as doing them no harm. On the contrary, Europeans viewed it as largesse. Such were the converts the Jesuits made in Africa, South India, and the islands of southeast Asia. Valignano concurred with the common opinion of the colonists that they were bringing these indigenous peoples not only the true religion but also a superior culture. He was, after all, a man who had grown up in the midst of the monumental architecture and high art of Renaissance Rome. But Valignano's thinking began to change when, after three years in India, he sailed to Macao, a peninsula on China's southern coast, cut off from the rest of China by a well-guarded wall. There he encountered Chinese and Japanese converts and their culture, and set about trying to learn why all previous missionary efforts at getting into China had failed.

Not unlike Europeans, the Chinese thought of their homeland as the center of the world. They called themselves the Middle Kingdom and, as

the name indicates, viewed their neighbors as geographically and culturally marginal. Foreigners were barbarians with little to offer that China
did not already have, so they could only pose a danger. Fearful of foreign
invasion and wary of spies, China chose to become hermetically sealed.
The government restricted foreigners to the peninsula of Macao. Only
twice a year, and under strict supervision, were foreigners residing on
Macao allowed to enter the mainland and travel the short distance to Canton, to serve as middlemen for the lucrative silk trade with Japan. (This
trade provided income for Portuguese merchants as well as for the struggling Jesuit missions, which needed a source of income other than the
charity of distant Europe—ever in jeopardy from bad seas and shipwreck.)

In 1578, on his way to visit the new churches in Japan, Valignano made
a stop in Macao. There he was dismayed to find that the Jesuit missionaries had become no more than chaplains to the Portuguese traders. They
had given up any hopes of ever preaching the gospel on the mainland.
And whatever Chinese or Japanese converts they made on Macao not only
had to learn about their new faith in Portuguese but assume Portuguese
dress and manners.

During this first visit to Macao, Valignano decided that missionary
efforts in China and Japan needed a new direction. He wrote from Macao
to the Jesuit provincial in India to send some able fathers who could devote
themselves to an intensive study of the Chinese language. After the better
part of a year on Macao, Valignano sailed to Japan, where he became even
more persuaded along his new line of thinking. Japan was like nothing he
had ever experienced, and nothing he had read could have prepared him
for it. As he would later write,

> The properties and qualities of this country are so strange, the mode of
> government of the state so different, and the customs and ways of liv-
> ing so extraordinary and so far removed from our own, that they are
> difficult to comprehend even for those of us who have been living here
> and dealing with the people for many years. How much more difficult,
> then, to make them intelligible to people in Europe.[19]

Valignano became convinced that the Japanese would never accommodate themselves to foreigners in any way whatsoever. The only way Christianity could be established in Japan was to educate the natives to run things themselves in their own way—and that could be done only by the missionaries earning the respect of the Japanese and learning their way of doing things. The Western missionaries would have to adapt themselves to the Japanese, not the other way around.[20]

Toward the end of 1581, Valignano composed a short handbook of decorum for the guidance of Jesuit missionaries.[21] If the missionaries were not to look ridiculous in the eyes of the Japanese, they had to know how to interact appropriately within Japanese society. That task was complicated, however, by a rigid hierarchical ranking that affected polite speech as well as correct behavior. Even a simple conversation was determined by rules of etiquette that took into account the social position of the speaker, the person spoken to, and the persons or subjects spoken about. If they were to avoid offending Japanese sensibilities, the Jesuits had to fit into the appropriate categories and know how to act accordingly. No one was to set himself up above his rank or step below it. Valignano was experienced in such matters: he had trained for a career at the papal court.

Japanese decorum distinguished sharply between priests and laity. On the advice of knowledgeable Japanese, Valignano boldly decided that the proper rank of the missionaries corresponded to that of Zen Buddhist bonzes. The superiors, priests, novices, lay helpers, servants—would all act according to the Zen model of decorum that would be expected at a Buddhist temple.

In his book on Japanese customs and decorum, Valignano prescribed how letters were to be written (when one wrote personally and when through an intermediary), how priests were to travel (never alone, never wearing the kind of straw hats worn by the peasants, and, when on foot, never holding their own umbrellas), how guests were to be received and entertained (in a special room near the entrance for the preparation of the traditional tea ceremony). To this end all Jesuit mission houses were to be constructed in a Japanese style with parlors for receiving visitors according to ceremonial custom. Proper decorum determined everything—the kind of tea one served one's guests, their place at the table, the appropriate gifts one presented to a visitor or to the local lord at the Japanese New Year. An unintended faux pas could be taken as a sign of disrespect or an embarrassing display of oneself as a boor.

Not surprisingly, Valignano had to defend some of his novel ideas to his fellow Jesuits, including the general in Rome. Some of his directives (like not carrying one's own umbrella) seemed to conflict with the spirit of Jesuit simplicity and poverty. He insisted, however, that if Christianity were to find a home in Japan, it could not appear inferior to Buddhism. More important, he argued, the missionaries had to learn from their mistakes:

> As a result of our not adapting ourselves to their customs, two serious evils followed, as indeed I realized from experience. They were the chief source of many others: First, we forfeited the respect and esteem of the Japanese, and second, we remained strangers, so to speak, to the Christians. Owing to our defective forms of social intercourse, we failed to make them feel at home with us.[22]

Schooled in the rules of rhetoric, the early Jesuits embraced the principle of accommodation—Ignatius wrote it into the *Constitutions of the Society of Jesus,* and the *compañeros* applied it in their vow at Montmartre. (Time and again amid his detailed instructions Ignatius would add the proviso that they should be followed unless circumstances indicated it would be better to do otherwise). So Valignano was acting in keeping with the Society's humanist origins and culture when he made accommodation a principle of Jesuit missionary efforts in China and Japan. Converts should not be required to become strangers to their own people and kin. Chinese and Japanese Christians should be able to feel at home in their new faith, which meant translating it into their own language and culture.

In response to Valignano's request, the provincial in India had sent to Macao a young Neopolitan Jesuit named Michele Ruggieri. His formidable task was to do nothing else but study Chinese, which, needless to say, was nothing like Italian. Spoken Chinese has five tones, each of which changes the meaning of the same sound. Instead of a phonetic alphabet, written Chinese has a different character or ideograph for every word. And if those were not troubles enough, the other Jesuit missionaries on Macao made Ruggieri's life miserable. They resented the hours he spent studying Chinese ideographs when he might have been doing something worthwhile, like ministering to the Portuguese. They assured him he was wasting his time; Chinese was impossible for a Westerner to learn, and he would never be allowed access to the mainland anyway.

Ruggieri proved them wrong. On three different occasions he accompanied the Portuguese merchants on their semiannual visits to buy silk in Canton. Though he was not a gifted linguist, he had learned enough of the language and culture to impress some senior Chinese officials. They gave him permission to set up a chapel in Canton in the quarter for foreign embassies, apparently seeing Ruggieri as different from the other Western barbarians. He knew, for example, how to behave appropriately toward them and make the customary profound bow, or kowtow. Most Europeans saw the kowtow as beneath their dignity. For the Chinese, Ruggieri observed, it was simply good manners.

Ruggieri, dispirited by the challenges posed by the Chinese language, asked Valignano to send the more gifted Matteo Ricci, then in India, to join him in the new enterprise. Valignano would have remembered Ricci from the novitiate in Rome, and he agreed to Ruggieri's request and wrote to India with instructions for Ricci to sail East. Prospects for the mission in China began to look up.

AN IGNATIAN HUMANIST IN CHINA

Matteo Ricci was born in 1552 in Macerata, Italy, near the Adriatic coast.[23] When a group of Jesuits arrived to establish a school in his hometown, he was one of the first pupils enrolled. He studied Latin and Greek and began making friendships that would last him a lifetime, even if maintained only through correspondence. His parents sent him at sixteen to study law at the Collegio Romano, the Jesuit college in Rome, where three years later he entered the Society of Jesus as a novice. Among his modest belongings were three books, including a Latin grammar and an illustrated volume on the glories of ancient Rome.

Ricci made the Spiritual Exercises and, after completing his novitiate, continued his studies in the humanities at the Jesuit college in Florence, birthplace of the Renaissance. After a year there he returned to Rome to study at the Collegio Romano, a school as cosmopolitan as the city. Ricci's colleagues came from all over Europe, with Latin their common language both in the classroom and in their private conversation. It was the language of their textbooks, like Cypriano Soarez's De Arte Rhetorica, required reading for Jesuit students in the 1570s. From that textbook, typical for the time, Ricci and his classmates studied classical usage, sentence structure, and the art of memorizing, which was regarded as the root of all eloquence. He learned the mnemonic device of creating dramatic images and then designing buildings to organize them, like "memory palaces."[24]

Under his Jesuit humanist instructors, Ricci applied himself to honing what would become his extraordinary memory skills. These he demonstrated years later by looking at and then recalling lists of 400 to 500 Chinese ideographs and by translating into Chinese any number of passages he had learned as a student in Italy. He eventually wrote a treatise on friendship, a collection of songs, and a book of discourses modeled after a Taoist classic, and in all of them drew from a rich store of classical humanist learning, much of it committed to memory. He quoted from Cicero's orations, Martial's epigrams, and long sections of Horace, Ovid, and Virgil. From the Greek classics he could quote Aesop's fables and Pindar's odes, passages from Homer, Plato's dialogues, and Aristophanes' *The Frogs*. As he wrote toward the end of his life, "I find myself so totally lacking in books that most of the things that I am now printing are things that I have been holding in my memory."[25]

Once he completed his studies in the humanities, Ricci moved on to philosophy and mathematics. He studied Aristotle and Euclid, geometry and astronomy. For four years at the Collegio Romano he studied under Christopher Clavius. From Clavius, Ricci learned the art of constructing sundials, clocks, and perpetual calendars. He learned how to use a quadrant to measure altitudes and astrolabes for calculating the motion of planets and stars. Ricci remained in correspondence with Clavius the rest of his life and, like any number of other Jesuits, might have followed him into the sciences. He was a likely prospect for a professorship in one of the Jesuit colleges, perhaps at the Collegio Romano itself, where the illustrious Robert Bellarmine had just joined the faculty.

But young Ricci put in a request that his superiors send him to the missions, and they approved. After studying Portuguese for the better part of a year at the University of Coimbra, Ricci set sail from Lisbon, taking leave of homeland, family, and friends he would never see again. Ricci followed the same difficult route that Xavier had taken, around the storm-ridden Cape of Good Hope, along the eastern coast of Africa to Mozambique, and then on to India. The voyage lasted six months. In September 1578, at the age of twenty-six, Ricci reached Goa.

In Goa, Ricci was assigned to teach Latin and Greek at the Jesuit college and to complete the theological studies he had begun in Rome. Two years later, while doing pastoral work in the coastal city of Cochin south of Goa, he was ordained a priest. A letter he wrote to the general during this period of his life gives an insight into Ricci's temper and character. Several of his fellow Jesuits had begun advocating policy changes regarding native candidates for the priesthood. Convinced of their intellectual and cultural superiority to the natives, these missionaries proposed that Indian candidates for the priesthood be given a less rigorous education than that which the Europeans received. Ricci was indignant at the proposed policy change and the discriminatory, not to say racist, attitudes behind it. Despite his relative youth and inexperience, Ricci expressed profound dissent with this kind of thinking. He pointed out that in Europe,

too, there were Jesuit priesthood candidates who did not do well in philosophy and theology.

> We don't refuse, for that reason, to teach all comers. All the more rea-
> son then, in the case of natives of this land, who, however much they
> know, very rarely receive much credit from white men. On the other
> hand, there is a universal custom in the whole Society to make no dis-
> tinction between classes of people, and even here in India there are so
> many Fathers, old, holy, and experienced, who open schools and are
> favorably disposed to all who come there. Secondly, in this way we
> encourage ignorance in ministers of the Church in a place where learn-
> ing is so necessary. . . . Thirdly, and this is the thing that most disturbs
> me, in my opinion they have none who show kindness to them except
> our people, and for this reason they have a special affection for us.[26]

The humanism of Ricci's Ignatian spirituality did not guarantee a resistance against the racism that generally infected European colonialists, but
it helped.

In 1582, in response to Valignano's request to the Jesuit superior in
India, Ricci left Goa for Macao. The following year he and Michele Ruggieri (another of the Jesuit recruits who had come to study Chinese at
Valignano's request; he had sailed from Lisbon to India with Ricci) traveled to the city of Zhaoqing on the south mainland of China, not far
from Canton. The local governor had learned of Ricci's skill with maps
and clocks and allowed the two Jesuits to set up a house that would
become the Jesuits' first mission on the Chinese mainland. The rest of
Ricci's life and career was spent in a slow, unsteady journey northward—
one that would eventually culminate in the imperial city of Beijing.

At the beginning of that career, the thirty-year-old Ricci applied himself
to learning Mandarin, the language of the Confucian classics and of China's
educated elite. He did so without benefit of dictionaries or grammars, with
only the aid of a Macao-born Chinese Christian. Besides learning Mandarin, Ricci had been assigned by Valignano to write up a comprehensive

report for him on China. He was to observe and describe as accurately as possible the people and their customs, government, and institutions. Though he would later correct a number of his early opinions, Ricci's was the first serious, reasonably accurate report to be written for the West.

Like the Jesuits in Japan, Ricci and Ruggieri dressed as Buddhist monks. They explained to the local governor on arriving in Zhaoqing, "We belong to an order of religious men who adore the King of Heaven as the one true God."[27] At the time the category of Buddhist monk seemed the most appropriate niche for them in Chinese society, and the governor confirmed their identity by placing a plaque on their mission house that read "Temple of the Flower of the Saints." Though Ricci preferred to read this as a reference to Mary, to whom their chapel was dedicated, the Chinese interpreted it to mean that their mission was a Buddhist temple.

This occasioned no little inconvenience for the two Jesuits, in that it designated their mission as the equivalent of an inn or public gathering place. It meant that mandarins, as they came to be called in the West, whatever their rank, could visit at any time of the night or day. The advantage was that Ricci had the opportunity to meet and converse freely with a segment of Chinese society he would never have reached otherwise. Decorum forbade the mandarins to visit the private residences of anyone not a member of their class.[28]

Mandarins, in the broadest sense, were an intellectual elite from whom were drawn the bureaucrats who governed China in a kind of meritocracy. One entered their number only by passing rigorous examinations in the Confucian classics. Ricci refers to these Confucian scholars in his journals as the "sect of literati" and describes them as ruling the country and as respected for their learning more than any other class. "Confucius is their Prince of Philosophers and according to them, it was he who discovered the art of philosophy. They do not believe in idol worship. In fact they have no idols. They do, however, believe in one deity who preserves and governs all things on earth."[29]

The Jesuits' first converts came mostly from the sick and elderly. Because their situation as resident aliens was too precarious, Ricci and

Ruggieri did not preach in the streets as Xavier had. Instead, they engaged in lengthy conversations with the Confucian scholars who came to their residence to meet the strangers from the West. Their visitors were curious to see their books and examples of Western art, rendered strikingly realistic by the technique of perspective. The mandarins also came to examine the map Ricci had made of the known world and were astounded at the many faraway lands that it claimed existed west of China. To his visitors' satisfaction, Ricci had prudently placed China in the center of the map, as the Middle Kingdom deserved. And when the conversation turned to matters philosophical, Ricci interjected information about the Westerners' Christian faith.

At one point, Ruggieri had to leave Ricci and the mission to return to Macao for funds and, at the governor's request, a clock. We can sense a nostalgia in Ricci's letters to his old school friends in Italy, indicating how important fellowship was to him. With Ruggieri gone, Ricci found himself without companions save for the Confucian scholars with whom he shared neither faith nor culture. The only thing to do was to learn and know theirs.

Finances were a constant worry for the mission, dependent on hazardous sea voyages and the silk trade. Furthermore, the Jesuits were expected not only to provide their visitors hospitality but also to engage in the ceremonial exchange of gifts. Yet the missionaries always seemed to have enough funds to survive, and this raised questions in the minds of some of their visitors. They began to suspect the missionaries of engaging in alchemy and knowing the secret of transforming mercury into silver. No matter what their level of education, alchemy and fortunetelling seemed to be two dominant passions of the Chinese.

Valignano directed Ruggieri to return to Europe to engage in fund raising. He also hoped that some appropriately splendid gifts from the pope to the emperor might guarantee them a permanent residence. Other Jesuits were assigned to join Ricci in the Chinese mission, which was relocated to Shaoshou, north of Canton. Here, in a residence utterly Chinese in architecture and appearance, Qu Rukuei entered Ricci's life.

A Confucian scholar three years his senior, Qu was quite sure that Ricci's knowledge of science included alchemy. To learn Ricci's supposed secrets, Qu asked him to become his teacher, and Ricci agreed. In a formal dinner for his mandarin colleagues and friends, Qu made the ceremonial kowtow to Ricci and declared himself Ricci's disciple. For the rest of his life he would be honor bound to acknowledge Matteo Ricci—Li Madou as the Chinese called him—as his master.

Ricci was able to wean his disciple from an interest in alchemy to mathematics, which at that time was only rudimentary in China. He lay open to Qu the world of Euclidian geometry with its axioms and deductions, and, when the opportunity arose, he related something about Christianity. Qu proved an adept student. He took careful notes and astounded his teacher one day with a series of perceptive questions about the Christian faith, all deriving from a Confucian scholar's perspective. The exchange proved significant for master and disciple alike. Qu eventually became a Christian, and Ricci learned the importance of relating Christianity to someone steeped in Confucian tradition.

Qu spread the word of his master throughout his network of colleagues and friends, many of whom also became friends of Li Madou. Through them Ricci deepened his knowledge of Chinese culture and the Confucian classics that lay at its foundation. It was becoming clear to Ricci that for all segments of society, not only the mandarins, China's dominant value system was Confucian. He began studying the Four Books at the heart of the Confucian classics and translating them into Latin.

All this time Ricci still shaved his head and wore the garb of a Buddhist monk. But after a year of almost daily conversations with Qu and his friends, he was convinced that dressing like a Buddhist monk was not the appropriate way to present himself. Ricci conferred with Valignano, who agreed with his view that Christianity was more compatible with Confucianism than with Buddhism. Their bonze attire was causing the Chinese to mistake the missionaries for members of a Buddhist sect.

Ricci had already adopted Chinese diet, manners, and sleep patterns. Now he began to let his hair and beard grow. In 1594 he put aside the coarse gray robe of the Buddhist monks and, to Qu Rukuei's delight, donned an ankle-length purple silk robe with loose flowing sleeves. On his feet he wore embroidered silk slippers and on his head a high square black hat not unlike a bishop's miter. He drew a line at the practice of letting one's fingernails grow to considerable length, but he did carry a fan. And if he thought to ask himself what Ignatius and Francis Xavier would have said to see a Jesuit in such splendid attire, he could presume that they would understand. After all, he was just building on the example of Francis Xavier, who appeared for his second audience with the daimyo of Yamaguchi dressed in silk. In good humanist, Jesuit fashion, he had accommodated himself to circumstances. He was not in Rome, but China. Li Madou had become a Confucian man of letters.

CONFUCIAN SCHOLAR

The following year, Ricci and the Jesuit mission received permission from the government to move farther north, to Nanchang. Here he began to meet scholars and high-ranking mandarins who had never known him in the garb of a Buddhist monk. With his excellent Chinese, good manners, and familiarity with the Confucian classics, they accepted Ricci as one of their own kind. His circle of influential friends and admirers broadened, and the number of visitors to the mission multiplied, as did the invitations to dine. Dinners among the literati were quite formal occasions, from a Western perspective conventionally short on food but long on ceremony and conversation. Ricci's Jesuit heritage put a high value on conversation, and he used the opportunities offered by the dinners to share ideas with his fellow scholars. From their respective Christian and Confucian perspectives, they talked philosophy, ethics, and religion.

Confucianism, called in Chinese the "teaching of the scholars," is the way of life propounded by K'ung Fu-tzu (551–479 B.C.E.). A political theorist and reformer, Confucius was not a religious leader in the ordinary Western sense of the word. His teachings were essentially a social ethic that both predated and continued to develop after him. The core of that tradition is found in the Analects (conversations) of Confucius compiled by his disciples. Here we find his answers to questions regarding life's meaning and the virtues required for a well-ordered society. In the second century B.C.E., the Han Dynasty of Chinese emperors adopted the Analects, along with other classical texts attributed to Confucius, as the state orthodoxy, which would dominate Chinese thinking for two millennia. Mastery of the Confucian literature became the basis for the civil service examinations of Ricci's day and up to the beginning of the twentieth century.

Ethics lay at the heart of Confucian philosophy, and at the heart of Confucian ethics was the virtue of *Jen*. Sometimes translated as goodness, benevolence, or kindness, *Jen* for Confucius is what makes a person a complete human being. Another justifiable translation is humaneness or humanity. "A disciple asked Confucius about humaneness (Jen). Confucius said, 'Love people'" (Analects, 12:22).

One can imagine Ricci's reaction, reading those words the first time and recognizing the affinity between them and his own faith and spirituality. He recognized, too, that in some respects at least, Confucians far surpassed most Christians, humanist or otherwise, in the love and reverence they showed to parents and teachers.[30]

Confucian ethics were organized around the so-called Five Relationships.[31] Three of them were familial: father and son, husband and wife, elder and younger brother. The other two were perceived in terms of familial models: the ruler-subject relationship resembling that of father and son, and the relationship of friends viewed as a form of brotherliness. These Five Relationships became the basis for understanding other relationships. Parental love of one's children was extended to love for all children; respect for parents extended to respect for all the elderly. Confucian society regarded itself, indeed all humanity, as a large family. "Within the four seas all men are brothers," declares the Analects (12:5). The maxim reads like a Confucian version of the humanist dictum, "I consider nothing human as foreign to me."

Friendship, as one of the Five Relationships, came up naturally enough in Ricci's conversations with the Confucian scholars. One of them, a nobleman residing in Nanchang, encouraged Ricci to put Western thoughts on the subject in writing. Ricci agreed, and in late 1595 completed a treatise on friendship. It was his first attempt, and the first altogether by a Westerner, to conceive and write a work in Chinese ideographs.

The mission library contained an anthology of Greek and Latin sayings on a variety of topics, including friendship. The book provided Ricci with ample material from the classics, church fathers, and even the Dutch humanist Erasmus.[32] From this and other sources Ricci put together first seventy-six, and in a later edition one hundred, maxims written in the form of proverbs, as found in the Confucian canon. We know from his letters how important friends were to Ricci, so there is certain poignancy to many of his maxims: "A friend is another self." "God commands us to make friends so that we can help one another." "Our most intimate friends are those with whom we can share our innermost feelings." "If there were no friends in the world, there would be no joy."

This collection of aphorisms, he later acknowledged, garnered Ricci and Europe more credit than anything he had done prior to that time. His prisms and clocks won him and the other Jesuits a reputation for ingenuity, but the treatise on friendship won them a reputation for learning and virtue. Ricci's own humanism and affability won the trust of the literati. As one of his new friends wrote in the preface to the 1601 edition of the treatise: "Ricci endured the discomfort of traveling 80,000 *li* in an easterly direction to China for the sake of friendship. He understands the ways of friendship."[33] Ricci would have probably described his motivation differently, but there is no doubting the ultimate truth of the comment.

At the same time in Nanchang, Ricci began discussing theories on memory with his Chinese interlocutors and teaching them mnemonic devices. The local governor, Lu Wangai, had three sons who were preparing for the triennial civil service examinations on the Confucian classics. The governor, as a young man, had passed his exams with distinction; now his sons needed to do so too, as success in the exams was imperative for acquiring any position of honor in China. In 1596 Ricci set about composing his second book in Chinese, a short treatise on the art of memory, which he presented as a gift to Governor Lu and his three sons.[34] Ricci knew, as did Ignatius and Xavier, that it never hurts to make friends in high places.

Whether trying to explain China to his friends back home or Western culture to the Chinese, Ricci was ever the humanist. He drew on classical analogies to compare Confucius to Seneca, the Buddhists to Pythagoreans, and Chinese governance to Plato's Republic. His treatise on friendship drew more from the pagan classics than from the church fathers. Almost the whole of his treatise on memory comes from Pliny and Cicero. And when he tried to describe his own state at that time in a letter to a friend, he compared himself to Aeneas in the underworld, the hero of Virgil's epic poem, laboring to complete a long arduous ascent.[35] Still hoping, like Xavier before him, to convert the emperor, Ricci kept his sights northward on the imperial palace in Beijing.

A detailed account of Ricci's ascent to Beijing lies outside the scope of this study and can be found elsewhere.[36] Suffice it to say that his journey north involved an initial failed attempt, followed by two years in the old capital of Nanjing, unfriendly encounters with a highly influential eunuch of the imperial court, and finally a second, this time successful, trip to Beijing in 1601. Ricci had been named superior of the mission in China for three years already and had been joined by several Jesuit colleagues. The fact that they were allowed at long last to establish a residence in Beijing was due in no little amount to the unusual gifts Ricci presented to the emperor, among them a large chiming clock and a harpsichord.

Ricci never met the emperor. In those days the only persons allowed into the emperor's presence were his wives and his eunuchs, who managed the affairs of the imperial palace and served as intermediaries between the emperor and the outside world. Ricci had simply left the gifts with the eunuch in charge of such matters. The emperor was delighted with the clock and became quite dismayed when it ran down and ceased to chime. Ricci and his Jesuit companion in Beijing, Diego Pantoja, were summoned to the palace to correct the problem. It was an extraordinary honor for anyone, let alone two foreigners. They were ushered into the inner courts of the Forbidden City, where no European had ever stood before, where they taught the grateful eunuchs how to wind and regulate the emperor's new clock.

The harpsichord was another matter. Though Ricci could assemble clocks, he was no musician. However, a Jesuit at the mission in Nanjing did have musical training, and Ricci, with considerable foresight, had him teach the newly arrived Fr. Pantoja how to tune the harpsichord and play several sonatas. As Ricci had hoped, the emperor was intrigued by the harpsichord and ordered the Jesuits to teach four of his eunuch musicians to play it. Pantoja was able to comply with the emperor's wishes, and over the course of a month taught each eunuch one piece. Two of the musicians learned quickly and asked for examples of Western songs. Better at words than music, Ricci wrote Chinese lyrics for eight songs, for which the eunuchs themselves wrote music. While his colleagues in Europe were authoring scripts for school plays, Ricci in China was writing songs for the imperial court.

Like Xavier before him, Ricci wrote lyrics that would teach moral and religious lessons. They were short and adapted to Chinese culture, but with roots in Ricci's training in the classics. Most of them harked back to the odes of Horace, with echoes of Seneca and Petrarch. Ricci wrote of the folly of the desire for long life; true longevity is measured not by years but virtue. He wrote of youth slipping away before we think about leading a moral life, how death spares no one, how the grace of God fills the world with harmonies much as music fills a hall. Reminiscent of Augustine's *Confessions,* he wrote of the restlessness of the human heart finding no peace except within. The eight songs were published and apparently won the esteem of the Confucian scholars. Whatever their literary merit, the songs would remind the emperor to govern the nation with virtue.[37]

Ricci's literary output came to include *Twenty-five Sayings,* a booklet on virtues that drew from the Stoic philosopher Epictetus and was conceived as a rival to a Buddhist work, *Forty-two Paragraphs.* In 1607 Ricci published a Chinese translation of the first six books of Euclid's *Elements of Geometry.* The following year he published a book entitled *Ten Paradoxes* or, more exactly, *Ten Truths Contrary to Public Opinion,* a reference to a (third century B.C.E.) Taoist classic. The ten chapters, or discourses, consist of conversations with Chinese scholars on a variety of moral and religious topics. Some of them were universal and perennial: how self-examination and self-reproach prevent mistakes; how the rich who are greedy cause the poor to suffer. But others were directed against what Ricci regarded as grave problems in Chinese culture—rampant superstition, the danger of seeking predictions of the future, Buddhist views of reincarnation, the promotion of fasting to prevent the slaughter and eating of animals.[38]

But the crowning and most original of Ricci's writings was *The True Meaning of the Lord of Heaven.* Published in 1603, it was in every way a tour de force—the mature product of two decades of conversations with Confucian scholars, of Ricci immersing himself in their culture, studying their classics. It was also a model showcase for Valignano's visionary theory of cultural accommodation. Some twenty years prior, two years after their arrival in China, Ruggieri and Ricci had published a Chinese translation of a catechism used by Jesuits in India. But the catechism, they learned, had serious flaws. It paid scant attention to Confucian scholarship, used the language of Buddhism, and presented the missionaries as "bonzes from India." Little wonder that most Chinese had viewed the Jesuits as members of a Buddhist sect. It was an error requiring correction.

INTERPRETING CONFUCIUS

In 1593, the same year the missionaries put aside the garb of Buddhist monks, Valignano urged Ricci to begin writing a book that would explain Christianity in categories that would be familiar to Chinese intellectuals. At the time, Ricci was in the process of translating the *Four Books* of Confucius into Latin, and the next year he set about studying the *Six Classics* of the Confucian canon. He wanted to achieve enough command of

China's cultural heritage to determine how much of it was compatible with Christian faith. He came to the conclusion that Confucius was "another Seneca" and that the Confucian canon embodied a moral philosophy reconcilable with Christianity. He wrote the Jesuit general, Claude Aquaviva, in 1595: "I have noted down many terms and phrases in harmony with our faith, for instance, 'the unity of God,' 'the immortality of the soul,' 'the glory of the blessed,' and the like."[39]

The True Meaning of the Lord of Heaven is framed as a dialogue between a Chinese and Western scholar. Years later critics would fault the book for omitting basic Christian doctrines and accuse Jesuits of watering down the gospel. The criticism was unfair, since the book was never intended to be a full exposition of Christian faith. Its purpose was propaedeutic; in Ricci's own words, it treated "only of certain principles, especially such as can be proved and understood with the light of natural reason. Thus it can be of service both to Christians and non-Christians and can be understood in those remote regions which our Fathers cannot immediately reach, preparing the way for those other mysteries which depend upon faith and revealed wisdom."[40] Quoting the Bible would obviously carry no weight with Ricci's Chinese readers. The only authorities to which he could appeal were the Confucian classics, and these he cited frequently as supportive of Christian faith.

But Ricci needed to interpret, not merely cite Confucian texts. Confucianism was a living tradition, and several centuries earlier, during the Sung dynasty (A.D. 960–1279), it had come under Buddhist influence, particularly its monism, which understood the Divine as an impersonal substance united with and uniting all things. The upshot was a development into what came to be called Neo-Confucianism. Ricci argued that when the Confucian classics referred to "heaven" *(T'ien)* or "the Lord on High" *(Shang-ti),* the "true meaning" of the term was that of a personal deity very much like the transcendent Creator God of Christianity. But Ricci knew full well that that was not how most Confucian scholars in his day understood the words.

Endorsed as the state orthodoxy, Neo-Confucianism understood "heaven" and "Lord on high" as impersonal. This, Ricci argued, distorted the original Confucian philosophy. He took the two terms as referring to the same divine reality and then created a new Chinese name for it, "Lord of Heaven," which he identified with the God of both Christianity and Confucius. He tried to prove that, not impersonal Buddhist monism, but Christianity's personal God accorded more fully with Confucian origins.[41] Not surprisingly, there were Buddhists and Neo-Confucians who challenged his novel interpretation. But more importantly, there were leading Confucian scholars who found his argument compelling and still others who, while not in complete agreement, at least accepted his interpretation as defensible and worthy of consideration.

Ricci's *True Meaning of the Lord of Heaven* is not a catechism, let alone a summa of Christian doctrine. It examines and argues for three fundamental principles of natural law that Ricci saw as common to Christianity and original Confucianism: the existence of a personal God, immortality of the soul, and eternal reward or punishment. Throughout the text one sees the influence of Thomas Aquinas as Ricci appeals to reason to dispute Buddhist doctrines like nirvana and reincarnation.

Ricci showed little sympathy for Buddhism, which he regarded as rife with idolatry and superstition. Because it was not a philosophy but a religion, it was necessarily in competition with Christianity and incompatible with it. A basic message of his book was "draw close to Confucianism and repudiate Buddhism." Put more positively, his aim was to demonstrate that one did not have to give up Chinese culture and its Confucian heritage in order to become Christian. On the contrary, he argued, Christianity completed the philosophical ethics of China's sages. But to prove that rapprochement between the two was possible, Ricci had to address Confucian practice as well as thinking.

In the abstract, the virtue of *hsiao,* or filial piety, which is central to Confucian culture, appears commendable and unproblematic, but it raised any number of practical difficulties for the missionaries. Confucian tradition had come to interpret filial piety as demanding that a son raise up progeny to remember and honor himself and his deceased ancestors. This assumption naturally raised questions about the filial piety of the unmarried Jesuits, so Ricci in *The True Meaning of the Lord of Heaven* addressed the issue with an apologia for celibacy.

Another, more pressing challenge to Jesuit efforts at convert making was the use of filial piety to justify polygamy. Though most Chinese men could afford only one wife, many wealthy Confucian scholars had plural wives to ensure progeny to honor them and their ancestors. Here the Jesuits drew the line. If a Confucian scholar expressed the desire to convert to Christianity, he first had to promise to make do with one wife. Accommodation to Chinese culture and mores clearly had its limits. An even knottier question, however, was whether those limits excluded the practice of the "Chinese rites."

Chinese tradition did not leave the observance of filial piety to subjective feelings or happenstance; it was determined by detailed rules of propriety and rituals. A devoted son was duty bound to care for his elderly parents during their lifetime, and at death to render them a proper funeral. Even after burial, deceased parents and ancestors were to be remembered with memorial tablets in each home, inscribed with their names and set up on family altars or shrines. Mourners performed various gestures of respect before the tablets—kneeling, bowing, lighting candles, burning incense. On certain prescribed occasions families gathered, set offerings of food and drink before the shrines, and later shared in a common meal. Similar rites were performed at shrines throughout China in memory of Confucius. On regular occasions a bull or a pig would be slaughtered, wine and food offered, and a banquet shared to honor "Master K'ung, the most holy teacher of antiquity."[42]

From their first encounters with the Chinese, Ricci and the other Jesuits had to confront the question of these ancestral and Confucian rites, which were so thoroughly embedded in the culture. How should one interpret these symbolic gestures? Were they religious or merely civil and social? Was Confucius being honored as divine? Did the Chinese believe that the spirits of the dead were somehow present in the memorial tablets inscribed with their names? The difficulty in determining the meaning of the rites was that several of their components—candles, incense, profound bows, the offering of food and drink—might well appear as religious in a Western context. But this was China, where the profound kowtow was simply the appropriate gesture of respect to be shown high-ranking civil officials. Was such a gesture to be taken as worship when directed to a memorial tablet?

Ricci's opinions on the ancestral and Confucian rites were at once sympathetic and discriminating, obviously drawn from conversations with Confucian scholars and their answers to his pointed questions. Ricci relates in his journals that the whole idea of the rituals honoring one's ancestors was "to serve them in death as though they were alive." Food was set out for the deceased, "because they know of no other way to show their love and grateful spirit toward them." Ricci relates being told that "this ceremony was begun more for the living than for the dead," to teach children how to respect living parents, seeing how they were honored in death. The Chinese did not regard their deceased ancestors as gods, nor did they ask them for favors. The same could be said of the rites honoring Confucius. Though candles were lighted and incense burned to express gratitude for Master K'ung's teachings, these things were done without prayers or petitions to him. So the rites, Ricci concluded, were free of idolatry and "perhaps" superstition.[43]

Ricci's qualifying "perhaps" derived from his awareness that superstition was rampant among the poorer, uneducated Chinese, many of whom worshiped Confucius as a god and practiced the ancestral rites as a form of magic. But such misunderstanding, in his opinion, did not vitiate the original and essential nonreligious nature of the rites, which he saw as legitimate and good. Superstition was not inherent in the rites. They did not have to be abolished just because they could be abused.

One is reminded here of the humane presupposition Ignatius Loyola put at the beginning of the *Spiritual Exercises*. Prefer to put a good interpretation on what someone says [or does] rather than condemn it. Ricci had only to remember how uneducated peasants back home in Catholic

Europe made superstitious use of relics, rosaries, and any number of other sacramental signs and symbols. Did Europeans place flowers on graves for the dead to smell them?

In December 1603, as superior of the Jesuit mission in China, Ricci issued a historic directive on ancestral and Confucian rites. Although the text is no longer extant, we know its contents. Ricci decided that it is licit and, for Christian missionary work to make any headway in China, even indispensable for Chinese Christians to observe the rites honoring their ancestors and Confucius. There is no conclusive evidence to prove that the rites are inherently superstitious and plenty of evidence to the contrary.[44] When they use the word *sacrifice* to describe the food brought to the Confucian ceremonies, it is "in a broad and indefinite sense." The ceremonies are not false worship because the Chinese honor Confucius as a great philosopher and teacher, not as a god.[45]

That tolerant, humanistic attitude allowed Ricci and the Jesuits to bring some remarkable Chinese intellectuals into the Christian fold. The most distinguished among them was Hsü Kuang-ch'i, who would go on to become the grand secretary of the Ming Imperial Government, the highest office in the land. A close friend to Ricci, Hsü became a valuable protector of the fledgling Christian community in China and living proof that one could be both a Confucian and devout Christian. How he could do so Hsü explained in a postscript he wrote for Ricci's *Twenty-five Sayings*. There Hsü describes how he searched through everything the missionaries said for even one word that was not in accord with the Confucian teachings of filial piety and loyalty to one's ruler. He could find none. He would later write that Christianity "supplements Confucianism and displaces Buddhism," which for some years had been precisely Ricci's point.[46]

At this time in his career, Ricci no longer needed to strive for acceptance. His celebrity was such that he was inundated with invitations to dinner and conversation. A steady stream of visitors made the last ten years of his life exhausting but the most productive yet for the missionary. Within his first five years in Beijing, there were more than one hundred converts; in 1608 Ricci wrote his brother back home in Macerata that

China now had "already more than 2,000 Christians, among them many scholars."[47] Compared to China's millions, the Christian community was miniscule. Most of the converts were from the ordinary ranks of Chinese society—merchants, craftsmen, and peasants—but included some members of the intellectual elite and high ranking officials.[48] The number of Christians was "not as great as might be wished," Ricci wrote, but he saw his task as one of preparing the way for others—not harvesting or even sowing the seed, but merely, as he put it, "clearing the forest."[49]

Given the hours he put into each day, Ricci did not expect to live a long life. He began thinking of those who would come after to continue the work he and his Jesuit colleagues had begun. The year before he died, he wrote of the importance of sending men to China who were not only "good, but also men of talent, since we are dealing with a people both intelligent and learned."[50]

Beijing in 1610 was filled with candidates for the triennial examinations, so the press of visitors eager to meet Ricci was even greater than usual. Some days he hardly had time to rest or eat until late in the evening. On May 3 he fell seriously ill, and a week later he died. Among the last things he said was, "I am leaving you before an open door which leads to great merits, but not without great effort and many dangers."[51] Ricci's words were uncannily prescient. Merit, effort, danger—his successors would encounter all three.

SUCCESSORS ADAM SCHALL AND FERDINAND VERBIEST

Hundreds of Confucian scholars joined the Jesuit missionaries and their Christian community in paying their last respects to Li Madou, the "wise man from the West" who had become one of them. In response to a petition to the emperor, imperial permission was granted for a villa near Beijing's western wall to be given over to the Jesuits for Ricci's tomb. Ordinarily such a grant was awarded only to outstanding public officials, not ordinary citizens, and certainly not foreigners. It served not only to honor Ricci's memory but also to provide imperial recognition and protection of the Jesuit mission. Some years later, the governor of Beijing honored the tomb with a plaque that read: "To one who loved righteousness and wrote illustrious books, to Li Madou, Far-Westerner."[52]

Ricci never met the emperor, but he came closer than anyone had a right to expect. Thanks to his Ignatian humanism, he found truth in Confucian texts, saw God at work in the lives of non-Christian Confucian friends, and laid the groundwork for rapprochement between Christianity and Chinese culture. Building on that foundation and taking his advice, his superiors sent "men of talent" to succeed him. Any number of remarkable Jesuits took up his mantle and efforts to make Christianity at home in Confucian China. Two in particular—Adam Schall and Ferdinand Verbiest—stand out for achieving a stature at least remotely comparable to Ricci's.

Adam Schall arrived in China nine years after Ricci's death.[53] Born in Cologne, educated in Rome, Schall like Ricci was gifted with a phenomenal memory. He came to master both literary and vernacular Chinese, but his greatest strengths lay in mathematics and astronomy. Even in China he made sure he kept abreast of the latest scientific developments occurring in Europe. His colorful career—too much for even a summary here—witnessed the political chaos that accompanied the fall of the last of the Ming emperors in 1644. The new Manchu (*Ch'ing*) Dynasty would come to rule China until the twentieth century. Schall's skill in predicting a lunar eclipse won the admiration of the new imperial regents, who very much wanted a reformed calendar. To that end they named Schall the director of the Bureau of Astronomy. He tried several times to decline the office, until his Jesuit superior instructed him to accept it lest he incur imperial disfavor and thereby endanger the mission.

Schall was now ex officio a mandarin himself, but of the fifth class. He would eventually be accorded honors taking him to the very first class, where, at the pinnacle of mandarin hierarchy, he would be distinguished with the title "imperial chamberlain." Even more remarkable was his relationship with the new young Manchu emperor, who refused to be a prisoner of the palace like the previous Ming emperors. The Manchu emperor regularly invited Schall to the palace and, in utter disregard for all previous tradition, frequently visited Schall's residence. The records tell of the emperor inspecting Schall's home and belongings, sitting on his bed, and inquiring about his Christian beliefs and way of life. The emperor even came to address Schall as *ma fa*, an affectionate Manchu term used for older members of one's family.[54]

Schall was sure the emperor wanted to become a Christian, but he was unable to accept what Schall told him of the church's disallowance of polygamy. (So much for the fiction about Jesuits being lax and watering down traditional moral obligations.) Despite the emperor's personal reluctance to convert, the Christian community grew exponentially. Certainly it did not hurt the Christian cause when the celebrated Nestorian tablet was discovered in 1625, telling of Syrian Christians coming to China in the seventh century. It was important for the Chinese to know that Christianity was not a modern import, but had come to China one thousand years earlier and been approved by the esteemed emperors of the Tang Dynasty. Christianity now had a demonstrable Chinese heritage. In 1627 there were 13,000 Chinese Christians; less than ten years later, 40,000; ten years after that the number had reached 150,000.[55]

At the death of the emperor, untimely in that his heir was too young to assume power, the imperial government passed into the hands of regents, and Schall became the victim of palace intrigues. Rival astronomers, who had long resented him for the favor the deceased emperor had lavished on him, accused Schall and his Jesuit companions of sorcery. Schall was stripped of his honors. A long investigation ensued during which Schall, in his midseventies, suffered an apparent stroke that left him paralyzed and speechless. He was exonerated only after his death in 1666, when he was buried alongside Ricci. Schall's honors were returned to him posthumously by the new emperor, Kangxi, who reigned for the next sixty years and looked to another Jesuit for counsel, Ferdinand Verbiest.

The Belgian-born Verbiest had been Schall's assistant and succeeded him as head of the calendar office, which came once again to be staffed by Chinese Christians trained in Western mathematics and astronomy. Verbiest tutored the new emperor in mathematics, introduced the thermometer into China, built new astronomical instruments, and in the course of the above became the emperor's friend. Thanks to the trust and admiration Verbiest inspired, the emperor issued an edict in 1692 comparable to the Emperor Constantine's fourth-century edict of Milan, which legitimized Christianity for the Roman Empire. The Kangxi emperor declared that Christians, no less than Buddhists, had a rightful place in Chinese society and culture. They commit no crimes and teach only good laws. Their temples to the "Lord of Heaven" ought to be preserved. "Therefore, let no one henceforth offer them any opposition."[56]

The emperor's edict protected the Jesuits and their converts from Chinese, but not European, opposition. Valignano's missionary method of adapting Christianity to China and Japan was not without its Catholic critics, both in and outside the Society of Jesus. Working deep within China, Ricci was at a safe distance from the influence of Europe's colonial powers and without the interference of missionaries who identified Christianity fully with European culture. His successors in China and India were not so fortunate.

ROBERTO DE NOBILI

Roman-born Jesuit priest Roberto de Nobili (1577–1656) was a contemporary of both Ricci and Schall and, like them, had a gift for languages.[57] He learned to read and write Tamil and Telugu and became the first European to study and master Sanskrit, the language of India's classic sacred texts. He arrived in India in 1605 and, following in the footsteps of Xavier and Ricci, began his work on the coast in Goa and Cochin with their transplanted Portuguese culture and barely literate natives. But the following year he was sent inland to the populous, sophisticated city of Madurai. There he encountered the high culture of the Brahmins, the highest class in the hierarchy of India's caste system.

Despite the best efforts of two generations of missionaries, no Brahmin had ever become Christian. De Nobili set about investigating the reason for this failure by trying to understand Hindu culture and religion from the inside. Assigned to study Tamil, the language of south India, de Nobili was fortunate enough to meet a knowledgeable, sympathetic Brahmin, a schoolteacher willing to talk to him about religion. In a series of long conversations, he learned that his black Jesuit robe and leather shoes were a hindrance to his work. De Nobili also learned that the Paranghi (as the Brahmins called the Portuguese and anyone associated with them—including the missionaries and their handful of lower-caste converts) conducted themselves in ways that were not only offensive to Indian social custom but defiling. Paranghi ate beef, drank wine, and mixed freely with all castes. They took untouchables into their service and ate food served by them.

Since the missionaries had the same language, customs, and diet as the Portuguese, they also were held in contempt. No Hindu could believe that they had any human or spiritual wisdom worth listening to. When asked by class-conscious Hindus to what caste he belonged, de Nobili pointed to his name as indicating that he was not a member of the despised Paranghis. Being a de Nobili meant that he was descended from nobility, making him a member of the high-ranking Raja caste and entitled to meet with the highest-ranking Brahmins.

Having learned of Ricci's successes in accommodating himself to a Confucian way of life, de Nobili requested and received permission from his Jesuit superiors to attempt the same thing with respect to Brahmin culture. That required distancing himself from Paranghi, including the Portuguese Jesuit with whom he had been living up to this time. De Nobili moved out of the tiled house into a hut nearby and began abstaining from all meat, fish, eggs, and wine. With the permission of his superiors, he shaved his head and began taking the frequent baths dictated by Brahmin custom. Since he was already a vowed celibate, he went beyond routine

Brahmin practice by assuming the lifestyle and dress of a *sanyasi,* one of India's revered ascetics. This was analogous to Ricci becoming a Confucian scholar, but in India at far greater cost to someone grown accustomed to a European lifestyle and diet.

As a *sanyasi,* de Nobili ate only once a day at four o'clock in the afternoon—a meal consisting of rice, vegetables, water, and milk. His dress consisted of a loincloth, a pale yellow toga, and a kind of cape that served as his only blanket at night. He wore a white linen turban on his head, and on his forehead, a rectangular mark made of sandalwood paste. On his breast he wore a cross on a cord made of five threads, two of white linen and three of gold. He had to forego any use of chairs or cots; for sitting or sleeping custom prescribed only a tiger's or goat's skin. Also disallowed was any travel by horseback; he would have to get around by walking barefoot.[58]

Even with all those measures, de Nobili discovered that Brahmins were reluctant to visit him in a locale populated by members of the lower caste. So once again he accommodated, purchasing some property in a Brahmin area of the city. There he resided in his hut with its chapel without leaving, an impressive indication for Hindus of his chastity and his practice of custody of the eyes. Curious Brahmins would have to come to him. And come they did, as word of his asceticism and learning spread.

De Nobili knew he would have to speak to the Brahmins in their own language and categories, with appeals to their own wisdom traditions. So he did as Ricci had done with his reading of Confucius. He learned Sanskrit and began what would be a lifelong study of classical Hindu texts like the Vedas, Bhagavad Gita, and Ramayana. By early 1610, only a little more than three years after his arrival in Madurai, Jesuit priest turned *sanyasi* ascetic Roberto de Nobili presented himself and was accepted as a teacher of spiritual wisdom, a Brahmin guru.

It was probably at this early period that de Nobili wrote the *Dialogue on Eternal Life* and the *Inquiry into the Meaning of God,* both Tamil-language treatises written and circulated to encourage Brahmins to enter into conversation with him.[59] The *Dialogue* is similar to Ricci's *The True*

Meaning of the Lord of Heaven, an idealized conversation. In it de Nobili borrows from Thomas Aquinas's *Summa contra Gentiles* and argues that Hinduism is not a religion that satisfies reasonable people and that, on the basis of reason, Christianity is the one "true Veda."

The *Inquiry* begins by identifying six characteristics that any intelligent person would agree must necessarily belong to the one true God. De Nobili then draws on descriptions of deities found in popular Hindu mythology to demonstrate why these deities do not meet those six criteria. Believing he had demolished the credibility of those stories, de Nobili fully expected his readers and interlocutors to come inquiring about his more reasonable religion and was frustrated when they did not. The power of Thomistic argument clearly persuaded him more than it did most Brahmins.

The product of a childhood spent amid Roman ruins, and educated to appreciate the Latin classics, de Nobili drew the same crucial analogy that Ricci did in China. He saw his position there as comparable to that of early Christians vis-à-vis Greece and Rome. While the church had drawn from the philosophy, literature, and legal principles of these pagan cultures, it rejected their mythology. In de Nobili's view, India enjoyed impressive philosophical theories and a fine legal system but erroneous religious beliefs and practices. He studied India's ancient texts so as to sort out and retain what he saw as true and good in the culture and dispose of the rest.

But de Nobili had more than one reason to study classics like the Vedas; he needed answers to several pressing practical questions. All Brahmins wore a three-stranded thread from their left shoulder and across the breast, and they shaved their heads except for a single tuft or lock of hair called the *kutumi.* Were these customs simply a badge of rank, or were they religious symbols and therefore prohibited to Christian converts? Members of all castes would mark their foreheads with scented sandalwood paste. Was this purely cosmetic, a social convention? Or again religious, and hence unacceptable for Christians?

De Nobili's investigations, both from reading texts and inquiring among Brahmins, convinced him that these were social and cultural rather than religious customs. This was the case he made in a "Report on Certain Customs of the Indian Nation," a Latin work he composed and in 1615 sent to the Jesuit superior general, Claudio Aquaviva.[60] Besides providing a valuable account of India's complex social structure, customs, and religion, it also served as something of a lawyer's brief. In it de Nobili cites numerous texts to support his view that India's culture and religion can be distinguished. He argued that no Indian should be required to give up the thread, the *kutumi,* or sandal paste as a price of becoming a Christian, as these were purely social and ornamental, and to make such a demand would mean that converts to Christianity in India must become outcasts in their own society.

De Nobili's asceticism and willingness to adopt Indian customs in every way he deemed possible won him Christianity's first Brahmin converts. But, as one can imagine, it also drew criticism from within his own ranks. His methods were an indirect but clear affront to those of other missionaries, including other Jesuits, many of whom regarded his practices as scandalous and illicit.[61] He had to defend himself against the charge that he was sinning against Christian charity. By conforming to Brahmin social norms, he was keeping aloof from India's lower castes, as well as from the other missionaries and their Westernized (Paranghi) Christian converts. He was accused of "pagan superstition" and even apostasy. Word got to Rome that he had left the church to become a Hindu.

More than once de Nobili had to defend his methods in writings addressed to his colleagues and superiors in India and Rome. He appealed to St. Paul, who described his own missionary method as one of being "all things to all men" (1 Cor 9:22). De Nobili pointed to the early church translating its original Jewish concepts into those of Greek philosophy. He cited the example of Francis Xavier, who dressed in silk when he appeared the second time before the daimyo of Yamaguchi. The word *Brahmin,* de Nobili argued, means "doctor." Brahmins are scholars, not managers of temples or priests. They were the "watch-dogs of Indian society and acknowledged masters in all matters that concerned religion and the sciences."[62] Christian converts from Brahmin ranks could evangelize the other upper castes of India. If only Christianity would be allowed to work like leaven, de Nobili argued, it would transform the culture slowly from within. But that would take time and patience.

After investigation by the Inquisition at Goa, de Nobili's case was sent to Rome, where in 1623 Pope Gregory XV pronounced in his favor. Brahmin and other Indian Christians were permitted to take and wear the thread and to grow the tuft of hair as a sign of social status. Jesuit missionaries in India subsequently divided themselves into two groups: one assumed the ascetic lifestyle of *sanyasis* and evangelized the upper castes, the other worked among the lower castes and untouchables.

It seemed at that point that Valignano's vision, pioneered by Ricci and de Nobili, had won the day. As once the church had melded its Jewish-Christian origins with late Hellenistic philosophy and letters to produce Byzantine and Roman Catholicism, it seemed ready to do the same in China and India to produce a Chinese and Indian Catholicism. That was what Ricci and de Nobili had hoped and worked for. And there were plenty of Jesuits willing to follow their examples—so long as the door Ricci had left behind remained open. Such, however, was not to be the case.

HUMANISM CENSURED AND EXONERATED

The "Chinese rites controversy," as it came to be called, erupted in 1645, thirty-five years after Ricci's death. Its tortured history involved Jesuits, Dominicans, Franciscans, a host of Vatican cardinals, twenty-six popes, and a Chinese emperor. Even a summary narrative of the controversy would be too convoluted to rehearse here. Let it suffice to say that Ricci's humanistic directives were overturned when, in 1704, the Vatican forbade Chinese Catholics to have any part in the ritual practices honoring their ancestors or Confucius. The ruling meant, in effect, that to become Christian, converts had to cease being Chinese, since it forbade them to do what in Chinese culture was requisite decency and good manners.

That same year the door began to close on Jesuit accommodation in India as well. The Christian community in Madurai had come to number 90,000, but the rites controversy in China and complaints by other missionaries led to a Vatican investigation of missionary practices there as well. Once again the Jesuits tried to defend themselves from their detractors. Another tangled dispute ensued, lasting for forty years until 1744, when missionaries in India were required to take an oath binding them not to tolerate a variety of Hindu practices. For the next 200 years, Catholic Christianity in China and India would remain alien European implants.

In 1939 the Vatican overturned the fateful decision regarding the Chinese ancestral and Confucian rites. The reasons given for doing so were essentially the same as those Ricci had offered 300 years earlier. The following year de Nobili was exonerated as well, when the Vatican abolished the oath required of missionaries in India. In 1965 the Second Vatican Council called for the adaptation of Christian life to indigenous cultures. It declared that "accommodated preaching" is the "law of all evangelization."[63] One can only conjecture how different China, India, and the Catholic Church might be today if those decisions had been made 250 years earlier.

Four hundred years after Valignano, Ricci, and de Nobili, their humanistic ideas and practices may possibly be given a second chance. At Vatican II the highest teaching authority in the Catholic Church gave official approval to the concepts of accommodation and inculturation—at least in theory. What those terms may mean in practice has yet to be seen, especially in light of the Vatican's (2000) document, *Dominus Jesus*. In that directive Catholics involved in interreligious dialogue were warned against allowing respect for the truth in other religions to appear too much like a relativism that sees all religions as equals.

Even with that anxious Vatican admonition, Catholic missionaries no longer need to be cultural imperialists. In an era in which cross-cultural studies and interreligious dialogue have become commonplace, it bears remembering that Matteo Ricci was the first Westerner to venture such undertakings. Granted, his motive was to convert the Chinese to

Catholicism, but to that end he studied ancient Chinese texts and entered into conversation with Chinese scholars on matters of morality and religion. The first practice was deeply rooted in his humanist training, the second in his Ignatian spirituality.

Going back to Ignatius's conversations with the women of Manresa, conversation is an integral part of the *Spiritual Exercises* and of the Jesuit "manner of proceeding." Today, at least as Ricci practiced it, we may prefer to call it ecumenical or interfaith dialogue. Considerable thought and literature has been devoted in recent years to the concept of dialogue— how it differs from debate and how it requires sympathetic listening and the willingness to learn, to grow in understanding, to be enriched, and even to be changed.[64] Ricci's dialogues with Confucian scholars resulted in the conversion of any number of Chinese to Christianity. But those dialogues together with his study of Confucian texts converted Ricci as well. Dialogue, as Ricci learned and we now better appreciate, often has unintended consequences. As a result of his conversations, Ricci not only changed his dress and lifestyle, but also his thinking and attitudes.

The same could be said about de Nobili. Being a European and a person of his time, he was quite sure he knew all he needed to know about God and salvation from his Christian faith, and all the basic truths about human nature from Thomistic philosophy. But as a humanist, he was ready to accept whatever wisdom he could find in Indian culture. His humanist principles allowed him to believe he could find evidence of impressive human achievements, ethical behavior, and spiritual insight even among people who worshipped idols. By observing India's culture and studying its religious traditions, he learned to think in Brahmin categories. He became comfortable using the imagery and ideas of his new culture to explain his own Christian faith.[65]

Neither Ricci nor de Nobili was uncritical of the culture in his new homeland. There was much to criticize: in China, widespread superstition and a social order oppressive of women; in India, the caste system with its treatment of untouchables and tradition of *sati,* which socially obliged Hindu widows to throw themselves on their husbands' funeral pyres.

But—both Jesuits realized—blanket condemnations got one nowhere. And notwithstanding the serious failings from a Western, Christian perspective, there was still much in these cultures worthy of respect—the sine qua non for the kind of interreligious dialogue in which Ricci and de Nobili pioneered.

Scholars experienced in interreligious dialogue now criticize de Nobili for trying to draw too neat a distinction between the supposed wheat of the culture and the superstitious chaff (myths, rituals) of religion. To this day the question of where Hindu religion ends and Indian culture begins has not been adequately resolved. The wisdom and values de Nobili attributed to India's culture have to be ascribed to the religious roots of that culture, with all that that implies.

Similarly, modern scholarship has gone beyond Ricci with respect to his jaundiced view of Buddhism. He simply did not study it deeply enough to recognize Buddhist affinities with certain aspects of Christian mystical tradition. But his sympathetic reading of Confucius, not his blind spot toward Buddhism, is what merits our considered reflection, if not imitation. Confucian thinking—though still a major influence—no longer has the hold on Chinese thinking and culture it once did. Nor will many of those who read this book have the opportunity to engage in Confucian-Christian dialogue.

Ricci's Ignatian humanism is what makes him relevant as a spiritual mentor for the twenty-first century. Wisdom, for Renaissance humanists, was universal; truth was where you found it. Ricci found them expressed in Chinese ideographs. His Ignatian spirituality trained him to seek God in all things. Ricci found God working in the hearts and lives of non-Christian Confucians.

Jews, Muslims, Hindus, Buddhists, Sikhs—all are no longer far-removed from what were once all-Christian ghettos. At a time when pundits anticipate global conflict between civilizations, survival as much as spirituality prompts us to seek inspiration in Ricci's humanity, warmth, and willingness to engage in conversation with people religiously and culturally different from himself. Both he and they were enriched by the exchange. As one of his Chinese admirers wrote, he understood the ways of friendship.

A measure of humanism at any time is the ability to be in solidarity with people who are culturally, racially, and socially different from ourselves. In light of the long-standing Christian animus toward other faiths, however, there is particular irony in the suggestion that a measure of one's Ignatian spirituality is the number of one's non-Christian friends.

FOUR

~

FRIEDRICH SPEE

If the reader allows me to say something here, I confess that I myself have accompanied several women to their deaths in various places over the preceding years whose innocence even now I am so sure of that there could never be any effort and diligence too great that I would not undertake it in order to reveal this truth. . . . One can easily guess what feelings were in my soul when I was present at such miserable deaths.[1]

The priest who wrote this passage relates how he went into the dungeons to hear the confessions of women accused of witchcraft. He tells us about examining the evidence against them, interrogating their judges, and learning firsthand how admissions of guilt were obtained under torture. In his role as confessor, he learned how these women had been compelled to lie, confirming their inquisitors' descriptions of the so-called "witches' Sabbath" and falsely incriminating others.

Having admitted their guilt, the accused women knew they had no chance of escaping death. But would they go to hell for lying about the others? The priest tried to comfort them and assure them of God's mercy.

We can only imagine what it was like for him to accompany the victims to the town square, where the stakes, straw, and jeering crowds waited. Imagine too how the victims' screams as they were burned alive echoed in his ears later those sleepless nights, convinced as he was that these women were innocent.

This first-person description of witch trials in seventeenth-century Germany appears in a 1631 Latin treatise entitled *Cautio Criminalis*. Its complete title, typical for that era, translates as *A Precaution for Prosecutors: A Book about the Witch trials, Necessary These Days for the Authorities in Germany, but also useful for the Counselors and Confessors of Princes, for Inquisitors, Judges, Lawyers, Confessors of the Accused, Preachers, and others. By an Anonymous Roman Theologian.*

The author did not remain anonymous for long, at least not within the inner ecclesiastical circles of Rhineland, Germany. Only a month after the book's appearance, Auxiliary Bishop Johannes Pelcking of Paderborn wrote a letter to a fellow bishop about a *liber pestilentissimus* ("most poisonous book") authored by one Fr. Friedrich Spee. This book, wrote the bishop, was filled with slanderous accusations against princes, magistrates, and judges and went so far as to compare witches to the early Christian martyrs. Unfortunately, the bishop lamented, so many copies had already been sold that repairing the damage would be most difficult.[2]

Bishop Pelcking was sure that the anonymous Roman theologian who wrote the *Cautio* was the Jesuit priest Friedrich Spee. Spee's Jesuit confreres and superiors knew this to be a fact, but the public at large did not learn the identity of the mystery author until early in the next century. The renowned German philosopher, G. W. Leibnitz, divulged the secret to his readers, paying lavish tribute to Spee's work not only as a humanist critic of the witch trials but also as the author of a book on the virtues of faith, hope, and charity.

Despite Leibnitz's praise, Spee continued to remain in relative obscurity. Of all the Ignatian humanists treated in this book, Spee is the least familiar to American and English readers. Until the appearance of the first English translation of Spee's *Cautio* in 2003, the most one could find were a few short articles and passing references to him in works on witchcraft or baroque German poetry. A good deal more has been written about him in German, especially since 1980 when his grave was rediscovered in a crypt beneath the Jesuit church in Trier.

Spee's obscurity outside of Germany, even among Jesuits, is not surprising. His reputation is linked to one of the darkest chapters in the history of the church and of the West altogether. Until more recent decades, church historians—usually men, most often churchmen—were professionally disinclined to give substantial attention to the hunting, torture, and burning of women for witchcraft. The topic is painful, involving church leaders who not only erred or tolerated an evil, but also often fully participated in mass judicial murder. The subject has been generally deemed an embarrassment to the church, Catholic and Protestant, best forgotten or treated only in passing.

Secular scholarship has not done much better. Recent decades have seen a rise of scholarly interest in witchcraft studies, and archival research has led to a sizeable literature.[3] But for the most part, the results of that specialized research and analysis have not found their way into general histories. And with some obvious exceptions (like Arthur Miller's *The Crucible* and dramatic presentations of the life of Joan of Arc), popular culture tends to regard witches as the stuff of Halloween parties, cartoons, and children's stories.

Young readers devour J. K. Rowling's best-selling adventures of Harry Potter, the most celebrated student at the Hogwarts School of Witchcraft and Wizardry. The wicked witch gets her comeuppance in Engelbert Humperdinck's *Hansel and Gretel*, nowadays an operatic Christmas treat for the whole family. And the very word *sorcery* conjures up images of a hapless Mickey Mouse trying vainly to subdue a bewitched broom to the music of Paul Dukas's "Sorcerer's Apprentice" in Walt Disney's animated classic *Fantasia*. But none of these cultural icons invokes the name of the devil. Demonology no longer enjoys a high profile, and our language has lost any sense of the dread and danger once associated with words like *entrancing, charming,* or *bewitching.*

Friedrich Spee (1591–1635) knew the danger firsthand. He lived most of his life in one of the epicenters of witch-hunting at a time when the fury was at its height. Not by chance, it was also a time of epidemic infection and the Thirty Years' War. And yet, when hunger and disease laid waste whole villages in some areas of Germany, he wrote poetry about the splendor of creation and hymns that are still sung in churches today. In a time of unrestrained patriarchy, he described God in feminine metaphors and wrote a book of spirituality intended primarily for women. But it's the *Cautio Criminalis* that most sets Spee apart from his contemporaries—a light whose intensity can only be gauged by the darkness that surrounded it.

WITCHCRAFT IN EARLY MODERN EUROPE

For most of human history, people in all cultures have believed in magic and witchcraft—in the superhuman powers of certain persons to foresee the future, to heal and help others (so-called "white magic"), or to do harm ("black magic"). The shaman was an integral part of primitive cultures, revered as a holy person in touch with the spirit world. Western civilization inherited a literature from ancient Greece and Rome filled with stories about amulets and love potions, magic spells, and witches who had the power to change themselves into animals or do the same to their victims.[4]

The other major source of Western culture, the Bible, also contains several references to witches and wizards communing with spirits. Though Mosaic law strictly forbade divination to learn the future (Lv 19:31), the prophet Isaiah relates that Israel in his day was filled with soothsayers (Is 2:6). Both the Hebrew and Christian Scriptures make allusions to sorcery and prohibit it as tantamount to idolatry (1 Sm 15:23; Gal 5:20). But, it should be stressed, neither testament asserts that divination and magic are nonexistent or fraudulent. On the contrary, their actuality is taken for granted.

The Bible affirms that magic is helpless against the power of God, but it does not deny that those who practice it can be effective. This was read in past centuries as an implicit affirmation that magical powers exist and that it is possible for ordinary human beings to tap into them. Demonic powers and magic were simply part of the worldview when the Bible was written; the biblical narratives tell of Moses and Aaron at Pharaoh's court, getting the better of his magicians and their "secret arts" (Ex 7:8–12, NRSV). But if the Bible took for granted the existence of witchcraft, it was emphatic in forbidding it. Practicing witchcraft was among the sins for which God had destroyed Israel (2 Kgs 17:17). Any Christian society that wanted to avoid the same fate was well advised to take the matter seriously and heed the explicit biblical command: "You shall not permit a sorceress to live" (Ex 22:18).

The gravitas accorded that Bible verse and its consequences constitutes the backdrop needed to take a proper measure of Friedrich Spee. We no longer believe in prosecuting and punishing people for witchcraft, and we righteously condemn those who did, regarding ourselves as morally superior. But as C. S. Lewis pointed out, the mere fact that we have become more sophisticated does not make us more moral. If we thought there were people who actually were using demonic powers to harm others, we would surely seek to punish them as criminals. We may have become more enlightened, but we have not necessarily become more humane.[5]

Most moderns associate the prosecution of witches with the supposedly Dark or Middle Ages. Witch trials are commonly assumed to have been the task of priest-inquisitors doing the work of the church. And, as a matter of fact, the first trial and execution for witchcraft was carried out by the Roman Inquisition in Toulouse, France, in 1275, during the so-called "High" Middle Ages. In the 1400s, especially in France, church inquisitors were responsible for a number of women being executed as witches, the case of Joan of Arc, of course, being the most famous. But the greatest number of witch trials and executions by far took place between 1550 and 1650, and most of those, more narrowly, between 1580 and 1630. In other words, not in the Middle Ages, but early modernity, at the dawn of a time associated with genius and Enlightenment. And in the main those trials and executions were in the hands of secular courts. When Spee wrote of inquisitors in his *Cautio,* he was referring to laymen.

There is much we still do not know about the waves of witchcraft trials that were conducted in various regions in early modern Europe. For one, we can only estimate how many people were executed. Records have been lost or destroyed, and many cases were never recorded at all because the accused were lynched, committed suicide, or died under torture. The most recent archival research estimates the total number of trials at 110,000 and the number of persons executed at 60,000. About half of those executions took place within the Holy Roman Empire.[6]

There are still open questions about why panics about witchcraft broke out at all, and why they occurred when and where they did. After Germany, other centers of intense witch-hunting were the British Isles with 5,000 (more than half of them in Scotland); 5,000 in the Scandinavian countries; and 9,000 in tiny Switzerland. In Italy and Spain, despite numerous investigations, very few prosecutions resulted in execution. The Spanish and Roman Inquisitions were generally skeptical of the accusations. In Rome only one execution is recorded for witchcraft.[7]

It's debated why the greatest number of witch trials and executions took place in Germany, Austria, Switzerland, and the territories immediately adjacent to them. War, famine, and epidemics certainly contributed to generalized feelings of anxiety and helplessness, a collective sense of being delivered over to mysterious evil powers. Economics, patriarchy, and social control of the masses have also been named as contributing factors.

At a time when Catholics and Protestants were intent on emphasizing their disagreements with one another, both confessional groups were in accord that witchcraft should be prosecuted. Martin Luther harbored no doubts that witches existed, that they could raise up storms and ride through the air. They were the "devil's whores" *(Teufelshuren),* he said, and should be exterminated. Luther himself excommunicated several witches in 1529. In 1540, when there were still relatively few witch-burnings in Germany, there were four executions in his hometown of Wittenberg.[8]

Catholic principalities like Cologne, Trier, Bamberg, and Würzburg, all of them ruled by prince-bishops, were major centers for witch trials. An eyewitness account of the 1581–93 persecutions in Trier speaks of civil leaders and clerics in the city being executed for witchcraft—two bürgermeisters, a judge, two associate judges, monsignorial canons, parish priests, and rural deans.[9] In 1628, the bürgermeister of Bamberg was tried and executed for witchcraft. The following year in Würzburg, the prince-bishop's chancellor wrote in a letter to a friend about the accusations of witchcraft being leveled against "four hundred in the city, high and low, of every rank and sex . . . clerics, electoral councilors and doctors, city officials, court assessors." Also accused were law students, thirteen or fourteen students soon to be ordained priests, and some three hundred "children of three and four years."[10]

These records can give the false impression that the witch hunts were indiscriminate in their choice of victims, that they struck men and women, rich and poor alike. Such, however, was not the case. "The most well-documented characteristic of those persons who were prosecuted for witchcraft is that they were predominantly, if not overwhelmingly, female."[11] Of the persons prosecuted in most regions of Europe, more than 75 percent were women. In some areas (Essex, England; Namur, Belgium; Basel, Switzerland), it was more than 90 percent. Why this was so is also not altogether clear.

A common feminist reading of this gender imbalance is that the witch hunts were a means of maintaining male domination in a changing society, that they were intended to make women feel guilty about their sexuality and to keep them in their place.[12] Critics of this particular interpretation point out that it does not explain why so many women accused other women. But it is, of course, a widely noted phenomenon that members of an oppressed group commonly identify with the prejudicial attitudes of their oppressors and ill-treat their own kind.

Another, more compelling explanation for the gender imbalance looks to the influence of stereotypes on attitudes and expectations. The misfortunes blamed on witchcraft more often than not related to women's areas of responsibility. There is nothing in the definition of a witch that excludes males. A man could just as easily practice harmful magic or, like the original sixteenth-century Faust legend reworked by Goethe, make a pact with the devil. But the stereotype of the witch that came down from ancient and medieval literature was always female, making women the more natural suspects.

Women in early modern Europe typically functioned as cooks, midwives, and healers, occupations that made them particularly vulnerable to accusations of sorcery. Women, not men, tended gardens and knew the qualities of herbs for cooking and healing. The idea of a man standing over a boiling cauldron was at the very least improbable.[13] Likewise, the image of a witch was that of a person morally weak and driven by carnal lust, qualities which the period in question attributed to women.

If contemporary research reveals anything, it is that no one interpretation explains everything. There was no one single cause for the early modern wave of witch hunts and trials—not politics, religion, economics, or misogyny. But if no one explanation fits all, neither is the number of typical cases unlimited. There are patterns, like that of the crone—the old single woman, so poor that she is dependent on her neighbors to stave off starvation. Very often a scold, she cursed those who denied her request for charity. And those who turned her down felt guilty, until some misfortune later occurred and they remembered her curse.[14]

But neither should we presume that the victims prosecuted for witchcraft were all innocent of trying. Artifacts and tools of the trade provide ample evidence that individuals did in fact practice sorcery, both white and black magic, in many different historical periods, and that they still do in our own. So, not surprisingly, in early modern Europe there were also cases, "at most only a few," where the accused did sincerely believe that the devil had granted their wishes.[15]

Among the more common stereotypes of the witch trials is that benighted clerics and judges initiated them from on high upon the hapless masses of common folk. More recent research indicates, to the contrary, that the gullibility and superstition of the masses were major factors in the desire to persecute witches, especially accompanied by a gloomy worldview that could become almost apocalyptic. In Germany there were village witch-hunting committees, and the authorities, especially in small states, often feared open revolt if they did not comply with their wishes. Under a sense of impending crisis, "exceptional crimes" called for exceptional measures.[16]

In Germany the belief that witchcraft was an "exceptional crime" was embedded in the 1532 "Carolina," the criminal code enacted for the Holy Roman Empire by Emperor Charles V. The code called for the secular courts to investigate and prosecute persons for witchcraft, whether they had injured others or not. Harmful or injurious witchcraft was punished by burning at the stake; the punishment for witchcraft that did no injury was left to the discretion of the judge and could be milder, like confiscation of property and exile. In practice, however, the milder punishment was supplanted by the legal reasoning of Lutheran jurist Benedict Carpzow (1595–1666), who held that the biblical command, "Thou shalt not allow a sorceress to live" (Ex 22:18) overruled the imperial legislation. If the Bible would not allow witches to live, neither should the penal law of Germany.[17]

The exceptional nature of the crime also explains how the Middle Ages and the imperial code justified the use of torture. From the times of the Roman Empire to the late eighteenth century, torture was a routine component of European judicial procedure. Today, even when legally prohibited, torture in various forms is standard practice in any number of countries around the globe—though it may be disguised under the euphemistic description of aggressive police interrogation. For documentary proof one need only consult agencies like Amnesty International. Even in the United States, in the aftermath of the 2001 terrorist attacks of 9/11, legal experts have begun to think the unthinkable and regard the use of nonlethal torture (even court-issued torture warrants!) as a matter meriting serious discussion. Generalized alarm about international networks of evildoers conspiring to unleash widespread destruction on innocent victims has put judicial use of torture in a different light. It is only the 20-20 vision of hindsight that permits us to view our anxieties about terrorists as justified and those of centuries past about witches as not.

The civil and religious authorities of medieval and early modern Europe did not have that benefit. So we really should not be appalled that in 1252, Pope Innocent IV allowed the use of torture to ferret out heretics, whom he equated with highway robbers and murderers as a menace to society. The same reasoning allowed the license for judicial torture to be extended to individuals suspected of witchcraft. Perhaps more surprising is the fact that the initial justification behind the use of torture was to protect not only society but innocent suspects. The idea was to learn some fact under torture that only the guilty party could know and to obtain a confession from the real culprit.

Debates about striking the proper balance between national security and personal civil rights are nothing new. Though obviously not comparable to the rights persons accused of crimes enjoy in most modern judicial systems, there were regulations intended to prevent judges from using torture arbitrarily. But in the case of suspected witches, the danger posed to society was seen as warranting disregard of the usual judicial constraints. Judges could apply and repeat torture without qualms, and they did so with the approval of learned jurists and theologians alike. Whereas in the Middle Ages witchcraft was seen exclusively in terms of harmful magic, by the sixteenth century witches were regarded as engaging in an anti-Christian, antisocial conspiracy with Satan. The point of the torture was not to punish but to uncover the conspiracy.[18]

If the general public called for the trial and execution of witches, one cannot ignore the complementary role played by the educated elite. The intellectuals were the ones responsible in the first place for forging an inseparable link between magic and the demonic. Illiterate commoners had no difficulty in accepting the effectiveness of magical causes alongside natural causality. They viewed magic as able to work directly, without any outside agency. But for intellectuals, especially those educated in the Aristotelian tradition, magic could have no reality without the participation of the spirit world.[19] To produce their extraordinary feats of magic, sorcerers and witches had to be in league with the devil.

DEMONOLOGISTS AND THE DEVIL

Belief in the devil had been a part of Christian tradition from its beginnings, part of its classical as well as biblical heritage. But when it came to the idea of witches, official Christian opinion was more skeptical the first 1000 years than it was the second. The so-called *Canon Episcopi* (Bishop's Canon), recorded circa A.D. 900, referred to "some wicked women" who sought the aid of the devil and actually believed that they traveled great distances and gathered in a crowd with others like themselves. The canon describes these women as "seduced by illusions," saying that their fantasies were produced by the devil and that anyone who believed them was "stupid and foolish." The canon was included in the Decretals of Gratian, the Middle Ages' most authoritative collection of church law.[20]

But by the fifteenth century, doubts began to be raised about the authenticity of the *Canon Episcopi*, thanks at least in part to the opinions of some of the church's most influential theologians. St. Augustine gave consideration to the obscure biblical passage about the "sons of God" marrying the "daughters of men" (Gn 6:1). He wrote of "a very general rumor," which many have verified and others have corroborated, that "certain devils" are constantly attempting to have sexual relations with women. This opinion, Augustine decided, was "so generally affirmed" that it would be "shameless" (*inpudentia*) to deny it (*City of God*, 15, 23).

Building on that opinion, St. Thomas Aquinas pondered how it might be possible for a spirit and a human being to have sexual intercourse. He believed it as factual that "some are occasionally begotten from demons" (*Summa Theologiae*, I, Q.51, art. 3, reply 6). Though he gave more attention to angels than demons, Aquinas did write on the latter as well, teaching that it was unlawful to invoke them, consult them about the future, or make use of their help. Such acts were wrongful precisely because they involved either a tacit or explicit compact with the devil (*Summa Theologiae*, II-II, Q. 90, art. 3; Q. 92, art. 2; Q. 95, art. 6).

With its central affirmation of faith in God's power and victory over evil, the Bible relegates the devil to the margins of salvation history. When one considers the massive theological output of both Augustine and Aquinas, the allusions they make to the demonic are relatively few and scattered at best. But there were enough of these scattered references for speculative intellects in the fourteenth and fifteenth centuries to create a whole literature and a full-blown demonology, which had its impact on church authorities. In 1325 Pope John XXII issued a papal bull (*Super illius specula*) in which he lamented the news he had received that Christians were making pacts with the devil and worshiping him. Pope John was so worried about witches that he had his personal physician and the bishop of his hometown executed for making attempts on his life by means of black magic.[21] (Little wonder it took more than 600 years before another pope took the name of John.)

The most important piece of papal legislation regarding witchcraft was a 1484 papal bull of Pope Innocent VIII (*Summis desiderantes affectibus*). It was occasioned by two Dominican priest-inquisitors, Jacob Sprenger and Heinrich Kramer, who had complained to the pope about high-ranking churchmen and laity hindering their attempts to root out witchcraft in Germany. Alarmed by their reports, the pope issued the fateful document in which he deplored the fact that men and women in Germany were entering into relations with the devil and doing harm to their neighbors and animals by means of black magic. Among the offenses attributed to witches, the pope listed such crimes as damaging harvests, crops, and vineyards; slaying infants in their mother's wombs; preventing women from conceiving; and preventing men from performing sexually. The pope put his full apostolic authority behind the two inquisitors. Anyone who would hinder their work was liable to excommunication, suspension, and "yet more terrible penalties."[22]

This papal bull, it can be argued, became the proximate cause for the outbreak of witch trials and executions, at least in Germany. Before this piece of papal legislation, there had been no systematic program for prose-cuting witches, and no reason to believe that Germany and its adjacent territories would become the locus for the great majority of subsequent witch trials.[23] As a practical commentary on the papal bull they had inspired, Fr. Sprenger and Fr. Kramer went on to write the *Malleus Malefi-carum* (The Hammer of Witches), with the papal bull invariably appended as an official seal of approval.

The *Malleus* opens with the authors arguing that witches exist and that any Christian who would dare deny their existence was "gravely suspect" of heresy.[24] With God's permission, witches do their harmful magic in virtue of their pact with the devil. Sexual intercourse with the devil is presumed rather than argued, with an appeal to the authority of St. Thomas Aquinas. The second part of the book deals with the various magical and evil deeds that witches perform and the remedies against them. Here we read about such matters as the way one makes a formal pact with the devil and how witches are transported from place to place. The third part of the *Malleus* comprises a handbook for prosecutors with detailed instructions on proper judicial procedure—how judges can recognize witches, protect themselves against their magic spells, and apply torture to obtain confessions.

Frs. Sprenger and Kramer filled their magnum opus with long exposi-tions and arguments in the disputatious style of the scholastic manuals and summas. Replete with copious references to the Bible, church fathers, and medieval theologians like Thomas Aquinas, the *Malleus* attempts to appear as a work of serious scholarship. But behind all its scholarly pretense lies a deep-seated hatred for women, described in the *Malleus* as "sluts" and "incomplete animals" whose evil deeds bring suffering to the world.

Although men were also capable of entering into a conspiracy with the devil, the possessive case of the title (*Maleficarum*) rendered the object of this would-be learned disquisition exclusively feminine. The authors pre-sume to prove that women are more susceptible to witchcraft than men on the grounds that the very word *femina* comes from *fe* (faith) and *mina* (less), an argument from etymology that women have weaker faith.[25] On page after page the authors of the *Malleus* betray an obsession with the idea of sexual intercourse with the devil, going on at length on how witches deprive men of their sexual organs. Along with their profound misogyny, a Freudian reading of Sprenger and Kramer's book discloses symptoms of two depraved, hallucinatory imaginations. There is good reason to believe that we are dealing here with two sexually fixated psychopaths.[26]

Whatever one may think of its authors' sexual fantasies, the *Malleus* was one of the biggest publishing success stories of its time. From 1487, the year it first appeared, to 1609, it went through twenty-nine editions, including two in Italy, eleven in France, and sixteen in Germany. But it was neither the first book published on witchcraft, nor the last.

French jurist Jean Bodin (1530–96), one of the founding fathers of political science, wrote on behalf of toleration when it came to Catholics and Protestants; but when it came to women, toleration gave way to pathology. Bodin's book, *De la Demonomanie des sorciers* (Paris 1580), together with the *Malleus,* became the basic texts for witch-hunters. In it he cites Plato to the effect that women stand midway between men and animals; men have more developed brains and women more developed viscera. Women are more susceptible to the devil than men (one man is worth fifty women), not because of the weakness of their sex but the "force of animal desire" (*cupidité*) that drives them. A likely explanation for Bodin's misogyny can be found in the pages of his book where he catalogues fifty different knots by which women use their magic to render men impotent; it is no unfair leap to suspect that the learned jurist suffered the affliction himself. In any case, Bodin, who allowed for the burning of both children and cripples as witches, counseled that the fire should be kept low, so that the victims would suffer at least a half-hour in preparation for the fires of hell.[27]

Kramer, Sprenger, and Bodin were joined by any number of other scholarly "experts" in demonology and witchcraft. Sex, violence, and occult conspiracies were clearly best-selling subjects even in those early days of publishing. But one other author in particular deserves further consideration here, if for no other reason than because he was a Jesuit.

Martin Delrio (1551–1608), born of Spanish parents in Antwerp, Belgium, was educated in Greek, Latin, Hebrew, Chaldean, five modern languages, and law. At nineteen he published an edition of Seneca in which he cited over 1,300 authorities. By any definition of the time, he was a humanist and a scholar. At age twenty-nine, he entered the Society of Jesus and went on to teach at several Jesuit universities. But of all his books and commentaries, Delrio is best known for his 1599 "inquiry" into the arts of magic (*Disquisitionum Magicarum*), a virtual encyclopedia on witchcraft. Later translated into French, it went through some twenty editions and became as renowned in its day as the *Malleus*.[28]

Citing classical and Hebrew references, Delrio discussed magic in general, diabolical magic, and such things as real and false apparitions. He explained why God allows witches to commit their crimes and assured his readers that devils obey witches not because they can be compelled but because of their pact (lib. 2, q. 30, sec. 2). He warned judges of their heavy responsibility to root out witchcraft, because this "most enormous, grave, and atrocious crime" involves apostasy, heresy, sacrilege, blasphemy, homicide, and sins against nature (lib. 5, sec. 1).

Unlike some of his fellow demonologists, Delrio favored allowing legal counsel for persons accused of witchcraft, and he cautioned judges to apply torture only with "prudence and fairness." Children under fourteen should not be tortured, nor should pregnant women, until they give birth (lib. 5, sec. 6). He insisted that judges adhere to the legal requirements of sufficient evidence before a suspect could be imprisoned or tortured. To the question why the devil does not help witches to escape, he answered that God simply does not allow it. It would be a scandal if the witches, the devil's servants, were seen as more powerful than God's servants, the judges (lib. 5, sec. 7).

A modern reader can't help but marvel at the assurance with which Delrio writes about what God does and does not permit and what most pleases and displeases the devil. Similarly striking is his erudition. Delrio read voraciously and knew all the important literary sources on the subject of witchcraft; he could quote them in Greek, Hebrew, and Latin. But along with impressive scholarship he displays amazing gullibility. He had no doubt that witches rode through the air to their meetings, for there were "well-founded" stories attesting to it, and he could produce eye-witnesses. He fully trusted as well the descriptions, which had been confirmed under torture, that detailed how witches would worship Satan with song, dance, and various orgiastic rituals.

Were these only old wives' tales, no more than wild dreams or possibly the delusions of delirious women? Delrio knew the arguments of the critics. He knew that there were stories of women accused of witchcraft whose husbands swore under oath that their wives had been in bed with them all night and never left their sides. He explained how it was possible for witches to deceive their husbands and gather with their cohorts at night even while appearing to remain at home in bed (lib. 2, q. 16). Delrio warned that those who ridicule the descriptions of the witches' Sabbath were treading on dangerous ground:

> Those who argue that [these descriptions] are dreams or ridiculous tales certainly sin against the reverence which is owed to Mother Church. For the Catholic Church does not punish crimes, unless they are certain and evident; it does not treat persons as heretics unless they have been caught in heresy by the evidence. For many years already, the Church has considered witches to be heretics and has commanded that they be punished by the inquisitors and handed over to the secular arm. This is clear from the books of Sprenger, Nider, Iaquerius, and Michaelis and from experience. Therefore, either the Church is in error or these skeptics are in error. Whoever says that the Church errs in a matter that pertains to faith, let that person be anathema.[29]

Here, remarkably enough, is an early claim for the Catholic Church's ordinary teaching being inerrant. Delrio makes the assertion almost 400 years before the First Vatican Council (1870) would formally proclaim papal infallibility a dogma. And in tying that claim to the prosecution of witches, Delrio reveals one of the reasons the witch hunts and trials went on for so many years at the hands of churchmen and secular courts alike, well into the "Age of Reason." The alternative to belief in witchcraft and the justification of the trials, torture, and witch-burnings was that both the church and state and their judiciaries had perpetrated monumental injustice. The alternative to the witch hunts was that church and state, the two institutions ordained by God to preserve order and justice, had put tens of thousands of innocent people to death. For Delrio and those like him, so sure of what God does and does not permit, contemplating that alternative was too awful to imagine. What would one do with the Bible's warnings against witchcraft? What would it mean for authority, the courts, the legal and judicial systems? How could one ever again trust the institutions that stood at the very foundation of social order?

In the name of inerrant church authority, Delrio sanctioned the witch trials and voiced suspicion against their critics. If ridiculing notions of a witches' Sabbath raised suspicions of heresy, finding fault with the witch trials could well be a clue that one was guilty of witchcraft.

> Judges are bound under pain of mortal sin to condemn witches to death who have confessed their crimes; anyone who pronounced against the death sentence is reasonably suspected of secret complicity; no one is to urge the judges to desist from the prosecution; nay, it is an *indicium* of witchcraft to defend witches, or to affirm that witch stories which are told as certain are mere deceptions or illusions.[30]

Such were the learned opinions that prevailed in early seventeenth-century Europe, respected by Catholics and Protestants alike. Only in the light of such beliefs can one appreciate the courage it took for Friedrich Spee to write a book against the witch trials of his day, even one published anonymously. He was going against mainstream public opinion and opening himself up to suspicions of heresy and witchcraft. Without question, he was risking his life.

Life and Career

The Spee family, which goes back to the twelfth century, belonged to the minor nobility and was raised in the eighteenth century to the rank of *Graf*, the German equivalent of an earl or count. When Friedrich was born in 1591, that grand-sounding title was still in the family's future. But even without it, Friedrich seems to have had a certain awareness about himself and his rank that probably came with his full name, Friedrich Spee von Langenfeld.[31] But despite ambitions to do great things with his life, he kept meeting with setbacks and failure.

We know of Spee's life only in its broadest outlines.[32] He was born February 25, 1591, in North-Rhine Westphalia, in the medieval town of Kaiserswerth, now part of metropolitan Düsseldorf. One of five children born to Peter and Mechtel Spee, he was apparently the oldest son, since he was given his grandfather's name and title. His father worked in the service of the prince-bishop elector of Cologne; there, at the age of ten, Friedrich began his study of the humanities at the Tricoronatum (Three Kings) College, operated by the Jesuits. The records show that he became a member and then an officer in the school's sodality, the movement Jesuits organized early on to foster spirituality among their students and laity. Their success in Friedrich's case was proven by the fact that, at nineteen, he quit the career path of his grandfather and father and entered the Society of Jesus.

A hint as to Spee's motivation is revealed in a letter he sent seven years later to the general of the Society of Jesus in Rome, Fr. Mutius Vitelleschi. In flawless, if florid, classical Latin, the twenty-six-year-old Spee wrote of his yearning to be a missionary: "India, my father, and those distant lands have wounded my heart." The dream of being a missionary, he wrote, drew him into the Society, and he asked to be sent where his heart already lay—but only, of course, if this was the will of God.

Several months later Spee was informed that his request could not be granted. Several German Jesuits (such as Adam Schall) had already been sent to be missionaries in the Far East. His homeland needed his labors. The general's decision was a disappointment, the first of many, for Spee, but the general was right, more than he or the young Jesuit could possibly know. Spee's entire life would be spent in Germany during decades racked with religious strife, anxiety about witches, epidemics, and war, and his life would be marked by all of them.[33]

The nineteen-year-old Spee joined the Rhineland province of the Jesuits and entered their novitiate at Trier. There on the Mosel River bordering France he made the Spiritual Exercises and studied the Jesuit constitutions. There too he undoubtedly learned of the terror that had gripped the region some twenty years earlier, thanks to Trier's suffragan bishop, Peter Binsfeld. Binsfeld had written a book on the detection and prosecution of witches and saw to it that his theories were put into practice; the executions ran into the hundreds.[34] Binsfeld had died, and the spate of witch hunts and trials had subsided by the time Spee arrived in Trier—but it was only a brief calm before another storm.

An outbreak of the plague forced the Jesuits at Trier to leave for Fulda, where in 1612 Spee took his first vows and began the program of study and formation that had become standard for all Jesuits. First, three years of philosophy (at the University of Würzberg). Then, according to Jesuit practice, an interruption from studies, as the young Master of Arts spent the next three years teaching Latin to schoolboys, first at the Jesuit school at Speyer and then at Worms. It was at Worms, in April 1618, that Spee learned that his ministry as a Jesuit would be spent in Germany and not the Far East. A month later an assassination attempt followed by an uprising in Prague led to the outbreak of what would become the Thirty Years' War; it was a conflict that would leave parts of Germany a wasteland and envelop the rest of Spee's life.

After his first stint in the classroom, Spee was sent to the Academy of Mainz, where for five years he studied theology and began trying his hand at creative verse. A letter dated 1621 from the Jesuit General in Rome, in response to Spee's request for permission to have some of his poems published, gently admonishes the young Jesuit not to rush into print, but to wait and complete his studies first. Greater maturity might lead him to express himself differently.[35] Good advice, but still disappointing.

In March 1622, Spee was ordained a priest and, after another year of studies, was assigned to teach philosophy at the Jesuit College in Paderborn. All expectations were that the rest of his life would center on the classroom. But the Jesuits' humanistic ethos resisted ivory towers, and even academics were expected to do pastoral work. So philosopher-theologian Fr. Spee began teaching catechism to children at a parish church. This activity appears to have been the motivation behind his writing various devotional songs and poems. Spee's charisma apparently extended to adult laity as well as youth, since he brought a number of Protestant nobles into the Catholic fold.

Spee's charm, however, did not win him the good graces of his immediate superior, Hermann Baving, rector of the Jesuit college at Paderborn, who evidently was an able administrator but an autocrat. Their relationship did not improve when Baving was promoted to provincial. After three years of teaching, Spee was due to make his tertianship, when he would once again make the Spiritual Exercises, study the Jesuit constitutions, and do some form of apostolic work. Because of the Thirty Years' War, German hospitals were filled with Spanish, French, and Italian soldiers; Spee wrote the general in Rome, requesting permission to do his tertianship in Milan, where he could learn Italian and be of more use ministering to the wounded troops. The general granted the permission, so long as Spee's provincial also agreed, but Baving did not. Frustrated once again, Spee made his tertianship in Speyer.

In late 1627, Fr. Iberus Fakenius, a Jesuit at the College in Cologne, became too ill to complete his course in metaphysics for the graduating senior class. Spee was assigned in midterm to fill in at his alma mater, and succeeded so well that in their closing ceremonies the following January the departing graduates paid tribute to him in a Latin doggerel in which they bid their teachers and schoolmates farewell. Playing on his name and the Latin for hope (*spes*), they wrote: "In Spee they placed hope, Friedrich was their hope" *(In Spe spes fuerat, spes Fridericus erat)*.[36] It's doubtful that they were the first to make this pun. Spee himself gave more than a little time to thinking about the virtue that, more than once, seems to have given him the strength to carry on.

The rest of 1628 did not go well for him. Spee requested permission to have a small book published—*De perpetua Dei laude* (On Praising God Constantly), and once again the general reminded Spee that standard procedure in the order called for him to go first with his requests to his immediate superior, Hermann Baving. In another letter that year, the general asks Baving to clarify his complaints that Fr. Spee "harbors misguided opinions about poverty in the order and about other things."[37] What the "other things" were is unclear, but it is likely that in Cologne, Spee began his ministry as confessor to women accused of witchcraft.

As if a strained relationship with his provincial were not bad enough, Spee suffered a further rebuff when efforts to have him appointed to the Jesuit college's regular faculty came to naught. The university dean and faculty council refused to honor Spee's Master of Arts degree because it came from Würzburg. Meanwhile, the prince-bishop of Cologne asked the Jesuits for a priest to work in the town of Peine, formerly Protestant territory and now, by virtue of imperial victories on the battlefield, back in Catholic hands. The combination of these events were all that Baving needed to get Spee out of Cologne and into the hinterlands.

Protestants and Catholics alike in that era of religious struggle accepted the principle that princes had the right to determine their subjects' religion *(cuius regio, eius religio)*. The fortunes of war, according to that axiom, often required families and whole towns to reconsider their religious affiliation, and those who preferred not to do so could leave their homes and lands behind. Spee was sent to pastor the country folk at Peine with the task of winning their hearts over to the old-time religion. His parishioners' first concern was that the new pastor might require a higher church tax for marriages and baptisms—but Spee informed them that he did not want any money from them at all.[38]

After several months the Jesuit rector of a neighboring school reported to the general in Rome that Spee was encountering considerable success in winning over the loyalties and affection of his new charges. We can surmise from his writings that Spee knew how to relate warmly with people in all walks of life. But there are always exceptions, such as Hermann Baving, and on a Sunday in April 1629, Spee met another one.

Spee was riding horseback to Sunday Mass in a small village near Peine, and an early morning fog hung thick over the fields. On a narrow path in a small woods, he was attacked by a would-be assassin who first shot at him with a pistol and then, when Spee tried to get away, struck him several times with a dagger. Spee escaped with a gallop and rode to the village church where the faithful were already gathered. He staggered into the church bleeding. Too weak and wounded to celebrate Mass, he led the gathered faithful in singing "Holy God, we praise thy name."[39]

Despite the authorities' best efforts, the assailant was never identified. Whatever the motivation, the assault afforded Spee an opportunity for convalescence in a quiet rural setting. Surrounded by the beauties of nature in summertime, he had the leisure once again to write verse. But his convalescence was cut short by a sudden opening that needed to be filled at the Jesuit college in Paderborn. Spee had first taught philosophy there as a young priest; he now returned to teach moral theology.

Moral theology was a specialty for Jesuit theologians, and Spee, popular with his students, was good at it. Among his students was the young and talented Hermann Busenbaum, who twenty years later would write a work on moral theology that would become a standard text for generations to come. In that book Busenbaum gratefully acknowledged the contributions made to his theological thinking by his old teacher.

But, once again, not everyone was gratified by Spee's theological ideas. Fr. Christian Lennep, the college rector, wrote to the general complaining that Spee was having an inordinate and adverse affect on the young Jesuits by openly raising doubts about the conduct of the witch trials. This, we may presume, was not only in personal conversations but also in the classroom, since Lennep asked for Spee to be removed from the faculty. The general agreed to an investigation but in the end decided to leave Spee at his post with an admonition to be more prudent.

In January 1631 Hermann Baving completed his tenure as provincial and was replaced by Fr. Goswin Nickel, a different personality type altogether. That was good news for Spee, but it came in tandem with the bad news that Baving was becoming the new rector at Paderborn. Almost immediately, Baving fired Spee from his teaching position. The dismissal was particularly humiliating because it came in the middle of the school year. Spee protested the injustice to the general, but before the squall stirred up by that insult could blow over, storm clouds rolled in promising even greater fury. Bookstands that April began selling the first edition of a new book entitled *Cautio Criminalis* by an "unknown Roman theologian."

The Jesuits at Paderborn knew Spee was the author of the *Cautio,* and they knew that he had not received the necessary permission for its publication. That was a serious breach of the Jesuit constitutions, an apparently deliberate act of disobedience. The new provincial, Goswin Nickel, investigated the matter and wrote to Rome. He explained to the general that, yes, Fr. Spee had written the *Cautio* but was not responsible for its publication. He had given the manuscript to an acquaintance for an opinion, and it was that unidentified other party who had taken it to a publisher as a "pious theft." The provincial and general were satisfied with Spee's explanation and admonished him only to take better care to safeguard his manuscripts in the future. Spee was reassigned to his post teaching moral theology back in Cologne.

Cologne continued to be a center for witch trials and executions, and there were Jesuits on both sides of the issue. Although Spee had colleagues who shared his thinking, others took strong exception. Three Jesuits, including the college rector, disagreed strongly enough with Spee to write the general and request that he take steps to have the *Cautio* put on the Index of Forbidden Books. The general rejected their petition, but Spee still had reason to be exasperated. Beset by continuous harassment, he petitioned the general to be transferred to a different province.

In June 1632, a second edition of the *Cautio Criminalis* appeared with some minor textual additions and corrections of typographical errors. This time Spee did not disclaim responsibility. One can only imagine the hostility that Spee had to live and deal with in his own Jesuit community. A letter from the general in Rome to the provincial, Goswin Nickel, questions whether Spee should be allowed to remain in the order. The general had reason to be concerned. From all appearances Spee was a maverick, heedless of the order's constitutions. His reckless actions were arousing controversy, bringing blame down not only on his own head but also on the entire Society.

Spee's situation was nothing if not grave. If he were dismissed from the Society and—as was more than likely—discovered by the authorities to be the author of the *Cautio,* what were his chances of escaping with his life? Deprived of the order's protection, he might well have to face prosecution alone, under suspicion of sorcery. As already seen in Delrio's writings, simply criticizing the witch trials was considered indicative that one was engaged in witchcraft.

But then something remarkable happened that still cannot be explained fully: Spee was not suspended or disciplined but assigned to teach moral theology at the Jesuit college in Trier. Scholars can only conjecture at the events behind the records. Certainly Spee had a friend and protector in Goswin Nickel. And it seems that the provincial shared Spee's opinions about the way in which the witch trials were being conducted. One plausible explanation why Spee was not disciplined for the second edition of the *Cautio* is that Nickel had authorized it.[40] Another hypothesis is that Nickel respected Spee's conscience. Certainly Spee was not bound to observe a rule if in his conscience it meant committing serious sin. Spee may have thought that trying to save innocent women from torture and execution justified this particular breach of the Society's legislation.[41]

In Trier Spee found himself among friends who valued him as a colleague and shared his views. A report by the rector of the Jesuit college there describes the *Cautio* as a "most useful and highly acclaimed book" and Spee as a priest "outstanding in piety and learning."[42] Here Spee was free to work in peace, teach his classes, and devote his spare time to writing poetry. Two manuscripts of Spee's poems have come down to us from this period, each written in his own hand.

But peace in Trier was short-lived. The city was a political football, lying on the boundary between Germany and France. It had been occupied first by the emperor's Spanish troops and then taken over by the French, who were allied with the Swedish and German Protestants. On March 26, 1635, at four o'clock in the morning, the townsfolk of Trier opened the city gates to the imperial forces. For four hours the streets of Trier ran with the blood of French and Imperial soldiers engaged in hand-to-hand combat. There in the midst of it all was Friedrich Spee, administering the last rites, carrying away the wounded, and comforting the dying. By eight o'clock, the emperor's army had won the day; five hundred French soldiers had been killed, another five hundred captured.

At a time when the devil claimed a high profile in European popular culture, Spee did not demonize the enemy. The records tell us that he collected food and clothing for the French prisoners of war and went to the imperial commander to plead with him to treat them with dignity and ultimately allow them to return home. In the months that followed, Spee regularly visited the military hospitals, overrun with wounded victims of the battle. Spee himself had written earlier of the appalling conditions that prevailed in the hospitals of his day, still centuries before anesthesia—the infected wounds, the foul smells, the screams of pain.[43] It was an exceptionally hot summer that year, and an epidemic broke out. Despite the personal risk, Spee continued to visit the wounded soldiers until he himself became infected. The records state simply that he died on August 7, 1635, at one o'clock in the afternoon, and was buried the same day.[44] He was forty-four years old.

THE *CAUTIO CRIMINALIS*

Friedrich Spee left behind two unpublished manuscripts: *Güldenes Tugend-Buch (The Golden Book of Virtues)* and a collection of poems and hymns entitled *Trutz-Nachtigall (The Rival Nightingale).*[45] Both of these works first appeared in print fourteen years after his death. The only works published during his lifetime—the *Cautio Criminalis* and a number of hymns—appeared anonymously. His thinking in moral theology would appear in the work of his more celebrated student, Hermann Busenbaum. Still he ranks among the most important authors of his time—a claim that needs no further warrant than the *Cautio,* which was one of the first sustained, public, detailed attacks of its kind against the witch trials and their use of torture.[46]

In his preface Spee explains with some irony that he wrote the *Cautio* for the authorities involved in prosecuting witches, especially those who would not care to read it [7].[47] Those likely to read it were already conscientious in their duties and would not need to; those who would not want to read it were those who should—if not the entire book then at least the last chapter, an overview of how the witch trials were being carried out in Germany at the time. This is the point on which Spee astutely focused his attack—not the "what" of the witch trials but the "how."

The *Cautio* consists of fifty-one chapters, each framed as a question. The first begins by asking straightforwardly whether witches and sorcerers really exist. Spee responds, perhaps to our surprise, "I answer, yes." It is a theoretical question, and Spee, without dwelling on it, gives a perfunctory answer. He then goes on to the second, more practical question, whether Germany has more witches than anyplace else. It would seem so, he answered, since it burns more. But the reasons he gives are the ignorance and superstition of people who immediately attribute a storm or sick animal to witchcraft. Spee did not question the existence of witches but whether all those accused and executed were really guilty. Precisely because of the way the authorities conducted the trials, innocent women were being executed. Nothing is more uncertain, he argues, than the number of witches in Germany [16–18].

Was Spee being disingenuous? Did he really disbelieve in the existence of witches but refuse to say so, to put heresy hunters off the track? There is no reason to think so.[48] Spee was not a post-Enlightenment skeptic when it came to reading the Bible; with Augustine and Aquinas, he was willing to grant that witches exist. But, against experts like Binsfeld and Delrio, he argued that their numbers were small. He never met one himself. But there have been judges who were particularly ruthless in the treatment of their victims, judges who were later accused themselves and under torture confessed to sorcery. In light of such diabolical behavior, Spee could well believe that they were guilty of conspiring with the devil [51].

Some seventy years earlier, in 1563, Johannes Weyer attacked the theory behind the witch hunts (the very idea of a pact with the devil) and was generally dismissed as a heretic. Spee took a more tactical (jesuitical?) approach by criticizing not the theory but the practice. (Analogously, death penalty opponents in the United States have proved unable to get widespread support to abolish the laws permitting capital punishment. They have more success convincing government officials and the general public of the need for a moratorium on the death penalty until such time as the fair application of the laws can be guaranteed.)

Because of the manner in which witch trials were being conducted, innocent people were being tortured and killed, and Spee did not mince words in allotting responsibility. Without mentioning names, he singled out four groups who were particularly at fault, because they were the ones who incited the princes to take measures against witchcraft. The first group consists of theologians and prelates, who sit peacefully in their comfortable studies, busy with their thoughts soaring in the clouds. "Experience has taught them nothing of events outside, of the squalor of the dungeons, of the weight of the chains, of the instruments of torture, of the lamentations of the poor. To visit the prisons, to speak with beggars, to turn an ear to the complaints of the poor is beneath their dignity and duty to study" [49].

Reading between the lines, one can imagine Spee muttering the names of Delrio and Bishop Binsfeld. Some of his Jesuit colleagues probably came to mind, when Spee included in this same category the "saintly and religious men who are completely inexperienced in the affairs and wickedness of men. As they are themselves simple and holy, they think all judges and inquisitors in these matters are like them and consider it to be the greatest crime if we do not revere all public courts as sacrosanct and incapable of error" [49].

The second group Spee indicts is comprised of lawyers for whom prosecuting witches has become a lucrative business. With fervent demonstrations of piety, they apply for the job of inquisitor, telling the princes of the grave dangers the witches pose and how measures must be taken to stop them. In the third group are the ignorant commoners who take revenge on their enemies by defaming them with slanders. If every silly rumor is not investigated at once, they threaten to go after the officials themselves and their families. Finally there are the inquisitors who do the devil's work and turn out themselves to be sorcerers, as a number of them, after being accused and tortured, have confessed [50–51].

Plainly the *Cautio* is not a calmly argued essay on jurisprudence. It is a shrill cry to stop a travesty of justice, and toward that end Spee used every rhetorical device he ever learned, especially when it came to torture. "It is incredible," he writes, "what people say under the compulsion of torture, and how many lies they will tell about themselves and about others; in the end whatever the torturers want to be true, is true" [83]. Spee describes the use of an iron press on the shinbone of the leg, how the press squeezes the flesh like "cake" with blood spurting out from both sides [77]. And this is only the first degree.

"It makes my blood boil," Spee writes, when he recalls speaking to two inquisitors about Jesuit theologian Adam Tanner. Tanner too had raised questions about the inquisitors' conduct.[49] Spee was not the first to express doubts about the witch trials, but he was the first to voice them so loudly and at length. The inquisitors told Spee how, if they got the chance, they would put Tanner on the rack [131]. Make me an inquisitor, Spee fumes, and I'll wring confessions out of all the priests and prelates in Germany [132]. Arrest and torture the Capuchins, Jesuits, and all the other religious clergy. They will confess. If any should deny it, repeat it three or four times. They will confess [85]. He tells of an inquisitor who after a few drinks boasted how he could wring a confession out of the pope himself [193].

Spee spoke the truth to power. He reproached bishops, religious superiors, respected academics, his fellow Jesuits, and virtually the entire legal profession. Not even the emperor was spared. But the princes were the primary target of his criticisms for their negligence, tolerating this gross injustice by leaving these matters to underlings. "They are ravaging their lands worse than any war could" [21].

Those in power should know how torture is being applied repeatedly without legal restraint. Spee appealed to their sense of decency. "Certainly there is not a single German nobleman who could bear to see his hunting dog mangled like this. Who then can bear it if a person is mutilated so many times" [87]? No longer can those with ultimate authority plead ignorance of the judicial criminality. Spee compares himself to a bellowing watchdog in the night, waking the household to imminent danger [138].

Spee's barking was not all oratory. He knew the literature produced by "experts" like Binsfeld and Delrio. But Spee had studied and taught logic, and he used it relentlessly to demolish the arguments of the demonologists. Time and again he shows the circularity of their reasoning: A is true because of B, and B is true because of A. One of the reasons the *Cautio* still attracts readers is its lively disputation format. Spee's most recent translator puts it aptly: "Disputations in which students argued opposing sides of a particular thesis were a fundamental part of Jesuit pedagogy, and Spee shows himself here to be a master of the art. The cut and thrust of argument and counterargument elevates the work above a dry, textbook discussion."[50]

To give just one example of Spee's mastery at the art of disputation: a monk was accused of being at a witches' Sabbath at the same time when the entire monastery swore he was chanting his prayers with the other monks in choir. Was it really the accused monk or an apparition of the devil? Would God allow the devil to assume the form of an innocent person? Delrio wrote that he had never read or heard of God allowing such a thing. The argument proves too much and thus nothing at all, Spee retorts. Any number of things have truly happened that Delrio never read or heard of [187, 189]. Spee derides Delrio and those like him who claim to know what God would and would not permit. God allowed the deaths of Christian martyrs and innocent children. Why not innocent people accused of witchcraft?

Delrio never went into the dungeons or spoke with the accused. He never experienced firsthand what the inquisitors meant by the first, second, and third degrees of torture. Spee did, and in the *Cautio* described the experience in detail. But in the final chapter, for readers who are too busy to read whole books and want only the bottom line, Spee summed up the "usual procedure" of the witch trials in a "brief overview." What is striking is how closely his summary corresponds with the findings of the most recent scholarship, particularly regarding the complicity of the general public.

It all begins with superstition, envy, and calumnies. Something goes amiss, and people clamor for an inquisition. All the divine punishments described in the Bible now come from witches. God and nature are no longer responsible for any mishap; witches do it all. The princes tell judges to investigate but they don't have any evidence and don't know where to begin. People start saying such delays are suspicious [214–15].

A specially commissioned inquisitor may be brought in, someone ignorant and unskilled or an indigent greedy man with a large family, who is paid a fee for every witch he burns. On the basis of a malicious rumor, a charge is brought against some poor old woman. An investigation is made into her life. If it has been evil, one may assume further malice; if it has been virtuous, that also is evidence, for witches regularly conceal themselves under the appearance of virtue.

The old woman is ordered into prison, where she either shows fear or does not. If she shows fear (for she has heard about the torture), that is evidence of her bad conscience. If she shows no fear (trusting in her innocence), that too is evidence, for witches are said to present themselves with heads held high. Because this is an "exceptional crime," the old woman is not provided defense counsel. Those who criticize this are called "witch-lovers" *(sagarum patronos)*.

To give some appearance of a fair trial, the old woman is read the allegations against her and given a hearing. If she defends herself well, this is taken as new evidence. If she were not a witch, she would not be so eloquent. As if she had not answered the accusations, the decree of torture is read. The old woman is then stripped and shaved of all her hair, including pubic hair, lest she have something hidden to prevent feeling the pain. Then she is tortured until she tells the truth, that is, until she confesses her guilt, since nothing else could possibly be true.

Inquisitors begin applying the first degree of torture, which in reality is quite horrible and "milder" only in comparison to the higher degrees. If she confesses, the court records say it was without torture. Why shouldn't the princes and people believe the truth of these confessions, when they were extracted without torture? If she does not confess, she can be tortured repeatedly, since there are no restrictions when it comes to "exceptional crimes." If she dies under the torture, they say that the devil broke her neck, and the executioner buries her body under the gallows.

If the old woman still refuses to confess, the judges may have her imprisoned for as long as a year. Contrary to the law, she cannot prove her innocence by withstanding the torture, since that would embarrass the inquisitors. She must be found guilty at any cost. Judges are reluctant to execute anyone for witchcraft without a confession, but, if they have to, they will. At this point, Spee interrupts his detailed narrative with a rhetorical appeal: for the love of God, if she must die, whether she confesses or not, how can any innocent person escape?

"You miserable woman! What are you hoping for? Why did you not declare yourself guilty when you first entered the prison? Why, you foolish and insane woman, do you wish to die many times when you can do it just once? Follow my advice, and before any torture just say that you are guilty and die. You will not escape, for this, after all, is the catastrophe of Germany's zeal" [219].

Once the accused confesses her guilt, she is forced to denounce other witches. Often the inquisitor will suggest names. Sometimes word leaks out, but that too has its advantages. If the persons denounced flee, it is evidence of a guilty conscience. If they do not, it is evidence that the devil is holding them fast. If they defend themselves to the inquisitors, this is taken as indicative of a bad conscience. The same thing happens when an enemy calumniates you. To keep still is evidence you are guilty. To protest your innocence is to arouse suspicion, and the calumny spreads wider. No matter what your sex or station, no matter how much wealth and honor you have, if you have an enemy who suspects you of practicing magic, you are not safe.

Spee closes the *Cautio* with a final appeal to the princes. Their immortal souls are in danger for countenancing the death of innocent people through their neglect. God will demand an accounting. Spee admits he has spoken out with passion. But he will not be numbered among those the Bible describes as dogs that will not bark (Is 56:10).

Despite the howls of his critics, Spee's bark was heard. Johann Philipp von Schönborn had met Spee and read the *Cautio*; later as prince-bishop of Würzburg (1642) and then Mainz (1647), he put an end to the witch trials in his territories.[51] But Spee seems to have influenced Protestants more than Catholics. In the same year Spee died (1635), Lutheran theologian Johann Meyfart made the first partial German translation. The first complete German translation (1647) is credited with influencing Queen Christina of Sweden to put a halt to the witch trials in her domains. Subsequent translations were made in Dutch, French, and Polish. At the turn of the century, Protestant jurist Christian Thomasius (1655–1728) is credited with overcoming the witch hunts in Prussia. He wrote how, after being fully convinced of the need for witch trials, the scales fell from his eyes while reading the *Cautio.*

One can see from the above description why Spee's book was so controversial. He blamed the witch trials on superstition and wrote that Germans were worse than other nationalities and Catholics worse than Protestants. He faulted not only judges and lawyers but also theologians (like Delrio), prelates (like Bishop Binsfeld), and gullible "pious clerics" (like his Jesuit colleagues).

Criticizing clergy was a time-honored Catholic custom. What was new here was Spee's outspoken reproof of the secular authorities, whom he held co-responsible for judicial murder. His courage is only magnified by the fact that he lived in an age when authority was virtually absolute.

For good reason Spee has been called a forerunner of the Enlightenment. Throughout the *Cautio* he appeals to what he calls healthy or right reason *(recta ratio).* He argues for such principles as the right to a fair trial, presumption of innocence until one is proven guilty, the right to competent defense, judicial impartiality and independence, and the prohibition of torture. In contrast to Spee's times, we take those legal principles for granted now, or at least we claim adherence to them in our Western democracies. Spee argued that "it is better to let thirty or more guilty men go than to punish one innocent" [46]. In the aftermath of terrorist attacks and contemporary discussions about balancing civil rights with security concerns, one can only wonder how many Americans would agree with Spee's liberal, civil-libertarian opinion today.

Especially notable about that particular opinion is that Spee did not base it on reason. He drew it from the Gospel parable of the weeds and wheat growing together till harvest time (Mt 13:24 ff.). He cited the parable several times in the course of the *Cautio* as a lesson that God does not will even a single innocent person to suffer the same fate as the guilty. With all his appeals to reason, Spee was not a rationalist. His courage to speak out against torture and the witch trials came not from philanthropy but out of his Christian faith and Ignatian spirituality.

IGNATIAN SPIRITUALITY
IN A BAROQUE AGE

As the *Cautio* exemplifies Spee's humanism, his Ignatian spirituality shines
out in the poetry of his *Rival Nightingale* and his *Golden Book of Virtues*.
These, unlike the *Cautio,* which he wrote in Latin for the educated elite,
Spee wrote in German for lay people, and they reflect the aesthetic taste
of the day. In many ways Spee's poems and book of virtues resemble the
church architecture and art of his time, both characterized by an exuberance of ornamentation and detail. Before long we want to say enough
already. We may admire their artistry and execution but our aesthetic sensibilities prefer more restraint.

Modern readers tend to have the same reaction reading Spee's book of
virtues with their seventy songs intended to "ignite all the hearts in the
whole wide world." Even more so with the fifty-one poems of the *Rival
Nightingale: A Poetic Spiritual Pleasure-Garden.*[52] The peculiar title seems to
come from Spee's resolve to prove himself a match for Martin Luther,
crowned by his admirers as the "Wittenberg Nightingale." In that age of
confessional one-upmanship, Spee was a Counter-Reformation Catholic
determined to prove that Protestants were not the only ones who knew how
to write good hymns in their native tongue. Catholics could praise God in
German too, and Spee was bent on giving them the words to do it.

Spee intended his verses to be sung, and some he set to music himself.
He had been writing in this genre since his earliest years as a Jesuit, when
he wrote songs for his catechism classes. Hymns were his first works to be
published and were to be found in various collections, although without
attribution, so that it is not easy to determine which ones are genuinely
his. Several of his hymns are still sung today in Germany, in both Catholic
and Protestant churches, and one of the poems in the *Rival Nightingale*
was set to music by Johannes Brahms.[53]

As a kind of overture for the entire book, Spee describes himself in the
first poem as a "rival nightingale," wounded by the "sweet arrow" of love

for Jesus. Spee's ardor can quickly become cloying with his repeated recourse to diminutives like "little flame" and "little flower." Equally alien to our tastes are the images drawn from classic Latin poetry, describing Jesus as the shepherd Daphnis or "chaste love, Cupid pure." Spee borrows too from the bridal imagery of the biblical Song of Songs, and, as have many Christian mystics, he writes of the feminine soul *(anima)* longing for Christ, her spouse. In verses reminiscent of the old Latin hymns sung by monks in their morning and evening prayers, Spee waxes lyrical over the beauties of creation. "When dawn dispels the night with its golden rays," joyfully he awakens and calls to God. "When murky gloom at eventide clothes us in dark shadows," he ponders his sins and the brevity of life. He closes with a challenge to the world to raise its voice in a songfest in praise of God.

At the outset of his book on the virtues, Spee informs his readers that it is not intended for scholars or to be read so much as put into practice.[54] In the Jesuit tradition of accommodation, Spee anticipated modern efforts to translate and adapt Ignatian spirituality to his readers. He relates how the book originated with his giving direction to a "spiritual daughter" who came to him weekly for confession and wanted to grow more deeply in her spiritual life. He complied by giving her very precise instructions on how to take a quarter- or half-hour each day for praying and practicing the virtues of faith, hope, and love.

Not surprisingly, Spee's book of virtues bears the stamp of Ignatius's *Spiritual Exercises.* As the Exercises ask for a so-called "application of the senses," Spee encourages his readers to use their imaginations and express their feelings. Imagine yourself, he tells them, conversing with the apostles, being faced with martyrdom, lying on your deathbed, or looking at all the sick people in the world. Repeatedly he asks his readers to pray with sighs of joy, sorrow, or longing. He has them listen to their hearts and whisper a short prayer with every beat.

Underlying Spee's virtue book is a theology that is, for the most part, traditional. Spee is quite conventional, for example, in his treatment of faith, which he describes as an intellectual assent to truths revealed by God and taught us by the church. In his chapters on faith, Spee has the reader pray over Bible stories, stories of martyrs, and the words of the Apostles' Creed.

For Spee, as for Ignatius, love is to be manifested more in deeds than in words, and the two great commandments are essentially one; you show your love for God by loving people. You bring greater glory to God by helping souls. Spee urges his reader to buy a poor person a loaf of bread. Care about children's education; buy schoolbooks for a student who can't afford them. More challenging still, overcome your disgust at the stench and visit a hospital, bring a meal to the sick, wash their linens, make their beds.

Thus far, nothing related here about Spee's spirituality could be called unconventional. Moreover, nothing so far suggests an answer to the question of where he got the courage to risk his life and write the *Cautio*. Was it perhaps not his spirituality but the fact that he was assigned to hear the confessions of the accused witches?

But Spee was not unique in receiving such an assignment. Indeed, some of his sharpest criticism in the *Cautio* is directed against priests who give no consolation to the accused women. Refusing to hear of any protestations of innocence, they only harangue the women to confess to the same crimes that they confessed to under torture. Spee tells us about a priest who accompanied almost 200 witches to their deaths, absolving only one or two of them after they had confessed their crime. God will demand an accounting from these ignorant priests, Spee thundered. They are asking for sacrilegious confessions, and the poor wretches who refuse to commit the sacrilege die without the sacraments "like a dog" [71].

It is in the context of experiences like these that we need to read the pages Spee devoted to hope. Here we can detect the source of Spee's courage, whether it was to write the *Cautio* or to minister to the wounded soldiers and risk the infection that eventually took his life. Here too we can surmise some idea of what he said to console the condemned women and to overcome their despair.

In a book meant for spiritual reading and pastoral use, Spee chose to forego a formal, scholastic definition of hope and described it instead with a variety of verbs. To hope means to long for, yearn for, sigh for God. It means we put ourselves completely in God's hands from whence we wait and look for all that is good. That we hope means that we "trust and count" on God (GTB 20).

Spee opens the section on hope with a series of rhetorical questions. Would you dare to doubt God's mercy even if you were the world's greatest sinner? Would you despair of God's mercy if you were at sea in a sinking ship with no priest present? Or—in a situation not dissimilar from that of the accused witches—would you despair if you were infected with a terrible disease and no priest would come near to give you absolution?

Citing Isaiah (49:15) Spee asks, "Can a woman forget her . . . child?" and goes on to describe God as father and mother; then, mixing metaphors even more, as sister and brother, help and refuge (GTB 128). Dwelling on God as having a motherly heart, he describes God as a "mighty empress" who loves each of us like her favorite child in danger of death. With an analogy even more original, he likens God to a heap of gunpowder immense as the earth. Could it help but explode if ignited? So too, it is God's nature to be merciful. Spee argues his point from the psalms and the prophets, and from the parables of Luke, which he describes as God's "true, infallible word" (GTB 151). The greater our misery, the more glorious God's mercy. God wills all people, even the greatest sinner, to be saved.

Like Ignatius in the first week of the *Spiritual Exercises,* Spee assumes the condition of human sinfulness. Our situation is such that all we can do is trust in God's gracious mercy. As Ignatius does in the Principle and Foundation at the outset of the *Spiritual Exercises,* Spee counsels his readers against hanging their hearts on any creature; only God can give you the peace you long for. Trust not in your own strength, but only in the power of God. When you feel lost and alone and think your heart will break, look at the crucified Christ, who prayed, "My God, my God, why have you forsaken me?"

Even though Spee's *Golden Book of Virtues* was first published posthumously, it still needed approval by the Society, and it was in connection with his thinking on trust that his Jesuit censors had the greatest difficulty. Fortunately, the original manuscript still exists and allows comparison with the published version to see where Spee's thinking on hope was considered too innovative for his times. Two major omissions from that first edition deserve notice here.

Spee encourages his readers to grow in faith and trust in God by reading the Bible. So far so good. But then he goes on to point out that one has to admire how much Protestants are strengthened and consoled in all manner of adversities by reading Scripture. Spee's censors took scissors to the text. In an era when Catholics and Protestants were slaughtering one another on battlefields, holding Protestants up as models of virtue for Catholics to imitate was out of the ordinary, to say the least.

Not just a paragraph, but an entire chapter hit the cutting-room floor when the censors came to Spee's treatment of purgatory and the issue of forgiveness of punishment as well as sin (GTB 158–62). Spee says nothing in his virtue book about doing penances; his emphasis is on trusting in God's mercy and grace. And in the situation of condemned women facing a death by fire there was no question of consoling them with the thought of dying into the flames of purgatory.

If we don't have the words Spee spoke to accused witches when he visited them in their cells or accompanied them to their deaths, we do have his theology of grace. In a conversation between himself and his reader, he asks a leading question. If a Turk, a Jew, or a pagan sinned his entire life but converted on his deathbed and was baptized, would he not upon dying escape purgatory and go straight to heaven as God's beloved child? Of course, is the answer, for that is traditional Catholic teaching. Would God then, Spee asks rhetorically, be any less generous to a Christian who receives the sacraments before dying? Spee finds the answer obvious.

He then becomes even more speculative. What if that Turk or pagan wanted to convert but was killed for his Christian faith before he could be baptized? Would he not enter heaven immediately as a martyr? Again the answer is yes; baptism of desire and of blood also have long histories in Catholic tradition. So, Spee asks his readers, are you willing to be a martyr? Are you willing to die a martyr's death? And if that Turk or pagan would be able to escape purgatory with a quick thrust of a sword or blade, would not the same be true for Christians who are willing to die for their faith but must suffer a slow martyrdom of many years struggling with the world, the flesh, and the devil?

Spee did not deny the existence of purgatory, but he professed that God has given us "infallible means" to escape it. He remained within the boundaries of Catholic orthodoxy but was breaking new ground with his thinking about "martyrdom of desire." It was the accepted view of Catholic theologians that an evil intention (like committing adultery in one's heart) was already sinful before the act. Spee was only carrying that line of thinking to its logical conclusions. If one could commit a sin in one's heart and reap the punishment, why couldn't one do a good deed in one's heart and reap the reward, including the reward for a heroic deed like martyrdom?

His censors did not think a book on spirituality for lay people was the proper place for trailblazing new paths in theology. The chapter was troublesome not only for its innovative thinking on purgatory but also for its affinity to Lutheran piety. Don't think about your works, Spee counseled his readers. Don't worry about your merits. "You should have a greater opinion of God's generosity, for that gives him glory. . . . Just put your trust in God's generosity and the blood of Christ; for it is not child's play that God died for you." Put yourself into the hands of God who is "a thousand times more gentle and generous than we imagine" (GTB 160).

Spee closed his section on hope with several reflections and exercises on the Lord's Prayer, where he cites the method suggested by Ignatius in the *Spiritual Exercises*. Say the prayer slowly; take as long as an hour if you wish; dwell on the meaning of each phrase. Would you like to say the Lord's Prayer in only a few words? Then simply pray, "Thy will be done." Put your hope and trust in God by praying those words throughout the day.

The French writer Charles Péguy once described hope as the little sister who walks between her big sisters, faith and love. Spee, whose very name engendered thoughts of hope, gave that oft-neglected virtue more serious reflection than it usually gets from theologians. Trusting in God's grace and mercy was the source of Friedrich Spee's courage to speak the truth to power, even at the risk of his life and vocation as a Jesuit.

As for his message to women tempted to despair as they looked forward to death by fire, the answer is the same. Though we don't have his exact words as he walked them to the stake, we can surmise them: "Just keep repeating, 'Thy will be done, thy will be done.' Put your trust in God's love and mercy. Think of those martyrs who gave their lives for their faith. Imagine yourself a martyr dying for Christ. The heavens are opening for you. Make your suffering and death a martyrdom."

As noted at the beginning of this chapter, the fact that Spee's *Cautio* compared the accused witches to the early Christian martyrs was one of the reasons Bishop Pelcking found it a "most poisonous book." Spee may have been treading close to the limits of Catholic orthodoxy at the time, but the fact that he regarded the executed women as martyrs was arguably the main reason he could write rhapsodic hymns about the beauties of dawn or ever get to sleep at night.

A Humanist for Our Times

Spee's baroque poetry might lead a contemporary reader to dismiss his spirituality as hopelessly outdated. His emotionality can be excessive, and his instructions on how to pray may seem charmingly naive. With all that, there is also much in Spee's personal spirituality that remains fresh and even daring. Living in what was—even more than our own—a man's world and a man's church, Spee wrote a book on spirituality specifically intended for laywomen.[55] This may not have been a total innovation; his contemporary St. Francis de Sales predated him by several years in a similar effort. But Spee's virtue book in its intended readership was still novel for its time, as was its feminist imagery. Such is God's love, as Spee saw it, that no one image suffices. "You must be my father and mother, my sister and brother" (GTB 128). The God of Spee's Ignatian spirituality transcended male imagery with a love that transcended all imagery. And this, perhaps, is one of the most valuable lessons Spee can teach us in our troubled times.

Spee lived in a culture convinced of divine punishment and demonic power. The devil was an undeniable reality, someone you might meet any moment walking home on a lonely path near a woods. In the midst of a bloody religious war, surrounded by pestilence and famine, it was not difficult to believe that God was like a vengeful Zeus, hurling down thunderbolts, or an irate Apollo, shooting poison arrows. Trying to appease God's anger by searching out scapegoats (Jews, witches, heretics) was easier than believing in a God who was merciful and "motherly." But Spee, undaunted, mindful of his name, held on to hope. Beleaguered by many of his own Jesuit confreres, he maintained his trust in the gracious God whom Ignatius said dwelled in all created things.

Looking back at a century marked by world wars and more than one instance of genocide, we have need of Spee's optimistic reading of Ignatian spirituality. In the long shadows created by Auschwitz, nuclear arms proliferation, economic policies that only widen the gap between rich and poor, and a "war" on terrorism with no end in sight, one might well ask, is it still possible to believe in a God of love for humankind?

A better question might be, dare we not? Given the atrocities of the last century and the inhumanity we now realize humans are capable of inflicting on one another, is it possible to put our hopes in humankind? It was only his hopeful trust in a gracious God that gave Spee the kind of heroic courage needed to speak out against a massive violation of human rights and make a difference.

Spee has been called a proto-Enlightenment figure for advocating recognition of the civil and human rights of women accused of witchcraft. But as much as the "Age of Reason," he also anticipated aspects of our own postmodernist times. Unlike Martin Delrio and his unsympathetic Jesuit confreres, Spee did his theological thinking where people were hurting—not in an ivory tower or a quiet, book-lined study, but where social and legal structures countenanced injustice. And the sources for his theological argumentation were not Scripture alone (as Protestants were wont), or Scripture and church tradition (as in the Catholic mode), but Scripture, church tradition, and experience. It was experience—going down to the dungeons, standing in solidarity with the victims—that made Spee a postmodern theologian ahead of his time.

Spee's humanism anticipated liberation theology and the contemporary Jesuit commitment to the faith that does justice. Spee did more than social service. Besides trying to alleviate the suffering caused by injustice, he practiced what today is called social analysis. He analyzed the ideological underpinnings of the witch trials (pointing an accusing finger at ivory-tower academics and gullible priests). He looked to the economics of the enterprise (drawing attention to the profits being made by lawyers and judges who got paid for every witch they executed). He assessed the role of popular opinion and superstition (no mishap merely natural), the legal and investigative structures involved in obtaining confessions (torture, denial of legal counsel for the accused). Then he discerned what he, one lone Jesuit priest-professor, could do and, in the words of Archbishop Oscar Romero, now an ideal of Jesuit education, became a "voice for the voiceless."

Spee knew that by speaking out for the alleged witches he was risking at the very least anything like a peaceful academic life. He was criticizing the status quo not only of Germany in general but also of the German Catholic Church, and not despite, but precisely because of his attachment both to his nation and his church. Criticizing one's government or church generally brings with it invidious insinuations about one's loyalties ("love it or leave it"). One is at best a nuisance, at worst a traitor. Spee was considered both and suffered harassment from Jesuit confreres who wanted him expelled from the Society and his book put on the Index.

After centuries of obscurity, Friedrich Spee deserves to be remembered by more than German Jesuits. These pages are one small attempt to bring his name to the attention of a wider, English-reading public. But more than simply remembered, he deserves to be honored and imitated for his heroic virtue. Obviously Ignatian spirituality has produced more saints than those who have been canonized.[56] Is it too much to hope that someday Friedrich Spee will be enrolled in the canon of saints? Certainly he exemplified what the New Testament and the Society of Jesus today mean by the "faith that does justice." Spee presaged the modern Ignatian awareness that being "friends of the Lord" means being "friends of the poor" and that oppression today has a distinctly "feminine face." In a culture more given to patriarchy than our own, Spee anticipated the need of Jesuits and other church leaders to "listen carefully and courageously to the experience of women."[57]

But considering Friedrich Spee for canonization might be too risky for church leaders. He did his thinking at the edges of orthodoxy. He was willing to criticize authorities. He put conscience ahead of personal comfort. Spee has too much in common with contemporary Christians willing to think critically about their churches and willing to go public. Church authorities might find it troublesome for Ignatian (or other Christian) humanists to have someone as independent and outspoken as Friedrich Spee for a patron saint.

FIVE

PIERRE TEILHARD
DE CHARDIN

The interview started badly. [Abbé] Gaudefroy [chair of geology at the Institut Catholique] began by saying that he distrusted the Jesuits because they were a secret society; that nobody was allowed to know their rules; and that their mail was opened by their superiors. Teilhard burst out laughing, opened a drawer, and took out the Exercises of St. Ignatius. "There you are," he said, "those are my rules. I haven't any others."[1]

Of all the words one could apply to Teilhard de Chardin, none characterize him more aptly than *quintessentially Jesuit.* One biographer has called him "the most Jesuit Jesuit in centuries,"[2] and with good reason. Teilhard was as much a world-class scientist as Christopher Clavius, Roger Boscovich, or Athanasius Kircher and as much an explorer of China and a cultural pioneer as Matteo Ricci or Adam Schall. His devotion to the Catholic Church and the Society of Jesus was as tested and proven as that of any Jesuit before, during, or since the suppression. His vision of the "human phenomenon" rooted in a "divine milieu" took its inspiration directly from the *Spiritual Exercises* with its vision of God in all things— raised exponentially to cosmic proportions. An expert on the distant past, he looked with Ignatian optimism into the distant future. A poet who wrote prayers, he was a humanist-priest whose altar was the universe.

THE HEART OF MATTER

Pierre Teilhard was born in 1881 in Auvergne in south-central France, the fourth of eleven children. On his mother's side he was related to Voltaire. But in stark contrast to the priest-eating savant, the family of Emmanuel and Berthe Teilhard de Chardin was fiercely loyal to the church. Though descended from nobility, they were not wealthy; their home was a modest seventeenth-century country house, from which one could see the mountains of Auvergne looming on the horizon. More accessible to young Pierre lay woods, meadows, and rocky soil veined with crystal.

Emmanuel Teilhard was a gentleman farmer, an amateur naturalist, and an avid student of history. He chose the books for his children's reading and supervised their Latin until they entered school. Pierre's mother, Berthe, rose before dawn every day, walked to Mass, and returned home for breakfast with her family. It was she who cultivated in Pierre a devotion to the Sacred Heart of Jesus—an image prominently displayed in the Teilhard home. More than a few contemporary Catholics find the image of Jesus' pierced heart a relic of an outmoded devotionalism, embarrassing and even irritating, but for Pierre Teilhard it symbolized the convergence of the divine and human and the cosmic energy that is love. Understood in this way, it epitomized Teilhard's spiritual vision and his life's work.

At age seventy-nine Teilhard, in a manner reminiscent of St. Ignatius, looked back on his life and career and wrote an autobiographical essay describing the experiences and influences that shaped his life and thought. He entitled the essay "The Heart of Matter," as succinct an expression of Teilhardian ideas and convictions as one could ask for. In it he wrote of a "certain 'love of the Invisible' that has always been active in me." He attributed this "sense of the Divine," as he also called it, to his mother's devotion to the humanity of Jesus as symbolized by the Sacred Heart. This he called the Christian half of his "fundamental being." But there was also what he called the "pagan" half, his "innate appetite for the Earth."[3]

As a boy, Teilhard had begun to feel himself "drawn by Matter." He recalls in his essay how, when no more than six or seven years old, he cherished the lock-pin of a plow and the hexagonal head of a bolt simply because they were made of iron and, so he thought, durable. Iron had "consistence," and consistence seemed to stand at the heart of what is necessary and incorruptible. Here, to his young mind, was an "iron God," the absolute in the form of the tangible. But he discovered soon enough that iron rusts. Disillusioned with iron idols, young Teilhard began looking for other signs of durability.

He found them in rocks. Auvergne has been described as a geologist's paradise, its soil rich with quartz and amethyst. Minerals replaced iron as Teilhard's engrossing passion, not just for their bright colors and transparency, but even more for their resistance to destruction. (Flowers and insects, on the other hand, seemed inconsistent and corruptible, so they held only passing interest for him.) He began collecting various types of stones, carefully labeling each specimen. It was a boyhood revelation to discover that rocks were the substance that made up the planet. Here was something ubiquitous and elemental, the very "stuff of things," as close to a tangible token of the absolute as the boy Teilhard ever hoped to find.

If these were the remembrances of someone else, they might explain how he or she grew up to become a geologist. But Teilhard was more than a scientist; his lifelong attraction to minerals was more than intellectual curiosity. He seemed to hunger for the impervious with a craving he called "spiritual." The universality and solidity of rock made it a kind of sacrament. It enabled him to enter into communion with a "sort of universal root or matrix of beings." Looking back over his life, Teilhard recognized that "even at the peak of my spiritual trajectory I was never to feel at home unless immersed in an Ocean of Matter."[4]

At age eleven Pierre began his formal education at a school operated by the French Jesuits. He thrived under its discipline and excelled in all his subjects, including Greek, Latin, literature, and science. But he never lost his passionate interest in rocks or his appetite for the certainty they represented for him. In light of Teilhard's considerable spiritual sensibilities and familial piety, his Jesuit teachers, not surprisingly, sparked a desire to enter their ranks. In the spring of 1899, shortly before his eighteenth birthday, Teilhard entered the novitiate of the Lyons province of the Society of Jesus. Here he made the thirty-day Spiritual Exercises of St. Ignatius, studied the constitutions of the Society, and made several lifelong friendships. In 1901 he took his first vows, writing to his parents, "If only you knew the joy I feel now that I have at last given myself completely and for ever to the Society."[5]

Together with his classmates, Teilhard was sent to the Isle of Jersey in the English Channel where he studied philosophy and elementary physics. But scholastic syllogisms intrigued him less than the island's minerals, and he felt obliged to subject his passion to the judgment of his spiritual director. Ignatian spirituality embraces St. Ignatius's ideal of detachment, but when it came to matters geological, Teilhard was hardly detached. His director assured the young scholastic that grace builds upon nature. The Jesus who was calling him to join in service in the Society desired the full development of his talents, his wholeness as well as his holiness. His qualms were pacified, and Teilhard felt free to pursue his geological interests.[6]

His superiors not only sanctioned but encouraged his propensity for the natural sciences, and from 1905 to 1908 Teilhard was assigned to teach chemistry and physics at a Jesuit junior college in Cairo. His letters from Egypt, especially those to his father, a fellow naturalist, are replete with meticulous observations of natural phenomena. His chief scientific interests in Egypt were its deposits of marine fossils, including whalebone and fish teeth—remnants of creatures once alive but now mineralized. The demarcation between minerals and life was not as firm as Teilhard once thought. He was still an amateur, but his correspondence and published research began to draw the attention of specialists.[7]

After his stint teaching in Egypt, Teilhard studied theology in England at a Jesuit house in Hastings. Here he met some of the finest minds in the

Society of Jesus, both among his teachers and his classmates—Léonce de Grandmaison, Pierre Rousselot, Joseph Huby, Jules Lebreton. Here he read Cardinal Newman's *Essay on the Development of Christian Doctrine* with its novel thesis that the expression of Catholic faith unfolds organically and develops through the course of history. Newman's ideas became seminal to Teilhard's thinking. So too did another book on development—Henri Bergson's 1907 *L'évolution créatrice* (Creative Evolution).

His work with fossils and his observations of natural phenomena had convinced Teilhard beyond any doubt that Darwin's theory could not be discounted; the universe was and is in a process of evolving. As he would later describe it in "The Heart of Matter," evolution was no longer an abstract notion for him but galvanized his entire being. Bergson's concept of creative evolution added fuel to a fire already kindled. The concept became, as he put it, "like an unsatisfied hunger, like a promise held out to me, like a summons to be answered."[8]

Up to this time, Teilhard had accepted that matter and spirit were fundamentally divergent. In accord with Catholic, neo-Platonic tradition, he had taken for granted the diversity of matter and spirit, body and soul. But Teilhard had always had a proclivity for seeing things as parts of a whole. Now he began seeing energy, matter, life, and spirit as interrelated constituents of a continuum. He agreed with Bergson about the illusory nature of permanence. Reality is a process of becoming—and what is becoming does not result from random chance. Evolution is spirit-directed, with matter being continuously spiritualized into life and reflective thought.

One must remember here that, within most Christian churches, Charles Darwin's *Origin of Species* (1859) still prompted bitter debate. And the same year Bergson's *Creative Evolution* appeared, Vatican authorities began a massive effort to halt the "modernist" trend in Catholic thinking. Any novel interpretation of the Bible or Catholic dogma—certainly any that conflicted with the traditional interpretation of the creation stories in Genesis—aroused suspicions of heresy. The Vatican placed Bergson's *Creative Evolution* on the Index of Forbidden Books. Roman professors of theology assured their students that evolution plainly contradicted reason; it was absurd to suggest that Dante or Shakespeare had descended from apes.

True-believing scientists were committed not only to evolutionary theory but also to the randomness of its operation. The evidence was such as to convince them that the diversity of species—including the origin of *homo sapiens*—results from random mutations, and that the survival of those species depends on their being suited to their environment. Humankind, then, owes its origins to chance. Here was the atheist's answer to the argument of a divine wisdom behind the laws of nature. The universe is not a watch requiring a watchmaker to be intelligible; natural selection explains whatever order exists. From the perspective of unbelief, evolution occurs without direction and without God.

Teilhard found himself situated between two worldviews generally regarded as inherently antagonistic.[9] In accord with his Thomistic, Jesuit conviction that science and faith are mutually compatible, he refused to erect a "watertight bulkhead" between them, but allowed science and faith full freedom to react upon each other. The result, he was convinced, was not schizophrenia but a synthesis. In Teilhard's vision of reality there was a positive fit between evolutionary theory and Christian belief. The originality of this idea was such as to arouse profound skepticism among his colleagues in both camps. Pursuing its implications, however, became his life's work. In accord with Ignatian tradition he set about attempting to mediate faith and science, for the sake of truth but also for the sake of his own psychic integrity.

In late summer, 1911, Teilhard was ordained a priest in the chapel of the Jesuit theological seminary in Hastings. He remained in England for another year, during which he had a curious brush with notoriety. An acquaintance of his, Charles Dawson, claimed to have discovered a skull and jawbone of a hominid, the so-called Piltdown Man. Teilhard had not yet begun his graduate work in science and accepted the claim that the two fossils were genuine, though he did not believe they belonged to the same creature. Years later, in 1953, the fossils were shown to have been chemically treated and planted as an elaborately contrived hoax. Teilhard did not want to believe that Dawson was guilty of the fraud. But whoever the perpetrator, Teilhard, along with other members of the scientific community, had been taken in by the deception.[10]

As a young priest, Teilhard said Mass and directed retreats. In any other religious community, that might well have composed the rest of his life's work. But his Jesuit superiors were supportive of his scientific aspirations and assigned him to pursue graduate studies at the Museum of Natural History in Paris, where he specialized in the area of paleontology. He became the acquaintance, friend, and eventually the professional peer of world-class experts on the fossilized remains of the first human beings and their more distant ancestors. In 1914 he was in his early thirties, living the rarified life of a scientist and scholar, when his peaceful academic existence shattered with the outbreak of World War I. From the experiences and ideas he recorded over the next four years would come the mature writings of the next forty.

WRITINGS IN TIME OF WAR

Although he could have sought duty as a military chaplain, Teilhard chose to serve as a stretcher-bearer on the front line. His assignment was to a mixed regiment of French and Moroccan riflemen, among the first units to face the enemy in any battle. Under enemy fire he comforted the dying, carried the wounded to safety, and learned firsthand the hell of life and death in the trenches. His biographers describe him wading through mud amid the fallen bodies at the battle of Verdun. On one occasion he volunteered to retrieve an officer who had fallen near a nest of machine guns. He returned with the officer's body on his back.[11] His courage won him promotion to the rank of corporal, a number of citations, and ultimately an appointment to the Legion of Honor.

Teilhard lost comrades, fellow Jesuits, and two of his brothers in the war. He lacked no personal experience of the evils human beings inflict on one another. Yet this "baptism into reality," as he called it, did not shake his childhood faith in God or his newfound faith in a material universe evolving into spirit. On the contrary, the trenches provided a matrix for his first groping expressions of that twofold faith. Surrounded by war and death—reality at its rawest—Teilhard spent his free time pondering absolutes. Fr. René d'Ouince, a close Jesuit friend, described him this way:

> Out on the front line, he thought all day long, and often at night. . . . He would make for the nearest wood and pace up and down for hours, consigning it all to notes at first light. At his next rest break, in some parish church or rundown sacristy, he would write . . . twenty or thirty pages in a meticulously neat hand.[12]

The first of his writings in time of war is entitled "Cosmic Life."[13] Teilhard described the essay, dated April 24, 1916, Dunkirk, as his "intellectual testament." Knowing he might never write anything else, he put down all the ideas and feelings churning within him. Dedicated "To *Terra Mater* [Mother Earth], and through her to Christ Jesus, above all things," the essay contains in embryo all that would become characteristic of his later thought.

"Cosmic Life" opens with an exuberant expression of love for life and for the energies and secrets of the material universe. An unsympathetic reader might infer that his exuberance was worldly, even pagan. But Teilhard was resolved to disprove the notion of any inconsistency between loving God and loving matter. He argues that every human person is "essentially cosmic" (15). Each of us is linked to all that is material, alive, and spiritual. We are interconnected elements in a continuum that reaches behind us and extends ahead. Teilhard entreats his Christian readers to become awakened to the cosmos and the "sacred evolution" going on in the whole of nature (17).

Cosmic consciousness requires abandoning "narrow individualism." Life is "in some way an extension of matter," and the matter common to all of us makes us ultimately "but one being" (23). But this "monistic" view of the universe does not mean that we are drifting involuntarily into a pantheistic Nirvana. On the contrary, "the true summons of the cosmos is a call consciously to share in the great work that goes on within it" (32). That "great work," which first brought forth organic and then human life, continues to operate within human society as we overcome our isolation as individuals and our segregation as social groups. We are in the evolutionary process of becoming spiritually integrated with humankind and thereby with the universe (45).

Lest he be reckoned more a pantheist than a Christian, Teilhard insisted that Christianity, for all its personal individualism, is at the same time "essentially a cosmic religion" (47). The God of Christianity is the God in whom "we live and move and have our being" (Acts 17:28). This is pantheistic language, bespeaking the ecstasy of union, or rather communion— the communion of saints—with a God that is both transcendent and immanent.

> God, who is as immense and all-embracing as matter, and at the same time as warm and intimate as a soul, is the Centre who spreads through all things. . . . No words can express the bliss of feeling oneself possessed, absorbed, without end or limit, by an Infinite that is not rarefied and colorless, but living and luminous, an Infinite that knows and attracts and loves (48).

To articulate his cosmic vision, Teilhard had to resort to the language of mystics and poets. But in searching his imagination for analogies, he often drew metaphors from modern science, which makes his writing highly unconventional. It was certainly a novel idea that human beings are somehow like molecules that, by coming together, stimulate otherwise dormant properties and thereby fertilize and complete one another (36). Teilhard also used more traditional metaphors, including that of the body of Christ. But he insisted that the union represented in that doctrine should be understood in the "strongest sense the words can bear" (51).

The Risen Christ, for Teilhard, is a "cosmic Christ," such as one finds in the New Testament writings of John and Paul, a reality that already exists but is also still becoming (59). For Teilhard as for St. Ignatius, God is "busily at work" within our lives and in our work, even in work that appears commonplace or profane. Whether spending hours in a laboratory probing some secret of nature, reaching out with love to another, or simply helping someone in a small way, no act is merely secular. It is part of the "holiness of evolution." Even more than a half century later, pairing these two words is jarring to our ears. But for Teilhard, evolution is the way God has created in the past and continues to create today. "The world is still being created"(60). What lies ahead is a new humanity in communion with God through earth, which Teilhard would later call a "Christogenesis."

Teilhard's "intellectual testament" represents an early attempt to put into words his vision of God at work in an evolving universe. For the next fifty years he would develop the implications of that vision. Already in this first essay, he began to be engaged with the apparent contradiction between his evolutionary worldview and Catholic tradition, more specifically between his ideas about evolutionary, human progress and the existence of evil. Even his sympathetic readers had difficulty reconciling Teilhard's optimism with the Augustinian Catholic tradition regarding sin, suffering, and death. But Teilhard had a unique perspective on Catholic tradition. He was a paleontologist who looked at space and time, the universe and the origins of life in terms of billions of light years, not just millennia.

Teilhard saw sin and suffering as necessary components of evolution. "In an organism as vast as the universe any amount of goodwill and countless resources remain unused, and a host of failures is the price that has to be paid for a few successes" (67). Observed in isolation, pain and suffering are inexplicable. Viewed in terms of an evolving universe, suffering punishes transgressions of life's laws and awakens effort against conditions inimical to human development (43). "One cannot build up a mountain without digging a great pit, and every energy has equal power for good and for evil. Everything that becomes suffers or sins. The truth about our position in this world is that in it we are on a Cross" (67).

Teilhard recognized that he was going against the classical Augustinian interpretation of suffering as a punishment for sin. He was saying that sin and suffering are inevitable aspects of evolution. "Physical and moral evil are produced by the process of Becoming: everything that evolves has its own suffering and commits its own faults." The cross, it follows, does not represent an expiation for sin so much as the arduous and painful travail of evolution in its present human, social phase (71).

Teilhard's "Cosmic Life" would be followed by other essays written during the war. His essay "The Priest" was rewritten in Asia as "Mass on the World." Both are prayers in which, bereft of altar, bread, and wine, Teilhard makes a sacrificial offering of the universe, its labors and sufferings. "The Mystical Milieu" introduces his readers to his peculiarly materialistic spirituality. It describes a mystical journey through a series of circles reminiscent of St. Theresa's interior castles, including consistency, energy, and spirit. It was obviously a journey Teilhard himself had taken. He was clearly the recipient of profound religious experiences and, like Ignatius Loyola, he attempted to describe them. The war and its aftermath were his Manresa.

MYSTICAL EXPERIENCES

In "The Heart of Matter," Teilhard appended two early writings as "particularly representative" of his state of mind during and just after the war. Like Ignatius's memoirs, they too were written in the third person, detailing matters so intimate and personal that Teilhard felt the need to relate them as stories. They disclose experiences that, as he put it, "allowed the light of day to pour into my soul," giving him inner peace and a confirmation that his cosmic vision was correct.[14]

Teilhard wrote the first story in October 1916, shortly before a major battle. He describes going into a church where he saw a picture of the Sacred Heart. He was reflecting on the impossibility of any artist depicting Jesus' humanity without being "over-exact" and limiting, when suddenly it seemed to him that the outlines of the picture were melting. "You might have said that the edge which divided Christ from the surrounding World was changing into a layer of vibration in which all distinct limitation was lost." The halo around Christ's head seemed to radiate into infinity. His garment was the warp and woof of matter, a florescence of matter. The whole Universe vibrated, writes Teilhard, and the very core of his being filled with an "explosive bliss that was completely and utterly unique." He describes himself as looking into the eyes of Christ and being completely at a loss to decipher the expression. Was it "unspeakable agony" or "triumphant joy"? He concludes, "All I know is that, since that occasion, I believe I have seen a hint of it once, and that was in the eyes of a dying soldier."[15]

Teilhard told of a similar experience when he was kneeling in a church before the Blessed Sacrament exposed in a monstrance. At first it seemed like a hallucination: the small white orb began to grow. It expanded until it seemed to be drawing close to him. Then its flow of whiteness enveloped and passed beyond him, overrunning all his surroundings. The brightness penetrated objects at their core and illuminated everything. "So, through the mysterious expansion of the host the whole world had become incandescent, had itself become like a single giant host."[16]

A third experience occurred not in a church but in the trenches at the battle of Verdun.[17] Teilhard, like many priests during combat, kept a pyx inside his jacket, a container like a pocket watch in which he carried the Blessed Sacrament. During a lull in the fighting, as he waited in his dugout, his thoughts turned to the sacrament he bore on his person. At other times he had experienced a sense of strength and joy at the thought of Christ's sacramental presence. But this time his thoughts fixed on the pyx and the separation it represented. He was so close to Christ, yet felt a barrier between them. Even after he opened the pyx and gave himself Holy Communion, he felt no inner penetration. The divine presence seemed to remain outside of him, receding from him even as it drew him on. But then he found a "new complexity" in the depths of his heart, a "marvelous substitution." In place of the sacrament was the universe and "the thousand entities which make up our lives: a suffering, a joy, a task, a friend to love or to console. . . ."

At this "revelation of the universe," Teilhard felt enraptured. He confessed that by temperament he was inclined toward pantheism, but he had never dared to give free rein to such tendencies for fear of their conflicting with his Catholic faith. These experiences convinced him that he had nothing to fear. Ours is a universe in which divine reality, spirit, and matter are intimately intermingled. Like Ignatius after Manresa, Teilhard was now assured that his earlier intuitions were sound.

> Now, since these various experiences (and others as well), I can affirm that I have found my interest in my existence inexhaustible, and my peace indestructible. I live at the heart of a single, unique Element, the Centre of the universe and present in each part of it: personal Love and cosmic Power.[18]

Teilhard wrote of another mystical experience that occurred in 1919, shortly after the war, while he vacationed with friends on the Isle of Jersey. Entitled "The Spiritual Power of Matter," he modeled his account after the biblical story of Elijah, taken up into heaven by a fiery chariot and whirlwind. It appears that Teilhard had come to see himself as something of a prophet—with all the estrangement and loneliness that accompany that unenviable calling. Biblical prophets knew not just the experience of oneness but also profound separation. Giving the ancient story new meaning, Teilhard related the power not only of a single, defined experience, but of a growing inspired intuition that consumed him.

Walking in a deserted place with a companion, Teilhard writes, he saw something in the distance. Gliding over the sand was what looked from afar like a small, vaporous cloud. It grew immense as it approached and then enveloped him. "Invaded" to the depths of his being, he fell to the ground. And like Moses before the burning bush, he asked the name of the power now within him.

I am the fire that consumes and the water that overthrows; I am the love that initiates and the truth that passes away. All that compels acceptance and all that brings renewal; all that breaks apart and all that binds together; power, experiment, progress—matter: all this am I (61).[19]

Here is a poetic apotheosis of matter deriving directly from Teilhard's experience of unitary reality. "Nothing is precious save what is yourself in others and others in yourself. In heaven, all things are but one. In heaven all is one" (62). Like other mystics, Teilhard wrote of a "wave of bliss" ensuing from his experience of oneness. But like the Hebrew prophets, he also felt a fire in his veins. He had a message to proclaim. There were errors to overcome, above all, the ancient fallacies of the Platonists and Manicheans. He experienced himself as given a charge:

Son of earth, steep yourself in the sea of matter, bathe in its fiery waters, for it is the source of your life and your youthfulness.

You thought you could do without it because the power of thought has been kindled in you? You hoped that the more thoroughly you rejected the tangible, the closer you would be to spirit: that you would be more divine if you lived in the world of pure thought, or at least more angelic if you fled the corporeal? Well, you were like to have perished of hunger.

You must have oil for your limbs, blood for your veins, water for your soul, the world of reality for your intellect: do you now see that the very law of your own nature makes these a necessity for you?[20]

"Never say 'matter is accursed, matter is evil,'" Teilhard is instructed, for there came one who said, "This is my body." Purity comes not from withdrawing from matter but from the deepest interpenetration. The noblest theorizing is empty compared to the plenitude of the smallest fact. And now Teilhard begins to see things from a broader perspective. He begins to feel pity for those who take fright at the span of centuries. Those who refuse to accept the reality of evolving matter are like Galileo's accusers.

Despite their denials, "it still moves." And their prohibitions begin to seem merely ridiculous. (Galileo's "it still moves" would eventually become one of Teilhard's favorite references, a plaintive recognition that his lot was not unlike that of the most famous scientist to suffer incomprehension at the hands of leading churchmen.)[21]

The prophet-visionary in Teilhard's autobiographical tale now realized that he would never be the same. His experience had placed him "on another plane," so that even his companions would find him a "stranger." Even "for his brothers in God, better men than he, he would inevitably speak henceforth in an incomprehensible tongue, he whom the Lord had drawn to follow the road of fire."[22] Matter had thrown off its veil of multiplicity, revealing its glorious unity. Teilhard's visionary surrenders himself in faith to the wind sweeping the universe onward. And here, falling to his knees in the fiery chariot that bears him away, he speaks a "Hymn to Matter" in the biblical cadences of a canticle:

> Blessed be you, harsh matter, barren soil, stubborn rock: . . . Blessed be you, mighty matter, irresistible march of evolution, reality ever new-born: . . . the sap of our souls, the hand of God, the flesh of Christ: it is you, matter, that I bless. . . . I acclaim you as the universal power which brings together and unites . . . I acclaim you as the divine *milieu*, charged with creative power, as the ocean stirred by the Spirit, as the clay molded and infused with life by the incarnate Word.[23]

After the war and the profound experiences described here, Teilhard returned to the academic life of the laboratory and the lecture hall, but he would never be the same. Being at once a scientist and priest-mystic, he moved in two diverse, more often than not antagonistic, circles. In Ignatian fashion he tried to reconcile them.

LIVING IN TWO WORLDS

Teilhard resumed his studies at Paris, where he completed his doctorate at the Sorbonne and began teaching at the Institut Catholique. In 1923 he accepted an invitation to join another Jesuit geologist in China, where he spent most of the next two years exploring for fossil remains. Both in Paris and Beijing, his research won him the respect of his colleagues in the scientific community. But science was only half his soul. He wrote at the time that, though science alone could not discover Christ, "Christ fulfills the desires which spring up in our hearts from the teachings of science." Similarly, "without biological evolution which produced the brain, there would be no sanctified souls."[24]

Though he was a staunch adherent to Catholic faith, Teilhard had also become a convinced evolutionist. In a letter to a friend in 1923, he wrote, "I don't know a *single* scientist who is not evolutionist."[25] But the Vatican guardians of theological orthodoxy were not scientists and were anything but evolutionists. A report sent to Jesuit headquarters in Rome related that Teilhard was interpreting the biblical Adam and Eve story as a parable rather than history, raising questions about his views on original sin. Teilhard was required to submit a statement affirming his belief in the traditional doctrine. Reluctantly—and, no doubt, with some mental reservation—he complied. Given the repressive climate in the church, Teilhard's Jesuit superiors in Rome thought it more prudent and safer for him and the Society if he continued his writing and lecturing at some remove from Europe. He was assigned to do his research in China. Teilhard had every reason to regard his oriental sojourn as an exile.

Literally as well as figuratively, Teilhard now lived in two worlds. His return visits to France were brief and sporadic. For the next twenty years he traveled and explored various regions of China as well as Somali, Ethiopia, India, and Burma. In 1929 he collaborated in the excavations that found the well-preserved skull of *Sinanthropus,* the so-called "Peking man" who had lived in Asia circa 400,000 years ago. All together he published some 170 articles and technical papers, primarily on the geological strata and fossils of North China and Asia. His work won him international stature, and he became a sought-after participant at scientific conferences.

His last and longest stay in China corresponded to the years of World War II. Upon his return to France at the end of the war, he found himself something of a celebrity. In recognition of his scientific achievements, the French government promoted him to the rank of officer in the Legion of Honor, and he was eventually offered the prestigious chair of prehistory at the Collège de France. But his early premonition still proved true: his fate was to be that of the prophet—not without honor except among his own people.

Earlier, in 1928, Teilhard's Jesuit superiors in Rome had directed him to confine his attention to science and to refrain from publishing any philosophical or theological writings. Now, twenty years later, after several meetings with the Jesuit general in Rome, Teilhard was told that he would not be allowed to accept the chair offered to him. Moreover, the prohibition against his publishing anything but pure science would remain in effect.

Hoping against hope that the strictures against his publishing would eventually be lifted, Teilhard had continued to unpack the ideas he first committed to writing in the trenches. He had sought to clarify his thoughts on evolution by writing them down and circulating them among a small circle of friends. Now he knew that he would never see his ideas in print. He would never learn what impact they might have or how they might be received by his peers in the academy or his co-religionists in the church. He would never have the benefit of scientific or theological critique so that he might improve his arguments or fine-tune his language.

Two of the works he would never see published stand out from the rest for their importance as attempts to mediate between science and Christian faith. The first, *The Divine Milieu,* was completed in China in 1927 and directed, he wrote, not only to believers but also to those who waver in their faith or who think they have grown beyond it.[26] Teilhard tried to convince them of the intellectual validity of Christian faith in the modern age. He assured his readers that those who listen to the "voices of the earth" have reason to follow the gospel path of Christianity.

The Divine Milieu specifically addresses readers who are aware that "the physical sciences are endlessly extending the abyss of time and space" (13). Confronted by such immensity, many question whether human beings still matter, or whether the Christ of the Gospels and his ancient Jewish God have not been eclipsed by a universe grown dazzlingly vast. Teilhard understood their feelings of anxiety or fascination, but he also felt he could teach them "how to see God everywhere," including in all that is "most hidden, most solid and most ultimate in the world" (15).

Like Ignatius in the *Spiritual Exercises,* Teilhard encouraged his readers "to see things as they are and to see them really and intensely." He calls it a "salutary exercise" to realize that the roots of our spiritual being go back into an unfathomable past. It has required the entire history of the universe for matter to become spirit, a spiritual history reflected in each one of us. Creation was not completed in the distant past but continues today in our work and actions. For those who see aright, nothing we do is devoid of spiritual significance. Our most natural and human labors are continuing creation and building the Kingdom of God (35).

God can be found in the most profane activity—and in our passivity as well. Another "salutary exercise" is to plumb the abyss that is our self and realize the depth and universality of our dependence. Teilhard drew here from his Ignatian spirituality, specifically the contemplation to attain love: all we are and have in life is a gift. What lies at the core of our being, the power to will and to love, is not of our own making. Even before the long decades of discussion over nature versus nurture, whether genes or cultural upbringing affect us more, Teilhard insisted to his readers that our identities, who we are, depends less on the work of our own hands than on what has been given to us (49). None of us is self-made. But then he went on to assure his readers that our receiving, be it from nature or nurture, does not imply passive resignation, whether to suffering or evil in the world.

Teilhard argued strenuously that Christian asceticism has nothing to do with detachment or flight from the world. Jesus revealed a kingdom within us, here and now, slowly transforming and unifying the hearts of humankind (107). The enchantments of earth do us no harm, any more than human endeavor and progress compete with God (137). Rather, God's presence and action in the world occur in us and through us.

Even from this brief description, one can see that there is a great deal in *The Divine Milieu* that is traditional. Teilhard's "salutary exercises" and vision of God's presence imbuing the universe are all conspicuously Ignatian. But there was also much that was novel both in his expression and in the implications Teilhard drew from his Ignatian heritage. Because of this originality, his theological censors never gave him the requisite permission for the book's publication.

Though Teilhard insisted that it was neither philosophical nor theological, *Le phénomène humain* suffered the same fate. Completed in 1940, it is at once his most ambitious, challenging, and celebrated work. The original English translation of its title into *The Phenomenon of Man* is regrettable. *Humain* is more inclusive than "man," and Teilhard's expressed purpose was to give an account of the "whole" human phenomenon.[27] Underlying and infusing that account is the reality of evolution, of which humanity is the axis and arrowhead. Even from a strictly scientific point of view, Teilhard argues, human beings are not an accident of random mutation but the key for understanding the universe.

Teilhard begins his description of the "human phenomenon" with the "profoundly 'atomic' character of the universe." Sand, the stars, even the ashes of the dead—all show that our lives are surrounded by and rest on dust. But the atoms are not inert and indivisible, as once thought, but alive with energy. And they are interrelated in a deeper unity, Teilhard argues, as he weaves a long, complex description of evolution—first at the macroscopic level with the origin of the galaxies and then with the advent and evolution of microscopic life on earth. Even at the lowest evolutionary levels, Teilhard perceived operative principles of increasing complexity, unification, and consciousness. But for the visionary Teilhard, evolution does not end with the appearance of intelligence or the evolution of human beings from lower species, but continues in the course of human social history.

Teilhard could not accept the idea of evolution going nowhere, coming to a dead end—as T. S. Eliot famously put it, "not with a bang but a whimper." If such were the case, he argues, people would become discouraged and cease striving; the age-old process of human development would self-abort. When it came to human progress, Teilhard was a true believer, and he wanted the world to share his optimism. In an effort to correlate evolution with Christian hope, Teilhard developed his concept of an Omega Point, the point of convergence where humanity not so much evolves as "involves" into what St. Paul describes as the "fullness" of Christ, where the divine and human meet. At the center of cosmic history stands the human person, and at the center of human history stands Christ. And the Omega Point of both histories is the same—a God who is "all in everyone."[28] Not the impersonal All of the philosophers but the supremely personal God of the gospel.

Clearly, Teilhard's portrayal of the "human phenomenon" is not based solely on scientific evidence. He integrates the facts of science with the convictions of Christian faith in a vision meant to persuade his readers that each requires the other. Both his elaborations upon the divine milieu and the human phenomenon ultimately have the same twofold aim—to show the world that it needs faith in Christ and to show Christians that they need faith in the world. Teilhard proved himself to be a Christian "apologist" of the highest order, in the original sense of one who explains his faith. As such he was also supremely Jesuit, a self-acknowledged missionary to a culture in which science and technology reigned supreme.

But no matter how sincere or apostolic his intentions, Teilhard's superiors refused to lift the strictures on his publishing; neither would they allow him to reside in France. In 1951 he accepted a research position in New York, where he lived the last four years of his life. He was often depressed and profoundly frustrated, but, remarkably, his letters during those last years betray no signs of bitterness. His superiors knew that they could take his faith and loyalty for granted. Teilhard seems to have successfully cultivated the Ignatian ideal of detachment. If his ideas had merit, they would win a hearing in God's good time. With the permission of a Jesuit superior, Teilhard bequeathed his unpublished manuscripts to a friend. There are, of course, limits to the obedience the church requires— even of Jesuits.

Along with his manuscripts and letters, those unpublished manuscripts also contained Teilhard's diary. The last page of that diary, dated Maundy Thursday, 7 April 1955, consists of a series of equations and phrases. Three times Teilhard describes his "credo" or vision of reality as a form of humanism—"Cosmos-humanism," "Humanism of Cosmogenesis," and "neo-humanism (ultra-Human)."[29] This last phrase is also found in the last essay he ever wrote, completed the month before he died. Entitled "The Christic," Teilhard wrote it as a summary of his essential message: the correspondence between a "converging cosmos" and an "emerging Christ." Love of God and faith in an evolving universe were "the two essential components of the Ultra-human." Both components of this new humanism were to be found "in the air" everywhere, but not necessarily in the same persons. In him, for whatever reason, the two had fused

> not as yet with sufficient force to spread explosively—but strong enough nevertheless to make it clear that the process is possible—and that sooner or later there will be a chain reaction. This is one more proof that Truth has to appear only once, in one single mind, for it to be impossible for anything ever to prevent it from spreading universally and setting everything ablaze.[30]

Teilhard died of a heart attack on Easter Sunday, April 10, 1955. A handful of mourners attended his funeral at St. Ignatius church in New York City, and his body was transported for burial at the Jesuit novitiate in Poughkeepsie, New York. Because the ground was too wet, digging the grave had to be delayed. As a consequence, no mourners were present for the burial.[31] Teilhard died and was buried in the obscurity he believed to be his destiny. But then his manuscripts were taken to a publisher. . . .

TEILHARD'S LEGACY

Appearing in print the same year its author died, *Le Phénomène Humain* became a literary phenomenon. Theologians and scientists do not ordinarily read, let alone applaud, the same book, but here was a unique synthesis of the intellectual, social, and spiritual achievements of the last hundred years. Ecologist Thomas Berry called it the closest thing we have to a "Summa of the modern mode of consciousness."[32] For like reasons, Mortimer Adler, the intellectual father of the Great Books movement, listed it among the great books of the twentieth century.

Teilhard's posthumously published essays now number thirteen volumes, not including several collections of letters. Their appearance from the late fifties to midseventies created a generation of devoted readers along with a host of books and articles of commentary and critique.[33] As one might expect, some scientists criticized Teilhard for going beyond the evidence and mixing science with mysticism. But this mixing was integral to Teilhard's intentions. He firmly believed that evolutionary science demonstrated what mystics had always affirmed—the unity of the universe.[34]

On the other side of the spectrum, the Vatican issued a *monitum* or warning in 1962 that not all of Teilhard's ideas could be accepted uncritically, and that seminary authorities should not allow his books to be placed on their library shelves. (The warning, however, said nothing about having his books available for purchase in the seminary bookstores.) The *monitum* was hardly surprising. Teilhard was unconventional in expressing his vision of reality. His notion of Christ's "cosmic nature" collided with the canonized divine-human, two-nature language of traditional Catholic theology. But there was also no denying his influence upon the Second Vatican Council, especially the world-affirming optimism of its Constitution on the Church in the Modern World *(Gaudium et Spes)*, a document that would itself be criticized by church conservatives for being too optimistic about human nature.

Sharing the optimism of Teilhard and that of the conciliar document was Pedro Arrupe, who in 1965 was elected the new superior general of the Jesuits. Despite the Vatican monitum, Teilhard continued to enjoy tremendous popularity, especially among Catholic intellectuals. In his first press conference as general, Arrupe was asked his opinion of Teilhard. His response, while tactful, was fully affirmative. Teilhard's thought was difficult to penetrate; he was not a professional theologian; still, there was more to praise in his work than to fault. Arrupe defended Teilhard as one of the leading thinkers of the day, whose writings were exercising a beneficial influence on the scientific community. His attempt to reconcile the world of science and that of faith was "completely in line with the mission of the Society of Jesus."[35]

By 1981, the centenary of Teilhard's birth, even the Holy See rectified its prior negative opinions. In a letter issued in the name of Pope John Paul II, the Vatican Secretary of State acknowledged Teilhard as "a man seized by Christ in the very depths of his being, and who struggled to honor at once faith and reason."[36] Teilhard's innovative thinking finally received a word of approval from his church's leaders—posthumously, like Galileo and the prophets to whose fate he had compared his own.

Among Teilhard's legacies is the fact that Roman Catholics generally do not join ranks with fundamentalist Protestants who denounce evolution as an unproven hypothesis. Thanks to Teilhard and a handful of intrepid biblical scholars, Catholic schools today, even at the primary level, regularly teach the Genesis stories of Adam and Eve as figurative rather than historical. Catholics need not choose between science and religion, as if the Bible and biology were in conflict. Even the 1981 Vatican letter praising Teilhard referred to his acute perception of the "dynamics of creation" and "his fearless optimism faced with the evolution of the world."[37]

Thanks much to Teilhard, Catholic theologians today generally interpret creation as an ongoing process, not an event that occurred once, sometime in the distant past. Within this ongoing, evolutionary process of creation, Teilhard placed the person of Jesus, the doctrine of redemption, and the whole history of salvation. Here is one of the most significant changes taking place in Christian theology today—a deeper appreciation, in the words of St. Paul, that "the whole creation has been groaning in travail" and "will be set free from its bondage" (Rom 8:21–22). Salvation and spirituality, within this Pauline-Teilhardian perspective, interrelate with the whole of creation.

Under the influence of Platonic philosophy, Christian writers for 2,000 years tended to divide matter and spirit into disparate, antithetical realities. Described metaphorically, living a spiritual life was viewed as an "ascent" to God (as in the "Purgatorio" and "Paradiso" of Dante's *Divine Comedy*), one that leaves the world behind. Love for God necessitated rising above, if not escaping from, the world and the flesh, both commonly regarded as the devil's domain. Teilhard is largely responsible for a fundamental shift away from this Platonic perspective. If, as he insisted, spirit is not alien or opposed to matter, but an outgrowth of it, we experience God precisely by uniting ourselves with the material world and with one another, ascending to the divine by converging with the cosmos.

In contrast to the traditional, otherworldly perspective, Teilhard's is a world-affirming as well as cosmic mysticism.[38] Very much in the tradition of Ignatian spirituality, Teilhard affirmed God's presence in all things, but he expanded the humanism of the tradition to cosmic proportions. He recognized that the beginnings of creation go back not a mere few thousand years but into what he called an "abyss of time." Today, even more clearly than Teilhard and his contemporaries in the 1950s, we know that the cosmos began to evolve some fifteen billion years ago. The evolution of life began nearly four billion years ago; the human species split from its primate relations about five million years ago. If, as Ignatius saw it, God is busily at work in creation, the enterprise has been going on much longer than Ignatius ever imagined. And the Ignatian ideal of helping to make God's presence palpable in the world has come to involve more than Ignatius—or even Teilhard—imagined.

Several decades now after his death, Teilhard deserves to be recognized as ahead of his time with respect to both his scientific and religious views. Yet, with the notable exception of evolutionary theorist Sir Julian Huxley, the biological community has paid little tribute to Teilhard's memory—perhaps because he was a priest, perhaps because he bewildered them. He used the word *science* in its broader, French meaning—as "knowledge" or "learning," like the German *Wissenschaft*—to include his visionary, theological, mystical ideas along with the raw data, hypotheses, and theories of "hard science" in the Anglo-American sense of the word.

Teilhard preceded most of his scientific peers in his appreciation of "deep time," the vast stretches of years it has taken for life to evolve to its present state. Without using the term, Teilhard's *Phenomenon* anticipated by several decades the idea of "punctuated equilibrium," which describes evolution as more like going up a flight of stairs than an inclined plane. He also anticipated evolution as the key integrating concept in science today, describing the process whereby atoms give rise to complex molecules, molecules to more complex cells, and cells to higher organisms. Teilhard was one of the first scientists in the last century to recognize that the entire cosmos is in a momentous process, and that its potential for life, including intelligent life, was there at the very beginning.

If Teilhard was ahead of his colleagues in the scientific community, what can be said of church leaders and theologians, who by and large still think and write as if Darwin never existed?[39] Teilhard realized early on the implications of evolution for religious thought, not only with respect to biblical creation stories but also to the very nature of God. Evolution, Teilhard knew, makes popular images of God as an Intelligent Designer (Watchmaker), Prime Mover (Puppeteer), or First Cause (Engineer) utterly inadequate. Ideas like an unfinished creation and deep time require new thinking about Providence.

Teilhard was more than open to the possible existence of intelligent life on counterparts to Earth in every galaxy of the universe (in other words, on millions of them). That possibility (which he saw as more likely than its contrary) has far-reaching implications for our thinking about sin, Christ, and redemption. He was adamant that the spatial idea of a "supernatural" had to be replaced by that of a future-oriented "ultra-human," that the God of evolution is an "ever-greater God," making it necessary to envision an "ever-greater Christ." What does a concept like salvation mean if humankind is, in Teilhard's words, "a *cosmic* phenomenon, not *primarily* an aesthetic, moral or religious one"? [40]

If evolution challenges traditional theology, it obviously does the same to traditional thinking about spirituality. Teilhard acknowledged the distance (he called it an "abyss") between his own religious vision of the universe and that of the "great Ignatius," but he insisted that there was no contradiction between them. As he wrote to a Jesuit friend just days before his death, he believed that the Ignatian Spiritual Exercises are "magnificently transposable in terms of a Universe in genesis."[41] In that same letter, with an eye to the worldly aspect of his own Ignatian spirituality, he referred to the need for "a special theological-mystical formation of laboratory priests, researcher-priests and worker-priests." Today, he would no doubt express himself in terms of the "extended Ignatian family" or the entire community of spiritual humanists. We do not rise to the divine by turning our backs on the Earth.

But for all his clairvoyance, Teilhard was not without blind spots. Despite his world-affirming mysticism, Teilhard was not appreciably responsive to the fragility of the Earth's ecosystem or the threat that human beings could pose to other forms of life on our planet. He was unabashedly optimistic about the powers of science and technology to discover answers and solve problems. Like most of his generation, he did not sufficiently appreciate the destructive aspects of progress. Endangered species, toxic waste, environmental pollution, acid rain—phrases now all too familiar to our ears, would have sounded strange to his. Teilhard appears unsuspecting of the dangers that unchecked urban and industrial expansion poses to the quality of human life or to hundreds of thousands of life forms that took hundreds of millions of years to evolve.

Despite their remarkable resilience, our planet and its biosphere require more care and cultivation than Teilhard realized. He was consumed by the idea of evolution, not ecology. He wrote of building the Earth, not protecting it. Obviously these ideas are not mutually exclusive. Our task, Teilhard insisted, is to continue God's creation. Forty years after him, no great leap of logic is required on our part to see that building the Earth entails its nurturance as well. By integrating spirit with matter and the human species with all other species of life on this planet, Teilhard's wide-ranging synthesis provides a singular foundation for the "ecological spirituality" that is being developed today.[42] Teilhard's take on Ignatian spirituality, not less than that of Ignatius, is open to accommodation.

Teilhard's "neo-humanism" includes the concept of a "living Earth" that gives rise to spirit. Even if Teilhard did not himself take it in that direction, his Ignatian humanism invites a sense of reverence and responsibility for all the variety and wonder of life on this planet. It allows us to see our lives and spiritual destiny as intimately intertwined with all the rest of life on Earth. This is the kind of development of Teilhard's thought that Thomas Berry presented in his own *Dream of the Earth*.[43] For many years the president of the American Teilhard Association, Berry augmented Teilhard's love of the Earth with a sense of obligation toward it. His arguments are compelling. Any humanism today that focuses only on human beings risks being irrelevant. Any spirituality that does not embrace the Earth in all its precious biological diversity lacks seriousness and integrity.

Much like Dante's vision of reality in the *Divine Comedy*, Teilhard's vision and his exposition of it are broad and complex. A summary such as this can only be suggestive, inviting the reader to turn to the works of Teilhard himself. Only time will tell whether Teilhard's work will enter the canon of classics. In the meantime, even after fifty years, he deserves to be read for his courageous integration of science and faith. For Teilhard, as for Dante, the force that moves the stars is the same that moves human hearts. In the context of his cosmic vision, if we embrace the humanist dictum that nothing human is foreign to us, neither is this tender and living Earth.

SIX

~

KARL RAHNER

I have encountered God directly and, as well as I could, I wanted to communicate such experiences to others. . . . I have experienced God, the nameless and unfathomable One, silent and yet near to me in Triune self-giving. . . . I have experienced not human words about God, but God's very self. . . . This experience is indeed grace, and there is really no one to whom it is denied. Of this I was quite sure.[1]

The words are Karl Rahner's and, though he put them into the mouth of Ignatius Loyola, the words spoke for both men. In the many interviews he gave toward the end of his life, Rahner always preferred to talk about his theology or the state of the church; he was rarely forthcoming about himself. So it comes as no surprise that, except with a small circle of trusted friends, he was reluctant to talk about his own experiences of God.[2] Something so personal has to be teased out of writings like this one, in which Rahner presumed to speak to his fellow Jesuits in Ignatius's name. If such a literary device insinuates a certain presumption on his part, it also testifies to a profound sense of identification with the kind of mystical experiences Ignatius claimed. Rahner would later call this essay his "spiritual testament." It provides as clear an insight into the man as he ever wrote and a key to what lies at the heart of his theology.

Karl Rahner was without question a towering figure in the religious thought of the twentieth century. Historians may well rank him someday alongside such theological giants as Origen, Augustine, and Thomas Aquinas; like them he changed the way Christians look at things. Virtually no area of Catholic theology is quite the same now as it was before him.[3] Today, in an age still marked by old religious hostilities and new fundamentalisms, most Roman Catholics along with numerous other Christians think differently and relate differently to people of other faiths and of no apparent faith—because of him.

Rahner insisted that today's Christians, and especially theologians, need to live in today's world. He criticized church leaders who preferred to live in intellectual ghettos or in some previous century presumed to have been more congenial to faith. Living out his own advice, Rahner subjected himself to the real-life questions, doubts, and sometimes despair brought to him by his twentieth-century contemporaries. He sought to answer their queries by boring into the teachings of the church, the fathers, and medieval theologians, and asking what those doctrines have to say to our day. In this way he revitalized some of the oldest fossils in Christian tradition, making something new of them.

The topics Rahner wrote about were as far-ranging as his theological output was vast. His bibliography contains some 4,000 titles—books, lexicons, dictionaries, but mostly articles written in response to specific pastoral questions. His books in various translations number some 2,000 volumes, with paperback sales in excess of a million copies. They speak, as one would expect, of God and Christ, sin and grace. But there are also reflections on provocative issues like the courage to remain in a sinful church, the ordination of women, and the maturity required to take responsibility for one's own decisions. Writing on such mundane matters as working, sleeping, laughing, and eating, he created as well a "theology of everyday things." Which is not to say that Rahner ever makes for easy reading.

The obscurity of Rahner's prose is proverbial. (An old chestnut has his brother Hugo promising to translate him someday into German.) Especially in his younger years, Rahner felt the need to nuance and qualify every statement to safeguard against any suspicions that he was straying beyond the bounds of orthodoxy. To prevent his being quoted out of context, he would write a sentence a half-page long; he could sum up an entire theology of a doctrine like grace in a series of secondary clauses.

Rahner's writing became less opaque in his old age, but even then he maintained his fondness for understatement and indirection, compounding conditional sentences with multiple participles. Some of his early works, though seminal, are among his most difficult, since in them he was addressing elites educated in the language and categories of German philosophy. But in his seventies he could speak to the questions of young people in their late teens and early twenties and answer them in language that spoke to their hearts.[4] Neither is it happenstance that two of his most accessible works, no less important or substantive than his more scholarly essays, are collections of prayers, one written at the beginning of his career and the other at the end.

Understanding Rahner requires patience and effort. It helps to know some of the philosophical terminology that would have been familiar to his educated German readers. Just as helpful is the realization that his experience of the Spiritual Exercises became the "existential root out of which he did his thinking."[5] Even at its most philosophical and abstract, there is a unity that runs like a thread through all his thinking, best described as Ignatian. Perhaps that should come as no surprise, considering that the Society of Jesus was Rahner's spiritual home for sixty-two years.

But being a Jesuit does not guarantee Ignatian thinking. Few Jesuits have examined the assumptions and implications of the Ignatian exercises as thoroughly as Rahner did. More than once he complained about his forebears and colleagues in the Society who forgot or neglected some of the basic insights of their founder. Rahner had read Augustine and Aquinas, Kant and Hegel; he had studied under Martin Heidegger. But when asked about the influences that had molded his theology, he answered candidly, "I think that the spirituality of Ignatius himself, which one learned through the practice of prayer and religious formation, was more significant for me than all learned philosophy and theology inside and outside the order."[6]

Of all the subjects studied in this survey of Ignatian humanists, Rahner's life is the least exciting. He was never wounded in battle or imprisoned by the Inquisition, as Ignatius was, though he did have a brush with the same kind of heresy hunters. Unlike Ricci or de Nobili, Rahner never left home for long. He did not have to suffer ignominy like Spee or exile like Teilhard. In his later years Rahner would describe his life as inseparable from his work. He refused even to consider writing his memoirs. The most he would do was to give interviews in which he would look back at one or another event or influence in his life and in that context try to explain some aspect of his theology. "I did not lead a life," he once remarked. "I worked, wrote, taught, tried to do my duty and earn my living. I tried in this ordinary way to serve God—that's it."[7]

Rahner's life may have been unexciting, but it did not go unexamined. And if thinking and theology were his life, it was his thinking about ordinary, uneventful lives like his own that made his theology attractive to so many readers: the fact that he was able to speak to people whose lives were equally everyday and uneventful. But within those everyday lives he was able to help them find mystery—the awesome mystery that is the human person and the absolute mystery that is God.

EARLY LIFE AND WRITINGS

Rahner's ordinary life began March 5, 1904, in the small Black Forest city of Freiburg im Breisgau. He was fourth of seven children in a modest, middle-class family. His father taught German, French, and history in a teachers' college, where he later became an assistant principal. That made him an official of the Grand Duke of Baden. Rahner grew up under a monarchy, and as a child his family celebrated the Kaiser's birthday.[8]

There was nothing about the young Karl Rahner that would indicate his future fame. He belonged to a Catholic youth group, similar to the Boy Scouts, with whom he enjoyed climbing up the mountain crest near Freiburg. Along with Protestant and Jewish boys in his neighborhood, he attended a state-sponsored *Gymnasium* (a six-year school equivalent to our high school and junior college), where he was an "average pupil who found lessons boring."[9] His diploma indicates that his overall score was "almost good."[10]

In his last year Rahner decided he wanted to become a priest. Hugo, Karl's older brother by four years, had entered the Jesuits three years earlier, and Karl decided to follow suit. Rahner's religion teacher, on hearing the news of Karl's decision, was skeptical and did not expect him to last. "No, Karl isn't suited for that. He's too withdrawn and grumpy. He should become something else."[11] Despite his teacher's opinion, Rahner lasted sixty years in the Society—but the adjective seems to have been appropriate. Years later writer Mario von Galli also characterized the already famous Rahner as having a "grumpy charm."

Rahner entered the Jesuits in 1922 and made the Spiritual Exercises for the first time. After spending two years in the novitiate, and before beginning his formal studies in philosophy, he authored his first published article under the title "Why Prayer Is Indispensable."[12] We do not know how it came to be published. It appears to be a sermon developing the biblical text, "Draw near to God and God will draw near to you" (Jas 4:8). If we did not know it was Rahner's first published work, the brief devotional piece could be described as unremarkable. But knowing it to be the youthful work of a future master, we find it telling that from the very beginning Rahner concerned himself with questions of spiritual practice.

He opens with a question, "What should your heart be like?" He goes on, "As the Holy, Eternal One would have it . . . like the heart of Christ . . . as you yourself would long for when God's Spirit fills you . . . when you long to lose yourself. . . . We must pray! For then we are far from the small everyday world that makes us insignificant and narrow. Then we draw near to God and become capable of 'touching our Creator and

Lord.'" The phrase is a direct quote from Ignatius's *Spiritual Exercises,* the twentieth annotation. Rahner continues, "But where God's-self is communicated to a creature . . . the soul recognizes its nothingness, emptiness, weakness. . . ." Here we find another direct reference to the *Spiritual Exercises.* The fifteenth annotation, which concerns God's self-giving, would become a constant refrain in Rahner's theology.

Since, as a Jesuit novice, he had just made the Spiritual Exercises and was studying them along with other Ignatian texts, it is not surprising that Rahner would refer to them in this, his first published essay. But anyone who knows his later work cannot help but notice topics in the earliest essays of his youth that he would later develop into major themes: his starting point with the human heart, emblematic for him of human emptiness and longing; his description of God as self-giving and capable of being sensibly "touched." If in later life Rahner complained about Jesuits not reflecting enough on the implications of Ignatius's spiritual insights, it was a fault he did not tolerate in himself.[13]

Rahner prepared for the priesthood at a time marked by a rigidity difficult to appreciate today. The lectures, textbooks, all of his studies were not only in Latin, but also framed in medieval, Neo-Scholastic categories nobody thought in anymore. The Vatican at the end of the nineteenth century had made it compulsory that all seminaries teach nothing but the philosophical and theological thought of St. Thomas Aquinas, but not in the original form with its questions, answers, and objections. Instead students memorized Latin definitions and distinctions from simplified handbooks. At Vatican behest, only the language of St. Thomas and of Aristotle before him was acceptable for the expression of Catholic faith. And no more than in the days when Renaissance humanists faulted its lack of warmth was it a language conducive to speaking to the human heart.

Rahner studied the Neo-Scholastic handbooks. His command of the tradition would stand him in good stead when he had to defend his orthodoxy before Vatican heresy hunters. But Rahner had a love of history that he inherited from his father and shared with his brother Hugo. Most likely under Hugo's influence, he spent considerable free time studying patristic writings, reading virtually all the church fathers of the second century. He was especially interested in what they had to say about mystical experience and how one knew when one had experienced God. In 1932 Rahner had his first scholarly essay published (in French!) on the "spiritual senses" according to Origen. The next year his second scholarly publication was on the "spiritual senses" in the Middle Ages, in particular in the writings of St. Bonaventure.

From Origen Rahner became convinced that all knowledge of God is more or less mystical, without a person necessarily having a genuine mystical understanding.[14] On the basis of Bonaventure's authority, Rahner would warn against putting too much weight on words like *knowledge.* Ecstasy is a matter of affectivity. "Mystical union is an entry into darkness, into a divine obscurity."[15] On the other hand, in a work on "Asceticism and Mysticism in the Patristic Period," Rahner expressed concern that spirituality not be seen as only a matter of experience and an enthusiastic heart.[16] Questions regarding spirituality must also be treated with critical reflection, which in turn requires historical investigation of church tradition. Rahner was never one merely to repeat the tradition, however. "Every age has its own questions," he wrote. The church fathers did not confront the same issues we do. We cannot expect them to answer our questions for us. Rahner studied the past but insisted on living in the present.

Thanks to one of his seminary professors, Rahner was exposed to more than medieval Thomism. He read Immanuel Kant, Martin Heidegger, and his fellow Jesuit, Belgian philosopher Joseph Maréchal. Like other Catholic thinkers, Maréchal was required to base his arguments on the thought of Thomas Aquinas, but he tried to correlate Aquinas's theory of knowledge with Kantian philosophy. Kant's critique of reason had seemed to destroy the possibility of our knowing anything beyond factual knowledge of the here and now. How could we know about an absolute, infinite God, when all we perceive in the world around us is relative and finite? Maréchal tried to use Kant's own method of asking what conditions are necessary to make a factual reality possible, thus transcending that reality. He developed what came to be called "transcendental Thomism." Rahner found the approach attractive and fruitful for his own future thinking. What conditions, he would come to ask, are necessary for one to have an experience of a self-giving, self-revealing God?

In 1932, in Munich, Rahner was ordained a priest. A year later, in Austria, he made his tertianship, a traditional break from studies during which Jesuits make the Spiritual Exercises a second time. It is also a time for Jesuits to work on retreat talks they will give based on the exercises. Rahner went further and used the opportunity to begin developing a theology of the Ignatian exercises and writing a commentary on them. His commentary would eventually appear as *Reflections on the Ignatian Book of Exercises.*[17] But, as even so cursory a summary as this makes clear, virtually everything Rahner wrote in his first years as a Jesuit bears the imprint of the Spiritual Exercises and the profound impact they had made on his thinking.

FREIBURG AND INNSBRUCK

After completing his seminary training, Rahner was given two years to earn a doctorate in philosophy at a German university; his superiors had decided that he would teach the history of philosophy in a Jesuit seminary. Rahner's heart had been set on teaching theology, not philosophy, but his superiors had spoken. In good Jesuit fashion—at least when it came to matters of mission and ministry—he acquiesced to their wishes. He decided to return to his hometown to study at the University of Freiburg, where he could hear the lectures of the renowned Martin Heidegger.

An antimodernist and conservative Catholic in his early years, Heidegger had broken with the Catholic Church in 1919, when he was thirty, though he continued to be influenced by religious thinkers like Luther and Kierkegaard.[18] In 1928, however, he shifted once again in his thinking and became positively hostile to Christianity, which he saw as a decadent falling away from the primordial experience of early Greek philosophy. He became an enthusiastic reader of Nietzsche and a supporter of National Socialism, confident that the Nazis could overcome what he regarded as the unwelcome effects of modernity and liberal democratic institutions. By the late 1930s he began to shift yet again, this time away from Nietzsche's anti-Christianity, and after the war he came full circle as he returned to a topic that had interested him in his youth, medieval mysticism. What is most pertinent here is that it was in the years 1934 to 1936, during Heidegger's anti-Christian period, that Rahner and a fellow Jesuit, Johann Lotz, chose to study philosophy at Freiburg.

At a time when Germany was ruled by brownshirts and Heidegger was still openly hostile to Christianity, particularly to Catholicism, Rahner and Lotz did not know how two Jesuits in clerical black would be received. So they registered as doctoral candidates with the safe, uncontroversial Martin Honecker, who held the chair of Catholic philosophy at Freiburg. They attended Heidegger's lectures, however, and were delighted when Heidegger accepted them into his seminar—no little honor for the two would-be philosophers.

Heidegger had become famous in 1927 for his book *Being and Time,* a descriptive analysis or phenomenology of Being—not Being as a concept *(Sein)* but as existence here and now, in a particular time and place *(Dasein,* the German for "being there"). Though Heidegger did not expressly raise the question of God in the book, Rahner, like other theologians (e.g., Rudolph Bultmann, Paul Tillich) found his thought suggestive for Christian thinking, especially the idea of the human person as "addressed" by Being and the notion of a "history of Being." It has been argued that much of Heidegger's thinking was amenable to Christian theology precisely because so many elements of it were drawn from Christian sources.[19]

Whatever the provenance of Heidegger's ideas, Rahner would come to credit him for teaching his students to read texts in a new way and to ask what is behind the text.[20] Heidegger would also confirm Rahner's natural bent to raise radical questions—above all, to confront the radical questionability of our existence. He taught Rahner to see human existence as constantly impacted, though not always consciously, by the distant horizon of death. He convinced Rahner that historicity, the fact that we exist in time and therefore history, affects every aspect of our being. Rahner found the idea not only philosophically compelling but theologically significant. A century earlier Kierkegaard had pointed out that the very concepts of time and history were Judeo-Christian discoveries. Rahner would later argue that historicity is a "profoundly Christian concept" precisely because Christian theology is about salvation, which it presents as revealed and mediated historically.[21]

Rahner would come to describe Heidegger as a "kind of mystagogue in philosophy."[22] The ancient, though now rarely used word, refers to a pedagogue who leads others into mystery, in this case the mystery of being. This was certainly high praise for someone who, at the time Rahner studied under him, was not only a self-described apostate but a ferocious critic of Christianity. Certainly under Heidegger, if not earlier, Rahner began learning from personal experience the importance of discernment; he could find truth in the thinking of even those hostile to the church and its teaching. Rejecting the idea of God did not necessarily make a person all wrong or completely wicked. It was a lesson Rahner would confront and reflect on more than once.

In the summer of 1935, after a year of seminars and lectures, Rahner commenced writing the dissertation required for a doctorate in philosophy. As noted above, he had registered as a doctoral candidate with the safe, conventional historian of Catholic philosophy, Martin Honecker. Since Catholic orthodoxy in those days was identified with the thinking of Thomas Aquinas, Rahner chose a topic that prima facie would seem equally safe—Aquinas's philosophy of human knowledge. But the conclusions he drew from it were anything but conventional.

Rahner wrote his dissertation on an article in the *Summa Theologiae* (Part I, Q. 84, art. 7) in which Thomas maintains that all human knowledge, even the most theoretical and abstract, begins first and foremost in the world of experience, with the intellect turning to images (phantasms) drawn from experience. From this Rahner argues for an original unity between the spiritual intellect and material sensibility; neither can be encountered in itself, we can only differentiate them from each other in their unity. Here Rahner breaks with the Platonic notion of the human person consisting of body and soul as two separate realities. We are essentially spiritual, but spirituality is not something separate or alien from matter. Spirit emerges from matter, when matter becomes aware of itself. Long before Teilhard's ideas on evolution appeared in print, Rahner was thinking along similar lines.

Clearly in conversation with Immanuel Kant, Rahner's dissertation begins and remains centered on the human person as thinking and knowing. But we are above all persons who question, who have the power of "reaching out" *(Vorgriff)* beyond our immediate experience of individual beings and asking the question of being itself in its totality. Here Rahner is clearly reading Thomas Aquinas while thinking like Martin Heidegger. But Rahner then goes beyond Heidegger when he concludes that we encounter ourselves most truly when we ask about ourselves and experience ourselves as infinite longing, as "reaching out" and striving but never being fulfilled. Finding ourselves in a material world not of our making, we encounter ourselves as spiritual, which is to say as human, when we find ourselves asking the question about God.

Rahner's dissertation is one of the most seminal, difficult, and original works he would ever write—too original, in the opinion of his dissertation director. Martin Honecker was a solid scholar with a command of historical data, but he was not himself a creative philosopher. What he expected from Rahner was an objective, historical presentation of Aquinas's thinking; instead he was handed a creative, subjective interpretation. Rahner was not merely reporting on Thomas's philosophy, he was doing philosophy by building on Thomas.

Dissatisfied with Rahner's submission, Honecker wanted him to rework parts of it (hardly an unusual request for any dissertation director to make). In the meantime, however, Rahner's superiors changed their earlier decision about his future career; someone was needed to teach theology at the Jesuit University of Innsbruck, Austria, where Rahner had studied as a seminarian. He was delighted. He never returned to his dissertation and never earned a doctorate in philosophy. Instead, three years later, his dissertation was published without revisions as *Spirit in the World*.[23] Martin Honecker, who died unexpectedly in 1941, never knew that he would go down in history—unfairly to be sure—as the man who "flunked" Karl Rahner.

Rahner returned to Innsbruck in 1936, where in short order he produced a theological dissertation on the church originating from the side of Christ, an investigative analysis of the symbolism in John 19:34.[24] He began teaching theology at the university in July 1937. That same year a little book of meditations he had written appeared in print. Eventually translated into English as *Encounters in Silence*, the original German title reads as "Words into Silence." The latter more accurately suggests the contents and tone of the prayers, which sometimes soar like poetry and other times cry out in protest, pain, and confusion, but invariably end in silent awe before the mystery that is God.[25] Here was Rahner translating into concrete terms what he meant by our humanity being constituted by "reaching out" for meaning, love, and fulfillment. His little book of meditations proved that Rahner could speak to people's hearts as well as their heads and would earn him a reputation far beyond theological circles.

Earlier that same year, Rahner was invited to participate in a study week at Salzburg. He used the opportunity to lecture on the philosophy of religion, theology, and their relationship. The result was a theological anthropology that Rahner, building on the ideas of his dissertation, published as *Hearers of the Word*.[26] Rahner asks the question: What is necessary for human beings to hear God's voice, to receive a revelation from the essentially Unknown God? God's free grace, certainly, but also the human capacity to listen and receive a possible revelation, which Rahner identifies with human spirituality, once again defined as "perpetual reaching out." In a world of finite beings, we reach out, never satisfied, in "infinite openness" for more, for Absolute Being, and thereby, even if unconsciously, for the Unknown God. In our reaching out for knowledge, for fulfillment—know it or not, like it or not—we are already standing before God and on the way to God.

But ours is a sensate spirituality; we are material beings in time and space and therefore history. We come to knowledge only by turning toward individual beings in time and space and therefore history. And we are also free to love or not, to listen or not, for a revelation from God, who may freely speak or not. And where we find freedom—indeed only where we find the uniqueness and unpredictability of freedom—there and only there do we find genuine historicity. Rahner argues Heidegger's point from a theological basis: temporality, or historicity, is intrinsic to human personhood.

Rahner draws corollaries from the foregoing that would become pivotal for his theology. To be spiritual, human beings must be essentially oriented toward history. If there is such a thing as a revelation from God, it is necessarily in history. We become more spiritual and have access to God only by entering and penetrating deeply into the historical time and place in which we live. Rahner breaks here radically with the centuries-old Christian Neoplatonism that saw spirituality as an escape from the merely temporal world. He regarded such attempts at escape as "inhuman" and "unspiritual." As sensate spiritual beings, we find God *in* the world, not outside it, and *in* history, not above it.

WAR AND ITS AFTERMATH

That Rahner could claim that we find God in the time and place in which we live is all the more remarkable when we consider that he was coming to these conclusions during the midthirties, when Adolf Hitler and the Nazis had taken hold of the reins of government in Germany. Rahner would come to describe the period as a time of "collective madness," and even in old age could not explain what he called the "Hitler phenomenon"—how such a "primitive man" could attract and sway even people of character and morality.[27] Rahner claimed no credit for not being swayed himself. As a priest, and particularly as a Jesuit, he would be labeled from the outset as *Reichsfeind,* an enemy of the Third Reich.

As an international order historically tied closely to the Vatican, the Jesuits had long been perceived as hostile to the interests of German nationalists; one need point only to the specifically anti-Jesuit (1872) legislation of Bismarck's *Kulturkampf* against the Catholic Church. The Nazis' pagan, anti-Christian, racist ideology was even more at odds with Catholicism and met with early opposition from Jesuits, most saliently from Fr. Rupert Mayer. Mayer was a former chaplain in the German army, had been decorated as a war hero, and was a powerful voice in the public life of Munich. His outspoken criticism of the Nazis is credited with contributing greatly to the Nazis' defeat in the plebiscite of 1923.

Though a number of individual Jesuits were initially taken in by Nazi posturing to be a bulwark against Communism, very early into the years of the Third Reich it was apparent that, not totally unlike its war against the Jews, Hitler's regime had initiated what has been called a "war against the Jesuits."[28] Even before the invasion of Poland and World War II, the Nazis began closing Jesuit publications and schools and confiscating Jesuit residences. Jesuits resisted Nazi efforts to incorporate Catholic youth groups into the *Hitler-Jugend*. Records indicate that already in April of 1935, the Gestapo had sent out confidential instructions entitled "Safeguarding against the Jesuits," which pointed out the Jesuits' public opposition to the Nazis.[29]

The Nazis put German Jesuits, more than other clergy, under particularly close surveillance. Any perceived opposition was excuse enough for the Gestapo to call them in for questioning. Harassed, in instances subjected to show trials, scores of German Jesuits were also sentenced to concentration camps, especially Dachau.[30] Among the more notable German Jesuits who actively resisted the Nazis was Augustin Rösch, Provincial of the Upper German province; his example is credited with steeling the courage of German bishops to mount similar resistance. The most famous Jesuit target of Nazi persecution, however, was Alfred Delp. For his active association with the Kreisau circle, a group that met to discuss matters like a spiritual foundation for a new kind of Germany after the Nazis' defeat, Delp was tried for treason in 1945 and condemned to death. He wrote from his prison cell shortly before his execution by hanging that he could have escaped the sentence if he had been willing to renounce his membership in the Society of Jesus: "The actual reason for my condemnation," he wrote, "was that I happened to be, and chose to remain, a Jesuit."[31]

Rahner knew Delp well indeed and had taught him Latin back in their seminary days. In 1943 Delp visited Rahner in Vienna, where Rahner spent most of the war years. Four months after the Nazis annexed Austria and marched triumphantly into Vienna (March 1938), they abolished the theological faculty at Innsbruck. Rahner and the other Jesuits were given three days to move out. They resided at a Jesuit college in the area until October 1939, when this too was expropriated. The local Nazi leader put Rahner under a "district prohibition," which banished him altogether from the Tyrol region of what was then "Greater Germany." Rahner was invited to work at a pastoral institute administered by the Archdiocese of Vienna.

If Rahner's was an ordinary, uneventful life, the war years in Vienna were the exception. Whether as a priest in the pulpit, a lecturer, or a pastoral counselor, he quietly presented the Christian vision of the human person, diametrically opposed to the Nazi propaganda that touted "Führer, Volk, and Vaterland." At the Pastoral Institute he would become a pastoral theologian, drawing from his knowledge to answer doubts of conscience. He addressed the questions not only of priests but also of lay people. He did pastoral work among students and began meeting with Lutheran theologians. In 1944, as the Soviet army beat back the Germans, Rahner was assigned to serve in the village of Mariakirchen in Lower Bavaria; there he spent the last year of the war giving pastoral care to the villagers and refugees from the advancing eastern front.

Looking back at the "collective madness" of the times and reflecting on the Jesuits' response to the atrocities of the Nazis, Rahner admitted that "resistance could have been greater and more explicit." But he pointed out that "Delp wasn't the only one who was killed by the Nazis. There is an entire list of other Jesuits, both German and Austrian, who were executed under National Socialism." He confessed his incomprehension, even in hindsight, as to what one should have done under those conditions.[32] If Rahner had ever entertained any illusions of optimism about human nature, they were certainly gone by the end of the war. He would regard sinfulness and guilt, along with spirituality, materiality, and historicity, as permanent, ineluctable structures of human existence.

Rahner spent the years immediately after the war amid the wreckage and debris left by the bombing of Munich. In 1948 he returned to Innsbruck, where the Jesuits had reestablished the faculty of theology, and there became the Ordinarius professor of dogmatics. One of the courses he was assigned to teach was the tract on grace, long an area of controversy with Protestants, and one to which he would devote considerable time and reflection. At the foot of the Austrian alps, his life as a Jesuit returned to normality as he taught his courses, preached at Mass on Sundays at the hospital church, heard confessions, and gave retreats based on the Spiritual Exercises.

As Rahner's reputation spread beyond Innsbruck, invitations began coming from all over Germany for him to lecture to various groups and audiences, often to answer quite specific questions of pastoral theology. He was also invited to join in academic dialogue with nontheologians who were not necessarily Catholic or even Christian. The 1950s saw him involved in three different discussion groups: one dedicated to matters of Christian unity; another to questions of faith and science; and a third concerned with Christianity and the modern world, focused primarily on faith and Marxism. These conversations would have a lasting impact on Rahner's thinking. Engaging on a personal level with atheists, agnostics, secular humanists, and Marxists, Rahner often found himself confronted with persons of integrity, conscience, and genuine good will, though ostensibly without faith. He found himself compelled to reflect even more deeply on the church's doctrine of grace.

WHAT IT MEANS TO BE HUMAN

By all accounts Rahner was a charismatic teacher who inspired loyalty and affection among his students. One former student tells of Rahner spending the entire first class of a semester not lecturing but simply asking theological questions—about topics interesting in their own right, issues left unresolved from the church's past, and problems raised by modern technology.[33] For Rahner, one question led to another, invariably coming to the perennial questions that constitute our human condition—questions about life's meaning, fulfillment, and purpose. Rahner's thinking does not begin with nature or the cosmos, as it did for Aristotle, or even with talk about God, as it did with Thomas Aquinas. Accepting modern philosophy's "turn to the subject" (Kant), he begins with human experience, above all the experience of ourselves and the radical questionability of our existence. His starting point and constant focus is what it means to be human.

Rahner's theology was an anthropology, a sustained reflection, drawn from the sources of Catholic theology, on the human person. Borrowing the word from Heidegger, he developed what he called *existentials,* features characteristic of human existence that make us different from other kinds of beings. Though distinguishable from each other intellectually, these existentials are not separable in reality; each implies and involves the others. Though we have already encountered their origins in Rahner's thinking, we would do well to review them here and see, at least in outline, how he developed them.

Spirituality. We are spiritual, which is to say, transcendent beings. Though we are aware of the limitations that time and space impose on us, we are also aware that we are the subjects of a questioning that transcends the limits of time and space. We reach out for truth, above all for truth about the meaning of human existence, and in doing so find ourselves, like it or not, asking questions about God. For Rahner, it is precisely our questions about God, reality, and our existence that define us as human persons. He goes so far as to say that if we were to cease asking such questions, we would cease being human and regress to the level of being clever animals.[34]

Freedom. For Rahner freedom is another name for spirituality. It is not the power to perform this or that specific action but the condition necessary for love, the one basic moral act in which we decide about ourselves by putting ourselves at the disposal of another. The same fundamental dynamic of reaching out that lies at the core of knowing, lies at the core of loving. What it means to be a human person is revealed and exercised in the act of freely loving another human being. It involves not part of our lives but the whole of ourselves, giving meaning and measure to everything else. We discover our true nature and possess ourselves, paradoxically, only by forgetting ourselves. Unfortunately, that is no easy task, since our spirituality and freedom are limited by our essential materiality.

Materiality. Human beings are not made up of separate bodies and souls; even less are we souls laden down with bodies like so much baggage. From the beginning of his theological career, Rahner argued for the essential unity of spirituality and materiality in the human person. Our loftiest, most abstract ideas are rooted in our sense experiences and imagination. The same is true of our most sublime moral decisions. Ours is a sensate spirituality, which must exist in matter in order to be spirit. We exercise our spirituality not by trying to escape the material world and the persons around us, but by reaching out to them.

Historicity. In reaching out for truth and love, we do so in time and space, which is to say, in a history marked by evolution and change. No thought of ours, no value, touches us outside a historical situation. Historicity affects every aspect of our lives. It is in time and history that we exist as spiritual and free beings, not only objects but also agents of change. We have always been capable of using or misusing our freedom and thereby changing ourselves, our history, and our physical environment; but now, because of modern science and technology, we can change them to an unprecedented degree.

Guilt. The freedom we exercise in history renders us not only responsible but also "threatened radically by guilt."[35] Guilt is a permanent possibility belonging to the whole of human life, whether or not we actually incur it. Inherent in every free decision is an implicit yes or no to ourselves and to our self-actualization. We experience a difference between what we are and what we ought to be. And knowing ourselves to be capable of coming into conflict with ourselves, we know ourselves to be free and accountable. But then the question arises—to whom or what are we accountable?

Rahner's is from the start a theological anthropology. God is the source and terminus of our spiritual reaching out, not reaching out toward an individual being within a universe of individual beings but reaching out to the absolute mystery that surrounds us like a horizon. Whether we know it or not, whether we will it or not, in our limitless reaching out for truth, we are reaching out for God. In reaching out and committing ourselves in self-forgetful love to another human being, we reach out to God. The human person is at the center of Rahner's Ignatian humanism, but so too is God. In the experience of ourselves as mystery, we experience the absolute mystery that is God. And we discover our true natures and most deeply experience the mystery of ourselves in the experience of loving another person.

For Rahner it is a fundamental principle of Christian teaching that the love of God and the love of neighbor are but two names for the same reality; one does not exist without the other.[36] Rahner concludes from all the foregoing that, though we distinguish them as not identical, the experience of God, our neighbor, and ourselves constitutes a single reality. God, our neighbor, and ourselves are present in every act endowed with transcendental freedom. In our use or misuse of freedom, in our willingness or unwillingness to give ourselves in love, we decide not only about things but also about ourselves. Implicit in the decision for or against ourselves is the decision for or against God. Appreciating the gravity of that decision and the nature of guilt is not possible, however, without consideration of one final dimension of human existence, what Rahner called the "supernatural existential," the universal and irrevocable invitation to divine grace.

HUMAN EXISTENCE
IN A UNIVERSE OF GRACE

Grace is one of the most fundamental and distinctive concepts in Christian theology. It is also one of the most complex and, thanks to sixteenth-century Reformation polemics, fraught with controversy. Analyzing the

Latin word *gratia,* Thomas Aquinas pointed out that it had three distinct but related meanings: the third meaning, thanks or gratitude, follows from the second meaning, that of gift, a free giving or forgiving; and this second meaning depends in turn on the first meaning of the word, which looks to the gift giver's generosity or graciousness *(Summa Theologiae,* I–II, q.110, art. 1). Following biblical usage, especially St. Paul, Catholic tradition uses the word in all three of its meanings but in the Middle Ages came to emphasize the second meaning over the first, the created gift of God more than the Giver.

This was the focus Rahner inherited from the Neo-Scholastic handbooks when he began teaching the subject; grace was defined as an unmerited supernatural gift. That concept was further analyzed and subdivided by the scholastics. There was actual grace, which was a passing or temporal help given by God to turn away from sin or to do good and grow in the sanctifying grace, which was the grace that really mattered. Sanctifying grace was defined as the grace that transforms us, that makes us children of God, heirs of heaven, and temples of the Holy Spirit. The gift of the Holy Spirit was designated uncreated grace. God dwelled within us, according to the handbooks, as a consequence of sanctifying grace. And what exactly was this sanctifying grace, sometimes also called "infused grace"? Was it some *thing* or, to put it into an Aristotelian category, a *substance?* The medieval scholastics, appealing to a Scripture verse about God's love "poured into our hearts through the Holy Spirit" (Rom 5:5), decided it was a quality. They defined sanctifying grace as a created quality, "infused" or poured into our souls, making us holy.

Rahner did not reject the scholastic theology of grace but, by changing its focus, revolutionized it. Already in the late 1930s he had begun thinking and writing on the Scholastic conception of uncreated grace; after the war he developed and argued his thinking more fully. Surely the self-gift of God's Holy Spirit was not to be classified as a mere consequence of a created gift. By all means, we are transformed by grace. The transformation, however, follows from God's uncreated self-gift, not the other way around. Rahner eventually dispensed with the Aristotelian categories altogether. Grace is most fundamentally God's self-gift, and, as Thomas Aquinas made plain, God by definition cannot be categorized. We may continue to speak of God's help or mercy and call it grace; these are still legitimate ways to use the word. They stem, however, from the more basic and most important gift God gives us, God's very self. From this self-giving, all other gifts flow.

Seeing grace essentially as God's self-communication is one of the most distinctive features of Rahner's understanding of grace. He insisted that it was nothing new, only a return to the biblical sources and church fathers. Another, more innovative, feature of Rahner's theology of grace is its universality. If there is one verse from Scripture that seems to have prodded Rahner's thinking more than others, it is that God "desires everyone to be saved and to come to the knowledge of the truth" (1 Tm 2:4, NRSV). Few theologians before him took that biblical teaching as seriously or probed its implications as thoroughly.

Catholic theologians had long distinguished between nature and grace. They described grace as supernatural, which is to say, unmerited and free, not in any way due to us because of our natures. Under the influence of St. Augustine and his pessimism about human nature, Catholic and Protestant theologians alike tended to see grace as given to some of us sometimes but not to others at other times. Rahner asked, why is that? Grace can be free and unmerited and still be bestowed lavishly. Grace is not withheld from anyone at any time, he argued. We exist in a universe of grace, surrounded by a God who like a horizon is ever receding and therefore Absolute Mystery but, as revealed by Jesus, is ever drawing near to us in gracious self-giving. Rahner put it this way: "It is not a rare and sporadic event just because grace is unmerited. Theology has been too long and too often bedeviled by the unavowed supposition that grace would be no longer grace if it were too generously distributed by the love of God."[37]

God's self-giving is and always has been universal and constant, Rahner contended. It is not restricted to unusual moments or special circumstances but has surrounded us at every moment from the very beginning of humankind. Being surrounded by a self-giving God is part of what it means to be human. Like our spirituality and freedom, grace is an ever-present characteristic, an "existential" of human nature. But because God's self-giving is a free gift, not due to us because of our natures, it is a "supernatural existential." It follows that "pure nature," the idea of human nature without God's self-giving presence, is just that—an idea, a theoretical, abstract possibility that has never existed in reality.

In Rahner's theology of grace, human beings have never been in a state of pure nature, without the presence of the self-giving God. And that being the case, never have we been unaffected by that presence. This is not to say, however, that all of us are affected in the same way. God's self-giving constitutes an invitation, a universal and constant offer to all of us, unbelievers and sinners along with the saints. But there is no assurance that all of us accept the offer. The New Testament and Catholic tradition allow us to hope that this is the case, but we cannot know for sure. Nor can we know with absolute certitude our own present or future condition, whether or not we have accepted God's invitation, or whether or not we will persevere in our acceptance. Rahner appeals here to the teaching of the Council of Trent as correctly descriptive of our human condition. The threat of guilt remains an unavoidable dimension of human existence; we cannot escape the possibility that we will reject God's offer. Only in death do we make our final, definitive decision to accept or reject it. This is no cause for anxiety, however; all we can do is accept our human condition and have faith—not in ourselves, but in the self-giving God revealed by Jesus.

This brings us to a third distinctive feature of Rahner's theology of grace, namely, where he locates it—at the level of our innermost spiritual, transcendental experience. Christian theology has always taught that God's free offer of grace requires a human response, that it must be accepted in an act of faith. We are saved by grace through faith. Because of this conviction, St. Paul and the apostolic church preached the gospel of Jesus to Jew and gentile alike. Because of this doctrine, missionaries later went out from Rome and Constantinople to evangelize Europe. By the Middle Ages the church was satisfied that its task had been completed; the gospel had been preached to the ends of the world—until the fifteenth and sixteenth centuries, that is, when the world suddenly proved to be much larger than medieval Europeans had ever imagined.

The age of discovery and exploration confronted Christian theologians with the realization that millions of people for more than a thousand years had been living outside the remotest possibility of Christian faith—and, therefore, it would appear, without the possibility of salvation. For missionaries like Ricci and de Nobili (see chapter 3), this constituted more than a speculative, theological problem; it was a matter of individual human beings whom they were encountering and befriending every day. Were they untouched by God's spirit and hopelessly damned? How could anything like that be reconciled with the doctrine of a loving God? Catholic theologians came to the conclusion that there was such a thing as implicit faith. They appealed to the Epistle to the Hebrews (11:6): "For whoever would draw near to God must believe that he exists and that he rewards those who seek him." So long as a person has explicit faith in God and God's judgment of human behavior, faith in Christ was implicit in it. One did not have to be a Catholic or a Christian to experience and respond to God's grace. Confucians, Hindus, those who practiced native religions and worshiped God under other names could be saved by their implicit faith.

Faith in this consideration, whether explicit or implicit, was conceptual, to be found at the level of the conscious intellect. Using the language of Kant, Rahner called it "categorical" faith. He argued, however, that the self-giving God addresses us at our deepest level of existence, deeper than our conscious intellects—at our spiritual, transcendental level, where we reach out for truth and meaning, where we reach out in self-forgetting love for another person and are only dimly aware and perhaps not at all reflective of the absolute mystery toward which we are also reaching. Rahner took for granted the church's teaching that good will alone was not enough and that faith is necessary for salvation. He locates the essence of faith, however, at the spiritual core of our being, where we experience ourselves as infinite longing. Here we encounter and experience, accept or reject the self-giving God with a "transcendental" faith, which may rise to the level of conscious awareness, and ideally does—but also perhaps may not.

Rahner argued against the notion, then prevailing among Catholic theologians, that grace was something purely metaphysical, beyond our experience. Although he appealed to the teaching of Thomas Aquinas, it was also the experiences of Ignatius Loyola and of Rahner's own personal experiences of God in the Spiritual Exercises that convinced him otherwise. We can and do experience God, God's very self, not only as the infinitely distant goal of our longing and striving but also as drawing near, touching and transforming us. He could also have appealed to Origen and Bonaventure, whom he read in his early years on the "spiritual senses." But he did not want to confine the experience of God to so-called extraordinary mystical experiences marked by ecstasy. Rahner's was a mysticism of everyday life. For him as for Ignatius Loyola, God can be experienced by anyone. All we need to do is learn to be attentive and listen. In the most mundane and secular of circumstances, we can and do experience the self-giving God at the inner core of our being. It is here that we are invited to a response that Rahner usually called transcendental faith; he also called it "anonymous" faith.[38]

Rahner's distinction between categorical and transcendental or anonymous faith lies at the basis of his controversial and much maligned notion of the "anonymous Christian." The phrase seems to patronize virtuous non-Christians by telling them that they are in fact Christians without knowing it. Would not a non-Christian, say a Buddhist, have the right to call Rahner an anonymous Buddhist? In fact, Nishitani, a well-known Zen Buddhist philosopher, once did, and Rahner responded that he felt honored by the designation since, from Nishitani's perspective, it implied that he regarded Rahner as enlightened.[39] Rahner recognized the problems with the phrase "anonymous Christian," but confessed that he did not know how to say it better within a Christian context.

For the record, Rahner's concept of anonymous Christianity arose as a response to a quite different question than that of Christian attitudes toward other religions. In one of the first essays in which he broached the notion, "The Christian among Unbelieving Relations," Rahner took up the pastoral question of how to deal with the anxiety suffered by parents, for example, when their child leaves the church.[40] The concept, in other words, is meant for internal, Christian consumption. And though it obviously has implications for Christian relations with other religions, it also deals with atheism and apostasy from within the church's ranks as not always or necessarily implying bad faith and guilt.

Rahner once described the intentions behind his theology as "completely, immediately, and genuinely pastoral."[41] Nowhere is that truer than here with his distinction between transcendental and categorical faith. Rahner took seriously the massive falling away from Christian faith taking place in Europe. The issue was more than academic for him; his dialogues with Marxist and secular humanists touched him personally. His relationships with them were marked by mutual fondness and respect, and he openly called several Marxist humanists "my friends." He shared their criticism of bourgeois religion and acknowledged with them that religion had been used (he would say misused) at various times to exploit people.[42]

But the misuse of religion does not disprove the existence of or human longing for God. Rahner would confront his nonbelieving dialogue partners with pointed questions. He rebuffed the notion that people of faith were suffering from an illusion while atheists were somehow brave in their rejection of God. Was it not more courageous to hold on to the conviction of ultimate meaning despite all disappointments? To Marxists he asked: Is it acceptable to sacrifice people of the present for the sake of a happier future generation? To liberal materialists: Is it acceptable to reduce humanity to a bundle of chemical processes influenced by society? To agnostics: Can the skeptical refusal to choose between faith and atheism produce anything more than a life of banality?[43]

Rahner never attempted to argue the existence of God. It is impossible to prove that reality coheres, that things ultimately make sense, since any "proof" would presuppose it. From the Christian tradition itself Rahner acknowledged that the so-called proofs for the existence of God are not so compelling as to overwhelm an individual and take away the burden of making a decision. Rahner respected the difficulties of his nonbelieving dialogue partners in making that decision. He could and did say: "I am someone who has been tempted by atheism." But at the same time he could also say: "There is nothing more self-evident to me than God's existence."[44] That evidence did not come from argument but from experience. We have it on the word of a close friend and collaborator that Rahner once put it this way: "I believe because I pray."[45]

Rahner's theology of grace—God's universal self-giving addressing us, often anonymously, at the innermost core of our beings—constitutes the unifying thread that pervades and colors virtually all the rest of his thought. The classic dogmas about Jesus, for example, came out of the static worldview and assumptions of fourth- and fifth-century theologians who thought in the categories of Greek philosophy. How, Rahner asked, do we reconcile them with our own evolutionary worldview? Rahner tried to answer that question by building on his anthropology and theology of grace. The universe is evolving, but is it all for nothing? Or does evolution look to a purposeful conclusion? There is a goal to evolution, Rahner argued, and Jesus reveals it. Jesus represents the divine self-giving that is the fulfillment of evolution and purpose of creation. He embodies the triumph of God's drawing near to humankind in a process that has been coexistent with the whole of human history.

Among the many titles the New Testament gives him, Jesus is called "savior"—because he changed history, not because he changed God. God's self-communication to humankind was made tangible in Jesus, as was God's will for all humankind to find its fulfillment. God's eternal salvific will was there from the beginning of human history and did not change as a result of human sin. Jesus did not have to persuade God to be gracious. His death did not change God's will, but revealed it. The cross was the culmination of a self-forgetting, self-emptying life and, together with Jesus' resurrection, constitutes a visible sign or sacrament of God's immutable self-giving.

Mystery is one of the earliest words used in biblical and Christian tradition to speak of God. Rahner used it so often that it practically became a hallmark of his theology. To speak of God is to speak about "absolute mystery," by which he meant that God is essentially beyond human comprehension and will always remain so. The revelation of God's self-giving in Jesus does not diminish God's mysteriousness but only increases it. Even in what Catholic tradition calls the "beatific vision," the triune God will remain inexhaustible to us, will remain "absolute mystery."

The doctrine of the triune God is not about three divine "persons" understood as three individuals, as that word *person* has come to be understood in modern usage. Such an understanding, Rahner insisted, is tantamount to polytheism. We no longer understand the word *person* in the same way as the church fathers who originally formulated the doctrine understood it, as a mode of subsisting, a way of being. With that change of meaning in the word, the doctrine has become a kind of curious arithmetical problem, virtually irrelevant to most Christians. Rahner sought to counter both these problems by arguing that the doctrine of the Trinity has everything to do with our daily lives, aspirations, and endeavors, which is to say, our salvation. To speak of the triune God of grace is to be redundant. The God who is given to us (as the Holy Spirit), who is revealed to us (as the Son or Word or Wisdom of God) always remains ineffable mystery (as the Father). To speak of the triune God is to speak of the self-giving God of grace.

Finally, Rahner's theology of grace obviously impacted how he thought about the church. Certainly, if grace is universal, the church is not an institution outside of which there is no salvation. But what, then, is the point of the church? What's the need for Sunday worship, prayer, preaching, and all the other normal practices of Christian life? Doesn't explicit Christianity lose its importance? Even more problematic, why should missionaries try to convert people to Christianity if they are already anonymous Christians in their innermost, transcendental experience? Because, Rahner would answer, transcendental experience seeks explicit expression; it is perfected by becoming conscious.

The Christian church exists where God's self-giving finds tangible expression, where grace is both symbolized and consciously experienced. In other words, the church is a kind of sacrament. It symbolizes God's grace as present within it but at the same time points to the self-giving God beyond its visible confines. The church, in short, has no monopoly on grace. Its missionaries do not bring God to non-Christians but can only make them aware of the God already addressing them, touching them in the innermost core of their lives. The concept of anonymous Christianity could have been expressed differently; Protestant theologian Paul Tillich used the term "spiritual community." No matter how one phrases it, the reality of grace beyond the church can never be a reason for dismissing the church. It provides a way for Christians to think about other people, not ourselves. It allows us to see Jews, Muslims, Buddhists, atheists as touched by God and quite possibly having something to teach us. In a universe where there is nothing untouched by grace, there is nothing alien to the church.

VATICAN II AND THE BEGINNINGS OF A WORLD CHURCH

One day in the early 1960s, Rahner received a telephone call from no less than Franz König, the archbishop of Vienna. Thirty years later the archbishop could still remember the conversation clearly. Pope John XXIII had announced his intention to summon all the bishops in union with the Holy See to what would be the Second Vatican Council. The archbishop decided to make use of his right to take a theological advisor with him to the council and invited Rahner. Would he accept? As König told it, Rahner answered in his amiable grumbling way: "How can you imagine such a thing? I've never been to Rome in my life. There are already people suspicious about what I am teaching and writing. What will the Romans say if I suddenly show up as a conciliar theologian?"[46]

Rahner was right. He had critics both among Jesuits and at the Vatican. Writings like his 1947 essay "A Church of Sinners" had raised questions as well as eyebrows; his interpretations of some dogmas were original to the point of scandalizing a number of conservative ecclesiastics. But Rahner also had friends in high places, like König. When in June 1962 Rahner was informed that he would have to submit all his future writings to the Vatican's Holy Office for prior censorship, admirers in the hierarchy and academic world protested directly to the pope at this insult to Rahner's orthodoxy. Pope John intervened personally, and the following year the Holy Office retreated. There would be no prior censorship, and Rahner would have no further difficulties with Vatican critics the rest of his life.

König had known Rahner personally since the war years, when Rahner worked at the pastoral institute in Vienna. He was familiar with Rahner's many essays, which since 1954 had begun appearing in collected book form and would eventually number sixteen volumes.[47] In 1957 Rahner had begun coediting a new edition of the prestigious Catholic encyclopedia, the *Lexikon für Theologie und Kirche*. König wanted Rahner as his advisor because of his theological expertise, but also because he knew Rahner made the effort to understand the minds and hearts of people immersed in modern secular society and to relate Catholic teaching in a way that spoke to them. The archbishop shared Rahner's pastoral convictions.

The challenge was already tangible for König. His desk was piling up with documents formulated and sent out to the world's bishops for their evaluation from various preparatory commissions in the Vatican. König wanted Rahner's opinions of these preliminary drafts. Pope John had put the curia in charge of preparing for the council, and the Vatican bureaucrats were known not to be enthusiastic about the council in the first place. They saw no reason for it, except perhaps to issue a new syllabus of the errors rampant in the modern world.

Rahner found much to criticize. Recalling those months before the council, König could still produce some of Rahner's comments. One, for example, read: "The authors [of this draft] have certainly never endured the distress of a troubled atheistic non-Christian who wants to believe but feels unable." Another: "No, these drafts do not accomplish all they can. They are the product of persons comfortably certain, who confuse their self-assurance with the firmness of faith . . . the work of good, pious professors . . . unselfish but simply unable to cope with the world today."[48]

Rahner and König had reason to be apprehensive. Most of the drafts contained the same old Neo-Scholastic language, the same defensive, accusatory tone that the Vatican had been using for centuries. The curia clearly was expecting the bishops to rubber-stamp what they had prepared and go home. So one can only imagine König's and Rahner's delight when, at the solemn opening of the council, Pope John XXIII chided the "prophets of gloom" in the church who see only disaster in our times and nothing good. Looking out at the world's bishops assembled in St. Peter's basilica, he was clearly referring to several of the curial cardinals seated before him.

Amid the baroque splendor of St. Peter's, emblematic of the Counter-Reformation, Pope John XXIII opened Vatican II with a speech that electrified the bishops and changed history.[49] He told them that he was envisioning a predominantly "pastoral" council, one that would replace severity and condemnation of errors with the "medicine of mercy." Their duty as bishops, the pope went on, involved more than guarding the inheritance of the past; they must also address the demands of the present. There is a difference between the substance of the church's tradition and the way it is expressed. The church's message needs to be presented in contemporary thought patterns. On that October 11, 1962, König and Rahner knew they were not alone in their pastoral enterprise; they had allies in Pope John XXIII and, as they would soon learn, in the majority of bishops as well. The pope made it clear that the texts prepared by the curia were not inviolable; they could be replaced by new working documents, and practically all of them were.

Pope John XXIII named Rahner an official *peritus* (expert) of the council and a member of the critically influential theological commission. That meant spending long days with bishops and other theologians, drawing up new drafts for the council's deliberations. Even more important, some would say, were the talks he gave in the evenings to various language groups of bishops on one or another topic on the council's agenda. In addition to his native German, Rahner was fluent in French, and his Latin was superior to most of the Vatican administrators who claimed it as the official language of the church. Rahner's command of Catholic tradition soon won the grudging admiration of even his most strident critics. Though he rarely had time to attend the general sessions, Rahner came to be regarded, in the words of one conservative theologian, as "the most powerful man" at the council.[50] But his influence was exerted behind the scenes.

Because he worked in committee with other bishops and theologians, no one conciliar document or even sections of documents can be ascribed to Rahner alone. That being said, traces of his influence can be detected in all but four conciliar texts, none more pivotal than the Dogmatic Constitution on the Church. There in the very first section of chapter 1, the church is described as a "kind of sacrament," a sign and instrument of God at work within but also beyond its visible confines. Chapter 2 of the Constitution speaks of Catholics "linked" by grace to other Christians, to people of other religious faiths, and even to people of conscience without any apparent faith in God: "Nor does divine Providence deny the help necessary for salvation to those who, without blame on their part, have not yet arrived at an explicit knowledge of God, but who strive to live a good life, thanks to His grace."[51]

Thanks greatly to Rahner, Vatican II put an end to the centuries-old sway over Catholic thinking held by St. Augustine's pessimistic view of humanity. Rahner's writing and speeches also contributed to the council's teaching on the intrinsic reliance of tradition on Scripture, the collegial relationship between bishops and the papacy, and the reinstitution of the permanent diaconate. If there is one single contribution Rahner made to the council that will prove to have the greatest impact on history, it would be his theology of universal grace and its implications for the Catholic church's relations to other churches, to the world religions, and to the modern secular world. One relates differently to people if they are viewed as kindred spirits within a community of grace rather than as outsiders.

Looking back at the council, Rahner saw it as a mere beginning—the first hesitant steps toward many more basic changes in Catholic teaching and structure and the dawn of a radically new era in the church's history. Vatican II, he wrote, marked the first time the Catholic Church officially realized and expressed itself to be a world church.[52] Prior to Vatican II, the Catholic Church, despite its claims to universality, was basically European. Even at Vatican I, the bishops representing Asia and Africa were European exports, missionary bishops of European or Euro-American origin. During the decades prior to the council, increasing numbers of native African and Asian bishops were named, but they made little impact on the church as they made their individual reports to a centralized Roman bureaucracy. Vatican II was a qualitative leap when the world episcopate came together as a body for the first time to assume supreme teaching and decision-making authority with the pope.

Rahner regarded Vatican II as a major break in the church's 2,000-year history; he could see only one precedent for it—the transition of Christianity from a Jewish sect to a gentile church. When St. Paul and his like began accepting gentiles as Christians without circumcision and observance of Jewish ritual law, the church was free to adapt itself to the Hellenistic culture of the Roman Empire. It continued to adapt itself as it spread out from the Mediterranean to the rest of Europe. But until Vatican II, subsequent changes within Christianity were minor compared to that caesura at the end of the first century. As Rahner saw it, church history has known only three great epochs: the brief period of Jewish-Christianity; the subsequent 1,900 years of European Christianity, exported by missionaries to other parts of the world but exclusively Hellenistic and European in its theology and culture; and the era just beginning, in which the church put an end to the European monopoly by adapting to other cultures as well and becoming a world church.

An inevitable consequence of a world church is a multiplicity of cultures and therefore theologies. Rahner was not surprised when, in the aftermath of Vatican II, countervailing efforts arose out of Rome to reinforce the former centralism and uniformity. But he saw no other alternative in our increasingly pluralistic world than an increasingly and permanently pluralistic church. He acknowledged that it will be painful for the church's leadership to adjust to this, with the situation aggravated by the breakdown of a relatively homogenous culture in what is now a post-Christian Europe. Though there are still pockets where traditional Christianity is taken for granted as part of the cultural landscape, these too are becoming fewer and smaller as secular culture becomes the norm, not only in the West but for the rest of the world as well.

In this new state of the world church, Rahner wrote on the need for "Pauline boldness" comparable to that which the church exerted when it revoked the requirement of circumcision for gentiles, changed the Sabbath, and augmented the Hebrew canon of scriptures with the New Testament. He called for greater autonomy for local churches to develop their own theologies and a canon law adapted to their particular cultures. What Rahner meant by Pauline boldness can be inferred from some of the questions he asked: Must the Eucharist be celebrated with grape wine even in Alaska? Must European marriage customs be imposed on African tribal chieftains accustomed, like Abraham, to living with more than one wife?[53]

For Rahner the breakdown of cultural Christianity in the West meant that the Catholic faithful no longer live in Catholic ghettos, and their leaders cannot afford to either. Cultural accommodation was required in post-Christian Europe no less than Asia, likewise implying openness to decentralization and reform. The papacy is essential to Catholicism, but it has changed in the past, and there is no reason why it cannot change in the future; the pope's function is nothing like that of a totalitarian head of state. A servant church is one that accepts itself and its institutions as means, never as ends in themselves. There is no divine law as to how the church should select its leaders. The people are not to be treated like sheep; they have a right to cooperate in decision making in the church, and as more than just consultors. If the church cannot find enough suitable celibate candidates for ordination to the priesthood, then celibacy should not be imposed. The ordained leader at the Eucharist and the leader of the community should be the same person, and Rahner saw no dogmatic reason why that person could not be a woman.[54]

Rahner became increasingly frustrated in the years after the council. The 1969 Synod of German bishops was a particularly keen disappointment; only two bishops responded positively to a paper he had helped to write on behalf of the ordination of married men. Rahner warned against pastoral needs being neglected and opportunities missed. His tone became sharper as he accused the bishops, not as individuals but as a group, of an institutionalized mentality and paternalism.[55] Though not ordinarily given to metaphors, he compared the church to a chess club. Those who carry the club are the members who play chess well. The officers of the club are necessary, important, and deserve respect for their service to the players, but they are not necessarily the best players themselves. The ones who make up the real core of the church are the ordinary Christians who love, serve, and speak out prophetically.[56]

Rahner came to use other metaphors as well, describing the situation of the church today as a "wintry season." The official church was not putting either the letter or the spirit of the council into practice. And faith no longer comes easy, as it once did when Christianity dominated European culture and faith was commonplace. Christians today find themselves in societies and cultures where the word *God* is virtually taboo, where not faith but a rationalist mindset and atheism are taken for granted.[57] The church must learn to exist in a "diaspora," as a minority surrounded by cultures marked by atheism and religious indifference. In such a diaspora situation, the church would be a network of grassroots communities composed of Christian mystics. Or, as he put it in a now oft-quoted passage: "The devout Christian of the future will either be a 'mystic,' one who has 'experienced' something, or he will cease to be anything at all."[58]

MYSTIC OF EVERYDAY LIFE

Rahner liked to call himself a dilettante.[59] Instead of lengthy volumes on one or two topics, he chose to write hundreds of brief essays on a broad range of subjects. He grumbled about those specialists in theology who focus their research and reflection so narrowly that they come to know everything there is to know about nothing of any importance. The task of theology, as Rahner saw it, is to serve preaching; and the task of preaching is to address people where they are, so they can recognize God at work in their concrete life situations.

The same driving force that lay behind Rahner's priesthood lay behind his theology—a pastoral concern for people and their spiritual lives. Rahner regarded guiding people in the Spiritual Exercises to be a Jesuit's primary task, something he did with regularity despite his time-consuming work teaching and writing theology. He saw no dichotomy between the two tasks. Directing Ignatian retreats and doing theology were two aspects of the same mystagogical enterprise—introducing people to the divine mystery in their lives. This he did, not by bringing God to people or people to God, but by making them aware of the God already experienced in their everyday lives.

The word *mystical* is generally used to describe both those experiences deemed so utterly beyond the limits of the ordinary that they are attributed to the presence of God and the sustained reflection upon verbalized expression of those experiences. In both understandings of the word, Rahner was a mystical theologian. For him the writings of mystics like Ignatius Loyola, Teresa of Ávila, and John of the Cross were as much a source for theological reflection as those of Augustine and Aquinas. Appealing to his early reading about the "spiritual senses," Rahner insisted that the so-called extraordinary experiences of great mystics are not substantially different from the everyday experiences we all normally have of God. The difference is not in the presence of God's spirit but in the psychological sensibility of the person experiencing that spirit. We all need to become more attuned. That's where Rahner believed we can learn from someone like Ignatius.

Once a radio interviewer told Rahner that he had never had an experience of God. Rahner responded emphatically: "I don't believe you; I just don't accept that. You have had, perhaps, no experience of God under this precise code-word *God*, but you have had or have now an experience of God—and I am convinced that this is true of every person." Rahner granted that the experience of God is necessarily difficult to describe. "What love is, what fidelity is, what longing is, what immediate responsibility is—are all things that are difficult to express and to think about. We start stuttering, and what we say sounds odd, provisional, difficult. But that doesn't prove that a person has not had experiences of fidelity, responsibility, joy, truth, love, and so on. And so it is with experiencing God."[60]

Rahner's thinking on mysticism grew out of his theology of grace and the human person. Not the word, linked in the popular mind with the singular and esoteric, but what it points to is what matters. "I think that people must understand that they have an implicit but true knowledge of God, perhaps not reflected upon and not verbalized—or better expressed: a genuine experience of God, which is ultimately rooted in their spiritual existence, in their transcendentality, in their personality, or whatever you want to name it. It is not a really important question whether you want to call that 'mystical' or not."[61]

In an attempt to help his readers recognize their implicit experiences of God, Rahner highlighted the often dreary reality of our situations. An astute student of Rahner's has noted how often he described our everyday lives by using words like *banal, humdrum,* and *routine.*[62] Here it is that perhaps the most universal experience of the infinite is discernable—in our experience of emptiness and longing. Our heart's desires are never satisfied. We are always on the lookout for the someone or something that we think will make the difference, that will give ultimate meaning and satisfaction to our lives. But it does not happen. Intelligence, power, wealth, prestige, a loving family—none of it seems to be enough. And this for Rahner pointed to an either-or situation: either God exists or life is absurd.

Rahner was once asked by an interviewer, "Is there one question that seems to you as a theologian to be perhaps the most important?" He replied: "Yes, there is such a question. It runs like this: Is human existence absurd or does it have an ultimate meaning? If it is absurd, why do human beings have an unquenchable hunger for meaning? Is it not a consequence of God's existence? For if God really doesn't exist, then the hunger for meaning is absurd."[63]

For Rahner as for St. Augustine, our restless hearts find repose only in God; nothing else corresponds to that infinite longing. Yet amid the restlessness and routine, there are moments of joy and blessedness, transient like flashes of light but giving promise of a light that is lasting. Rahner wrote of an Ignatian affirmation of joy in the world but insisted that a young and happy heart is not necessarily closer to God than one that is tired and disillusioned. While he did not entirely discount the experiences of charismatic Christians, he preferred to dwell on the less enthusiastic experiences of God's spirit, in his words, that "sober intoxication of the Spirit, of which the Fathers and the liturgy speak, which we cannot reject or despise, because it is real."[64]

Like Ignatius, Rahner encouraged his readers to recognize God in all things, even the most commonplace: when we forgive without reward, do our duty without thanks, when we dare to let ourselves hope despite our guilt and failures—there is God and the experience of God. Where we affirm another's absolute worth no matter what that person's failings, where we remain silent rather than strike back, where we offer the biblical glass of water to someone thirsty or a kind word to someone in distress—there is God and the experience of God.[65] Where anyone, including the atheist and agnostic, protests injustice, suffering, and meaningless death, harboring a hope so deep that it can go undetected—there is God and the experience of God, for nothing else grounds that hope or our standard of "what not ought to be."[66]

Such is Rahner's mysticism of everyday life, based upon an anthropology that even some of his friends found too individualistic. Rahner was faulted for not sufficiently emphasizing the social nature of human existence and as a result neglecting the economic and political responsibilities that come with Christian discipleship. Rahner countered the criticism by arguing that the sociopolitical task of the modern Christian is implicit in his identification of the love of God and love of neighbor. True love of neighbor in our day must involve more than private relationships between individual persons; it must be willing to exercise social criticism of political and social injustice.[67] Along this vein, Rahner endorsed the direction that the Society of Jesus was taking under Father Pedro Arrupe, integrating faith with work on behalf of justice. Similarly, he supported the work of lib-eration theologians in Latin America as having a rightful place among the multiple theologies of today's world church. As he wrote in a letter to the bishops of Peru, "The voice of the poor must be made heard."[68] Rahner sent that letter from a hospital bed two weeks before he died.

Exemplifying Terrence's dictum, nothing human was alien to Rahner's interests. His former students have told of his love for ice cream, fast cars, and toy shops. He seems to have had an almost insatiable curiosity for learning how things work, not dissimilar from the singular way he tried to get inside the minds and hearts of his conversation partners, whether they were Marxists, atheists, scientists, or ordinary folk. As one friend described it, no matter how contrary their thinking was to his own, Rahner wanted to know how and why people thought and felt as they did. He did not try to contradict or correct their thinking but simply to understand it, to find whatever truth he could within it, and to know the experience on which it rested.[69] From there he tried to direct their attention to the whole of reality and absolute mystery that surrounds it.

As a priest and theologian, Rahner tried to find healing words for hurting or troubled hearts, for people who saw themselves as ill-treated by the church or disappointed by God. Yet his spiritual works of mercy did not divert him from people's more mundane needs. Friends have told of his bringing bags of groceries to a widow and typing the thesis of a student

in academic trouble. On the occasion of a festive academic gathering cele-
brating his eightieth birthday, after an address relating his experiences as
a Catholic theologian, he somewhat sheepishly returned to the podium
and asked those present if they would contribute toward a new motor
bicycle for a missionary in Africa.

In the course of that address, Rahner spoke of the too often forgotten
theological dictum that our words about God are mere analogies, stuttering metaphors more unlike than like the mystery they seek to represent.
He acknowledged and did not regret the fact that he had thought and
written more about grace than about sinfulness. Compared to God's self-
giving, human sinfulness is of secondary importance and is often less the
result of malice than of human weakness, impulse, or stupidity. He also
encouraged theologians to turn to scientists to learn more about God. The
Bible can tell us all we need to know about our salvation, but we have to
look to science to tell us just how awesome is the mystery that has brought
so awesome a universe into existence. And he told of waiting for death,
that "colossal, silent emptiness" that will in truth be filled with the light
and the love of the absolute mystery that we call God.[70]

Only a few weeks later, Rahner died. In that last address he had remarked
in passing, "I hope that the great founder of my religious order, Ignatius
Loyola, will concede that at least a little bit of his spirit and spirituality is
perceptible in my theology." Rahner's life and writings demonstrate his
right to that hope. He understood Ignatian spirituality and its humanist
contours as few before him. Finding God in all things, he found grace to
be constitutive of human existence so that non-Christians, even secular
humanists, can be touched by the absolute mystery that we call God, and
that God can teach and touch us through them.

SEVEN

PEDRO ARRUPE

Dn. <#7 Spirituality =

Have we Jesuits educated you for justice? You and I know what many of your Jesuit teachers will answer to that question. They will answer, in all sincerity and humility: No, we have not. If the terms "justice" and "education for justice" carry all the depth of meaning which the Church gives them today, we have not educated you for justice.[1]

It would have been at this point, early on in Pedro Arrupe's address, that his audience began to squirm. Arrupe knew that the men seated before him were not expecting anything like this. They had come to Spain from all over Europe to attend the 1973 International Congress of Jesuit Alumni at Valencia. These prosperous, well-dressed products of Jesuit schooling expected to be congratulated on their successful careers and commended for their loyalty to the church and their alma maters. They had not come to be told that there had been deficiencies in their Jesuit education.

One of Arrupe's tasks as superior general was to raise funds for Jesuit institutions and ministries. Since his days as a missionary in Japan, he had become adept at extending a tin cup. (A vintage quip has it that God raised up Franciscans to exemplify Christ's poverty, Dominicans to model good preaching, and Jesuits to get money from the rich.) So Arrupe was taking a risk to speak as he did.

Arrupe's Valencia address marked a defining moment in his career. In it he challenged his audience to "humanize" the world, nurture respect for all persons, live more simply, do away with luxuries, and dismantle unjust social structures. To claim a love for God that does not result in justice is a farce, he said, not mincing any words. And now the Jesuit alumni at Valencia and the rest of the world discovered what Jesuits had already learned, as the next day's international press criticized Arrupe and his speech as "radical."

Arrupe—Don Pedro, as his friends and associates called him—was the most unlikely of radicals. Before becoming superior general, he was notorious for not reading newspapers. When he occasionally showed some awareness of current events, friends would tease him with "Look! Don Pedro has decided to come down from his planet!"[2] The Jesuit electors who chose him superior general in 1965 had no reason to suspect that Arrupe would be anything but solidly conservative. He seemed hardly the type to stir up controversy. Even less would his electors have imagined that he would shepherd them and the Society of Jesus into a new era of their history.

Some critics have characterized this new era as a revolution; I would argue that it is more accurately described as a return to origins. As a novice master in Japan, directing retreats in the Spiritual Excercises, Arrupe had to become deeply immersed in Ignatian spirituality and foundational documents, all influenced (as seen in chapter 2) by the humanist values of the Renaissance. His writings and speeches evince that immersion. How much or whether he recognized the humanist influences on Ignatian spirituality makes no difference. What matters is that Arrupe came to embody a retrieval and elaboration of the original *this-worldly* aspect of Ignatian spirituality. If Arrupe was a radical, it was only in the sense that he took Jesuits and Ignatian spirituality back to their roots.

Early Years

Pedro Arrupe was born November 14, 1907, not fifty miles from Loyola, in Bilbao, capital of Spain's northern Basque province. He would become the first Basque to succeed Ignatius Loyola as superior general of the Jesuits. Together with that oft-noted fact, commentators also repeatedly remarked on how much Arrupe's beaked nose, high forehead, and slight build gave him a striking physical resemblance to Ignatius.

The Arrupe family was middle-class and devoutly Catholic, something not to be taken for granted in a Spain that for more than a century had been rife with anticlericalism. Pedro's father, Marcelino Arrupe, was an architect and a founder of one of the first Catholic newspapers in Spain, *La Gaceta del Norte*. His mother, Dolores, the daughter of a medical doctor, died when Pedro was only ten years old, leaving his long-grieving father and four doting, older sisters to make up for the loss.[3]

Arrupe was remembered as a normal boy, happy, good at soccer, and an excellent student. At eleven he joined the local chapter of the Sodality of the Blessed Virgin Mary, the same Jesuit youth movement to which the young Friedrich Spee belonged in the seventeenth century (see chapter 4). At fifteen Arrupe wrote a prophetic piece for the Sodality publication in which he described Francis Xavier's work in Japan as something to be emulated. But Arrupe's father had set his sights on the boy becoming a doctor, and at graduation from high school Pedro left home to study medicine at San Carlos University in Madrid.

With its broad boulevards, theaters, and sidewalk cafes, Madrid was a teeming metropolis and a far cry from the secure haven that was Bilbao. The times were tense; the 1920s in Spain were already marked by the social and political unrest that would explode a decade later into full-blown civil war. Russia's Bolshevik revolution only a few years earlier had emboldened Spanish socialists and communists. When anarchists assassinated the prime minister in 1923, General Primo de Rivera led a coup, setting up a military dictatorship in place of the civil government.

At first Arrupe lived with a married sister and brother-in-law, but the second year he moved into a student residence. His first year at the University, he won top honors in anatomy; his second year, he ranked first in his class in physiology. By his own admission, he enjoyed reading physics, chemistry, and biology more than literature. Not that he was a drudge— he and his friends enjoyed music, including musical comedy and grand opera. They would buy tickets for the cheap seats, where they made up a cheering section for their favorite singers. Gifted with a fine singing voice himself, Arrupe was later remembered by colleagues in Japan for entertaining them on picnics with his repertoire of Basque folk songs.[4]

When Arrupe came to look back at his four years in Madrid, two incidents in particular stood out in his memory. Both had to do with his involvement in the St. Vincent de Paul Society, a lay organization dedicated to providing aid to the poor. Arrupe's family, while not rich, lived comfortably, and he had had no firsthand experience of true destitution. So when the Society sent him to the poverty-stricken suburbs of the city, he was entering a new world. One day he met a young boy eating a roll.

"Are you having an afternoon snack?" Arrupe asked.

"No," the boy answered, as he munched away.

"Okay, then, what are you doing?" Arrupe recalled smiling, but then the smile froze on his face as the boy replied, "I'm having my breakfast."

"But it's four in the afternoon," Arrupe protested.

"I know," the boy said. "But this is the first time I'm eating today. For you this is snack time; for me it's breakfast."

"Did you skip your noon meal today?" Arrupe asked. "Does your father work?"

"I didn't skip it. We never eat more than once a day. And my father does not work, because I don't have one."[5]

The second such experience occurred with his close friend Enrique Chacón. The two university students had been assigned to visit a widow named Luisa in a slum neighborhood of Vallecas. After climbing up the dilapidated staircase of a run-down apartment building, they found the door they were looking for, only to hear deafening shouts coming from the other side. Hesitantly they opened the door and looked in. Suddenly there was silence, as six half-dressed children fled behind the skirts of the two women standing before them.

After explaining who they were and why they had come, Enrique and Pedro handed out caramels to the children and began to learn how two women and six children, all boys, survived with little or no money, living together in one room. While one of them went out to earn something, the other stayed behind to watch the children. Mornings they ate garlic soup; in the afternoon beans and bread. At night all eight of them shared the same bed with its soiled mattress, three boys at the head, three at the foot, and in the space between them the two women. If the weather was cold, the boys stayed in bed under a blanket, since they had no clothes warm enough for the outdoors. Enrique and Pedro left the money they had brought for the women and distributed the rest of the caramels. Returning to the street, they walked home in silence.[6]

Like his encounter with the boy eating his breakfast at four in the afternoon, his visit with the two widows seared itself on Arrupe's memory. Some thirty years later, when writing about his years in Madrid, it was those two experiences more than any others that he recalled in painfully minute detail. In the years ahead he would experience privation himself. The way other world travelers visit museums and tourist sites, Arrupe visited barrios, ghettos, and slums. But he seemed never to forget—even to the point of remembering the smile that froze on his face—encountering a child's hunger for the first time.

LOURDES

In 1926 Arrupe was at the end of his fourth and last year of undergraduate medical studies in Madrid when he was suddenly called home to Bilbao. His father was seriously ill. Marcelino Arrupe had been a pillar of faith and strength to his family, and his death was a blow to the nineteen-year-old Pedro and his sisters alike. As a way of finding some solace in their mourning, they decided to make a pilgrimage together to Lourdes. Situated in southern France, the celebrated Marian shrine was not far from Bilbao, just the other side of the Pyrenees.

Lourdes had been a little-known village until 1858, when Bernadette Soubirous, a simple country girl, claimed to have had heavenly visions there of a beautiful lady. Ever since then a steady stream of pilgrims and curiosity seekers had made their way to Lourdes from all corners of the globe. They came for one reason—miracles. Next to the grotto where she had her visions, Bernadette uncovered a stream of water capable, it seemed, of wonders. Hundreds of crutches and tokens of gratitude decked the shrine basilica and its grotto, testifying to cures unexplainable by science. While not everyday occurrences, the cures were frequent enough to draw visitors by the hundreds of thousands annually.

Life in Lourdes in 1926 centered around the shrine. Souvenir shops sold rosaries, statues, and properly emblazoned bottles to be taken home filled with water from the grotto. One walked to the shrine alongside invalids on stretchers and families pushing children in wheelchairs.

Shortly after arriving at Lourdes, Arrupe sought out the Office of Verification, where he offered his services. On the basis of his four years in medical school, he was authorized to examine any cures alleged to be miraculous. More than once during his years at San Carlos University, Arrupe had heard one or another professor scoff at Lourdes as rank superstition. As a man of faith and science both, he wanted to see for himself and, if necessary, to attest to what he saw. Arrupe spent three months at Lourdes, and with the same kind of exquisite detail with which he described his first encounters with poverty, he would later recall his remarkable experiences there.

One afternoon he was in the basilica shrine for the customary procession and benediction with the Blessed Sacrament. A bishop was conducting the service that day, carrying the Blessed Sacrament and stopping every few yards to make the sign of the cross with the Sacrament over the hundreds of miracle seekers lined up in rows. All around him Arrupe heard prayers whispered in French, Spanish, English, Italian, German—"Lord, if you wish you can cure me," "Our Lady of Lourdes, take pity on us," "Lord, speak but the word and I will be healed."

Suddenly a commotion broke out in the basilica. A nun who had been paralyzed with Pott's disease rose from her stretcher, fell on her knees before the Sacrament, and exclaimed, "I'm cured." Arrupe later examined the nun, studied the X-rays of her deteriorated spine, and verified that indeed her cure could not be explained by medical science. There was no doubt in his mind that the love of God and the faith of that nun had wrought a miracle.

Another time Arrupe was present when doctors took X-rays of a seventy-five-year-old woman from Brussels. Surgeons in Belgium had discovered an advanced case of stomach cancer. When she was told only a miracle could save her, she decided that a miracle it would have to be. Against medical advice she made the trip to Lourdes, where she was immersed in the waters. Back at the Lourdes hospice, she found herself hungry for the first time in years. In three days she was walking around the town in splendid good health. When Arrupe and other medical doctors from the Verification Bureau read her X-rays, they found not the least trace of the cancer.

A third cure Arrupe experienced was that of a young man in his twenties. One of Arrupe's sisters had pointed him out earlier in the day, visibly suffering from infantile paralysis, a look of defeat on his face as a nurse wheeled him among the throng. Once again it was during the procession with the Blessed Sacrament that the young man rose to his feet, convinced he was cured. Once again Arrupe was allowed to examine the young man's case and to attest that there was no natural explanation for his cure.[7]

Arrupe left Lourdes profoundly moved. He would come to regard his months there as the birth of his vocation.[8] He had no doubt but that he had been privileged to experience firsthand the wondrous power of faith, not just once but three times. He returned to Bilbao and then to Madrid, where in the fall he would begin his graduate studies in medicine. Arrupe found everything to be exactly the same as it was before—but he was different. He had no doubt that he had experienced miracles, but the dominant culture at the San Carlos medical school was determined by a faculty who had long given up on religion in the name of science. They had no time for stories about miracles.

Arrupe felt out of sorts. His friends told him he looked "out of it," and he admitted they were right. He was thinking about what he wanted to do with the rest of his life and was not sure that it included being a medical doctor. Some afflictions, he knew, needed a different kind of healing than that which physicians could provide.

Looking back later at those days, Arrupe confessed he did not know when exactly the idea first came to him to become a Jesuit. He was sure it evolved slowly, but once he decided, he moved quickly. On his way back to Bilbao for Christmas, he stopped at Loyola and inquired about entering the Society. He was told there were no problems. He waited until after the holidays to tell his sisters of his plans; they were stunned but ultimately supportive of his decision.

Not at all supportive, however, was Professor Juan Negrín, a leading member of the medical faculty and one of Arrupe's teachers. A well-known socialist and agnostic (who would go on to become prime minister of the Spanish Republic), Negrín wrote Arrupe's sisters imploring them to dissuade him from this career change. To Negrín's mind it was barbarous that, with a brilliant career before him and great contributions to make in the field, Arrupe would leave medicine to become a priest.

Negrín also refused to sign a document granting Arrupe an award for being recognized as the foremost student in medicine. Later he made the trip all the way to Loyola to visit Arrupe and explain why he had refused to sign. It was nothing personal, he said; in fact, he liked Arrupe very much. He was just hoping that he could lure him back into medicine and away from religious life. Arrupe smiled, and the two men embraced.

THE SOCIETY OF JESUS

On January 15, 1927, Arrupe entered the novitiate at Loyola and with it a regimen of training that went back to Ignatius and the constitutions of the Society. The routine was as unvarying as it was traditional—prayer, examination of conscience, some brief free time, and manual labor in the garden. Overseeing his development was the master of novices, under whose direction he made the full thirty-day Spiritual Excercises. In the shadow of the fortress where the Exercises first germinated, he learned to discern spirits and listen for the voice of God.

After two years as a novice, Arrupe took his first vows and began studying Greek and Latin classics like all the Jesuits who had gone before him. It was at this time that he first wrote to the superior general in Rome, requesting to follow in the footsteps of Francis Xavier and be sent as a missionary to Japan. To his disappointment, his Jesuit superiors responded ambiguously, taking positive note of his aspirations but without guaranteeing they would be realized. Arrupe would have to wait and see what the years ahead would bring.

The uncertainty of his future corresponded to the uncertainty of the times. He was at the beginning of courses in philosophy when Spain entered into a decade that would take it from street fights to a fratricidal civil war. In April 1931, electoral victories for liberal, labor, and socialist parties led to the abdication of King Alfonso XIII, and Spain declared itself a socialist republic. That summer the new government promulgated a new, markedly anticlerical constitution. As was often the case, the Jesuits were the first to feel its provisions. In October Spain's socialist government dissolved the Society of Jesus, nationalized its assets, and ordered all Jesuits out of the country. Arrupe would continue his studies at the Jesuit college in Marneffe, Belgium: "the beginning of my exodus," as he would describe it, and "the first step of my formation as a missionary."[9]

After two years of philosophy in Belgium, Arrupe was assigned to pursue theology in Holland at Valkenburg, where he was exposed to some of the finest scholars the Society had to offer. Because of his undergraduate training in medicine, Arrupe's interests focused on the ethical questions being raised by medical science. The choice was more than fortuitous. It was 1933, and the rise of national socialism in Germany gave new prominence to its racial theories and new urgency to questions of racial enhancement by means of eugenic sterilization.

Arrupe was not unprepared, but was still quite astounded, when in 1936 an acquaintance who was president of a Spanish Catholic medical association arranged an invitation for him to participate at an international congress on eugenics in Vienna. Despite feelings of inadequacy— he was only in his third year of theology and not yet a priest—he accepted the invitation and delivered two papers before an audience of distinguished scientists and academics. They received his papers warmly, but their applause and kind words for the young Jesuit did not assuage his feelings of intimidation and inadequacy.

Looking back at his vocation as a Jesuit, Arrupe would come to regard his experience in Vienna alongside that at Lourdes for the impact it had on him. He learned important lessons at that eugenics congress, like the critical importance of scientific work and the influence it can have on society. He learned that theologians should presume to engage scholars on moral issues only after acquiring a respectable command of their disciplines. And he experienced the virulence of the racism that was gripping Nazi Germany and Austria. It was, as he put it, a "culture shock."[10]

Arrupe returned to Belgium, where on July 30, 1936, the eve of the feast of St. Ignatius, he was ordained a priest. Just weeks before, all-out civil war had erupted in Spain, so none of his family could be with him. A month later Arrupe's provincial sent him a telegram informing him to make immediate arrangements to travel to the United States. The newly ordained Fr. Arrupe set sail for the United States, where he would continue his formal education and add to his Spanish, Latin, French, and German a conversational command of English.

Arrupe completed his fourth year of theology at Saint Mary's College, Kansas. His formal education had come to a close, but the life lessons continued. What was supposed to be a vacation in San Antonio, Texas, turned into a trip to Mexico, where an anticlerical government was hunting down and arresting priests for doing pastoral work. Ignoring the risk, Arrupe dressed in lay clothes and "kept busy" at a school with children from Spain who were orphaned because of the civil war. He would write of his time with these little exiles as a "moving human experience," being helpless to do anything but listen to their stories, wipe away their tears, and pray.[11]

Returning from Mexico, Arrupe did his tertianship in Cleveland, Ohio, a second immersion into Ignatian spirituality, like that of his novitiate. Once again he made the full thirty-day Spiritual Excercises and studied the constitutions. While in Cleveland he received word that his longtime prayers were going to be answered. He was being assigned to do mission work in Japan.

Out of the more than two years he spent in the United States, the last three months were plausibly the most significant. He was invited to do pastoral work at a maximum security prison in New York where more than 500 Spanish-speaking prisoners were held for crimes ranging from armed robbery and rape to murder. The experience opened his eyes to a world of iron gates, grills, and shouted obscenities. It didn't help his nervousness when a guard asked, "Which lion should we let out of the cage for you, Father?" Arrupe went down the list—Rodríguez, Alvarez, García, López, Sánchez—and at random chose number 279. "You picked the worst one," the guard told him. "I hope he doesn't kill you."

Number 279 turned out to be the first of Arrupe's success stories. He was able to get this prisoner and many others to talk about their lives and families, and he found that even the most hardened criminals softened when asked about their children. He remembered a prisoner from Panama, a self-confessed and convicted murderer, who told how he would walk home from work just to save ten cents so he could buy his children candy. Arrupe remembered too his farewell visit; the prisoners were at recreation on the baseball field. It turned into a "sort of a party" as the "friends" he had made began singing old Spanish songs, and he responded with a Basque song of his own.[12]

Arrupe was not naive about human nature; he knew what terrible crimes people can commit. But he also knew that the men he had met in prison were capable of repentance and change. They had come to New York from all over Latin America hoping for a better life, but, pushed to the margins of society, they perpetrated outrageous acts and fell off the edge. He found the contradictions in their lives and characters a mystery. Arrupe would later write that, had he not already set his heart on Japan, he could well have spent the rest of his life as a priest ministering to prisoners in New York. But in September 1938, he set sail from Seattle, bound for Japan.

INCREDIBLE JAPAN

Arrupe's first months in what he would call "incredible Japan" were spent in Tokyo. Here he set about studying Japanese, notoriously difficult and unlike any of the languages he already spoke with some fluency. Tokyo also initiated him into Japanese culture, so alien from anything he had ever experienced. He learned to pray while kneeling on a straw mat and sitting back on his heels. He learned to breakfast on seaweed rice, bean-paste soup, and green tea. And by working with impoverished Korean immigrants, generally despised by the Japanese, he learned that racism is not an exclusively Western phenomenon.

After eighteen months in Tokyo, Arrupe was assigned to a mission in the industrial town of Ube. His Japanese was still shaky, and the thrill of being a missionary in Japan had worn off. He wrote later of experiencing profound loneliness and discovering the reality of missionary life to be quite different from what he had expected.[13] Those feelings abated with time, improved language skills, and his reassignment to the parish church of Yamaguchi. He found himself not only in an ancient, former capital and imperial city, but also serving in a church founded by Francis Xavier himself.

It was 1941, and the war that had embroiled Europe for more than a year was literally on the other side of Pedro Arrupe's world. But all that changed the morning of December 8, when Arrupe and his parishioners heard the news over the radio: on December 7 Japan had declared war against the United States. Japanese armed forces had attacked and destroyed the U.S. fleet anchored at Pearl Harbor.

Arrupe knew that war would mean consequences for him. Just how soon he learned later that day, when members of the Japanese military police came to the church with orders to search the premises. Though he was a Spaniard, Arrupe had spent two years studying in the United States, and the Japanese authorities were notoriously suspicious of foreigners of any stripe. When they found his Latin prayer book and letters in various languages, including some in English from the United States, they were sure they had evidence against Arrupe.

Arrupe was taken to military police headquarters where he was interrogated through the night. Why had he left Spain? Why did he go to the United States? Why did he preach peace when Japan was preparing for war? At the end of a long night, the military police ordered him to be held in the maximum security prison. There he was given a uniform and put into a cell with no table, no chair, no bed—only a metal receptacle and a straw sleeping mat on a stone floor. He was to be kept in solitary confinement, on what charges and for how long he had no idea. Only at the end of his imprisonment did he learn he was being held for espionage.

Arrupe remembered his imprisonment in terms of the cold December sun setting at four in the afternoon, fourteen-hour nights, and absolute silence.[14] Once a day a guard brought him a bowl of turnip leaf soup or a vegetable and rice stew. At irregular intervals he would be taken out of his cell for interrogation. What was his name; who were his parents; where did he go to school? If he was a priest, why was there a letter in his possession indicating he had attended a medical conference in Vienna? Why had he given up studying medicine to become a priest? Arrupe answered the questions politely and as best he could.

One day Arrupe overheard his guards discussing what came first, water or the clouds. Let's ask the foreigner, one of them suggested. And with that Arrupe found himself talking to his guards about beginnings, creation, and soon enough God. His conversations with his guards became a daily occurrence. At these catechism sessions Arrupe, like missionaries before him, learned how difficult it was to express Christian ideas of God, sin, and eternity when the words implied different meanings in Japanese. How does one translate the symbol of the Good Shepherd, he would ask, in a land without shepherds or sheep?

Christmas came and passed without ceremony. Arrupe spent his days praying and studying his Japanese dictionary. At midnight on January 11, he was awakened and led out of his cell to be interrogated once again, this time by the chief of the military police. Once again the same questions about his early life, daily routine, political views, religious beliefs. What did he think about God? Did he consider the emperor to be God? (No, Arrupe answered.) His conversations with his prison guards proved helpful. The questions went on without stopping for a day and a half. Arrupe was exhausted, but he knew that one wrong answer could mean the difference between life and death. He answered slowly, patiently, and carefully.

Finally, at the end of thirty-seven hours, his chief interrogator read aloud a statement beginning with the words "I, Pedro Arrupe," summing up his testimony about his reasons for being in Japan. Arrupe found it a remarkably accurate expression of his beliefs as a missionary and priest. If he agreed to its contents, he was to put his fingerprint at the bottom of the document. Arrupe obliged, and a half hour later he was free to go.

Looking back at his thirty-five days in solitary confinement, Arrupe refused to fault the Japanese military police or their methods. He insisted that he was treated no better or worse than any other prisoner. Not sure whether or not he was a spy, the Japanese authorities decided to judge his guilt or innocence by observing his behavior under duress. By never complaining, by remaining dedicated to his prayers and study, he proved to his jailers that he was what he claimed to be. "I believe this was the most instructive month of my entire life," he reflected later. Strengthened by an inner dialogue with the "guest of my soul," he now had a new awareness of silence, solitude, and severe poverty.[15]

Arrupe returned to his church, where his former prison guards visited him occasionally and played table tennis in the parish hall. The following March the Jesuit superior, Fr. Lasalle, visited him in Yamaguchi. The novice master at the Jesuit novitiate in Nagatsuka was ill and could not continue on the job. Lasalle thought that Arrupe would be the right choice to replace him. Arrupe protested his inadequate command of the Japanese language and culture but to no avail. Upon formal notice of his reassignment, Arrupe proceeded to the novitiate at Nagatsuka, nestled up in the hills three miles outside Hiroshima.

HIROSHIMA

The novitiate at Nagatsuka had been built in the style of a Japanese pagoda. Since the days of Xavier, Valignano, Ricci, and de Nobili, Jesuit missionaries to the Orient had tried to fit into the landscape without appearing entirely foreign. Along these lines, if he were to teach his Japanese students in a way that touched their hearts, Arrupe knew he had to learn more than their language. He needed to penetrate into their minds and culture. He began taking lessons from a Zen master of the tea ceremony. He studied the art of making controlled bows and measured gestures, learning to do something simple with solemnity.

Arrupe also applied himself to the Zen arts of calligraphy and archery. He would spend an hour a day painting Japanese characters with a brush in such a way as to identify with the forms. He learned to draw back a bow in a slow deliberate action, releasing the arrow with consummate tranquility. On a visit to a nearby Buddhist monastery, he observed the novices in meditation. He began assuming the same posture during his own daily hour of meditation each morning, sitting Zen-style on his heels.

As novice master, Arrupe was responsible not only for the spiritual formation of his charges but also for their sustenance. Wartime rations were meager, and the diet at the novitiate austere. Arrupe became a familiar sight, riding the three miles to Hiroshima on his bicycle and scrounging for whatever food he could find. Former students remember him shining the shoes of the novices during siesta or once, dressed in swimming clothes, cleaning out the novitiate's sewage system. To teach the novices to let go of their egoism and learn humility, Arrupe would have them go to Hiroshima and walk behind horses, collecting their manure with a bucket and spade.[16]

In May and June of 1942, the battles of Coral Sea and Midway put a halt to Japanese advances in the Pacific and turned the tide of the war. In the course of the next two years, U.S. victories at Guadalcanal and New Guinea ended Japanese occupation of distant islands, so that in the summer of 1944, U.S. aircraft could begin using China as a base to bomb the Japanese mainland. Arrupe remembered the practice drills in which even the elderly took part to learn to defend themselves from U.S. invaders. He noticed bronze statues disappearing from the parks so their metal could be used for the war effort. At the same time he was struck by the Japanese assurance that victory would ultimately be theirs. For all but a few Japanese, the possibility of surrender was inconceivable.[17]

This conviction of Japanese victory held fast despite massive U.S. bombing strikes on Japanese cities. In one such bombing, an estimated 35,000 Japanese perished in the city of Kobe. Japanese homes were made of wood, paper, and straw, and the fires that resulted from the bombing of Tokyo resulted in the death of more than 90,000 Japanese. For some reason, Hiroshima had been spared the bombings that had devastated other cities, despite the fact that it was a principal port for transporting troops and housed the second general headquarters of the Japanese military. Unlike Kobe and Osaka, Hiroshima did not manufacture munitions and was not a large industrial center, so its inhabitants thought they would be spared. They gradually learned to take no notice when every morning at 4:30 an American B-29 bomber on reconnaissance appeared in the skies and then flew away. Its punctuality was such that its sound served to remind Arrupe to begin preparations for 5:30 Mass.

On the morning of August 6, 1945, the unexpected appearance of a lone B-29 bomber in the sky at 7:55 set off the usual air-raid alarm. When, five minutes later, the plane suddenly changed course and left the city, an all clear sounded. Then at 8:15, two B-29s were sighted, flying six miles high, too far for antiaircraft fire. At a certain point each made a violent turn, one to the right, the other to the left. One, the *Enola Gay*, dropped a bomb. The other dropped a trio of parachutes carrying measuring instruments that would transmit back readings from the ground. The pilots were told they had only forty-three seconds to get far enough away.

The Jesuits had two houses in Hiroshima, a parish church in the center of the city and the novitiate where Arrupe and thirty-five young Jesuits lived in the hills on the outskirts. Arrupe was in his room with another priest when they saw a blinding flash of light. They jumped up to see what had happened and opened the door facing the city. A hurricane blast threw them to the ground, shattering doors and windows all about them. Bricks, tiles, and glass rained down on them for seconds that seemed like hours. Once he was able to stand, Arrupe hurried through the house to discover with gratitude that no one had been hurt.

Arrupe and several others rushed outside to the garden to look for a crater or some sign of what they took for a nearby bomb blast. They found nothing. The trees, flowers, and rice fields surrounding the novitiate all seemed quite normal. After about fifteen minutes, seeing first smoke and then flames rising in the distance, they climbed a hill to get a better view. There, three miles away, they could see Hiroshima, its wood, paper, and straw houses enveloped in a lake of fire, a mushroomlike cloud billowing up into the sky.[18]

They did not know yet that they had experienced the first explosion of an atom bomb. They did not know about the dangers of radiation. They only knew that they had Jesuit colleagues, including their superior, Fr. Lasalle, living in the parish church at the heart of the city. Before they could set out to find and, if possible, help them, scores of wounded and bleeding victims of the bomb blast began streaming up the hills away from the burning city below. Arrupe quickly converted the chapel into a hospital ward and began administering first aid. The library and other rooms were cleared of glass and debris to make room for more makeshift beds, 150 in all.

Sent out on foot or on bicycles to find food, the students returned with gifts of meat, fish, and eggs. Neighbors depleted their gardens of potatoes and squash. At four that afternoon, a Jesuit brother from the city arrived to tell Arrupe that the Jesuit church and parish house had burned to the ground. The priests were alive but too weak and injured to move. Arrupe, with several others, collected poles and boards for stretchers, food, and medicine, and set out for the city.

Arrupe's words conjure images of Dante's *Inferno* when he describes Hiroshima on that evening. His first sight was of a group of young women dragging themselves along the road, clinging to one another, one of them blistered and burned, with blood coursing down her face. On and on in a steady procession the victims came. A child with a piece of glass embedded in his left eye, another with a wooden splinter protruding like a dagger from between his ribs. A young man half-crazed called for help to release his mother, buried under the rubble of what had been their home. Even more heartbreaking were the cries of children searching for their parents.

By ten that evening Arrupe and his colleagues found what had been the Jesuit residence. All five of the priests had been injured, one of them critically, slowly bleeding to death from glass fragments embedded in his body. After Arrupe removed the glass fragments with a razor blade, they put him on a stretcher and slowly made their way back to the novitiate, stopping every hundred yards to rest. When they came to the river, Arrupe encountered another spectacle worthy of Dante. People fleeing the burning city had sought relief on the river's shores at low tide. Now, in the middle of the night, as the tide began to rise, they lay wounded and half-buried in mud, too exhausted to move. The cries of the drowning victims that night would echo in Arrupe's memory the rest of his life.[19]

At five in the morning, the Jesuits finally arrived with their wounded colleagues back at the novitiate. Anywhere there was floor space, there lay the injured. Having spent a night walking through hell, Arrupe knew he needed more than sleep to help him face the tasks before him. He donned his vestments and proceeded to offer a Mass that, like all else during those extraordinary days, he would never forget.

The bodies of the wounded so covered the chapel floor that he had to be careful where he stepped. During most of the Mass he faced the altar, his back to the congregation. But at one point the liturgy called for him to turn away from the altar, face the congregation, extend his arms, and say *Dominus vobiscum* (The Lord be with you). Looking at those faces contorted with pain, not comprehending what he was doing but visibly hungry for the slightest comfort in their agony, Arrupe froze. He stood, his hands outstretched, unable to move. Scientific progress and technology were being used to destroy the human race. Christ's words in Luke's Gospel came to his lips, "Father forgive them, they know not what they do." Arrupe prayed for the tormented victims before him, that they be given faith and strength to bear the pain. "I do not think I have ever said Mass with such devotion," he later wrote.[20]

That same morning one of the novitiate employees informed Arrupe that he had found a sack of bottles filled with what looked like medicine. Would they be of any help? The bottles proved to be a godsend: they contained boric acid. He ordered sheets and underwear torn up to make bandages, and instructed the Jesuits on how to clean and dress wounds, keeping them moist with an antiseptic solution of boric acid to prevent blood poisoning. The discharge from the wounds adhered to the bandages, which the Jesuits would change four or five times a day. The medical treatment was primitive but it kept the wounds relatively clean. And it worked.

The most serious case Arrupe treated in those days was a young man, age twenty-two. Hardly able to move himself, half his body covered with burns, he was dragged to the novitiate by his wife of one month. Arrupe hesitated. The pus had hardened underneath the burns. Cleaning the wounds would be painful, and there was no anesthetic. The young man assured the priest he could take the pain. With his desk serving as an operating table, Arrupe felt like an executioner. For two and a half hours he reopened, cleaned, and dressed the wounds, as the young man writhed in agony beneath his hands.

Just as memorable were the children. The bomb had exploded during school hours, leaving thousands of children separated from their parents, many of them severely wounded, wandering in the streets unable to fend for themselves. The Jesuits sought out as many as they could, bringing them to the novitiate, where they began treating them at once to prevent infection and fever. One of them had been hit by a falling beam and suffered a scalp wound that ran from ear to ear, filled with clay and pieces of glass. Again, with no anesthetic available, the poor child's screams filled the house. They had to tie him to a cart, take him outside, and finish cleaning and dressing the wound on a nearby hill.

The day after the explosion, cars and trains began arriving from Tokyo and Osaka, and the people of Hiroshima learned that they had been the victims of the first atomic bomb. It was a new word in everyone's vocabulary but not much help, since no one knew its full effects on the human organism. Rumors spread with warnings not to go into the city, that a gas in the air there kills for seventy years. But the Jesuits knew that unless the tens of thousands of dead bodies there were cremated, the consequent epidemic would be just as dire. Disregarding the danger of the unknown, they went into the city and began with other brave souls to pile bodies into pyramids, pour on fuel, and set them on fire, as many as fifty or sixty at a time.

When Ignatius gathered together his society of companions to help people by doing whatever needed to be done, he could not have conceived that it would someday entail cremating corpses. But caring for the victims of radiation in Hiroshima was not too far a cry from caring for victims of syphilis in Venice. Thanks to Arrupe's medical expertise and leadership at the makeshift hospital, all but two of the victims treated at the novitiate survived. With the help of the Japanese police, all the children in the house were reunited with their families. And the following April, the young man who had been dragged to the novitiate by his wife left with her, the two of them walking down the hill, newly baptized and, as Arrupe recalled, smiling.[21]

POSTWAR YEARS

Three days after the first atomic bomb fell on Hiroshima, a second demolished Nagasaki. At noon on August 15, millions of Japanese dutifully crowded around loudspeakers and radio sets, as they had been instructed to do the day before. They listened with disbelief as their emperor announced the government's unconditional surrender to the Allied forces. Most were ready to fight to the death, in hand-to-hand combat if necessary. They were not prepared for the humiliation of surrender. Japan had not suffered a defeat in more than 2,500 years. Arrupe marveled at the discipline the Japanese demonstrated. He recalled the sadness, the tears flowing down waxen, expressionless faces. Looking back twenty-five years later, he had no doubt that the war ended ultimately not because of the atomic bomb but at the order of the emperor.[22]

The bomb blast that devastated Hiroshima had stopped the clock in Arrupe's office. He left it there as a reminder of the day that changed the world and his life. In the following weeks and months, existence for the Jesuits and Japanese alike was marked by a struggle for survival and by tending to the victims, including those of a strange, new disease that came to be called radiation sickness.

The American occupation of Japan began in October. There was apprehension on both sides, but the absolute submission of the Japanese and the courtesy of the American troops helped to melt mutual fears and animosity. The Japanese began to rebuild their cities, and the Jesuits, their novitiate.

With all he lived through that August 6 and after, Arrupe thought he had nerves of steel. Five years later, however, he found himself in Bogota, Colombia, watching a documentary film on Hiroshima. All the horror and tragedy he had experienced over the course of months had been captured on celluloid and concentrated into an hour and a half. It was too much for him. Embarrassed, his vision blinded by tears, he had to walk out. Unreal images on a screen let loose memories too many and too real for him to endure a second time.[23]

Even if he could have or wanted to, Arrupe was not allowed to forget his experiences of August 1945. As a "survivor of Hiroshima," he had become a celebrity. In 1949 he left for what would become an eighteen-month speaking tour that took him one-and-a-half times around the globe. Three other speaking tours of six months each followed in the mid-fifties and early sixties. Looking back thirty-five years, Arrupe figured that he spoke to Western audiences about Hiroshima and Japan more than a thousand times, always met with the same rapt attention. Hiroshima was no mere past event but a symbol of an ever constant and ominous presence, reminding people that the nuclear destruction of the human race was a very real possibility.

A privileged witness to the dawn of the nuclear age, Arrupe described Hiroshima as a satellite that now accompanied the earth on its rotation, a sword of Damocles poised over our heads. Hiroshima revealed the vanity of all that can disappear in a flash and, at the same time, the substance of spiritual truths and values. During the war Americans and Japanese had demonized one another, as adversaries invariably do. From his years of personal experience, Arrupe knew the admirable qualities of both peoples, and he saw how the defeated Japanese and victorious Americans slowly grew to admire one another and to recognize one another's humanity.

Don Pedro, the priest, made no claim to expertise in politics, but he knew the human heart. He pointed to history to prove that neither wars nor violent revolutions had ever solved human problems. And he saw the same virus lying at the root of all wars and violence: worse than the destruction caused by violence, he wrote, is the hatred that gives rise to it. The hatred that resorts to violence has been with humankind since its infancy, when wars meant swords and slingshots. Now, in the age of nuclear weapons, international peace conferences and arms limitation treaties will be futile until peoples stop demonizing one another. Peace, Arrupe wrote, can only come of love, and love can only come with discovering God within ourselves and "in the rest of humanity."[24]

Arrupe's first international speaking (and fund-raising) tour came at the suggestion of the Jesuit general, Fr. John Baptist Janssens. Arrupe met him after being elected to represent Japan at a meeting of Jesuit delegates in Rome. Four years later the general appointed him superior (vice-provincial) over all the Jesuit missions and ministries in Japan, some 200 Jesuits hailing from twenty-nine different nations. That same year he began a second speaking and fund-raising tour that took him throughout Latin America and Western Europe.

With his headquarters now in Tokyo, it was Arrupe's responsibility to visit every Jesuit house in Japan at least once a year, meeting personally with every Jesuit. His task was to listen as each Jesuit opened his mind and heart to him, and then to advise, console, encourage, and exhort. The Jesuits he supervised in those days came to describe him as an indomitable optimist, perhaps too trusting of people, a visionary with great ideas who needed to be surrounded by realists, hard on himself but always kind to others.[25]

Arrupe also found time to become a prolific author. After he published a book in Spanish on "incredible Japan," in 1951, there followed a life of St. Francis Xavier in Japanese, a translation of works by St. John of the Cross, and a commentary on the *Spiritual Exercises.* In the course of the 1950s, Jesuits in Japan established ten new missionary posts, built new churches, and expanded the University of Sophia. In 1958, Jesuit head-quarters in Rome made Japan an autonomous province and Arrupe a provincial.

That year also saw the death of Pope Pius XII and the election of Angelo Roncalli as Pope John XXIII. In contrast to his aloof, ascetic-appearing predecessor, Roncalli was rotund and jovial, endearing himself almost immediately to people both in and outside the Catholic fold. Well on in years, pundits dubbed him a "transition pope" who would not live long enough to make any serious impact on the church. They were right on the first score (his papacy lasted only four and a half years), but his impact was such as to make him a transition to a very new and different period in church history.

Pope John XXIII lost no time in making his mark; early in 1959 he announced his intentions to convene an ecumenical council of the world's bishops. The purpose of the council was not to condemn heresy or error but to "update" the Catholic Church and, he hoped, promote closer unity among Christian churches. Living in postwar Paris as a papal diplomat to France, Roncalli experienced how foreign the church had become in the minds of most moderns. Much of the church's worship and teaching had simply become unintelligible. Traditional language and customs needed to be scrutinized and, if necessary, translated into a new idiom so that the church's message could once again touch people's minds and hearts.

As a Jesuit missionary in Japan, Arrupe understood the challenges entailed in Pope John's program. "Updating" *(aggiornamento)* in the church was a logical corollary of "accommodation," a hallmark of Jesuit missionary activity from the beginning. If Europe had become post-Christian, no less a mission territory than Japan, then church leaders had better learn the language, thinking, and culture of the people they wanted to engage. Arrupe knew from long hours of hard work and study how difficult this could be. And how absolutely necessary.

Pope John embodied what he preached. When he spoke, people took notice, particularly of his social encyclicals, *Mater et magistra* (Mother and teacher) and *Pacem in terris* (Peace on earth). He disturbed consciences when he pointed to the responsibilities of the wealthy and criticized economic policies determined solely by the marketplace without regard to human dignity and justice. In some cases he touched raw nerves. *(Mater, si; magistra, no,* one conservative American Catholic gibed notoriously.) But Arrupe found the pope's social teaching singularly consonant with his experiences.

In 1962, on the other side of the globe from Rome, Arrupe was a spectator like most everyone else, reading about the bishops' debates at the early sessions of the Second Vatican Council in magazines and newspapers. Pope John XXIII, who died in June 1963, was succeeded by Pope Paul VI, who vowed to continue the council's program of renewal. That fall on the first Sunday of Advent, the initial intimations of that renewal became visible with the introduction of vernacular into parts of the Latin Mass. It took five centuries, but Valignano and Ricci were at last vindicated, as the

Japanese Catholics at Don Pedro's Mass participated for the first time in their own language.

The death of Superior General John Baptist Janssens in October 1964 meant that Jesuits would have to choose a new general, and that Pedro Arrupe, as the Japanese provincial, would be one of the electors. The following May, when Arrupe arrived in Rome for the Thirty-first General Congregation, he found, thanks to his speaking and fund-raising tours, that many of the faces among the more than 200 delegates were familiar to him. Those delegates knew, even though the work of the council was still going on, that the new general would have to deal with dramatic changes in both church and society. His vision would have to be global in every sense. It took only three ballots for the delegates to elect Pedro Arrupe Superior General of the Society of Jesus.

SUPERIOR GENERAL

His origins had inclined Arrupe early on to identify with his fellow Basque, Francis Xavier. Now, after almost thirty years as a missionary in Japan, he unexpectedly found himself the twenty-seventh successor of Ignatius Loyola. With Rome as his new address, Arrupe, once notorious for his disinterest in politics, was thrust into the center of world and church affairs, both in singular states of upheaval. It was 1965 when Arrupe took the helm of the Society of Jesus—the middle of one of the most turbulent and pivotal decades in modern history.

In 1961 the Soviet Union had put a cosmonaut into space, setting off a race to the moon. That same year a barbed-wire fence was put up in Berlin, gradually to become a wall and a symbol of a world divided into armed camps. For ten days in October 1962, Cold War nerves grew more tense as the Cuban missile crisis brought two nuclear superpowers to the brink of no return. And a generation of postwar baby boomers born under the cloud of Hiroshima began coming of age. In the United States, boycotts and marches against racial discrimination became mass movements for civil rights, and hippies squared off with hardhats over long hair and a self-styled sexual revolution and counterculture. In 1963 an assassin's bullet felled President John F. Kennedy, and later in the decade the same fate befell his brother Robert and civil rights leader Martin Luther King.

When Arrupe became general in 1965, no assumption, institution, or aspect of the status quo in Europe or North America could be presumed above question or criticism. Within that social climate Vatican II initiated a series of changes. Latin virtually disappeared from the liturgy; altars were moved out from walls so Mass could be celebrated facing the congregation; people were encouraged to put away their rosaries and read the Bible. Laity were told that they too, not only the clergy, are the church and have a right to share in its worship and ministry. Almost overnight prayer services with Protestants went from forbidden to encouraged. Trained for generations to accept constancy as a sign of their church's superiority, Catholics wondered what would change next. It was only a small step to begin asking what *should* change next. With the repeal of "no meat on Friday," Catholics questioned not if but when their pastors would be married priests.

Innovation, like dissent, continued through the decade: the first heart transplant, transistor radio, audiocassette, photocopier, fax machine. The birth control pill had been introduced earlier, in the 1950s, but in 1968, contrary to widespread expectation, Pope Paul VI restated the traditional ban on all artificial contraception *(Humanae vitae)*. Catholic laity, priests, and theologians dissented openly, and even bishops distanced themselves from the pope's position. In 1969 the United States put two astronauts on the moon but proved unable to end the war in Vietnam, provoking hundreds of thousands of protestors to join in antiwar demonstrations. At the same time, tens of thousands of priests and nuns left clerical and religious life, including thousands of Jesuits.

After electing Arrupe superior general, the Thirty-first General Congregation elected his four general assistants and made a modification to the Society's constitution. Though elected for life, the general could abdicate his office on the grounds of illness, old age, or infirmity. Arrupe settled into his new office but kept up his old routine. He still rose at 4:00 A.M.

and did his morning meditation Zen-style on a mat. After Mass and breakfast, he would study until nine and then begin the work of reading and
answering letters, writing talks, and meeting visitors. In his office, facing
his armchair, hung a picture of Ignatius Loyola and eventually, opposite it,
a photograph of the earth taken from the moon—both eloquent symbols
of his new responsibilities as he saw them.[26]

His election as general meant that Arrupe was invited to participate at
the fourth and final session of Vatican II. The assembled bishops listened
intently and with some curiosity as he spoke to them regarding the proposed draft on the church in the modern world. On the issue of atheism,
he stressed that the church's response had to be social, not just cerebral,
formulated in the center of world affairs, not from some intellectual ghetto.
In another address he drew on his missionary experience and spoke to the
church's need to become at home in diverse cultures and learn from them.

Those two concerns—"inculturation" and the "integration" of faith and
justice—would become hallmarks of Arrupe's tenure as superior general.
He would go on to write a letter on inculturation to the world's Jesuits,
defining it as an "incarnation of the Christian life and message" that not
only finds expression in other cultures but animates and transforms them
as well. His letter described the challenge of inculturation as universal.
Continents and countries, once presumed to be possessed of Christian cultures, were no longer so. He challenged Jesuits to risk the personal shock
of being immersed in cultures or subcultures foreign to them, whether
they be the worlds of outcasts and slum dwellers or those of artists and
intellectuals.[27] Four-hundred years after Valignano, Ricci, and de Nobili,
their principles had at last found a champion in high places.

With the close of Vatican II, Arrupe began a tour of Jesuit missions in
Africa and the Middle East. The following years took him to the United
States, including Alaska, and also to Canada and Latin America. Once
again he entered into the lives of people housed in slums and of children
who eat only once a day. He remembered being invited to the hovel of an
old man who wanted to thank him for his visit to their parish church. He
sat Arrupe down on a rickety old chair from which he could see the

sunset. The old man didn't know how else to show his thanks, since he had nothing else to give him.[28]

INTEGRATING THE SERVICE OF FAITH AND PROMOTION OF JUSTICE

In 1971 Pope Paul VI convened the Third Synod of Bishops, and Arrupe along with representative bishops from around the world gathered to deliberate questions pertaining to the priesthood and social justice. Media attention focused primarily on the priesthood and celibacy, but for Arrupe the discussions on social justice were of equal if not greater importance for the church. The synod's key outcome, a Vatican document entitled "Justice in the World," continues to affect Catholic thinking to this day.

To the chagrin of those who prefer church pronouncements diplomatically subtle, the synod was critically blunt regarding the "concentration of wealth, power, and decision making in the hands of a small public or private controlling group." The synod also rejected making distinctions too neat between the church's spiritual and social missions: "Action on behalf of justice and participation in the transformation of the world fully appear to us as a constitutive dimension of the preaching of the Gospel, or, in other words, of the Church's mission for the redemption of the human race and its liberation from every oppressive situation."[29]

Here was the church at its highest levels saying that its aims and identity are not just otherworldly. In 1971, speaking to North American Jesuit provincials, Arrupe made a similar point, noting that the gospel has social and economic dimensions that make it impossible for the church or its priests to be completely apolitical. Certain government policies cry out to be denounced. "We cannot remain silent, in certain countries, before regimes which constitute without any doubt a sort of institutionalized violence."[30]

Arrupe took as a challenge the 1971 synod's declaration that action on behalf of justice is a "constitutive dimension" of the church's mission. He had noted in a 1966 letter to Latin American Jesuits how the Society had historically tried to make an impact on the world by influencing dominant social classes and educating future leaders.[31] It had not focused on social justice or the underprivileged. One can imagine Arrupe doing an Ignatian examination of conscience as head of the church's largest teaching order and putting to himself the same question he put two years later to the alumni at Valencia, "Have we Jesuits educated you for justice?"

Arrupe's Valencia address came to be titled "Men for Others." The phrase, borrowed from Lutheran theologian Dietrich Bonhoeffer and now rendered more inclusively as "men and women for others," has become a watchword and criterion of Ignatian spirituality and Jesuit education. Arrupe unpacked the implications of the phrase for his Valencia audience. To be a follower of Jesus, the "man for others," means bringing good news for the poor. Just as we are never sure that we love God unless we love our fellow men and women, so too are we never sure that we have love at all unless our love produces works of justice.

By works of justice Arrupe did not mean individual acts of charity. He spelled out what the term implies for our times: First, a basic attitude of respect for all people, forbidding us ever to use others as instruments of our own profit. Second, a firm resolve not to profit passively from the active oppression of others, refusing to be a silent beneficiary of injustice. Third, a decision to work with others toward dismantling unjust social structures, so as to set free people who are weak and marginalized.

To follow Jesus this way, Arrupe continued, is a work of "humanizing the world," which in turn means striving to overcome the egoism that dehumanizes both persons and institutions. Making his message more concrete, he made three suggestions.

Live more simply. Don't give in to the pressure to compete socially, to acquire every luxury people in your social set regard as necessities. If this produces surplus wealth, give it to those for whom the necessities of life are still luxuries.

Draw no profit from unjust sources. Work so far as possible to reduce your own privileges in favor of the truly underprivileged, in your own society and in the Third World.

Become change agents. Work with others to undertake reform of unjust social structures in your society, assisting the poor and oppressed who, in the last analysis, must become the principal agents of change.[32]

As noted earlier, conservative newspapers were harshly critical of Arrupe's talk, but there were also words of appreciation, including a letter from the Vatican communicating the thanks of Pope Paul VI. When critics accused him of being radical, Arrupe would respond that he was simply applying the social teaching of the popes. But ripples in the press paled in comparison to the criticisms being voiced in certain quarters by Jesuits themselves. Though never the majority, conservative Jesuits averse to change were heard to grumble that just as one Basque founded the Society of Jesus, another was destroying it. (So much for the stereotype of blind Jesuit obedience.)

The dismay expressed by Arrupe's Jesuit critics did not result from a single talk but from an entire series of pronouncements. The road down which Arrupe seemed to be taking the Society alarmed them. The direction of that road was made clear in a 1971 presentation to North American provincials on "The Social Commitment of the Society of Jesus." Arrupe asked why there was an "appreciable gap" between the Jesuits' publicly expressed intentions with respect to social commitment and reality. He wondered if Jesuits had "sufficiently assimilated" the vision of the first week of the Spiritual Excercises, with its focus on the "mystery of iniquity." Very much part of that mystery was the existence of unjust social structures.

Well aware that phrases like "unjust social structures" raised specters of Marxism, Arrupe distanced his views from a humanitarianism devoid of faith. But reforming socioeconomic structures, he was convinced, was a "truly Christian and ecclesial," and not merely secular, enterprise. To stand by silent was to be complicit in an injustice that constitutes in our day the "great sin of the church." As priests, Jesuits were not to become involved in partisan politics, but that did not mean they could not adopt a political stance that happened to be consonant with that of a particular party.

Precisely as priests, Jesuits have "the inalienable duty of prophetically denouncing injustice."

Arrupe asked Jesuits to look at and analyze the social and economic realities of the contemporary world and the attitudes and values underlying them. It was an appeal not for a Marxist critique but for what the *Spiritual Exercises* calls "consideration of things as they are." He asked Jesuits, once they have diagnosed the social situation, to discern how they can best respond. Arrupe knew that there would be disagreements among his confreres. This was, after all, a break with the exclusively spiritual vision of ministry to which many Jesuits had become accustomed. He was calling them to a kind of conversion, but it was by entering into the familiar process Jesuits still refer to as "our way of proceeding."[33]

Vatican II had called upon religious orders to "renew" themselves and their way of life in light of the council's teaching and the spirit and intentions that led to their original founding. Arrupe took this as a central mandate for his tenure as superior general, and to fulfill that mandate he rightfully saw the need to convene a general congregation. In preparation for it, he asked the world's Jesuits to make recommendations for matters the congregation should consider.

Jesuits from India pointed to abject poverty as the most striking trait in today's world; they spoke to the Jesuit tradition of not only helping people in need but also prioritizing those needs and responding to the most urgent. Jesuits from Asia appealed to the Society's early ministry of reconciling adversaries and the need today to help reconcile widely disparate social classes. Brazil's Jesuits wrote of mobilizing forces in favor of people who were most needy so that Jesuits could rediscover themselves as the "light infantry" of the church.[34]

Recommendations such as these were compiled into propositions and distributed for comment. The proposition on justice merely requested that the general congregation declare social justice to be one of the commitments of the Society and approve a program of reflection on it. Even in that lackluster articulation, some provinces, like Spain and Central America, were deeply divided. A not-inconsiderable minority criticized the proposition as distorting Jesuit identity: the Society should be one of priests, not social workers. Most Jesuits agreed with the proposition but urged the congregation to avoid "beautiful but ineffective ideals" in favor of concrete, workable proposals.

When the delegates to the Thirty-second General Congregation (GC 32, for short) convened in December 1974, their deliberations on justice took them far beyond a "program of reflection." In attaching priorities to the Society's various works and ministries, they came to view justice issues as a "priority of priorities." Justice, the delegates decided, was integral to the Society's traditional service of faith. The 1971 Synod of Bishops had already said as much, but popes and bishops say many things that get forgotten. Here was the highest legislative body of the church's largest religious order taking that teaching of the synod and making it part of their very self-definition.

Before they took that momentous step, Arrupe wanted to be sure that the delegates fully realized what they were doing. A sober silence hung over the hall as Arrupe assured the congregation that, if the Society truly committed itself to work and not just beautiful words, the promotion of justice would be done "from the cross." Critics would accuse them of Marxism and subversion. Friends and benefactors would withdraw their financial assistance and support. Church and civil authorities would not understand. They were embarking on a "more severe way of the cross," one required by "Ignatian evangelical radicalism," as Arrupe called it, but one that would have "ultimate consequences." Arrupe used that phrase— "ultimate consequences"—twice in his brief address.[35] If they had not already, the delegates became conscious then that they were making history. But any sense of self-importance vanished with the dawning realization that in consequence of their decision, there would be martyrs.

Decree Four of the Thirty-second General Congregation has become a watershed document for its articulation of Jesuit mission as "the service of faith, of which the promotion of justice is an absolute requirement." Immediately following that statement, which the decree describes as "normative," is a reference to reconciliation, one of the Society's original purposes as expressed in its foundational Formula of the Institute. The delegates were at obvious pains to present the linking of faith and justice as part of their Jesuit heritage, not an innovation. "In one form or another," they argued, "this has always been the mission of the Society."

Referring to those places in the *Spiritual Exercises* where Ignatius asks for a long look at the world as it exists today, the decree points to millions of people suffering from the unjust distribution of wealth and from the consequences of racial, social, and political discrimination. It calls for dismantling false images of God that prop up and legitimize unjust social structures. But to intellectual criticism must be joined a conversion of the heart. The delegates at GC 32 were convinced that "it is now within human power to make the world more just," but added, "we do not really want to." Injustice and exploitation, they said, are not inevitable but result from human selfishness.

In accord with Jesuit tradition, the decree called for applying various intellectual disciplines to today's social problems. "We cannot be excused from making the most rigorous possible political and social analysis of our situation." From analysis and discernment would come "committed action," and "from the experience of action will come insight on how to proceed further." And all this was to be done not solely as a Jesuit undertaking but in collaboration with other Catholics, Christians, believers, and even nonbelievers "who hunger and thirst after justice."[36] The delegates to GC 32 gave their overwhelming approval to Decree Four and its new articulation of the Society's mission. Arrupe had no doubts that the Society's actions would be misunderstood and that as "ultimate consequences" there would be martyrs. But he had no inkling that, figuratively at least, he would be one of them.

The general congregation had also decided to discuss the possibility of allowing Jesuit brothers—who take the usual three vows of poverty, chastity, and obedience—to take a fourth vow, promising to serve wherever the pope asks. Up to that time, only Jesuit priests were allowed to take the fourth vow. Arrupe and the assembled delegates had assumed that this was a question open for reconsideration. But when word of this discussion got to the Vatican, an alarmed Pope Paul VI sent for Arrupe and let it be known in no uncertain terms that he considered this distinction between Jesuit brothers and priests to be essential and in no way open to revision.[37] The pope was concerned that any blurring of the distinction would encourage attempts to change the Jesuits as a "society of priests" and by extension the nature of the ordained priesthood. The congregation was to discontinue any discussion of the matter. When Arrupe informed the delegates of the pope's decision, they acceded without demur.[38]

The general congregation ended on March 7 and sent its decrees to the pope for his approval of their publication. A few weeks later a letter to Arrupe from Cardinal Jean Villot, the Vatican secretary of state, communicated the pope's approval but expressed concern that certain statements were "somewhat confusing" and could give "grounds for misinterpretation." The pope was concerned that Decree Four on the integration of justice into the service of faith would lead Jesuit priests into becoming involved in activities more appropriate for lay people. Such involvement, he was afraid, might cost the Society its priestly identity, leading it to become a "secular institute."[39] The pope was sensitive to the breadth of Jesuit influence. Given his fears about erasing the distinction between priests and brothers within the Society, he was apprehensive that the new directions the Jesuits were taking might blur the lines between clergy and laity altogether.

Arrupe convinced the pope that Jesuits were just as committed to their priestly mission as they had ever been. But GC 32's call for integrating the service of faith with the promotion of justice required a balancing act, one which Arrupe managed with all the skills and dexterity he could muster. As one of his close Jesuit associates put it: "On the one hand he had to convince people that the Society is not becoming a group of social activists, abandoning its traditional priestly ministries for the promotion of the faith. On the other hand he had to control enthusiasts for whom *justice* was the new catch-word that took priority over everything else."[40]

For the next six years Don Pedro Arrupe visited Jesuit houses around the globe, listening to, encouraging, and admonishing his confreres to keep their own balance. During his years as general, Arrupe spoke and wrote on a broad range of topics—ecumenism, education, racism, missions, simplicity of life, and Jesuit identity as well as faith and justice. Arrupe approached all these issues in similar fashion: with one eye on Ignatian spiritual tradition (with Ignatius Loyola's picture looking down at him from one office wall) and the other on a global network of increasingly interconnected peoples enveloped by problems anyone with less faith and optimism would find too overwhelming to contemplate (and the lunar perspective of the blue-and-white planet Earth when looking down from another heavenly body).

One of the most critical problems with which Arrupe grappled was the plight of refugees around the world, particularly the "boat people" of southeast Asia. The fall of Saigon in the summer of 1975 prompted tens of thousands of Vietnamese to flee their homes and seek refuge in Thailand or Malaysia, risking their lives on small, rickety wooden boats. Their numbers would be joined by refugees fleeing Laos and Cambodia. In 1980, when Arrupe wrote to the provincials asking their support for an organized Jesuit response to the problem, there were nearly 16 million refugees and displaced persons worldwide.

That initiative materialized into the Jesuit Refugee Service. Still housed some twenty-five years later at Jesuit headquarters in Rome, it continues to address a global crisis affecting 45 million refugees, 80 percent of them women and children. But refugees were to be found not just in camps far off in southeast Asia; there were homeless people from the African nations of Eritrea and Somalia literally at the Jesuits' doorstep. Arrupe remembered the first Jesuits' response to the famine of 1538. He set up a center *(Centro Astalli)* to provide food and shelter for the refugees from African famine. The center continues to take in some 300 refugees every night—in the very same building where Ignatius Loyola took in homeless people off the streets of Rome. Once again, Arrupe had taken the Society back to its roots.[41]

Since concern for the displaced and homeless had become practically a signature mission for Arrupe, it is fitting that his last plane trip involved a visit to a refugee camp. On the morning of August 7, 1981, Don Pedro was returning from visiting Jesuits working in the Philippines and in refugee camps in Thailand. Arriving at the Rome airport after a long flight from Bangkok, he reached down to pick up his suitcase and found he could not close his right hand around the handle. He began sweating profusely. His companions rushed him to a hospital, where doctors confirmed everyone's worst fears. He had suffered a cerebral thrombosis.

The stroke left him partially paralyzed on his right side. Pedro Arrupe, whose energy even at seventy-four had seemed boundless, was suddenly an invalid. Once capable of conversing in seven languages, he was now reduced to speaking only in his native Spanish, and even that haltingly. His typewriter, once heard clacking at all hours of the morning and night, was silent.[42] Arrupe was moved from the hospital to the infirmary of Jesuit headquarters, where he underwent therapy and received visitors, struggling to remember their names. But even in his weakened condition, history continued to swirl about him.

Fr. Vincent O'Keefe had been one of Arrupe's assistants from the beginning of his tenure as superior general. At the time of Arrupe's stroke, the New Jersey-born American Jesuit had already been serving as the vicar general of the Society, handling its day-to-day business when Arrupe was away. When it became clear that a full recovery from his stroke was neither imminent nor likely, talk began at the Jesuit headquarters about the procedures to be followed for the election of a new superior general. The Jesuit constitutions called for the convening of a general congregation to hold the election.

But in a historically unprecedented move, Pope John Paul II intervened and suspended two of the normal operating procedures set down in the Society's constitutions. The convocation of a general congregation would wait, and the Society would be governed not by its vicar general but by the eighty-year-old Jesuit Paolo Dezza. If the pope expected Jesuit outcries of protest, he was pleasantly surprised that there were none. He later said that he was testing the Jesuits' obedience, a test, he acknowledged, they passed admirably.[43] In 1983 Don Pedro resigned his office, and delegates to the Thirty-third General Congregation elected as his successor Fr. Peter-Hans Kolvenbach.

And Arrupe was proven right. There have been martyrs, as of this writing more than forty. In El Salvador, Jesuit Rutilio Grande was gunned down in 1977; and most famously, at the University of Central America in 1989, Ignacio Ellacuría and five other Jesuit professors, their housekeeper, and her daughter were killed. Ellacuría and his colleagues were all guilty of teaching their students to contemplate injustices in their society and discern what needed to be done.[44] Almost immediately there were Jesuits who volunteered to take their place.

In 1990, fifteen years after the "Arrupe Congregation," Superior General Kolvenbach sent a letter to Jesuit provincials inquiring if the formula "promotion of justice" was still adequate in articulating the Jesuit mission, or if it needed to be modified. Their response was that it did indeed express the Ignatian vision but that it needed to be understood broadly. Some Jesuits and critics alike had interpreted the word too narrowly by limiting it to mean only economic justice. Cultural differences among nations required legitimate differences in how Jesuits saw and promoted justice. The promotion of justice concerns not only the struggle against poverty, but also defense of human dignity and rights, and opposition to discrimination based on race, religion, caste, or gender. One Jesuit author, closely associated with the superior general, summed up this broader notion of justice as the "promotion of the human in all its dimensions."[45]

In 1995, Jesuit delegates at the Thirty-fourth General Congregation affirmed the direction in which Arrupe had taken them. They acknowledged that, interpreted broadly, the promotion of justice was integral to Jesuit origins, heritage, and identity. They spoke of fostering a "culture of life" and promoting concern for the environment as a matter of justice for "future generations who will inherit whatever we leave them."

The delegates at GC 34 also addressed the "Situation of Women in Church and Civil Society."[46] They pointed out the almost universal "feminization of poverty" and the "feminine face of oppression." Acknowledging Jesuit complicity and that of the church in the problem, they called for conversion and invited Jesuits everywhere to begin by listening to the voices and experiences of women. The delegates called for solidarity with women and based it explicitly on their commitment to promote justice. Arrupe would have remembered his visit to Vallecas—the two widows and their six boys, living in one room, sleeping in one bed—and would surely have approved.

After ten years of paralysis, the last year during which he was rendered virtually silent, Don Pedro Arrupe died in February 1991. But his legacy remains enshrined in hundreds of Jesuit schools, colleges, and universities explicitly committed to educating "men and women for others." The integration of faith with justice remains a central focus of every Jesuit enterprise, enlisting the commitment and energies of hundreds of thousands of non-Jesuits who share in the Ignatian vision and find it attractive but are not necessarily sure of what it is that attracts them. Could it be the Renaissance humanism that lies at the historical origins of both Ignatian spirituality and the Jesuits who foster it? It was to these origins that Arrupe returned the Society of Jesus.

IGNATIAN HUMANIST

Under the leadership of Pedro Arrupe, the Society of Jesus became what French historian Jean Lacouture has called the "third company."[47] The first company, born when Ignatius and his companions at the University of Paris vowed to remain together, ended when Pope Clement XIV suppressed the Society in 1773. The restoration of the Jesuits by Pope Pius VII in 1814 resulted in a very different kind of Society of Jesus, Lacouture's "second company." Popes and the Vatican curia came to regard Jesuits as intellectual counterparts to the Swiss guard, an elite corps charged with defending Catholic barricades against the onslaught and errors of modernity. Instead of critically accommodating to new cultures and ideas, Jesuits were expected to be uncritical apologists of papal teaching, medieval tradition, and Neo-Thomist, "perennial" philosophy.

Lacouture contends that Jesuits began to change in the 1930s with their struggle against racist fascism. A good case for dating the transformation could be made for August 15, 1945, Hiroshima. Whatever its remote origins, if one grants that there is today a changed or "third" Society of Jesus, different from the "second," there can be no doubt that Pedro Arrupe is singularly, though not solely, responsible. His years as superior general (sometimes called the "Arrupe era"), and above all Decree Four of GC 32 (the "Arrupe Congregation") formalized the difference, which Arrupe himself acknowledged.

It was argued at the outset of this chapter that the changes wrought during the Arrupe era were not an innovation but a return to the secular or *this-worldly* aspect of Ignatian spirituality, which itself was grounded in the Renaissance humanism of its origins. The Thirty-second General Congregation admitted as much when it connected the integration of faith and justice with the early Jesuit focus on reconciling enemies. It could also have pointed to Jesuits nursing syphilis patients in Venice or begging food and shelter for the homeless victims of the Roman winter of 1538. The Arrupe challenge for Jesuit schools to educate "men and women for others" is profoundly rooted in the humanist ideal of reforming church and society by educating people for an active life of service to the community. Obviously sixteenth-century humanists had no idea of reforming social structures, but they were conscious and explicit about cultivating character by communicating values and "promoting the human in all its dimensions."

His efforts to make the promotion of justice integral to the service of faith, retrieving the this-worldly aspect of Ignatian spirituality, is a major and obvious warrant for calling Pedro Arrupe an Ignatian humanist. But it is not the only one. Arrupe, like Francis Xavier (and even more like Alessandro Valignano, Matteo Ricci, and Roberto de Nobili), reflected the willingness of the humanists to learn from other cultures and take truth where they found it. The same might be said of goodness, beauty, and grace. Following in the ranks of his late Renaissance forebears, Arrupe found truth and beauty in the classics and practices of Zen Buddhism and goodness and grace in its adherents.

Arrupe studied the Zen tea ceremony, calligraphy, and archery so he might better understand Japanese culture and more ably communicate his own faith and values. But, convinced that no culture is perfect, he saw the enrichment as reciprocal. Inculturation, with which he has become identified, meant combining oriental intuition with Western rationalization. "Why should all people in all nations speak, eat, and dress like Europeans?" he asked.[48] Or pray like them, he might have added, pointing to the straw mat on which he meditated Zen-style even after leaving Japan.

As much as Ricci and de Nobili, though, there is something about Arrupe that is remniscent of Friedrich Spee. They both experienced the horrors humans are capable of inflicting on one another and yet remained hopeful and optimistic. On at least two different occasions, interviewers accused Arrupe of being an "incorrigible optimist."[49] He was happy to accept the charge. His optimism, inspired by faith, is what Superior General Kolvenbach singled out about his predecessor at his funeral.

Arrupe had every reason to adopt the Augustinian view of the human race as a *massa damnata*. If one accepts the barbed definition of a pessimist as an optimist who is better informed, Arrupe had every right to be a pessimist. From his first visit to the slums of Madrid to the shacks of Latin American peasants who had nothing to share but a sunrise, from looking into the eyes and hearts of convicted criminals in a New York penitentiary to solitary confinement in a Japanese prison cell, from the cries of children searching for their parents amid the rubble that was Hiroshima to the plight of refugees uprooted from their homes by war in southeast Asia, Arrupe was informed. He had every right to be cynical about human nature and call it realism.

Arrupe was neither utopian nor naive. His optimism arose from a calculated choice to hope and trust. Arrupe put his hope and trust in the God whose healing power and presence he experienced at Lourdes, the God he had experienced in the Spiritual Excercises as busily at work in all aspects of the world and people's lives. He believed that what our era needs most is hope. Particularly now, when former bearers of hope have become causes for fear: when technology gives us ever more sophisticated weapons, when biological research and genetic engineering raise specters of human clones, when political leaders on the right and left are willing to use terror and torture to serve their ends.[50]

Arrupe's hope and trust radiated optimism. His humanity and warmth radiated love. His acceptance of his paralysis and suffering the last ten years of his life radiated holiness. By that time any Jesuit talk about a second Basque general undoing the work of the first had muted. On the contrary, long after his death, Jesuit houses continue to display his image alongside that of Ignatius. That gesture bespeaks recognition of his saintliness, but also his peculiar stature. More than the second Basque to serve as general of the Society of Jesus, history is proving Don Pedro Arrupe to be its second founder.

EIGHT

A SPIRITUALITY FOR THE TWENTY-FIRST CENTURY

Readers picking up a book the first time and leafing through its pages sometimes turn to the back, looking for a bottom line or a summary of what went ahead. That this book provides neither is not because of authorial sloth or unconcern for busy people. There is simply too much to recap, and it would be presumptuous of me to instruct readers as to what should have engaged their interest or spoken to their hearts. Besides, to write about spirituality is to reflect on something highly personal and subjective. So I can only tell the reader what has engaged my interest and spoken to my heart.

A DYNAMIC TRADITION

Perhaps the most striking thing for me, looking back at this undertaking, is what a wide-ranging odyssey it has been. Though conceived in late-medieval Spain, Ignatian spirituality, when still in its infancy, became imbued with Renaissance humanism in Paris and Rome. The humanistic values of his Ignatian spirituality allowed Matteo Ricci to appreciate the classics of China, where it took on exotic new forms. On the banks of the Rhine, Friedrich Spee's humanistic spirituality gave him the courage to cry out in protest when early modern European Christians hunted and burned alive their fellow townsfolk for practicing witchcraft. From battle trenches at Verdun, Teilhard de Chardin looked out into a vastly expanded, evolving universe. At Hiroshima in August 1945, Pedro Arrupe contemplated the newfound capacity of human beings to destroy themselves. Under the great dome of St. Peter's Basilica in Rome, thanks to Karl Rahner, bishops spoke of God and grace in the hearts and lives of persons once scorned as heretics, infidels, and enemies of the church.

Ignatian spirituality in the twenty-first century is not what it was when Iñigo de Loyola first began giving people spiritual exercises. We no longer share many of his most basic assumptions. The earth is no longer at the center of the universe. A scientific worldview no longer permits us to take God's existence for granted. Homogeneous Christian cultures supportive of personal faith are relics of the past, confined at most to ghettos. Whatever their religious heritage, people in the West today live their spiritual lives in a secular, pluralistic context. And still, countless Christians find Ignatian spirituality a meaningful way of living their faith. As I have tried to demonstrate in these pages, that is thanks in great measure to its deep-seated humanism with its aptitude for accommodation.

Ignatian spirituality is a dynamic, living tradition and, as its name implies, biographical. It assumed its mature form over the course of Iñigo's lifetime. But even after being formalized in the text of the *Spiritual Exercises,* though maintaining its essential identity, Ignatian spiritual tradition continued to develop. It illustrates Cardinal Newman's oft-quoted observation that "in a higher world it is otherwise, but here below to live is to change, and to be perfect is to have changed often."[1] The story of Ignatian spirituality is one of a pilgrimage not yet ended.

The dynamic nature of Ignatian spiritual tradition can be seen in the documents of the thirty-four general congregations of the Society of Jesus. Those documents reflect and formalize the experiences and contributions of Ignatian humanists like Ricci and de Nobili, Teilhard, Rahner, and Arrupe. If Friedrich Spee has not made an impact on Ignatian spirituality as an individual, he exemplifies numerous other virtually anonymous Ignatian heroes who have done so, serving along with Spee as "voices for the voiceless." In the eighteenth century, in the interiors of Paraguay and Bolivia, Jesuits spoke out in defense of native tribes against efforts of Catholic colonials to enslave them. Today they speak out for third-world populations against multinational corporations whose policies are to exploit them as cheap labor.

This study has been admittedly sympathetic in its portrayal of several remarkable Jesuit humanists. But it has also been fair and not fawning with respect to the Society of Jesus as a body of flawed and fallible human beings. There were Jesuits who insisted that Ruggieri and Ricci would never learn Chinese, and who, when Roberto de Nobili adopted certain Hindu spiritual practices, accused him of engaging in pagan superstition. Jesuit Martin Delrio used his humanistic scholarship to defend the witchcraft trials. And, when Friedrich Spee had the temerity to speak and write against the trials and the use of torture to gain confessions, Spee's immediate Jesuit superior made his life miserable. Teilhard's Jesuit colleagues sent his privately circulated essays to his superiors in Rome, who then proceeded to censor his writings and send him into exile in China. When Pedro Arrupe took seriously the words of the popes and the Second Vatican Council concerning the faith that does justice, his conservative Jesuit confreres accused him of undermining the priestly identity of the Society of Jesus and jeopardizing its future.

Evidently, making the Spiritual Exercises doesn't guarantee one becoming a humanist any more than a saint. That said, embracing Ignatian spirituality, especially as it has continued to evolve, does lend itself toward forming a certain humanist mindset. One of the not-too-subtle objectives of this study has been to help retrieve and reclaim *humanism* as a serviceable descriptive for Christians who wish to challenge the secularist monopoly of the term and to distance themselves from the exclusivist claims of Christian and other fundamentalists.

⌐ 'Radical' non-fundamentalist xtians being desc. by "Humanism" is the/one of the obj. of Author

A Religious Alternative to Fundamentalism

One doesn't need a degree in social analysis to notice that formerly sharp boundary lines separating Christian churches from one another are blurring in comparison to the gaps widening within each church. Catholics—whether Roman, Orthodox, or Anglican—together with Lutherans and other Protestants who acknowledge the existence of truth and spiritual riches in other churches and faith traditions often have more in common with each other than with their coreligionists who do not—who see only darkness and damnation beyond their particular communities and biblical interpretations. The latter—those who have nothing to learn or gain from other churches or religions, who make exclusive claims on grace, truth, and divine favor—have come to be called fundamentalists.[2]

But how should we describe Christians or other believers who are willing to accept truth wherever they find it, to see God at work in the lives of outsiders? Liberals? Modernists? Those terms are mired in historical and political ambiguities. Ecumenical is another possibility, but refers to relationships among Christians. The same gaps that separate coreligionists within the Christian churches are present within other religious traditions, as manifested in recent years by Jewish, Muslim, and Hindu fundamentalist violence. How can one best describe those Christians, Muslims, Jews, and other religious persons who are willing to learn from one another, who are receptive to seeing God's hand at work outside of their own community? I would suggest that historical usage affords us no better word than *humanist*.

Granted, the word has been applied to a variety of disparate persons and groups, but it has not become so broad as to lose all meaning and usefulness. It may require adjectives to qualify it, but the term cannot be applied indiscriminately. Any ideology that divides the human race into *us* and *them* cannot be called humanistic. Any belief system that makes claims based on being a chosen people or master race cannot be called humanistic. Ethnocentrism, anti-Semitism, homophobia, chauvinism—

none of them can be called humanistic. Humanism of any kind is irreconcilable with racist, nationalist, sexist, religious, or cultural claims of superiority or self-sufficiency.

Humanism by its nature draws wide circles. Roman playwright Terence's dictum provides as good a definition as any: "I consider nothing human foreign to me." But the circle of concern does not exclude the rest of the living creatures with whom we share this earth. We may be superior to other animal species, but we are not unrelated and are certainly not self-sufficient. We are part of a network of life dependent on the rest of this living planet for our own survival. Teilhard de Chardin's concept of a cosmic spirituality was ahead of its time, but right for ours. A twenty-first-century spirituality must be able to embrace the planet and not just the people on it.

If Ignatian spirituality is an evolving tradition respectful of experience, espousing it means being open to learning from past mistakes, in this instance, with respect to environmental degradation and ecology. In the concluding contemplation on love, the *Spiritual Exercises* would have us view all creation as gift. Gifts bring responsibilities with them. The Exercises speak of God indwelling and at work in all creation, thereby giving plants and animals a certain sacramental significance. We are different from the animal world but, we have come to learn, not as different as we thought. Any humanist tradition must be respectful of future generations and their right to inherit an environmentally healthy, biologically diverse planet. The biblical injunction to take dominion over the world (Gn 1:28) makes us stewards and guardians of creation, not owners with the right to do with it as we please. For Ignatius, as for the biblical book of Genesis, it is God's world, not ours.

Ignatian spirituality is humanistic, but its humanism is theocentric. Secular humanists consider that a contradiction in terms, and partisans for precise language would have reason to agree. Humanism, if it is to mean anything, would seem to require an anthropocentric focus, one that concentrates on matters of human dignity, achievement, and enrichment. Conceding that point, I would answer that the focal point of Ignatian spirituality is the human person—but as unpacked and expounded by Karl Rahner, not as a mere rational or tool-making animal.

In Rahner's theological development of Ignatian spirituality, what makes us human is precisely our experience of the infinite, the fact that we are never satisfied. We are the subjects of unlimited longing, finding infinity not outside ourselves but within. We ask questions about totality and ultimate meaning, and by so doing find that we are asking the question about God. God and humanity are not rivals. One does not love God less by loving someone more; in reaching out to love another person, we are reaching out for God. To speak about love for God and love for human beings is to speak of the same reality. And in the experience of ourselves as mystery, we experience the absolute mystery that is God. A theocentric Ignatian humanism is not a contradiction in terms, if its focus is on a humanity that is waiting, looking, listening, hoping, reaching out beyond the finite for an infinite more.

CONTEMPORARY BIBLICAL SCHOLARSHIP

But what of the Christ-centeredness of Ignatian spirituality, especially Ignatius's image of a crusader Christ? Could a Christology be less politically correct or more out of sync with our twenty-first-century sensibilities? Ignatius read the Gospel stories through the lens of a would-be knight, in thrall to late-medieval romantic notions of chivalry. And he took the Gospel stories to be straight historical, eyewitness accounts of all that Jesus said and did. He did not have the benefit of modern biblical scholarship and our contemporary appreciation that the Gospels are faith interpretations of a post-Easter exalted Christ as much as they are narratives of historical events. In short, can one reconcile the crusader Christ of Ignatian spirituality with what modern biblical studies tell us about the person behind the overlay of faith interpretation, the Jesus of history? I would answer yes and contend that they relate quite congruently.

One must obviously get behind Ignatius's medieval imagery to see the Jesus of Ignatian spirituality as a man consumed with a sense of mission. In the synoptic Gospels that mission is called the "reign" or "kingdom" of God, and it constituted the focus of everything Jesus said and did. After Easter, the New Testament church spoke more of being "in Christ" or "in the Holy Spirit," and described itself as carrying on Jesus' mission in terms of "divine mystery" and "reconciliation." Whatever image or metaphor one uses, the idea behind them all is bringing people into touch with the power and presence of God and thereby empowering them to make a difference in how they relate to one another and live their lives.

Biblical scholars today generally agree that Jesus' ministry centered on the reign of God and that Jesus recruited apostles and disciples around himself to symbolize and serve the cause of that reign. Both those historical certitudes are pivotal to Ignatian spirituality. As pointed out in the first pages of this book, retreatants making the Spiritual Exercises pray over Jesus' mission and the quite individualized invitation of Jesus to "come, follow me" (Mk 10:21). The Jesus of Ignatian spirituality conforms to the Jesus of Mark's Gospel, the earliest of the four, for which God's reign and discipleship are central themes.[3]

The meaning and implications of that image, "reign of God," have inspired shelves of commentary and lengthy debates that need not detain us here. What is noteworthy is that modern scholarship has learned a deeper appreciation for the Jewishness of Jesus, and that we have a better understanding of what sets him apart, thanks to increased awareness of the social conditions under which he lived. Both those avenues to understanding the Jesus who walked the shores of the Sea of Galilee 2,000 years ago confirm the this-worldly, justice-oriented, humanistic aspects of Ignatian spirituality.

Judaism in the time of Jesus was—and still is—concerned with the here-and-now more than with the hereafter, with correct, ethical behavior (orthopraxy) more than with correct thinking (orthodoxy). Jesus was thoroughly Jewish in his thinking, one of his people and not an exception. He

The sad thing is that some of the Sullivan scholars are "contemporaries" in my p.o.v. — & they refuse to ∆, see cannot & or differenciate themselves from pol + soc. consequences.

announced the imminent reign of God and offered an answer to the question Leo Tolstoy phrased as "how then shall we live?" Jesus called his disciples to a way of life that was distinctive from that of their contemporaries, one that required trust—in him and in the divine power and presence they experienced in him. They had to trust because of the risk he was asking them to take. They had to trust him, because the countercultural way of life to which he invited them had social and political consequences.

We need go no further than the prayer Jesus taught his disciples to realize he was not solely about otherworldly matters (Mt 6:9–13; Lk 11:2–4). Central to the Lord's Prayer are a political symbol ("Thy kingdom come") and a reference to cold, hard economic facts of life ("forgive us our debts, as we also have forgiven our debtors"). With good reason, praying those words has been described as subversive.[4] Lest there be any doubts, Matthew, the most Jewish of the Gospels, explains that "thy kingdom come" means praying for God's will to be done "on *earth* as it is in heaven." Another indication of what Jesus' Jewish audience understood him to mean is found in former Pharisee, St. Paul, for whom God's reign is justice and peace as well as joy in the Holy Spirit (Rom 14:17).

The social world of Jesus' day was marked by a sole political superpower, a system of taxation that supported a massive military, and wide disparities between rich and poor. Persons who could not pay their taxes lost first their land and property and then their freedom. Taxation and slavery were foundational to the Pax Romana. Slaves who fled their servitude—or anyone who threatened the political economic status quo—faced execution on a cross, an effective means of state-sponsored terror guaranteed to keep the peace. Throw into that mix Zealot terrorists for whom the Roman yoke was a blasphemy and for whom it was permissible to take civilian life in the name of God.

It was within this context that a countercultural Jesus invited people to enter the reign of God, to risk joining him in a countercultural movement where God is Abba and disciples are brothers and sisters who forgive debts and share their daily bread. Jesus' mission was spiritual—in him people encountered the power and presence that the Hebrew Scriptures

NOT RELIGIOUS.

called the spirit of God—but it was not apolitical. His words and behavior implied social and economic consequences, for which Jesus paid with his life.

For the better part of 2,000 years, Christian theology has tended to focus on two phrases of the Apostles' Creed: "born of the Virgin Mary, suffered under Pontius Pilate." As formulated in the creed, Jesus' life and ministry were reduced to a comma. Traditional theology (in the Eastern Orthodox churches) has tended to view Jesus' life as simply an unfolding of his incarnation or (in the Roman Catholic and Protestant West) as a prelude to his death. But it was Jesus' life as a "man for others" that served as the incarnate epiphany or revelation of a "God for others." And it was Jesus' life that serves to explain what led to his death on a cross. His was a way of life deemed subversive to Roman law and order.

If traditional Christian theology generally focused on the incarnation and death of Jesus, traditional piety did not, and it was during a traditional reading of the life of Christ that Ignatius experienced God. Ignatius eventually wrote down his Spiritual Exercises, so that those who made them could experience God's grace in a way analogous to his own. His image of Christ may have been one of a crusader Christ, but it reconciles readily with the historical record of a Jesus calling his contemporaries into a community where they experience the power and presence of God—a Jesus who called people to a way of life that risks giving and forgiving, trusting that God will provide daily bread.

In short, the Jesus of Ignatian spirituality corresponds closely to what we know today about the first-century Jesus of Nazareth and why he called disciples in the first place. Ignatian spirituality is all about a discipleship modeled after a Jesus "for others." That our twenty-first century differs from the first or that of Ignatius goes without saying. But the analogies—political corruption, greed, economic exploitation, religious fanaticism, terror—are sufficient to recommend Jesus' way of life. It is one that draws strength (consolation) from an experience of God and then looks to how to make a difference, integrating the risk that is faith with the justice that is required by love.

DARWIN, AUSCHWITZ, AND GOD

If the Jesus of Ignatian spirituality fits our twenty-first-century percep-
tions of a first-century Jesus of Nazareth, can we say that same thing of
God? Ignatius in the *Spiritual Exercises* [102] has God gazing down at us
from the top of a three-tiered universe. In his meditation on the origins
of sin, Ignatius, like everyone else in his day, assumed that the biblical stories about Adam and Eve were historical and accurate [51]. Science and
modern biblical scholarship have rendered those assumptions inadequate
to the extreme.

Teilhard de Chardin was among the first Christian thinkers to perceive
the implications of modern astronomy, paleontology, and evolutionary
theory not only for biblical interpretation but also for the very foundations of a faith in God. Karl Rahner, in his last public address before he
died, encouraged theologians to turn to scientists to learn more about
God. The Bible can tell us what we need to know about salvation, he said,
but we have to look to science to tell us just how awesome is the mystery
that brought so awesome a universe into existence.

Our image of God after Darwin and the Hubble telescope cannot
responsibly be the same as it was before. The images of God in Ignatius's
memoirs and *Spiritual Exercises,* drawn from the Bible, are necessarily
naive. They could not help but reflect a prescientific age and culture. But
even the biblical authors realized that their images were metaphors—limp,
stuttering attempts to express in analogies the mystery that they called
holy and beyond all telling.[5] The Prophet Mohammed represented both
Jewish and Catholic Christian tradition when he spoke of God's utter-
ances as symbols and metaphors (Qur'an, 24:35). So Karl Rahner was simply being traditional, and not particularly Ignatian, when he chose
"Absolute Mystery" as his preferred reference to God. He was being very
Ignatian, however, when he encouraged theologians to turn to scientists
to perceive in creation some deeper glimpse of the Creator.

Ignatian spirituality is founded on the Thomistic conviction that there
is not and cannot be a contradiction between science and religion. Church

leaders have not always acted on that principle—to what will be the church's long-remembered embarrassment and discredit. (Galileo's encounter with the guardians of orthodoxy will not be forgotten, nor should that of Teilhard.) But the history of Jesuit education is replete with the names of scientists who did act on that principle, who dedicated themselves to research and discovery, convinced that they were doing God's work. There was something very Ignatian about Teilhard's vision of a spirituality rooted in the earth.

Pierre Teilhard is paradigmatic of an Ignatian humanism that sees science not as a threat to faith but as a source of deeper knowledge and awe. As we peer into the vast expanses of the universe, our thinking about God and ourselves can't help but be impacted by the realization that our sun is but one of several hundred million stars in our galaxy, which is itself but one of several hundred million galaxies. We can't help but feel insignificant, dwarfed by the knowledge that the age of the universe must be measured not in thousands but billions of years. Even without benefit of a high-powered telescope, however, the psalmist in the Bible had the same sense of human smallness, and still a sense of human greatness, without knowing that our body chemistry is composed literally of the stuff of stars (Ps 8).

The challenge to any twenty-first-century spirituality is more than God after Darwin; it's also God after Auschwitz. For philosopher-novelist Albert Camus, the suffering of one innocent child exemplified and raised the foremost objection to a too-easy faith in a heavenly father figure. His difficulty—reconciling a benevolent God with human suffering—was nothing new. The tens of thousands of deaths caused by the (1755) Lisbon earthquake was enough to convince Voltaire that this was not the "best of all possible worlds." His solution was that we simply tend our gardens without trying to understand or explain when or why "bad things happen to good people." But simply tending our gardens becomes escapist and immoral when we are confronted by the massive death tolls of the last century.

Can the God of Ignatian spirituality be reconciled with Nazi death camps, Stalinist-created famine, or Cambodian killing fields? Where was

God when apostate German Christians gassed, shot, and worked to death Soviet POWs, homosexuals, Poles, Gypsies, and Jews? The only possible answer is: with the Soviet POWs, homosexuals, Poles, Gypsies, and Jews. Where was God when the burning Twin Towers of Manhattan collapsed on firefighters, police, and rescue workers who were only there because they were trying to save other peoples' lives? The only possible answer is: with the firefighters, police, and rescue workers.

There is a life-size crucifix I once saw in a church in Germany, ordinary except for the fact that—a casualty of war—the body of Jesus has no arms. The parishioners decided to leave the crucifix in that truncated state as a reminder to onlookers that *they* are to become Christ's arms. The God of Ignatian spirituality is the God who "acts in the manner of one who is laboring" (*Spiritual Exercises,* 236). Ignatius speaks of God dwelling and at work in all creatures, in all plant and animal life, and in us. He does not speak of God pulling strings like a cosmic puppeteer, nor of a *Deus ex machina* who makes all things right at the end of a melodrama.

The traditional image of God as operating outside of creation was a part of the traditional image of a three-tiered universe. The self-giving God of Ignatian spirituality works within the universe, within human hearts and lives, giving men and women the strength to give of themselves. For Ignatius, as for St. Paul, the God who was in Christ reconciling the world now entrusts to us the work of reconciliation (2 Cor 5:19). The God who became incarnate continues to "help souls"—to heal the sick, forgive sins, and feed people who are hungry—but, as before, with human hands.

It was an image of God that died in Auschwitz, an image that should have died in the Lisbon earthquake or long before. A God who pulls all the strings is a god responsible for genocides. That is not the God revealed in a crucified Jesus, nor the God revealed in an exalted Christ. The optimism and indefatigable efforts of a Pedro Arrupe, who witnessed the horrors of Hiroshima, who knew firsthand the squalor of third-world slums, were only possible because of an Easter faith that makes the human enterprise a Divine Comedy. And in this play God is there all the while, not an appendix to the plot descending miraculously at the end of all the action. Jesuit poet Gerard Manley Hopkins caught the truth of the matter in two lines: "for Christ plays in ten thousand places, / lovely in limbs, and lovely in eyes not his."[6]

A TWENTY-FIRST-CENTURY CHURCH

This attempt to think about Ignatian spirituality and its relevance for the twenty-first century is not anything new. In 1995, Jesuit delegates from around the world did the same thing at their Thirty-fourth General Congregation. With a hard look at where they were—thirty years after Vatican II, twenty since the "Arrupe congregation" (GC 32)—they deliberated the challenges and opportunities that the dawning millenium presented to Jesuits and their institutions. → △ in CHURCH PRACTICE.

The congregation's immediate, narrower concern was for the thousands of Jesuit priests and brothers bound together in a vowed life of apostolic service. But they also spoke to the wider circle of non-Jesuits with whom they shared their Ignatian spirituality and vision (referred to in this book as the "extended Ignatian family"), to whom they offered the benefits of four centuries of experience and their "companionship" [337].[7] Most tellingly, the congregation did not speak of laity assisting Jesuits in their ministries but rather of Jesuits assisting laity in theirs. Jesuits are to be not only "men *for* others" but also "men *with* others," sharing their spiritual inheritance but also listening and learning from others [334].

GC 34 looked at the social conditions that mark the global situation today. Some of the problems listed include famine, religious and racial persecution, lack of political freedom and social justice, exploitation and sexual abuse (especially of women and children), the disregard for human life, and the disparity between wealthy nations and the poor. (The congregation considered global, not national, situations, so it did not point specifically to the United States, where, as of this writing, 1 percent of the population owns 40 percent of the nation's wealth.) Within this context, reflecting on the experiences of the years since the (1975) Thirty-second General Congregation, the Society of Jesus recommitted itself to the faith that does justice. The delegates cited the words of their superior general, Peter-Hans Kolvenbach: "The Society continues to insist on the promotion of justice. Why? Because it corresponds to our very spirituality" [73].

Lest Jesuits be accused again of diluting the gospel with Marxism, GC 34 insisted that the promotion of justice is rooted in Scripture and church tradition and that it is integral to Ignatian spirituality. The *Spiritual Exercises* fosters a "contemplative identification" with "a Christ on the move," who preaches the Kingdom where people live and work [7]. Being "friends of the Lord" (as Ignatius and his companions first called themselves) entails being "friends with the poor" [34]. In that same vein, the church does not exist for itself but for "the whole of human society"—a church "for others"—making real the reign of God "not only in the life to come but also in this life" [24].

Coming from all parts of the world, the delegates at GC 34 did their own take on the peace slogan "Think globally, act locally." The struggle for justice confronts changing needs relative to specific cultures and circumstances. For some it may mean working for structural change in the social-political-economic arena; for others, working for peace and reconciliation through nonviolence. For some it means working to end discrimination based on race, religion, gender, ethnicity, or social class; for others, working to counter growing poverty while wealth becomes ever more concentrated. Each of us is challenged to focus on one or another of these problems, doing what we can to help resolve it [54]. For those intellectually and academically equipped to do so, the challenge is not only to alleviate the consequences of injustice with service but to provide a social analysis and theological reflection of its causes [400].

Against the backdrop of Ignatian spirituality and the social challenges facing our day, GC 34 dedicated an entire document to "the situation of women in church and civil society." The delegates saw it as an outgrowth of GC 32 and its commitment to the promotion of justice. In a grateful acknowledgement of the growing numbers of lay and religious women who are directing retreatants in the Spiritual Exercises, the congregation credited them for both enriching and reshaping Ignatian tradition [370]. But the delegates acknowledged as well the "legacy of systematic discrimination against women," which they described as "embedded within the economic, social, political, religious, and even linguistic structures of our societies" [363]. Most unprecedented of all, the delegates made an acknowledgement of Jesuit complicity by contributing, "however unwittingly," to male domination. "We have been part of a civil and ecclesial tradition that has offended against women. And, like many men, we have a tendency to convince ourselves that there is no problem" [369].

To demonstrate the contrary, GC 34 gave a global overview of the problems. In various cultures women are excluded from educational opportunities or bear a disproportionate burden in family life. They receive a lesser wage for the same work and are treated as objects in advertising and the media. The congregation pointed to the "feminization of poverty" and distinctive "feminine face of oppression" [364]. It also detailed the violence to which women are subjected in some parts of the world—female circumcision, dowry deaths, the murder of unwanted infant girls, an international sex tourism trade that treats women as commodities [362].

The congregation called for Jesuits—and by extension all men who share Ignatian values—to demonstrate conversion by aligning themselves in solidarity with women [373]. This requires that men "listen carefully and courageously to the experience of women," doing so "in a spirit of partnership and equality" [372]. Though they vary from culture to culture, some practical ways of demonstrating this solidarity include resisting situations where women suffer exploitation [375] or violence [376] and supporting liberation movements that encourage their entry into social and political life [375]. Closer to home, the delegates called for Jesuits and their institutions to provide appropriate involvement of women in their ministries and institutions, including formation [377], consultation, and decision making [378]. The congregation also called for the "use of appropriately inclusive language in speech and official documents" [380].

The Jesuits' 1995 document on women was widely hailed in reform-minded Catholic circles and even imitated by the Vatican. But the Jesuit document was a not-too-subtle allusion to several hot-button items of controversy in the Catholic Church at large, matters like inclusive language, clericalism, and the involvement of women in ministry and decision making. Women's issues—along with those related to sexuality, authority, and dissent—are among the topics that GC 34 described as creating "strong tensions" in the Roman Catholic church, leading to "conflictual, even explosive situations" [310]. Because these issues and conflicts affect all Catholics, not only Jesuits, the stance GC 34 took in response to them can prove instructive for those willing to share their Ignatian heritage.

Jesuits—who as individuals take a vow of obedience and as a society have a unique, historical bond to the pope—are obviously obliged in ways nonreligious are not to pay heed to the decisions of church authorities. One cannot help but remember here Ignatius's "What I see as white, I will believe to be black if the hierarchical Church thus determines it."[8] Yet, contrary to the common stereotype of unquestioning Jesuit obedience, GC 34 recognized that Jesuits are not bound to passively acquiesce to church authority. There are times when a Jesuit may feel justified or even obliged to speak out in ways that do not win the Society general approval. "To do so does not put the Jesuit in a stance of disobedience or revolt" [311]. The congregation went on to explain: "Ignatian obedience, in accord with the tradition of Catholic theology, has always recognized that our first fidelity must be to God, to the truth, and to a well-formed conscience. Obedience, then, cannot exclude our prayerful discernment of the course of action to be followed, one that may in some circumstances differ from the one suggested by our religious and Church superiors" [311].

If loyal, respectful dissent of this kind is legitimate for Jesuits, certainly it is not disallowed for those who share their spirituality. On the contrary, thinking critically about conditions in the church and investing oneself in its reform is a sign of solidarity with the church. Vatican II spoke of the church as a pilgrim in need of "continual reformation" in its conduct and discipline.[9] It also spoke of church leaders not having the answers to all questions, of laity being permitted, "sometimes even obliged," to express their opinions on matters concerning the welfare of the church.[10] In other words, respectful criticism of the church and a desire for its reform is both a Catholic right and responsibility. It is also part of the Ignatian spiritual tradition.

Looking back at the Jesuits whose lives and thinking have been surveyed in this book, one cannot help but notice that all of them thought outside the box that was the customary Catholic way of doing things in their day. All of them were bona fide, even if undeclared, reformers. Ignatius taught that God speaks to people outside the usual ecclesiastical channels. Ricci and de Nobili criticized the identification of Christianity with European culture. Spee spoke out against the complicity of scholars and church leaders in the witch trials of his day. Teilhard pitted evolutionary science against the literal interpretation of the biblical creation stories. Rahner spoke out in favor of married priests and the ordination of women. Arrupe criticized a too facile disjunction of spirituality and secular matters that allowed priests to remain complicit in situations of social, economic, or political injustice.

All these Ignatian humanists enjoy respect and admiration today, even from high-ranking Catholic churchmen. Yet during their time or subsequently, all of them ran afoul of church authorities and were put under a cloud. Under suspicion of heresy, Ignatius was imprisoned by the Inquisition. The Vatican jettisoned the ideas of Ricci and de Nobili and for centuries forbade their use. Spee's immediate superior wanted him expelled from the Jesuits. Teilhard was forbidden to publish his ideas during his lifetime and was not allowed to accept a prestigious lectureship in his homeland. Until his friends put a quick end to the humiliation, Rahner was obliged to submit his writings to Vatican censors. Despite his profound deference to papal authority, Arrupe suffered public embarrassment at the hands of a Vatican distrustful of Jesuit loyalty under his administration.

Asceticism is a time-honored component of both Catholic and Ignatian spirituality. From a twenty-first-century humanist perspective, however, and contrary to ascetic practices of old, one need not seek out pain or suffering, certainly not for its own sake. If one speaks out and actively works for justice in society or for reform in the church, pain—criticism, rejection, verbal abuse, or worse—invariably comes as part of the package.

CONVERSATION WITH PEOPLE OF OTHER CULTURES

Reading through the documents of GC 34, one finds certain ideas cropping up repeatedly, such as, not unexpectedly, the faith that does justice. But recurring just as often are references to culture and dialogue, which the delegates defined as a "spiritual conversation of equal partners that opens human beings to the core of their identity" [101]. In fact, the congregation saw culture and dialogue as so central to Ignatian spirituality and so closely connected to the linkage of faith and justice that it described them as integral to one another. For that highest legislative body in the Society of Jesus, the faith that does justice is "inseparably" the faith that engages other cultures in dialogue [49].

Perhaps that should not be surprising. When one looks back at the Ignatian humanists surveyed here, conversation is what made a major difference in their lives and thinking. Ignatius began developing his Spiritual Exercises after conversations with women at Manresa convinced him that he could help people open up to experiences of grace like his own. Ricci spent so many hours a day conversing with Confucian scholars that he learned to think like them. Spee first questioned and listened to women accused of witchcraft, did the same with their inquisitors and torturers, and only then denounced what he knew to be judicial injustice. Scientist-priest Teilhard de Chardin embodied the dialogue between science and religion in his person. Conversations with self-described agnostics prompted Rahner to plumb the deeper meanings of faith and grace. Arrupe visited Zen monasteries, where he learned from Buddhist monks, and Latin American slums, where he learned from people too poor to share anything more than a sunset.

Given our inclination to associate spirituality with monastic quiet, it might seem unlikely at first that Ignatian spirituality should value something so ostensibly at odds with silence, something so commonplace as conversation. Of course, there is nothing common or ordinary about a genuine conversation. In contrast to chitchat about the news or gossip about people, conversation is about sharing ideas and dreams, aspirations and anxieties, about things that matter, what we hold dear, life, death, what we hang our hearts on. Because it "opens human beings to the core of their identity," GC 34 spoke of this kind of conversation as a way of serving God's mystery of salvation, bringing us into contact with God active in people's lives. The congregation cited the words of Pope John Paul II: "As we open ourselves in dialogue to one another, we also open ourselves to God" [101]. Obviously conversation in this sense is about listening as much as talking.

The pope's words, cited here, were originally addressed to "Leaders of Non-Christian Religions" in Madras, India. The context too for GC 34's reflections on culture and conversation was that of a worldwide Jesuit network of ministries and institutions. Gathered from what were once far-flung shores, the delegates addressed the pluralism and diversity not only distinguishing their diverse locales but characterizing them. And within this context the congregation made two statements that fifty years ago would have been unthinkable. One of these addressed dialogue and collaboration with other Christian churches: ecumenism is not a concern only for experts but "a new way of being Christian" [328]. The other concerned conversation with non-Christian believers: "to be religious today is to be interreligious" [130]. Both statements evoked the challenge of Pope Paul VI, who envisioned dialogue as a new way of being Church.[11]

The delegates to GC 34 viewed ecumenical and interreligious dialogue as integral to any twenty-first-century Christian spirituality that seeks to be relevant, but especially one that is Ignatian. As "a new way of being Christian," ecumenical conversation listens. "It seeks to see things from the other's point of view and to take seriously the other's critique of one's own communion and its historic errors and failings." Taking a cue from the preamble in the *Spiritual Exercises* [22], it seeks to put the best interpretation on the words and actions of one's conversation partners. Putting aside the polemics that have divided Christians for the better part of 450 years, ecumenical conversation "seeks what unites rather than what divides; seeks understanding rather than confrontation; seeks to know, understand, and love others as they wish to be known and understood, with full respect for their distinctiveness" [328].

Just as ecumenism is not just for experts, interreligious conversation is no longer the monopoly of foreign missionaries. Workplaces, college campuses, and suburban neighborhoods routinely bring together people of diverse ethnic, racial, and religious backgrounds. One does not have to visit New York City or Chicago to encounter men with yarmulkes or turbans on their heads, or women dressed in saris or headscarves. Virtually all of us in the United States have opportunities to enter into conversation with persons of non-Christian faith traditions. And long before 9/11, but even more since, conversation leading to mutual understanding among people of different religious traditions has been recognized as indispensable for creating the conditions that make for global peace.

A precondition for genuine interreligious conversation—in contrast to a self-righteous monologue—is the kind of optimistic theology of grace one finds in Ignatian spirituality, and which was canonized at Vatican II, thanks greatly to the influence of Karl Rahner. Interreligious dialogue is not a matter of Christians one-sidedly admonishing benighted pagans or infidels. Within the plurality of religious traditions, the delegates at GC 34 found a "plurality of religious experiences." Interreligious conversation helps us to recognize these religious traditions as "graced with an authentic experience of the self-communication of the divine word and of the saving presence of the divine Spirit" [134]. In a genuine encounter with people of other religions, "we discover deeper dimensions of our Christian faith and wider horizons of God's salvific presence in the world" [135]. The congregation cited the words of Pope Paul VI, spoken in Bombay, in the heart of India's Hindu culture: "We are all pilgrims setting out to find God in human hearts" [134].

When the Jesuit delegates at GC 34 spoke of conversation with people in other cultures and subcultures, they thought beyond the parameters of non-Catholic churches or non-Christian religions. They took into account the more than one billion people with no religion at all [128]. This included those cultures in what was once called Christendom, where many people believe they have gone beyond Christianity or any other religious commitment. In some of these cultures, the delegates noted, religion has been so restricted to the personal and private spheres of life that any public expression of faith comes to be seen as eccentric or embarrassing. For many of our contemporaries in the post-Christian West, religious faith of any kind is deemed as detrimental to the health of the human race.

Conversation with people committed to a secular, post-Christian, or postmodern culture is not easy. GC 34 admitted that it's threatening—but it is equally indispensable. Secular attitudes and values dominate academe and the centers of mass media and popular culture. And we find the culture resonating within ourselves. We can no longer gaze out into starry skies and find an easy faith. We have to look into our deepest selves to find an experience of God and realize that even there we hear the whisper of doubt. In the words of GC 34, "the boundary line between the Gospel and the modern and postmodern culture passes through the heart of each of us." The impulse to unbelief is not foreign to our personal experience, and "it is only when we deal with that dimension in ourselves that we can speak to others of the reality of God" [104].

Our postmodern contemporaries have given up on God-talk. We can't ignore the critical questions raised by our agnostic interlocutors or answer them in a traditional language utterly foreign to their experience. Again, to cite GC 34, "only when we make sense of our own experience and understanding of God can we say things which make sense to contemporary agnosticism" [104]. We can still speak, however, of the "absolute mystery" of which Rahner wrote, rooted in a mystical tradition that speaks only of a God beyond images or words.

With Rahner and Vatican II, however, it is important to realize that faith resides in the heart more than the intellect, and that grace does not depend on correct thinking. Neither does the self-giving God of grace depend on the church or on any other religious community or institution. In this vein, the Jesuits at GC 34 said something quite germane to the idea of a wider spiritual humanism: "There is a fragmentation of Christian faith in God in postmodern culture, in which human spirituality becomes detached from an explicitly religious expression. People's spiritual lives have not died; they are simply taking place outside the Church" [105].

Ignatius would have found it difficult to accept that people could live spiritual, grace-filled lives outside the confines of explicit Christian faith. But both the spirituality that bears his name and the Catholic Church to which he was so fiercely attached have come to accept that conclusion—thanks greatly, I have argued here, to the humanistic principles described and illustrated in these pages. There are people working for justice, reaching out in love, living lives of grace—outside the church, but inside a spiritual communion that it takes a spiritual humanism to recognize. Ignatian humanism is an explicit subset or variety of that broader, more encompassing spiritual humanism.

Ignatian humanism is but one of many schools of spirituality in the Catholic Church, and it is but one of many genuine varieties of humanism. But it is one that I, and thousands like me, find personally meaningful, congenial, and, most important, relevant to our twenty-first-century exigencies and experience. Its origins in a premodern era of turmoil and transition accord with our postmodern era of turmoil and transition.

With its focus on a countercultural Christ, Ignatian humanism bolsters living a life "for others." Fostering attentiveness to Absolute Mystery, it offers hopeful optimism to the ofttimes discouraging work on behalf of justice. Opening our eyes to new horizons of grace, it allows us to extend our hands to people we once dismissed as outsiders and discover in them, perhaps to our wonderment, kindred spirits.

Totem pole

Notes

Introduction: Ignatian Humanism

1. Ronald Rolheiser, *The Holy Longing: The Search for a Christian Spirituality* (New York: Doubleday, 1999), 5–12.

2. Rolheiser, *Holy Longing,* 7.

3. Tony Davies, *Humanism* (London: Routledge, 1997), 3.

4. See H. J. Blackham, *Humanism* (Harmondsworth, England: Penguin, 1968); Martin C. D'Arcy, *Humanism and Christianity* (New York: World Pub. Co., 1969); R. William Franklin and Joseph M. Shaw, *The Case for Christian Humanism* (Grand Rapids, MI: Eerdmans, 1991).

5. Blackham, *Humanism,* 13–17.

6. See Davies, *Humanism,* 35–71.

7. See David Lonsdale, *Eyes to See, Ears to Hear: An Introduction to Ignatian Spirituality* (London: Darton Longman & Todd, 1990), 1, 3–4; Joyce Hugget, "Why Ignatian Spirituality Hooks Protestants," *The Way Supplement* 68 (Summer 1990): 22–33; Graham Chadwick, "Giving the Exercises and Training Directors in an Ecumenical Context," *The Way Supplement* 68 (Summer 1990): 35–41.

8. *Documents of the Thirty-fourth General Congregation of the Society of Jesus* (St. Louis: Institute of Jesuit Sources, 1995), 175 [# 370]. The phrase is used by the General Congregation to describe the many religious congregations of women who have adopted the Spiritual Exercises and Jesuit constitutions as the basis for their own spirituality and governance. I take the liberty of broadening the concept here.

9. See Ronald Modras, "The Spiritual Humanism of the Jesuits," *America,* 4 February 1995.

10. Hugo Rahner, *Saint Ignatius Loyola: Letters to Women,* trans. Kathleen Pond and S. A. H. Weetman (New York: Herder and Herder, 1960).

11. An outstanding scholarly example of this change is Katherine Dyckman, Mary Garvin, and Elizabeth Liebert, *The Spiritual Exercises Reclaimed: Uncovering Liberating Possibilities for Women* (New York: Paulist Press, 2001).

CHAPTER 1: IGNATIAN SPIRITUALITY

1. Ignatius of Loyola, *A Pilgrim's Testament: The Memoirs of St. Ignatius Loyola,* transcribed by Luís Gonçalves da Câmara, trans. Parmananda R. Divarkar (St. Louis: Institute of Jesuit Sources, 1995). Citations bracketed in the text refer to the standard section numbers used for most editions of the memoirs.

2. "Da Camara's Preface," *A Pilgrim's Testament,* xxvii.

3. The paradoxes in Ignatius's life (courtier-contemplative; administrator-mystic) as a source of the paradoxes in the lives and spirituality of Jesuits are the focus of the helpful book by William A. Barry and Robert G. Doherty, *Contemplatives in Action: The Jesuit Way* (New York: Paulist Press, 2002).

4. This book will follow the convention of using capital letters and italics to refer to the printed text; "Spiritual Exercises" without italics to refer to the process or contents of the Ignatian text, and "spiritual exercises" to refer to these types of exercises generally.

5. Recent biographies of Ignatius in English include Philip Caraman, *Ignatius Loyola: A Biography of the Founder of the Jesuits* (San Francisco: Harper and Row, 1990); Cándido de Dalmases, *Ignatius of Loyola, Founder of the Jesuits: His Life and Work,* trans. Jerome Aixalá (St. Louis: Institute of Jesuit Sources, 1985); Harvey Egan, *Ignatius the Mystic* (Wilmington, DE: Michael Glazier, 1987); Mary Purcell,

The First Jesuit: St. Ignatius Loyola (Chicago: Loyola University Press, 1981); and André Ravier, *Ignatius of Loyola and the Founding of the Society of Jesus,* trans. Maura Daly, Joan Daly, and Carson Daly (San Francisco: Ignatius Press, 1987). For a psychological biography of Ignatius from a Freudian perspective, see W. W. Meissner, *Ignatius of Loyola: The Psychology of a Saint* (New Haven, CT: Yale University Press, 1992). A biography with special insight into Ignatius's Spanish background is José Ignacio Tellechea Idígoras, *Ignatius of Loyola: The Pilgrim Saint,* trans. Cornelius Michael Buckley (Chicago: Loyola University Press, 1994).

6. Tellechea Idígoras, *Ignatius of Loyola,* 50.

7. Quoted in Hugo Rahner, *The Spirituality of St. Ignatius Loyola: An Account of Its Historical Development,* trans. Francis John Smith, S.J. (Westminster, MD: Newman Press, 1953), 8.

8. Tellechea Idígoras, *Ignatius of Loyola,* 72.

9. H. Rahner, *Spirituality of St. Ignatius Loyola,* 118n52.

10. John W. O'Malley, "Some Distinctive Characteristics of Jesuit Spirituality in the Sixteenth Century," in John O'Malley, John W. Padberg, Vincent O'Keefe, *Jesuit Spirituality: A Now and Future Resource* (Chicago: Loyola University Press, 1990), 4.

11. George Ganss, ed., *Ignatius of Loyola: The Spiritual Exercises and Selected Works,* with the collaboration of Parmananda R. Divarkar, Edward J. Malatesta, and Martin Palmer, and a preface by John W. Padberg (New York: Paulist Press, 1991), 26.

12. Tellechea Idígoras, *Ignatius of Loyola,* 154.

13. Katherine Dyckman, Mary Garvin, and Elizabeth Liebert, *The Spiritual Exercises Reclaimed: Uncovering Liberating Possibilities for Women* (New York: Paulist Press, 2001), 32–33.

14. For a detailed psychological analysis of this process, see Meissner, *Ignatius of Loyola,* 69.

15. Quoted in H. Rahner, *The Spirituality of St. Ignatius Loyola,* 53.

16. Ganss, *Ignatius of Loyola.* Brackets in the text refer to the standard passage numbering for this and all editions of the *Spiritual Exercises.*

17. See Marian Cowan and John C. Futrell, *Companions in Grace: A Handbook for Directors of the Spiritual Exercises of St. Ignatius Loyola* (St. Louis: Institute of Jesuit Sources, 2000), 14. Directors may offer questions and hypothetical models to clarify the retreatants' experiences and information when there is a problem arising from misinformation. Directors are never to be judgmental, appear shocked, or give homilies.

18. Karl Rahner, *Spiritual Exercises,* trans. Kenneth Baker (New York: Herder and Herder, 1965), 23–27.

19. Joseph A. Tetlow, "The Fundamentum: Creation in the Principle and Foundation," *Studies in the Spirituality of Jesuits* 21/4 (September 1989): 4–8, 49–51.

20. Hugo Rahner, *Ignatius the Theologian,* trans. Michael Barry (New York: Herder and Herder, 1968), 53–93.

21. Quoted in H. Rahner, *The Spirituality of St. Ignatius Loyola,* 26–27.

22. Karl Rahner, *Spiritual Exercises,* trans. Kenneth Baker (New York: Herder and Herder, 1965), 23–27.

23. David Lonsdale, S.J., *Eyes to See, Ears to Hear: An Introduction to Ignatian Spirituality* (London: Darton Longman & Todd, 1990), 37.

24. Ganss, *Ignatius of Loyola,* 389–90.

25. For a probing theological consideration of this phrase within the context of Ignatian mysticism, see Harvey D. Egan, *The Spiritual Exercises and the Ignatian Mystical Horizon* (St. Louis: Institute of Jesuit Sources, 1976). For a psychological interpretation, see W. W. Meissner, *To the Greater Glory: A Psychological Study of Ignatian Spirituality* (Milwaukee: Marquette University Press, 1999), 272–73.

26. Meissner, *To the Greater Glory of God,* 226–31.

27. This classic phrase commonly identified with Ignatian spirituality is found in the *Constitutions of the Society of Jesus* [288] but recurs with slight variations throughout Ignatius's writings. See Ganss, *Ignatius of Loyola,* 292.

28. K. Rahner, *Spiritual Exercises,* 272.

29. Paul Coutinho, *The Ignatian Ideal and Jesuit Reality* (Anand, India: Gujarat Sahitya Prakash, 1999).

30. Gerard Manley Hopkins, *Poems of Gerard Manley Hopkins,* 3rd ed. (New York: Oxford University Press, 1961), 70.

31. From almost the very beginning, Jesuits began writing "directories," which were guidebooks for directing the Exercises, including how to accommodate them. For an English translation of these early manuscripts, see Martin Palmer, *On Giving the Spiritual Exercises* (St. Louis: Institute of Jesuit Sources, 1996). A modern example of such a guidebook is Cowan and Futrell, *Companions in Grace.*

32. Among those women in the United States who have made contributions in this vein are Marian Cowan, Kathrine Dyckman, Mary Garvin, Elizabeth Liebert, and Elizabeth Meier Tetlow.

33. Examples of this are Lewis Delmage, *The Spiritual Exercises of Saint Ignatius Loyola: An American Translation from the Final Version of the Exercises, the Latin Vulgate, into Contemporary English* (New York: Joseph F.Wagner, 1968); David Fleming, *The Spiritual Exercises of St. Ignatius: A Literal Translation and a Contemporary Reading* (St. Louis: Institute of Jesuit Sources,1978); Elisabeth Meier Tetlow, *The Spiritual Exercises of St. Ignatius Loyola: A New Translation* (Lanham, MD: University Press of America; London: College Theology Society, 1987).

34. Joseph A. Tetlow, "The Most Postmodern Prayer," *Studies in the Spirituality of Jesuits* (January 1994).

35. Principal credit for this retrieval goes to George A. Aschenbrenner, "Consciousness Examen," *Review for Religious* 31 (January 1971): 14–21.

36. Dennis Hamm, "Rummaging for God: Praying Backward through Your Day," *America,* 14 May 1994, 22–23.

37. For a helpful summary of how the various phases of Ignatius's life influenced the Spiritual Exercises, see Lonsdale, *Eyes to See,* 8–27.

38. For a detailed exposition of the Pauline foundations of Ignatian spirituality, see Gilles Cusson, *Biblical Theology and the Spiritual Exercises,* trans. Mary Engela Roduit and George E. Ganss (St. Louis: Institute of Jesuit Sources, 1988).

39. O'Malley, "Some Distinctive Characteristics," 18.

40. Ganss, *Ignatius of Loyola,* 423–24.

CHAPTER 2: RENAISSANCE ORIGINS

1. Ignatius of Loyola, *A Pilgrim's Testament: The Memoirs of St. Ignatius of Loyola,* transcribed by Luís Gonçalves da Câmara, trans. Parmananda R. Divarkar (St. Louis: Institute of Jesuit Sources, 1995), 120. This translation is also found in George E. Ganss, *Ignatius of Loyola: The Spiritual Exercises and Selected Works* (New York: Paulist Press, 1991), 65–111.

2. The most complete history of the Society of Jesus in English is still that of William V. Bangert, S.J., *A History of the Society of Jesus,* 2nd rev. ed. (St. Louis: Institute of Jesuit Sources, 1986). The best history in any language of the early years of the Society is the magisterial work of John O'Malley, S.J., *The First Jesuits* (Cambridge, MA: Harvard University, 1993). An abbreviated English translation of a popularly written two-volume French work is that of Jean Lacouture, *Jesuits: A Multibiography,* trans. Jeremy Leggatt (Washington, DC: Counterpoint, 1995).

3. Besides the memoirs of Ignatius cited above, the beginnings of the Society of Jesus are recounted in the autobiographical "Memoriale" of Pierre Favre. See Edmond C. Murphy and John W. Padberg, *The Spiritual Writings of Pierre Favre,* trans. Edmond Murphy and Martin E. Palmer (St. Louis: Institute of Jesuit Sources, 1996).

4. Wallace K. Ferguson, *The Renaissance in Historical Thought: Five Centuries of Interpretation* (New York: Houghton Mifflin, 1948), 8.

5. Paul Oskar Kristeller, *Renaissance Thought: The Classic, Scholastic, and Humanist Strains* (New York: Harper, 1955), 9.

6. Ernst Cassirer, Paul Oscar Kristeller, and John Henry Randall Jr., *The Renaissance Philosophy of Man* (Chicago: University of Chicago Press, 1948), 16.

7. The exception seems to have been the writings of St. Thomas Aquinas. Despite the Gothic nature of their structure and method, Italian humanists, especially in Rome, admired their order, clarity, and simplicity of expression—classical virtues that appealed to the humanists. See John O'Malley, "The Feast of Thomas Aquinas in Renaissance Rome: A Neglected Document and Its Import," *Rivista di Storia della Chiesa in Italia,* 34 (1981): 1–27.

8. Wallace K. Ferguson, *Renaissance Studies* (London, Ontario: University of Western Ontario, 1963), 19.

9. Kristeller, *Renaissance Thought: The Classic, Scholastic, and Humanist Strains,* 86.

10. Cassirer, Kristeller, and Randall, *Renaissance Philosophy of Man,* 5.

11. Paul Oskar Kristeller, *Renaissance Thought and Its Sources,* ed. Michael Mooney (New York: Columbia, 1979), 145–47.

12. Petrarca, "On His Own Ignorance," in Cassirer, Kristeller, and Randall, *Renaissance Philosophy of Man,* 104–05.

13. Kristeller, *Renaissance Thought and Its Sources,* 181–96.

14. The classic expression of this identification of the Renaissance with the rise of individualism is Jacob Burckhardt, *The Renaissance in Italy: An Essay,* 4th ed., rev. (London: Phaidon, 1951).

15. Johan Huizinga, *The Waning of the Middle Ages: A Study of the Forms of Life, Thought, and Art in France and the Netherlands in the XIVth and XVth Centuries* (London: E. Arnold & Co., 1924). See also Ferguson, *Renaissance Studies,* 29; and *Renaissance in Historical Thought,* 329–85.

16. Pico della Mirandola, "Oration on the Dignity of Man," in Cassirer, Kristeller, and Randall, *The Renaissance Philosophy of Man,* 223–25; see also Kristeller, *Renaissance Thought and Its Sources,* 169–81.

17. See Kristeller, *Renaissance Thought and Its Sources,* 196–210.

18. On the matter of Ignatius's education, see George Ganss, *Saint Ignatius's Idea of a Jesuit University* (Milwaukee: Marquette University, 1954), 9–17.

19. O'Malley, "Feast of Thomas Aquinas," *Rivista di Storia della Chiesa in Italia* 34 (1981): 22–23.

20. John W. O'Malley, "Renaissance Humanism and the Religious Culture of the First Jesuits," *Heythrop Journal* 31 (1990): 477.

21. See Joseph A. Tetlow, *Ignatius Loyola, Spiritual Exercises* (New York: Crossroad, 1992), 51–52.

22. O'Malley, "Renaissance Humanism," 476.

23. O'Malley, "Renaissance Humanism," 477.

24. The story goes back to the life of Ignatius written by Jeronimo Polanco after the death of Ignatius and after several of Erasmus's writings had been placed on the index of forbidden books. For an examination of the relationship between Ignatius and Erasmus, see John Olin, *Six Essays on Erasmus* (New York: Fordham, 1979). Olin shows that, aside from the satire in the *Praise of Folly,* there was much in common between the two. See also Marjorie O'Rourke Boyle, "Angels Black and White: Loyola's Spiritual Discernment in Historical Perspective," *Theological Studies* 44, no. 2 (June 1983): 241–57.

25. John W. Padberg, "Ignatius, the Popes, and Realistic Reverence," *Studies in the Spirituality of Jesuits* 25 (May 1993): 10–11.

26. See George E. Ganss, "Thinking with the Church: The Spirit of St. Ignatius's Rules," *The Way Supplement* 20 (1973): 72–82; also Cowan and Futrell, *Companions in Grace,* 170.

27. See John H. Wright, George E. Ganss, and Ladislas Orsy, "On Thinking with the Church Today," *Studies in the Spirituality of Jesuits* 7, no. 1 (January 1975): 1–44.

28. John W. O'Malley, "Some Distinctive Characteristics of Jesuit Spirituality in the Sixteenth Century," in John W. O'Malley, John W. Padberg, and Vincent O'Keefe, *Jesuit Spirituality: A Now and Future Resource* (Chicago: Loyola University Press, 1990), 11.

29. O'Malley, *First Jesuits,* 33.

30. O'Malley, *First Jesuits,* 34.

31. John F. D'Amico, *Renaissance Humanism in Papal Rome: Humanists and Churchmen on the Eve of the Reformation* (Baltimore: John Hopkins University, 1983), 3–11.

32. O'Malley, *First Jesuits,* 171–72.

33. For an extended treatment of this early social ministry, see O'Malley, *First Jesuits,* 178–85.

34. See George Ganss, *Saint Ignatius's Idea of a Jesuit University.*

35. O'Malley, *First Jesuits,* 211, 219.

36. O'Malley, *First Jesuits*, 242.

37. See Judith Rock, *Terpsichore at Louis-le-Grand: Baroque Dance on the Jesuit Stage in Paris* (St. Louis: Institute of Jesuit Sources, 1996), 11, 39.

CHAPTER 3: MATTEO RICCI

1. Louis J. Gallagher, S.J., trans., *China in the Sixteenth Century: The Journals of Matthew Ricci: 1583–1610* (New York: Random House, 1953), 30.

2. Gallagher, *Journals*, 93.

3. For a convenient history of Catholic thinking in this area, see Francis A. Sullivan, S.J., *Salvation outside the Church? Tracing the History of the Catholic Response* (New York: Paulist Press, 1992).

4. Xavier's letters and other writings are collected in *The Letters and Instructions of Francis Xavier*, M. Joseph Costelloe, S.J., trans. (St. Louis: Institute of Jesuit Sources, 1992). The most complete biography is the monumental work by Georg Schurhammer, S.J., *Francis Xavier: His Life and Times*, 4 vols., trans. M. Joseph Costelloe, S.J., (Rome: Jesuit Historical Institute, 1982).

5. Xavier, *Letters*, 15.

6. Andrew C. Ross, *A Vision Betrayed: The Jesuits in Japan and China, 1542–1742* (Maryknoll, NY: Orbis, 1994), 17.

7. Xavier, *Letters*, 61–62.

8. Xavier, *Letters*, 67.

9. Xavier, *Letters*, 122-23, 194-95.

10. Xavier, *Letters*, 219.

11. Xavier, *Letters*, 219.

12. Schurhammer, *Francis Xavier*, 4:223–26, 229.

13. Schurhammer, *Francis Xavier*, 4:228, 235.

14. Gallagher, *Journals*, 118.

15. Schurhammer, *Francis Xavier*, 4:638.

16. The most thorough treatment on Valignano in English is Josef Franz Schütte, *Valignano's Mission Principles for Japan*, 2 vols., trans. John J. Coyne, S.J. (St. Louis: Institute of Jesuit Sources, 1980). Another fine scholarly book-length study is J. F. Moran, *The Japanese and the Jesuits: Alessandro Valignano in Sixteenth-Century Japan* (London: Routledge, 1993). Excellent shorter treatments are to be found in George H. Dunne, S.J., *Generation of Giants: The Story of the Jesuits in China in the Last Decades of the Ming Dynasty* (Notre Dame, IN: University of Notre Dame, 1962) and Andrew C. Ross, *A Vision Betrayed: The Jesuits in Japan and China, 1542–1742* (Maryknoll, NY: Orbis, 1994).

17. Schütte, *Valignano's Mission Principles*, 2:35n125.

18. Ross, *A Vision Betrayed*, 38.

19. Moran, *Japanese and Jesuits*, 29.

20. Moran, *Japanese and Jesuits*, 54.

21. For a detailed description of the contents, see Schütte, *Valignano's Mission Principles*, 2:155–90.

22. Schütte, *Valignano's Mission Principles*, 2:163.

23. The most complete biography of Ricci is the two-volume work of Henri Bernard, S.J., *Le Père Matthieu Ricci et la Société Chinoise de son temps (1552–1610)* (Tientsin: Hautes Études, 1937). In English there is the scholarly biography of Jonathan D. Spence, *The Memory Palace of Matteo Ricci* (New York: Viking, 1984) and the more popular biography by Vincent Cronin, *The Wise Man from the West* (New York: Dutton, 1955). All of them draw on Ricci's *Journals*, cited above. Shorter treatments of Ricci's life and career are to be found in Dunne, *Generation of Giants*, and Ross, *A Vision Betrayed*, also cited above.

24. Ricci's prodigious memory and his *Treatise on Mnemonic Arts* are the principal focus of Jonathan D. Spence, *The Memory Palace of Matteo Ricci*.

25. Spence, *Memory Palace*, 141.

26. Cited in Ross, *A Vision Betrayed*, 121–22. Also emphasized by Dunne, *Generation of Giants*, 25.

27. Ricci, *Journals,* 147.

28. Ross, *A Vision Betrayed,* 123.

29. Gallagher, *Journals,* 94.

30. Gallagher, *Journals,* 72, 80.

31. Julia Ching, *Confucianism and Christianity: A Comparative Study* (Tokyo: Kodansha International, 1977), 97.

32. The book *Sententiae et Exempla* was compiled by the Portuguese humanist Andreas de Resende, also known as Eborensis. A 1590 edition of the work was part of the Jesuit mission library. See Pasquale M. D'Elia, S.I., "Il Trattato sull'Amicizia," *Studia Missionalia* 7 (1952): 425–515, and also by the same author, "Further Notes on Matteo Ricci's *De Amicitia,*" *Monumenta serica* 15 (1956): 356–77. I am grateful to the Ricci Institute for Chinese-Western Cultural History, University of San Francisco, for making available to me the unpublished English translation.

33. Cited in Paul A. Rule, *K'ung-tzu or Confucius? The Jesuit Interpretation of Confucianism* (Sydney: Allen & Unwin, 1986), 20–21.

34. Spence, *Memory Palace,* 3–4.

35. Jonathan D. Spence, "Matteo Ricci and the Ascent to Peking," in *East Meets West: The Jesuits in China, 1582–1773,* ed. Charles E. Ronan, S.J., and Bonnie B. C. Oh (Chicago: Loyola University Press, 1988), 15.

36. See the works listed in note 23 above.

37. Gallagher, *Journals,* 378; Spence, *Memory Palace,* 197–99;

38. Douglas Lancashire and Peter Hu Kuo-chen, S.J., translators' introduction to *The True Meaning of the Lord of Heaven,* by Matteo Ricci, ed. Edward J. Malatesta, S.J. (St. Louis: Institute of Jesuit Sources, 1985), 16–17.

39. Lancashire and Kuo-chen, translators' introduction, *True Meaning,* 14.

40. Cited in Dunne, *Generation of Giants,* 96–97.

41. Ross, *A Vision Betrayed,* 148–49.

42. George Minamiki, S.J., *The Chinese Rites Controversy from Its Beginnings to Modern Times* (Chicago: Loyola University Press, 1985), 3–10.

43. Minamiki, *The Chinese Rites Controversy,* 17–20. See also Ricci *Journals* 96–97.

44. Ray R. Noll, ed., *100 Roman Documents Concerning the Chinese Rites Controversy (1645–1941),* trans. Donald F. St. Sure, S.J. (San Francisco: Ricci Institute, University of San Francisco, 1992), vii.

45. Rule, *K'ung-tzu or Confucius,* 47.

46. Willard J. Peterson, "Why Did They Become Christians" in *East Meets West: The Jesuits in China, 1582–1773,* ed. Charles E. Ronan, S.J. and Bonnie B. C. Oh (Chicago: Loyola University Press, 1988), 145–47. For a similar analysis of the Jesuits' early Confucian converts and how they viewed Christianity, see Rule, *K'ung-Tzu or Confucius,* 58–69.

47. Dunne, *Generation of Giants,* 101, 104.

48. Ross, *A Vision Betrayed,* 166. Ross argues against the claim that Jesuits, in contrast to other religious orders, favored a "top down" missionary strategy that favored the elite over the ordinary people of China. It was the Jesuits' acceptance by the scholars that made their outreach to the masses possible.

49. Cited in Tacchi Venturi, S.J., *Opere Storiche del P. Matteo Ricci* (Macerata, Italy: Filippo Gioretti, 1913), II:246–47.

50. Dunne, *Generation of Giants,* 105.

51. Gallagher, *Journals,* 563; Cronin, *Wise Man from the West,* 272.

52. Ross, *A Vision Betrayed,* 153.

53. English works on Schall and Verbiest include Dunne, *Generation of Giants;* Ross, *A Vision Betrayed;* and Arnold H. Rowbotham, *Missionary and Mandarin: The Jesuits at the Court of China* (New York: Russell & Russell, 1966).

54. Ross, *A Vision Betrayed,* 170.

55. Dunne, *Generation of Giants,* 314.

56. Ross, *A Vision Betrayed,* 174–76.

57. English works on Roberto de Nobili are Vincent Cronin, *A Pearl to India: The Life of Roberto de Nobili* (New York: Dutton, 1959); S. Rajamanickam, *The First Oriental Scholar* (Madras: De Nobili Research Instititute, 1972); S. Rajamanickam, *Roberto de Nobili on Indian Customs* (Madras: De Nobili Research Institute, 1972).

58. S. Rajamanickam, "Madurai Mission—Old and New," in *Jesuit Presence in Indian History,* ed. Anand Amaladass (Anand, India: Gujarat Sahitya Prakash, 1988), 304–06.

59. Both are to be found in English translation in Anand Amaladass and Francis X. Clooney, *Preaching Wisdom to the Wise: Three Treatises of Robert de Nobili, S.J., Missionary and Scholar in Seventeenth-Century India,* (St. Louis: Institute of Jesuit Sources, 2001).

60. See Amaladass and Clooney, *Preaching Wisdom to the Wise.*

61. Jesuit missionaries Gonçalo Fernandes, Diego Gonsalvez, and Jacobo Fenicio also studied and wrote about Indian culture and Hindu religious beliefs and practices contemporaneous with or even before de Nobili but were all convinced of the superiority of Western Christian culture. See Amaladass and Clooney, *Preaching Wisdom to the Wise,* 28–33.

62. S. Rajamanickam, "Madurai Mission" in Amaladass, *Jesuit Presence,* 307.

63. *Dogmatic Constitution on the Church in the Modern World,* 44; *Decree on Missions,* 22.

64. On the nature and potential impact of dialogue, see Leonard Swidler, "The Dialogue Decalogue: Ground Rules for Interreligious, Interideological Dialogue," *Journal of Ecumenical Studies* (Winter 1983): 1–4.

65. Amaladass and Clooney, *Preaching Wisdom to the Wise,* 18–19.

CHAPTER 4: FRIEDRICH SPEE

1. Friedrich Spee von Langenfeld, *Cautio Criminalis, or a Book on Witch Trials,* trans. Marcus Hellyer (Charlottesville: University of Virginia Press, 2003), 39.

2. Joachim-Friedrich Ritter, *Friedrich von Spee, 1591–1635: Ein Edelmann, Mahner und Dichter* (Trier: Spee-Varlag, 1977), 68.

3. Current interest goes back to the book by Julio Caro Baroja, *The World of the Witches* (Chicago: University of Chicago Press, 1965), and the title essay of H. R. Trevor-Roper's collection, *The European Witch-Craze of the Sixteenth and Seventeenth Centuries, and Other Essays* (New York: Harper Torchbooks, 1969). The latter essay certainly contributed to *witch-craze* becoming the most common term employed to describe this phenomenon but this term implies that the prosecution of witches was somehow the product of a collective psychosis or mental disorder, and this is certainly not the case. For one of the most reliable and authoritative works on the subject, see Brian P. Levack, *The Witch-Hunt in Early Modern Europe* (London: Longman, 1987), 2.

4. Baroja, *The World of the Witches*, 17–40. The most celebrated classic source is Apuleius, *Metamorphoses;* the Loeb Classical Library has an English/Latin edition edited and translated by J. Arthur Hanson (Cambridge, MA: Harvard University Press, 1989).

5. C. S. Lewis, *Mere Christianity* (New York: Macmillan, 1952), 12.

6. Levack, *Witch-Hunt,* 19–21.

7. See Herbert Haag, *Teufelsglaube* (Tübingen: Katzmann, 1974), 442; Anne Llewellyn Barstow, *Witchcraze: A New History of the European Witch Hunts* (San Francisco: Pandora, 1994), 181; Levack, *Witch-Hunt,* 20–21.

8. Haag, *Teufelsglaube,* 469.

9. Alan C. Kors and Edward Peters, eds., *Witchcraft in Europe, 1100–1700: A Documentary History* (Philadelphia: University of Pennsylvania, 1972), 217.

10. Kors and Peters, *Witchcraft in Europe,* 251–53.

11. Levack, *Witch-Hunt,* 124. See also Barstow, *Witchcraze,* 25; and Wolfgang Behringer on recent witchcraft studies in Austria, Germany, and Switzerland in Jonathan Barry, Marianne Hester, and Gareth Roberts, eds., *Witchcraft in Early Modern Europe: Studies in Culture and Belief* (Cambridge: Cambridge University, 1996), 93.

12. Barstow, *Witchcraze,* 147–65.

13. Levack, *Witch-Hunt,* 126–27; Behringer in Barry, Hester, and Roberts, *Witchcraft in Early Modern Europe,* 94.

14. Barstow, *Witchcraze*, 26

15. Barry, Hester, and Roberts, *Witchcraft*, 39.

16. Behringer in Barry, Hester, and Roberts, *Witchcraft*, 87.

17. Haag, *Teufelsglaube*, 457.

18. Michele Battafarano, ed., *Friedrich von Spee: Dichter, Theologe und Bekämpfer der Hexenprozesse* (Trento: Luigi Reverdito, 1988), 224–26.

19. Richard Kieckhefer, *European Witch Trials: Their Foundation in Popular and Learned Culture, 1300–1500* (Berkeley: University of California, 1976), 78–80.

20. Rosemary Ellen Guiley, *The Encyclopedia of Witches and Witchcraft* (New York: Facts on File, 1987), 52.

21. Haag, *Teufelsglaube*, 452.

22. The full text of the papal bull is to be found in Montague Summers, trans., *Malleus Maleficarum* (New York: Benjamin Blom, 1928), xliii–xlv.

23. Haag, *Teufelsglaube*, 453.

24. Summers, *Malleus*, 9.

25. Summers, *Malleus*, 44.

26. Haag, *Teufelsglaube*, 454.

27. Haag, *Teufelsglaube*, 456.

28. Russell Hope Robbins, *The Encyclopedia of Witchcraft and Demonology* (New York: Crown, 1959), 121.

29. Martin Delrio, S.J., *Disquisitionum Magicarum Libri Sex (1617)* Lib. II, q. 6, p. 182. Author's translation. "Praeteria qui haec afferunt somnia esse & ludibria, certe peccant contra reverentia Ecclesiae matri debitam. Nam Ecclesia Catholica non punit crimina, nisi certa & manifesta; nec habet pro haereticis, nisi qui in haeresi manifeste sunt deprehensi; striges autem iam a plurimis annis pro haereticis habet, & iubet per inquisitores puniri, & brachio saeculari tradi, ut patet ex libris Sprengeri, Nideri, Iaquerii, Machaelis, & docet experientia. Ergo vel Ecclesia errat

vel isti Pyrrhonii errant: Ecclesiam in re ad fidem pertinente errare qui dicat, anathema maranatha sit."

30. Cited in Robbins, *Encyclopedia,* 123.

31. Although even early on his name appears as Friedrich von Spee, the correct form, followed here, is Friedrich Spee von Langenfeld.

32. The biographies of Spee are at this time all in German. Among the most helpful for its extended documentation is Joachim-Friedrich Ritter, *Friedrich von Spee, 1591–1635: Ein Edelmann, Mahner und Dichter* (Trier: Spee-Verlag, 1977). Others are Emmy Rosenfeld, *Friedrich Spee von Langenfeld: Eine Stimme in der Wuste* (Berlin: Walter de Gruyter, 1958); Karl-Jurgen Miesen, *Friedrich Spee: Pater, Dichter, Hexen-Anwalt* (Dusseldorf: Doste, 1987); Karl Keller, *Friedrich Spee von Langenfeld (1591–1635): Leben und Werk des Seelsorgers und Dichters* (Geldern: Keuck, 1990); Walter Nigg, *Friedrich von Spee: Ein Jesuit Kampft gegen den Hexenwahn* (Paderborn: Bonifatius, 1991).

33. Ritter, *Friedrich von Spee,* 13–14.

34. In this period (1587–1593), records indicate that 368 people in and around Trier were burned as witches. Cf., Barstow, *Witchcraze,* 59.

35. Ritter, *Friedrich von Spee,* 155.

36. Rosenfeld, *Friedrich Spee,* 41. The entire verse reads:
Ah caput a toto seiunctum est corpore, Iberus,
In Spe spes fuerat, spes Fridericus erat.
Spe Friderice vale, fueras languente magistro
Tu desperatis spes, per amice, Sophis.

37. Ritter, *Friedrich von Spee,* 20.

38. Rosenfeld, *Friedrich Spee,* 50.

39. Ritter, *Friedrich von Spee,* 23–24.

40. Gunther Franz, "Friedrich Spee und die Bücherzensur," in *Friedrich Spee zum 400. Geburtsag: Kolloquium der Friedrich-Spee-Gesellschaft Trier,* ed. Gunther Franz (Paderborn: Bonifatius, 1995), 94.

41. Marcus Hellyer, translator's introduction to *Cautio Criminalis* by Friedrich Spee, xiv.

42. Ritter, *Friedrich Spee*, 82.

43. Friedrich Spee, *Güldenes Tugend-Buch*, ed. Theo G. M. van Oorshot (Munich: Kösel, 1968), 355–56.

44. Ritter, *Friedrich Spee*, 132.

45. I wish to express my gratitude to G. Ronald Murphy, S.J., of Georgetown University for his assistance in coming up with an appropriate English translation of this somewhat peculiar use of the German *Trutz*.

46. Battafarano, *Friedrich von Spee*, 229–30. Well over half a century before Spee (1563), Protestant court physician Johannes Weyer wrote against the belief in witches and the idea of a pact with the devil as fantasy.

47. Bracketed references in the text will be to Hellyer's English translation of the *Cautio*.

48. Pamela Reilly, "Friedrich von Spee's Belief in Witchcraft: Some Deductions from the 'Cautio Criminalis'," *Modern Language Review* 54 (1959): 51–55.

49. Bavarian Jesuit Adam Tanner devoted a number of pages to questioning the conduct of the witch trials in his four volume (1627) *Theologia Scholastica*. Tanner considerably influenced Spee, who cites him several times in the *Cautio*. At least in Bavaria, Tanner's *Theologica* seems to have made a greater impact on Catholics than did Spee's anonymous work. See Wolfgang Behringer, *Witchcraft Persecutions in Bavaria: Popular Magic, Religious Zealotry, and Reason of State in Early Modern Europe*, trans. J. C. Grayson and David Lederer (New York: Cambridge University Press, 1997).

50. Marcus Hellyer, translator's introduction to *Cautio Criminalis*, xxix–xxx.

51. Friedrich Spee, *Cautio Criminalis*, herausgegeben von Theo G. M. van Oorschot, mit einem Beitrag von Gunther Franz (Tübingen: Francke, 1992), 632.

52. Friedrich Spee, *Trutz-Nachtigal*, ed. Theo G. M. van Oorschot (Bern: Francke, 1985). See the work of G. Richard Demler, especially his "Friedrich Spee: Poet, Priest, Reformer" in *America*, 166:95–97 (Feb. 8, 1992).

53. Kurt Küppers, "Trutz-Nachtigal," in Michael Sievernich, S.J., *Friedrich von Spee: Priester-Poet-Prophet* (Frankfurt: Knecht, 1986), 83.

54. Friedrich Spee, *Güldenes Tugend-Buch,* ed. Theo G. M. van Oorschot (Munich: Kösel, 1968), 11. Henceforth referred to in the text as GTB.

55. The laywomen in question were probably a group of "Devotissen" who lived in Cologne. "Devotissen" were women who wished to grow in the spiritual life outside the cloister. Cf., Battafarano, *Friedrich Spee,* 48.

56. Even though he has not been canonized, two writers in our time who regard Spee as exemplifying the heroic sanctity of a saint are Karl Rahner, in Sievernich, ed., *Friedrich von Spee,* 139; and Protestant biographer of saints Walter Nigg, *Friedrich von Spee: Ein Jesuit kämpft gegen den Hexenwahn* (Paderborn: Bonifatius, 1991).

57. *Documents of the Thirty-fourth General Congregation of the Society of Jesus* (St. Louis: Institute of Jesuit Sources, 1995), 34, 364, 372.

CHAPTER 5: PIERRE TEILHARD DE CHARDIN

1. Robert Speaight, *The Life of Teilhard de Chardin* (New York: Harper & Row, 1967), 113.

2. Jean Lacouture, *Jesuits: A Multibiography,* trans. Jeremy Leggatt (Washington, DC: Counterpoint, 1995), 416.

3. Pierre Teilhard de Chardin, *The Heart of Matter,* trans. René Hague (New York: Harcourt Brace Jovanovich, 1979), 41.

4. Teilhard, *Heart of Matter,* 20.

5. Speaight, *Life,* 30.

6. Teilhard, *Heart of Matter,* 46.

7. Claude Cuénot, *Teilhard de Chardin: A Biographical Study* (Baltimore: Helicon, 1965), 9.

8. Teilhard, *Heart of Matter,* 25.

9. Pierre Teilhard de Chardin, *How I Believe,* trans. René Hague (New York: Harper & Row, 1969), 10.

10. The only reason for mentioning this incident here at all is an article that Harvard biologist Stephen Jay Gould wrote in 1980, twenty-five years after Teilhard's death, in which he charged that Teilhard knew of the forgery and "probably" helped Dawson with it. Closer investigation showed that Gould's accusation relied on the flimsiest of circumstantial evidence. One book-length investigative report concluded that Dawson acted alone. Evidence discovered in 1996 points to a staff member of London's Natural History Museum as the perpetrator. See Harold J. Morowitz, *The Kindly Dr. Guillotin and Other Essays on Science and Life* (Washington, DC: Counterpoint, 1997), 21–27.

11. Cuénot, *Teilhard,* 24–25.

12. Lacouture, *Jesuits,* 408.

13. Pierre Teilhard de Chardin, *Writings in Time of War,* trans. René Hague (New York: Harper & Row, 1968), 13–71.

14. Teilhard, *Heart of Matter,* 61.

15. Teilhard, *Heart of Matter,* 62–65.

16. Pierre Teilhard de Chardin, *Hymn of the Universe* (New York: Harper& Row, 1965), 47–48.

17. Teilhard, *Hymn of the Universe,* 50–55.

18. Teilhard, *Hymn of the Universe,* 54.

19. Teilhard, *Hymn of the Universe,* 61.

20. Teilhard, *Hymn of the Universe,* 63–64.

21. Pierre Leroy, *Letters from My Friend Teilhard de Chardin (1948–1955),* trans. Mary Lukas (New York: Paulist Press, 1980), 103.

22. Teilhard, *Hymn of the Universe,* 67.

23. Teilhard, *Hymn of the Universe,* 68–71.

24. Speaight, *Life*, 112.

25. Speaight, *Life*, 116.

26. Pierre Teilhard de Chardin, *The Divine Milieu: An Essay on the Interior Life* (New York: Harper & Row, 1960), 11.

27. Pierre Teilhard de Chardin, *The Phenomenon of Man*, with an introduction by Sir Julian Huxley (New York: Harper & Row, 1959), 29. A new edition and translation of the work by Sarah Appleton-Weber corrects that problem, *The Human Phenomenon* (Brighton, England: Sussex Academic Press, 1999). References in these notes are to the 1959 edition.

28. Teilhard, *Phenomenon*, 308.

29. Teilhard, *Heart of Matter*, 104.

30. Teilhard, *Heart of Matter*, 102.

31. Speaight, *Life*, 332. The Jesuits subsequently sold the novitiate buildings and property, so that Teilhard's grave is presently on the grounds of a school for the culinary arts.

32. Thomas Berry, *Teilhard in the Ecological Age* (Chambersburg, PA: Anima Books, 1982), 4.

33. Among the most detailed, Henri de Lubac, S.J., *The Religion of Teilhard de Chardin*, trans. René Hague (New York: Desclee, 1967) and Emile Rideau, *The Thought of Teilhard de Chardin*, trans. René Hague (New York: Harper & Row, 1968).

34. See Thomas King, S.J., *Teilhard de Chardin* (Wilmington, DE: Michael Glazier, 1988), 65.

35. Pedro Miguel Lamet, *Arrupe, Una explosión en la Iglesia* (Madrid: Tenas de Hoy, 1989), 271.

36. Lacouture, *Jesuits*, 435.

37. Lacouture, *Jesuits*, 434.

38. See King, *Teilhard*, 62–65.

39. A major exception to the mainstream of Catholic theologians in this regard is John F. Haught, who was himself influenced and inspired by Teilhard. See Haught's *Science and Religion: From Conflict to Conversation* (New York: Paulist Press, 1995); *God after Darwin: A Theology of Evolution* (Boulder, CO: Westview, 2000); and *Responses to 101 Questions about God and Evolution* (New York: Paulist Press, 2001).

40. Leroy, *Letters from My Friend,* 137, 174.

41. Leroy, *Letters from My Friend,* 133, 215.

42. See, for example, Mary Evelyn Tucker, *The Ecological Spirituality of Teilhard* (Chambersburg, PA: Anima Books, 1985).

43. Thomas Berry, *The Dream of the Earth* (San Francisco: Sierra Club Books, 1988).

CHAPTER 6: KARL RAHNER

1. Karl Rahner, "Rede des Ignatius von Loyola an einen Jesuiten von Heute" [St. Ignatius of Loyola Speaks to a Jesuit of Today], *Schriften zur Theologie* (hereafter *Schriften*), (Einsiedeln: Benzinger) 15 (1954): 374–75 (author's translation). Cf., *Ignatius of Loyola*, trans. Rosaleen Ockenden (London: Collins, 1979).

2. See Paul Imhof and Hubert Biallowons, eds., *Karl Rahner in Dialogue: Conversations and Interviews, 1965–1982,* trans. Harvey D. Egan (New York: Crossroad, 1986), 191.

3. J. B. Metz in Paul Imhof and Hubert Biallowons, eds., *Karl Rahner: Bilder eines Lebens* (Zurich: Benziger; Freiburg im Breisgau: Herder, 1985), 166.

4. Karl Rahner, *Is Christian Life Possible Today?* (Denville, NJ: Dimension Books, 1984).

5. Foreword in *Schriften*, 12:8.

6. Ibid.

7. Quoted in Herbert Vorgrimler, *Understanding Karl Rahner: An Introduction to His Life and Thought* (New York: Crossroad, 1986), 44.

8. Karl Rahner, *I Remember: An Autobiographical Interview*, trans. Harvey Egan (New York: Crossroad, 1985), 30.

9. Vorgrimler, *Understanding Karl Rahner*, 48.

10. Imhof and Biallowons, *Karl Rahner: Bilder eines Lebens*, 12.

11. Rahner, *I Remember*, 26.

12. "Warum uns das Beten nottut," reprinted in Herbert Vorgrimler, ed., *Karl Rahner, Sehnsucht nach dem Geheimnisvollen Gott* (Freiburg: Herder, 1990), 77–80.

13. Karl Rahner, "The Logic of Existential Knowledge . . . ," in *Dynamics of Faith* (New York: Herder and Herder, 1964), 85.

14. Karl Rahner, "The 'Spiritual Senses' According to Origen," in *Theological Investigations* (New York: Crossroad, 1979), 16:81–103.

15. Karl Rahner, "The Doctrine of the 'Spiritual Senses' in the Middle Ages," in *Theological Investigations* (New York: Crossroad, 1979), 16:123.

16. Karl Rahner, "Aszese und Mystik in der Väterzeit," in Karl Rahner, *Sämtliche Werke* (Zurich: Benziger; Freiburg im Breisgau: Herder, 1996), 3:125–390. See especially pages 125 and 389.

17. Karl Rahner, *Spiritual Exercises*, trans. Kenneth Baker (New York: Herder and Herder, 1965).

18. For a discussion of the various shifts and phases in Heidegger's thinking, see John D. Caputo, "Heidegger and Theology," in Charles B. Guignon, *The Cambridge Companion to Heidegger* (Cambridge: Cambridge University Press, 1993), 270–88.

19. Ibid., 280.

20. Rahner, *I Remember*, 46.

21. Karl Rahner, "Unity of Spirit and Matter," in *Theological Investigations*, 6:171; "Theology and Anthropology," in *Theological Investigations*, 9:35, 43.

22. Rahner, *I Remember*, 46.

23. Karl Rahner, *Spirit in the World,* 2nd ed., trans. Willam Dych, S.J. (New York: Herder and Herder, 1968).

24. "Ex Latere Christi" in Karl Rahner, *Sämtliche Werke* (Zurich: Benziger; Freiburg im Breisgau: Herder, 1996), 3:3–84.

25. Karl Rahner, *Encounters in Silence* (Westminster, MD: Newman Press, 1960).

26. Karl Rahner, *Hearers of the Word,* 2nd rev. ed., trans. Michael Richard (New York: Herder and Herder, 1969). A subsequent translation by Joseph Donceel, generally considered superior to the Richard translation, is to be found in Gerald McCool, *A Rahner Reader* (New York: Seabury, 1975).

27. Rahner, *I Remember,* 52.

28. The term is that of Jesuit Vincent A. Lapomarda in the fullest, treatment of the subject, *The Jesuits and the Third Reich* (Lewiston, NY: Edwin Mellen Press, 1989).

29. Lapomarda, *Jesuits and the Third Reich,* 13.

30. Lapomarda, *Jesuits and the Third Reich,* 55, n. 58.

31. Alfred Delp, *The Prison Meditations of Alfred Delp* (New York: Herder and Herder, 1963), 166. Loyola Press has recently published *With Bound Hands: A Jesuit in Nazi Germany: The Life and Selected Prison Letters of Alfred Delp,* translated and compiled by Mary Frances Coady. This is the first time that much of the material in this collection has been available in English.

32. Rahner, *I Remember,* 50–51.

33. Thomas O'Meara, "A History of Grace," in *A World of Grace: An Introduction to the Themes and Foundations of Karl Rahner's Theology,* ed. Leo J. O'Donovan (New York: Crossroad, 1981), 76.

34. Karl Rahner, *Foundations of Christian Faith: An Introduction to the Idea of Christianity,* trans. W. V. Dych (New York: Seabury, 1978), 21–22, 32–33, 48.

35. *Foundations,* 99–104.

36. Karl Rahner, "Reflections on the Unity of the Love of Neighbor and the Love of God," in *Theological Investigations,* 6:231–49. See also "Christian Humanism," in *Theological Investigations,* 9:188.

37. Rahner, *Theological Investigations*, 4:180.

38. Karl Rahner, "Anonymous and Explicit Faith," in *Theological Investigations*, 16:52–59.

39. Karl Rahner, "The One Christ and the Universality of Salvation," in *Theological Investigations*, 16:219.

40. Karen Kilby, *Karl Rahner*, Fount Christian Thinkers Series (London: Fount/HarperCollins, 1997), 36. I recommend this excellent little book most highly for its accessibility and insights into Rahner.

41. Rahner, *I Remember*, 21.

42. Vorgrimler, *Understanding Karl Rahner*, 113.

43. Imhof and Biallowon, *Karl Rahner: Bilder eines Lebens*, 113; Vorgrimler, *Understanding Karl Rahner*, 113.

44. Rahner, *I Remember*, 5.

45. Karl-Heinz Weger in Imhof and Biallowons's, *Karl Rahner, Bilder eines Lebens*, 114.

46. Franz Kardinal König, "Erinnerungen an Karl Rahner als Konzilstheologen," in *Karl Rahner in Erinnerung*, ed. Albert Raffelt (Düsseldorf: Patmos, 1994), 151.

47. *Schriften zur Theologie* (see n. 1), translated into English as *Theological Investigations* (Baltimore: Helicon Press, 1961).

48. König, in Raffelt, *Karl Rahner in Erinnerungen*, 152–53.

49. Walter M. Abbott, ed., *The Documents of Vatican II* (New York: America Press, 1966), 710–19.

50. Vorgrimler, *Understanding Karl Rahner*, 98–99.

51. Dogmatic Constitution on the Church, 16, in Abbot, *Documents of Vatican II*, 35.

52. Karl Rahner, "Basic Theological Interpretation of the Second Vatican Council," in *Theological Investigations*, 20:77–89.

53. Ibid., 79.

54. Karl Rahner, *The Shape of the Church to Come,* (New York: Seabury/Crossroad, 1974), 53–63, 108–21.

55. Imhof and Biallowons, *Karl Rahner: Bilder eines Lebens,* 124.

56. Imhof and Biallowons, *Karl Rahner in Dialogue,* 106.

57. Karl Rahner, *Faith in a Wintry Season: Conversations and Interviews with Karl Rahner in the Last Years of His Life,* ed. Paul Imhof and Hubert Biallowons, trans. Harvey D. Egan (New York: Crossroad, 1990), 35, 39.

58. Rahner, *Theological Investigations,* 7:15.

59. Rahner, *Faith in a Wintry Season,* 19.

60. Imhof and Biallowons, *Karl Rahner in Dialogue,* 211.

61. Rahner, *Faith in a Wintry Season,* 115.

62. Harvey D. Egan, S.J., *Karl Rahner: The Mystic of Everyday Life* (New York: Crossroad, 1998), 59. I am indebted to Egan for his valuable insights into Rahner as a mystical theologian.

63. Rahner, *Faith in a Wintry Season,* 163.

64. Karl Rahner, *The Practice of Faith: A Handbook of Contemporary Spirituality* (New York: Crossroad, 1983), 84.

65. Rahner, *The Practice of Faith,* 80–84.

66. Imhof and Biallowons, *Karl Rahner in Dialogue,* 89–90.

67. Ibid., 185.

68. Imhof and Biallowons, *Karl Rahner: Bilder eines Lebens,* 146.

69. Albert Görres in Imhof and Biallowons, *Karl Rahner: Bilder eines Lebens,* 80.

70. The address "Erfahrungen eines katholischen Theologen" [Experiences of a Catholic Theologian] is to be found in Raffelt, *Karl Rahner in Erinnerung,* 134–48.

CHAPTER 7: PEDRO ARRUPE

1. Pedro Arrupe, S.J., *Justice with Faith Today: Selected Letters and Addresses,* ed. Jerome Aixala, S.J. (St. Louis: Institute of Jesuit Sources, 1980), 2:125.

2. Pedro Arrupe, S.J., *One Jesuit's Spiritual Journey: Autobiographical Conversations with Jean-Claude Dietsch, S.J.,* trans. Ruth Bradley (St. Louis: Institute of Jesuit Sources, 1986), 19.

3. George Bishop, *Pedro Arrupe: Twenty-eighth General of the Society of Jesus* (Gujarat, India: Gujarat Sahitya Prakash, 2000), 20–23. Bishop's is the most detailed biography of Arrupe in English. The most detailed altogether is the Spanish biography by Pedro Miguel Lamet, *Arrupe, Una explosión en la Iglesia* (Madrid: Temas de Hoy, 1994). Both are based greatly on Arrupe's autobiographical memoirs: *Pedro Arrupe, Este Japón increíble: Memorias del P. Arrupe* (Bilbao: Mensajero, 1957) and *One Jesuit's Spiritual Journey.*

4. Arrupe, *One Jesuit's Spiritual Journey,* 51.

5. Arrupe, *Este Japón,* 10.

6. Arrupe, *Este Japón,* 10–13.

7. Arrupe, *Este Japón,* 15–19.

8. Arrupe, *One Jesuit's Spiritual Journey,* 18.

9. Arrupe, *Este Japón,* 22.

10. Arrupe, *One Jesuit's Spiritual Journey,* 18–19.

11. Arrupe, *One Jesuit's Spiritual Journey,* 20. See also Lamet, *Arrupe, Una explosión,* 98–101.

12. Arrupe, *Este Japón,* 33–42.

13. Arrupe, *One Jesuit's Spiritual Journey,* 20.

14. Arrupe, *Este Japón,* 109–10.

15. Arrupe, *One Jesuit's Spiritual Journey,* 21. See also *Este Japón,* 111–21.

16. Lamet, *Arrupe, Una explosión,* 169–85; Bishop, 81–91.

17. Pedro Arrupe, *Recollections and Reflections of Pedro Arrupe, S.J.,* trans. Yolanda T. De Mola, S.C., with an introduction by Vincent O'Keefe, S.J. (Wilmington, DE: Michael Glazier, 1986), 17–18.

18. For detailed descriptions of Arrupe's experience of the bombing of Hiroshima, see Arrupe, *Este Japón,* 156–73; Lamet, *Arrupe, Una explosión,* 187–214; Bishop, *Pedro Arrupe,* 117–56.

19. Arrupe, *Recollections,* 29–31.

20. Arrupe, *Recollections,* 33. See also, *One Jesuit's Spiritual Journey,* 33–34.

21. Arrupe, *Recollections,* 34–39; *One Jesuit's Spiritual Journey,* 34.

22. Arrupe, *Recollections,* 55–56.

23. Arrupe, *Recollections,* 53.

24. Arrupe, *Recollections,* 68–69.

25. Bishop, *Pedro Arrupe,* 206.

26. Arrupe, *One Jesuit's Spiritual Journey,* 10.

27. Pedro Arrupe, *Other Apostolates Today (Selected Letters and Addresses III)* (St. Louis: Institute of Jesuit Sources, 1981), 173, 179.

28. Arrupe, *One Jesuit's Spiritual Journey,* 34–37.

29. Cited in Jean-Yves Calvez, S.J., *Faith and Justice: The Social Dimension of Evangelization* (St. Louis: Institute of Jesuit Sources, 1991), 17–18.

30. Arrupe, *Recollections,* 165.

31. Pedro Arrupe, *La Iglesia de hoy y del futuro* (Santander, Spain: Sal Terrae, 1982), 286–87.

32. Arrupe, *Justice with Faith Today,* 123–38, especially 130 and 136–37.

33. Arrupe, *Justice with Faith Today,* 29–59.

34. Cited in Calvez, *Faith and Justice,* 29–30.

35. His address to the Congregation (December 20, 1974) can be found in Arrupe, *Faith with Justice Today,* 317–20.

36. The entire text of Decree Four can be found in *Documents of the 31st and 32nd General Congregations of the Society of Jesus* (St. Louis: Institute of Jesuit Sources, 1977), 411–38.

37. The Autograph Letter (February 15, 1975) of Pope Paul VI to Arrupe can be found in *Documents of the 31st and 32nd General Congregations,* 539–40.

38. Arrupe, *One Jesuit's Spiritual Journey,* 96.

39. Letter (May 2, 1975) of the Cardinal Secretary of State to Arrupe, *Documents of the 31st and 32nd General Congregations,* 545–49. See also Arrupe, *One Jesuit's Spiritual Journey,* 96–97.

40. Michael Amaladoss, "Sent on Mission," in *Constitutions of the Society of Jesus: Incorporation of a Spirit* (Rome: Secretariatus Spiritualitatis Ignatinae, 1993), 340.

41. For his personal reflections on his creation of the Jesuit Refugee Service, see Arrupe, *One Jesuit's Spiritual Journey,* 77.

42. Vincent O'Keefe, S.J., introduction to Arrupe, *Recollections and Reflections,* 9–11.

43. For full details of the events surrounding the papal intervention and other aspects of Arrupe's tenure as superior general, the historical record must await publication of Father O'Keefe's memoirs of Don Pedro.

44. For the full stories of the El Salvador martyrs, see Martha Doggett, *Death Foretold: The Jesuit Murders in El Salvador* (Washington, DC: Georgetown University Press, 1993) and Teresa Whitfield, *Paying the Price: Ignacio Ellacuría and the Murdered Jesuits of El Salvador* (Philadelphia: Temple University, 1995).

45. Amaladoss, "Sent on Mission," 342–43.

46. *Documents of the Thirty-fourth General Congregation of the Society of Jesus* (St. Louis: Institute of Jesuit Sources, 1995), 171–78.

47. Jean Lacouture, *Jesuits: A Multibiography,* trans. Jeremy Leggatt (Washington, DC: Counterpoint, 1995).

48. Arrupe, *One Jesuit's Spiritual Journey,* 60–62.

49. Arrupe, *Justice with Faith Today,* 269–271; Arrupe, *One Jesuit's Spiritual Journey,* 81–84.

50. Arrupe, *One Jesuit's Spiritual Journey,* 81–84; Arrupe, *Justice with Faith Today,* 270–71.

CHAPTER 8: A SPIRITUALITY FOR THE TWENTY-FIRST CENTURY

1. John Henry Cardinal Newman, *An Essay on the Development of Christian Doctrine* (Garden City, NY: Image Books, 1960), 63.

2. Because of its pejorative connotations, fundamentalists generally prefer to call themselves by other names, by which they regard themselves as the only true Christians (or Jews or Muslims) and reject the characteristics described in this book as humanistic. *Fundamentalist* here does not mean someone with convictions but with an exclusionary bias.

3. David M. Stanley, "Contemporary Gospel-Criticism and 'the Mysteries of the Life of our Lord' in the Spiritual Exercises," in *Ignatian Spirituality in a Secular Age,* ed. Geroge P. Schner (Waterloo, Ontario: Wilfrid Laurier University Press, 1984), 26–46.

4. See Michael H. Crosby, *Thy Will Be Done: Praying the Our Father as Subversive Activity* (Maryknoll, NY: Orbis, 1977) and *The Prayer That Jesus Taught Us* (Maryknoll, NY: Orbis, 2002).

5. Even the most determined literalist must recognize the poetic license in Isaiah 6:1, with its description of God sitting on a throne with the fringe of his garment filling the temple.

6. Gerard Manley Hopkins, "As Kingfishers Catch Fire."

7. *Documents of the Thirty-fourth General Congregation of the Society of Jesus* (St. Louis: Institute of Jesuit Sources, 1995). The bracketed numbers in the text refer to paragraphs in the published documents.

8. *Spiritual Exercises* [365]. See chapter 2 above.

9. *Decree on Ecumenism*, #6, in *The Documents of Vatican II*, ed. Walter M. Abbott (New York: America Press, 1966), 350–51.

10. *Constitution on the Church*, # 37, in *The Documents of Vatican II*, ed. Walter M. Abbott (New York: America Press, 1966), 64–65.

11. Paul VI, Encyclical letter *Ecclesiam Suam*, n. 63. See Claudia Carlen, ed., *The Papal Encyclicals* (Wilmington, NC: McGrath, 1981), 5:148–49.

INDEX

Europe, 235
evil, problem of
and God, 181–82, 192, 295
evolution
Rahner on, 228
Teilhard on, 179–80, 182–83, 184, 190, 193–95
examination of conscience. See Spiritual Exercises
experience of God. See experience, mystical
experience, theology and, 157, 160, 172
experience, mystical, 23, 25, 209, 237–40
exploration, Jesuits and, 82–83

F
faith, 19, 63, 70–71, 166
biblical meaning of, 43–44, 292
implicit, 225–27
science and, 66–67, 180, 191–93. See also trust
family, extended Ignatian, xix, xixn8, 297
famine, Roman winter of 1539, 77
fathers of the church, 68–69, 123, 209
Favre, Pierre, 24, 76, 52–53, 78
feelings. See affectivity
Foucault, Michel, xiii
Francis de Sales, St., 170
Francis Xavier, St., 52–53, 88–93, 89
freedom, 31, 46, 62–63,
Rahner on, 215, 220
friendship, Ricci on, 104, 108
fundamentalism, religious, 197, 288–90, 288n2

G
Galileo, 188–89
General Congregation, Thirty-second, 270, 273–76

General Congregation, Thirty-fourth, 279–80, 297–300, 302–06
Germany, witch-hunting in, 136, 139
Goa, 88, 101
God, 92, 167, 213, 221
Absolute Mystery, 224, 229
as gracious, 167, 223–24
existence of, 199–200, 228, 239
experience of, in Rahner, 238–40
Ignatius and, as schoolmaster, 16–17, 22
images of, 171, 199–200, 275, 294–96, 294n5
in the Spiritual Exercises, 294, 296
Rahner on, as Triune, 229–30
reaching out for, in Rahner, 213, 221
revealed in Jesus, 296
Teilhard on, 194, 200
Golden Legend, The. See Voragine, Jacopo de
gospels, nature of, 290
Gould, Stephen Jay, 181n10
grace, 42
God's Self-gift, 31, 223
harmony with nature, 66, 67, 178
liberality of, 41–43
Rahner on, 218, 222–28
Spee on, 168–69, 171
Spiritiual Exercises on, 31–32
universality of, 87, 223–24, 304, 306
Vatican Council II on, 233–34
Grande, Fr. Rutilio, 279
gratitude, 35
Gregory XIII, Pope, 82
guilt, 221
Gutenberg, Johannes, 87

H
hatred, 264
Haught, John, 199n39
Heidegger, Martin, 211–12
hell, 92

Swidler, Leonard, 127, 127n64
Synod of Bishops, Third (1971), 270, 274

T
Tamil, 89
Tanner, Adam, 158n49
Teilhard de Chardin, Pierre, 175–81
  Divine Milieu, The, 191–93
  Le phènomène humaine, 193–95
  legacy of, 196–201, 295
  mediation of faith and science, 190–96
  mysticism of, 181–89
Terence, 83
terrorism, 139–40, 163, 292
theocentrism, 289–90
theology, 172, 237
Thomas à Kempis, 14
Thomas Aquinas, 42, 69, 141–42, 212–13
  humanism and, 57n7, 63, 66–67
Thomas More, St., xii
Thomasius, Christian, 162
Tillich, Paul, ix, 230
time, deep, 198, 199
Toland, John, xiv–xv
Tolstoy, Leo, 292
torture, 139–40, 145
  Spee on, 158–59, 161–62
translation, 36–37, 92
Trent, Council of, 224–25
Trinity, God as, 40–41, 229–30
trust, 19, 43–45, 292
  optimism, basis for, 282–83, 296
  Spee on, 166–70
truth, universality of, 63–64, 128, 281–82

U
umanisti, xiii, xiv, 56, 66. *See also* humanism, Renaissance

universe, unity of the, 196
V
Valignano, Allesandro, 93–99, 105
Vatican Council II, 196–97, 231–37, 265–66, 268, 269
  church reform, 300–301
  inculturation, 126
  ministry, 46
  religious life, renewal of, 273
Venice, 73–75
Verbiest, Ferdinand, 120
via antiqua. See Scholasticism
Villot, Cardinal Jean, 276
virtue, 59–61
Vitelleschi, Mutius, Superior General, Fr., 148
vocation, 46, 78–79
Voltaire, xiv, 84, 295
Voragine, Jacopo de, 8, 29
vow (1534), of Ignatius and companions, 51–52

W, X, Y, Z
wealth, disparity of, 268, 270, 275, 297
Weyer, Johannes, 156n46, 157
will of God, 22
witchcraft trials, 133, 138–40, 158, 160–62
  recent research on, 134–41, 160
women, xxii, 13–14, 18–19, 34, 78
  General Congregation 34 on, 279–280, 298–300
  ordination of, 236
  poverty of, 279–80, 299
  Spee and, 170n55, 171, 173
  witchcraft, persecuted for, 137–38, 143–44
World War II, 255–63
world, 46, 47
Xavier, Francis. *See* Francis Xavier, St.
Zen Buddhism, 257
Zipoli, Domenico, xix